Inclusion and Exclusion in the Global Arena

EDITED BY

MAX KIRSCH

Routledge
Taylor & Francis Group
New York   London

Routledge is an imprint of the
Taylor & Francis Group, an informa business

Routledge   Routledge
Taylor & Francis Group   Taylor & Francis Group
270 Madison Avenue   2 Park Square
New York, NY 10016   Milton Park, Abingdon
                                         Oxon OX14 4RN

© 2006 by Taylor and Francis Group, LLC
Routledge is an imprint of Taylor & Francis Group, an Informa business

Printed in the United States of America on acid-free paper
10 9 8 7 6 5 4 3 2 1

International Standard Book Number-10: 0-415-95242-5 (Softcover) 0-415-95241-7 (Hardcover)
International Standard Book Number-13: 978-0-415-95242-2 (Softcover) 978-0-415-95241-5 (Hardcover)
Library of Congress Card Number 2006010485

Library of Congress Cataloging-in-Publication Data

Inclusion and exclusion in the global arena / edited by Max Kirsch.
    p. cm.
    ISBN 0-415-95241-7 (hardback : alk. paper) -- ISBN 0-415-95242-5 (pbk.)
    1. Globalization--Social aspects. 2. Marginality, Social. 3. Indigenous peoples. I.
Kirsch, Max.

    HN18.3.I54 2006
    305.5'68089--dc22   2006010485

Visit the Taylor & Francis Web site at
http://www.taylorandfrancis.com

and the Routledge Web site at
http://www.routledge-ny.com

Inclusion and Exclusion in the Global Arena

CONTENTS

ACKNOWLEDGMENTS

The editor and publishers wish to thank the following for permission to use copyrighted or revised versions of copyrighted material:

Urban Anthropology and Studies of Cultural Systems and World Economic Development for the special issue on Inclusion and Exclusion in the Global Arena (Max Kirsch, ed.), which originally published the articles by Jack Goody, June Nash, Helen Safa, and Max Kirsch (volume 32, number 1, spring 2003).

Renee Sylvain, "Disorderly Development: Globalization and the Idea of Culture in the Kalahari, " *American Ethnologist* (volume 32, number 3, August 2005).

Eric Wolf, "Incorporation and Identity in the Making of the Modern World, " in his *Pathways to Power* (Berkeley: University of California Press, 2001).

Nancy Sheper-Hughes, "Dangerous and Endangered Youth: Social Structures and Determinants of Violence, " *Annals of the New York Academy of Science* (2004, 1036).

INTRODUCTION
Inclusion and Exclusion in the Global Arena

Max Kirsch

This collection is an outgrowth of a special issue of *Urban Anthropology* that was meant to focus analyses on the general areas of participation and exclusion in an era of economic and social integration. The claim of the authors who contributed to the special issue was that many studies have discussed the way in which globalization has changed the nature of boundaries, space, and the movement of peoples, but that there exists a wide gap in a literature that rarely addressed the reactions of local communities or discussed the inclusion of some stakeholders in decision making while excluding others, particularly in regard to the global integration of industry, and the legislation of planning and trade. This gap has often led to narrow, specific, and sometimes misleading ways of presenting the results of globalizing processes. With contributions from Jack Goody, June Nash, Helen Safa, and Max Kirsch, the original collection sought to bridge this gap by providing case studies that lead to alternative ways of viewing current conceptual frameworks of globalization and its consequences. It focused on the conceptual divisions among the constructs of space and place, indigenous strategies for autonomy, polity and global planning mechanisms, and the role of transnational corporations in community disintegration and resistance.

1

In the present volume, a group of distinguished scholars expand the aims of the special issue with case studies that address a set of issues and questions that are now central to anthropology and more broadly, the social sciences. Particularly since the advent of neoliberal policies enacted by governments around the globe, a renewed but ongoing debate about globalization, its processes and its effects on peoples, communities, regions, and nations has driven theory and policy discussions toward the differential pressures on economic and social participation, autonomy, social movements, human rights, and the attributes of power as they are applied to problems of basic human survival. *Inclusion* and *exclusion* seem appropriate organizing references for this discussion, for much of the current literature comments on the forces that are powering the current processes, which include those peoples and places that may be well integrated, as well as those who may be or become disenfranchised in the current politics of globalization. Any particular case study will produce instances of both, depending on the unit of analysis and the problem addressed. When we speak of inclusion and exclusion, then, we need to delineate *what kind* of inclusion, what it represents, and the resources and the specificity of place where groups, communities, corporations, states, governments, and civil society intersect. This intersection is by necessity political and economic, or what Pierre Bourdieu refers to as "a field of struggles," encompassing agents with varying resources and with constraints and possibilities built into their position. He stresses that for global managers "far from being faced with a weightless, constraint-free world in which to develop their strategies at leisure, they are oriented by the constraints and possibilities built into their position and by the representation they are about to form of that position and the positions of their competitors as a function of the information at their disposal and their cognitive structures" (Bourdieu 2005, 199–200). This leads us to a starting proposition that underlies the analysis of power as it is regarded among agents and actors.

The following papers, then, revisit the enduring debate regarding the binaries of capital-intensive versus less-developed regions, their inhabitants, and communities, and suggests that our analyses need to be generated by on-the-ground ethnography that can inform our understanding of the world as it presently exists. While the enduring characteristics of inclusion and exclusion are delineated in each of these essays, together they put forward that we need to move away from analyses that stress the abstractions of *space* without including the components of how space is constructed, formulated, and reflected in a widespread ideology that values the free-flow and unfettered organization of capital over the people who inhabit fluid communities where capital intervenes and is confronted by localized responses.

GLOBALIZATION AND ITS THEORISTS

Globalization often has the connotation, within both specialized and more public circles, of being a monolithic and homogeneous concept. It is conceptualized as a natural process that has integrated the world with winners and losers that correspond to the industrial centers and peripheral outposts. Many readers will recognize this binary designation as one that assimilates a recurring debate fostered by the publication of *The Modern World System* in 1974. In this seminal volume, Immanuel Wallerstein argued that a world system had developed that separated areas and regions into "cores," "peripheries," and "semi-peripheries," depending on their roles in the world economy. Peripheral areas serviced the core states with capital, labor, and commodities. The controversy around this argument centered, first, on the role of the periphery in shaping the practices of the core; many have also questioned the sudden emergence of the world system in Wallerstein's conceptual framework. Eric Wolf's *Europe and the People without History* (1982) notably argued that there was an active precapitalist world system that had to be accounted for if modern capitalism was to be correctly understood. Similarly, Goody (Chapter 1, this volume) argues that world systems and similarities in social behavior were present long before the current discussions around the creation of global cultural homogeneity. In particular, Goody reminds us that trade routes in the fourteenth century brought about similarities in consumption and artistic forms, and that other configurations of globalization have existed since the appearance of stone-age axes, representing part of a "unity of mankind." He uses as units of analysis families, marriage, education, and the globalization of the demographic transition as examples of universal variables that can be used to compare modern globalizing societies.

Early on in the discussions of world systems analysis, June Nash (1981) reminded us that anthropology has had a world focus since its inception, and that at the time of her writing, anthropologists were recognizing that their fields of study were no longer isolated communities separated from their neighboring or far-off regions and states. In her seminal article, "Ethnographic Aspects of the World Capitalist System" (1981), she recalled two past presidents of the American Anthropological Association, both of whom counseled that our subjects were well integrated into existing social networks:

As a result of world integration, Colson warned, "Not only is our basic subject matter suspect, but often enough we are told that we are now superfluous given that the 'primitive' cultures, which some assume we study, are disappearing and everyone is now, or is soon to be, a member of a world society dominated by giant industrial bureaucracies and contending imperialism." While she forecasts as a central problem of the 1980s the "implications of the large-scale organizations within which so many of us now spend our lives," Bohannon asserts that the most important topic might be the "'world problematique' concerning population, pollution and conservation of resources." (Nash 1981, 394–5).

One of the primary concerns with Wallerstein's argument was that he insisted on designating the world system as *the* world system. He contemplated his analysis within a context of a single entity, uncomplicated by multiple modes of production, uneven and combined development, or processes of development and change that went from the periphery and semiperiphery to the core and vice versa. In creating such a model, many contended that the binary of power, that between the core and the periphery, could not tell us much about how peoples dealt with those bureaucracies and contending imperialisms noted by the presidents of the American Anthropological Association, nor could they account for changes on the ground that were being witnessed by fieldworkers and theorists alike. Competitive capitalism presents complex relationships among core industries and countries; states still play an important role in protecting favored multinational organizations and in the creation of free trade zones along with protected commodities. The multivaried resistance to managerial strategies are often lost in the analyses of overly simplified processes, which present all-encompassing pretexts for the analyses of world schema.

Since Wallerstein's provocative and widely debated formulation, the workings of global processes have taken an even stronger place in the anthropological literature, as it has in other disciplines and in the realm of civil society. The current focus is not so much the created binary between *core* and *periphery*, as it is the disappearance of boundaries and communities as capital-intensive states as industries overpower potential obstacles to their expansion (and the ideologies that accompany them) with ideology, industrial reorganization, capital reallocation, or force. As new currents of analysis have come to the fore, *space* and *place* have become recurrent issues in anthropological analyses as processes of globalization continue to challenge the assumptions of community-based ethnographic research. A growing trend in our discipline claims that we now inhabit a *spaceless* world, where the flow of people, commodities, and capital powerfully overshadows the activities of peoples attempting to maintain community lifestyles, beliefs, and traditions.

The possibilities of redefining or eliminating boundaries in our studies have raised questions of voice and agency for the people we engage and the resulting narratives that we provide. The incorporation of globalization and its consequent emphases on time, access to resources, and control over labor and social reproduction have altered the way we approach ethnographic analysis. In this attempt to integrate shifts in political influence resulting from global processes, we may create dichotomies that marginalize the local and its role in determining the course of globalization. While the strategies of global are often aimed at controlling geographical spaces, they may also reinforce the resistance of local struggles based on the politics of place.

Thus, what is often forgotten in the postmodern analysis of late-capitalist accumulation is the sense of place, where people live, resist domination, and maintain their communities. That localized responses have not been prominent in the literature is documented by Nash in her "Globalization and the Cultivation of Peripheral Vision" (2001a), and which she backs up with over forty years of fieldwork in a Mayan community (Nash 2001b).

The inclusion or exclusion of social actors in the processes of globalization, enculturation, and development are products of power and policy, but they are also, often, the failure of analyses to recognize the role that stakeholders play in the development of social organization and production. In this way, our analyses do reflect the ideology of our social surroundings, as the media and the *mouthtalk* of government agencies and multinational corporations assure us that boundaries no longer exist, only possibilities for increased expansion and profit. In addition, the relegating of local regions as the passive "victims" of globalization promotes the same social ideation as the promises of increasing stock prices and the consequent accumulation of wealth, despite what may be temporary setbacks.

Reemphasizing the local and the importance of place in furthering our understanding of the processes of globalization presents the possibilities of examining those who are benefiting from current social policies and those who are meant to lose in the strategies presented by world bodies such as the World Trade Organization, the World Bank, and the International Monetary Fund, and carried through in practice by multinational organizations whose primary concern is the accumulation of capital. In approach, the propositions that these multilateral organizations put forward resemble in kind the doctrines of "modernization" developed by Walter Rustow and his colleagues at the University of Texas (1960) and quickly adopted by government policy developers as a way of rationalizing why some economies were "developing" and others seemed wedged in some sort of premodern nexus. The policies and theoretical assumptions developed under this rubric simply assumed that if national economies would only follow the correct "stages of economic growth," the world capitalist system could function smoothly while guaranteeing better living standards for all. The allure of these postulates was, of course, that the theory could not be found at fault. If economies failed to develop, then there was obviously something amiss with the plans, and more often the attitudes, of its managers and citizens. If economies succeeded in developing a more "modern" competitive capitalism, then we had more data proving the venture correct and sustainable.

Like the proponents of modernization theory, promoters of unfettered globalization assume that geographic boundaries only create obstacles to the development of healthy economies where peoples can be free to find improved lifestyles and better employment in any part of the world they choose. Even the secretary general of the United Nations, at a special UNESCO conference on "open boarders" wondered optimistically about a world where migrations could occur without boarders and the suppression of boarder controls (Pecoud and Guchteneire 2005). The premise is that migrants would be treated with the same rights and freedoms as citizens, a fantasy that completely ignores the fate of migrants in the world today.

WORLD SYSTEMS THEORY REVISITED

Whether regarded as an inevitable phenomenon or studied as part of ongoing social change, studies of globalization are now at the forefront of the social sciences. Fortunately, if Sassen's work (1998, 2000; Chapter 2, this volume), is an indication, we are now moving from the blind assertion that globalization is occurring, to the necessary inquiry of globalization as a phenomenon that requires conceptual frameworks and empirical investigations. Sassen starts with the postulate that questions of place and scale are not self-evident in the globalizing arena, and that we need to study the variety of dynamics that are a part of globalization if we are to understand how it is operating in specific places. This emphasis provides empirical detail that transcends the usual focus on the power of corporations over governments and economies, marking instead the components of production that characterize changes in skill level, operational fluidity, and the centrality of the local. By taking as her example the telecommunications industry, she shows that the nonmobile parts of the global infrastructure contradict the tacit knowledge that globalization is a narrative of eviction moving through unblocked space. Sassen emphasizes that the local itself is in need of investigation. As she tells us:

> a critical reconceptualization of the local ... entails an at least partial rejection of the notion that local scales are inevitably part of nested hierarchies of scale running from the local to the regional, the national, the international. Localities or local practices can constitute multiscalar systems—operating across scales and not merely scaling upwards because of new communication capabilities.

The local and its relationship to any conceptualization of globalization is thus more than the local's integration with other forms of social organization. The qualitative difference between what is occurring in local fields and how those fields interact with exogenous forces are two kinds of inquiry. We can move, for example, from the determination that the local sphere interacts with multinational corporations through a variety of venues and actions, to Bourdieu's (2005) problematique (as Bohannan would have it) of "core" and "periphery" useful only as a symbolic force created by "superimposing two sets of oppositions" (2005, 127). The local thereby becomes the venue whereby bureaucratic structures carry out their decisions at "external outposts" as the first set of oppositions. The second set of oppositions are the bureaucracy itself "and everything external to it: 'subjects' or 'citizens,' and also 'local communities' or, in other words, between the 'public services' and the 'private interests,' between the 'general interest' and the 'particular interest'" (127). In this instance, all of these structures carry out their actions through existing and developing structural constraints, and policy and regulatory measures are themselves reinterpreted though sets of interactions among agents. Complementing Sassen's argument, then, he writes,

> This means that we cannot conceive the relationship between the "national" and the "local" the "centre" and the "periphery" as a relationship between a universal rule and its particular application, between conception and execution. The view one gets from the "centres" of power, the view that makes one tend

to perceive (geographically or socially) "peripheral" religions and forms of worship as magical rituals, regional languages as (provincial) dialects, etc. foists itself insidiously on social science and it would be easy to demonstrate that many uses of the opposition between "centre" and "periphery" (or between the *universal* and the *parochial*), apart from making effects of domination vanish between a semblance of descriptive neutrality, tend to establish a hierarchy between the two opposing terms (126).

The case examples presented here show that globalization and its effects vary as it takes different forms in an arrangement that is geographically site specific. It is not a monolithic force but a series of processes that change and are changed by its interactive sphere. Castells puts it this way: "Globalization proceeds selectively, including and excluding segments of economies and societies in and out of the networks of information, wealth and power that characterize the new dominant system" (1998, 162). The *local* then, may include social fields as complex and differentiated as any description of the global arena. Elites, governments and their agents, workers, communities, and struggles all exist within "local" frameworks that are themselves historically specific and include the categories of class, status, and power that compose that arrangement. Any ethnographic exposition of the local quickly and easily exposes the complexity of the social field and the relationships of inclusion and exclusion presented.

Too, analysis of globalization is affected as much by the theoretical orientation of its analysts and the general environment in which they are writing as empirical events on the ground. Wolf's (1969) caution that our social analyses and definitions of concepts are products of the processes and changes in the wider social organization still holds in an age of increasing complexity. Indeed, one of the theoretical innovations that feminism brought to social science theory was the necessity of proclaiming one's point of view—and one's politics—as an obligatory and essential ingredient of any investigation. The differences among those who would analyze an ethnographic site and the processes of globalization from the point of view of postmodernism or poststructuralism, and those who would insist on a more materialist analysis are political. Postmodernism and poststructuralism, for example, focus on the self and the deconstruction of collective community. Any descriptive tool that attempts to include or compare a variety of realities becomes *essentialist*—an accusatory label that Nash (Chapter 4, this volume) welcomes. These are not proactive tools, for in their rush to deconstruct any notion of a group or identity—no matter how fluid and temporary they might be—they leave us without a basis to *construct* alternate social descriptions and possibilities. These modes of analysis dismiss agency, and run the danger of forgetting that observable norms do exist, are enforced through socialization, and are fundamental to the exercise of power. What these constructions do instead is codify differences in social realities into arguments about theory, rather than grounding them in society and history. The realities of ethnography—the observation of real people going about their daily lives in tandem with the struggles that emerge from a world capitalist system—will ultimately prove these theoretical constructs incompatible with a scientific, and a humanistic, anthropology.

Smith and Mantz (Chapter 3, this volume) aptly demonstrate the result of these differing approaches by posing two interpretations of the place and nature of cities in the current literature. In one account, the city has become a digital divide "shaped by connectivity and bandwidth constraints" inhabited by fragmented subjects ruled by the intangencies of software. The other view is the more traditional one, where cities act as centers of administrative and economic activity and are bound by networks. These cities are more in danger of rapid social change as natural disasters and managerial deterioration threaten their very existence in an era where militias may dominate city buildings or volcanoes and hurricanes may wipe out the infrastructure altogether. Smith and Mantz ask: "How is it possible for two social observers, writing at roughly the same moment in history, to make such radically opposed pronouncements about the state of the world, of the nature of being in it, and of the capacity of humans to change it?" They answer that we are really observing two sides of the same coin, and that the answer lies in unpacking the connections and place of cities as local arenas operating within connections that integrate them into wider social issues and phenomena. The case example they use is the city of Goma in the eastern Congo, which that was almost entirely destroyed by a volcano. Despite this widespread destruction coupled with ongoing warfare among neighboring countries, this area mines 80 percent of the world's supply of columbite-tantalite, a silicate that is needed for all microchips found in digital technology today. This fact undeniably ties the eastern Congo into a transnational market transversed with middlemen and militias that ensure the trade of what is locally known as *coltan*. The existence of a mineral that is needed for the functioning of the kind of city described by our first observer, combined with the relations of production that exist to coerce workers into producing this mineral, presents an ironic twist to the digital divide that is hard to imagine in the world of academic theorizing. In the author's words:

> The fact that most of the world's supply of coltan is located in the Congo also means that the cultural dispositions associated with postmodernism (the emphasis on subjectivity, ambiguity, flexibility, multivocality, and the generative power of consumption as a form of agency and politics) are dependent on genocide, ecocide, incarceration, and perhaps more importantly for those seeking an antidote to the overriding focus on consumption in contemporary thought, *production* in the Congo (this volume).

Smith and Mantz note a specificity about the eastern Congo and about Goma that combines the abstract world of postmodern transactions and the commodity that is being produced there. While Goma provides an obvious example of what can be missed if we concentrate on binaries that do not integrate the intricate specificity of global transactions and processes with local realities, each of the papers in this volume tells a story equally dependent on sound ethnographic research. Development theory then becomes more than abstract renditions of what Wolf refers to as action upon action (1999, 45) or contexts of space through which capital flows among markets. It becomes the description and inclusion of the place where peoples, workers, and communities experience life and attempt to maintain and defend their existence.

DEVELOPMENT THEORY, SOCIAL COHESION, AND THE NEW INDIGENISM

Beyond ongoing arguments about the nature of globalization and the interaction of the global and local contexts, our recent epoch has witnessed an upsurge in demands for local autonomy, particularly among indigenous peoples. Indigenous peoples no longer simply symbolize the public stereotype of a more simple and more natural way of life. As anthropologists have discovered when their subjects turn up at American Anthropological Association meetings, indigenous peoples no longer consider themselves outside the realm of international politics, if they ever did. Indigenous movements have become vital parts of a civil society that is challenging the view that passivity on the local level is to be expected, particularly in undercapitalized areas of the world.

Anthropologists are attending to the widespread growth of indigenous movements around the world, from Christian assertions of identity recognition in Japan and the reassertion of Welsh in Great

Britain, to the Zapitistas in Mexico, Mayas in Guatemala, Brazil's Landless Workers Movement, Cherokee culture in the United States, and the ethnic movements of the Philippines. In all of these developments exists the common cause of place-based autonomy from outside control. For here what drives the maintenance of resistance is the pursuit of community stability.

In their chapters, both Lee and Conklin provide examples of how indigenous peoples and indigenous movements have gained a new respect in the global arena. This respect is a result, primarily, of 1) an intensifying public concern with the environment and an assumption that indigenous peoples can illustrate the values required for environmental policies that safeguard the earth's resources, and 2) a disquiet that indigenous peoples and small-scale societies are in danger of extinction as global processes overwhelm what were perceived to be autonomous, self-bounded social formations. The third element, that of the activism of indigenous peoples themselves, has not as often been noted by journalists and say, environmental activists, though it is this aspect that has most effectively catapulted indigenous concerns to the center of the world stage. The political stake that has been undertaken by what Lee calls the "small peoples" has been a result of a globally uniform drive for claims on agendas that would otherwise see them disappearing into a vast underclass. Lee's paper shows how small peoples have, by necessity, reinvented themselves, including the definition and use of the term *indigenous*. Rather than be simply defined as another group of poor citizens of the south, or an encapsulated underclass, many indigenous groups have used their status to defend their autonomy from the strategies of dislocating state and multinational agendas and their inclusion into arenas that at least provide a promise for the maintenance of community and lifestyle, and sometimes an acknowledgement of past wrongs. But with this integration comes the problems that have infected the populations of the world, sometimes in an even more exaggerated form: alcoholism, suicide, ill-gotten gains, and a process of internal differentiation that mimics the inequities of the global order. What is preserved, however, is a sense of place and rootedness that migrants and children of migrants often lack. This fact by itself makes, as Lee warns in his essay, "indigenous" a category "that postmodern anthropology ignores at its peril." If the past two decades have witnessed a new respect for indigenous concerns and beliefs, it has done so against a backdrop of academic theorizing that noticeably ignores the specific histories and alternate ways of being that characterize small peoples. Although the novel theories of globalization would have us visualizing an interconnected world that subsumes all

12 • Inclusion and Exclusion in the Global Arena

peoples in "*a) ethnoscapes, b) mediascapes, c) technoscapes, d) finances-capes, and e) ideoscapes*"—visions of boundaryless territories in which everyone becomes a migrant and citizen of the world (cf. Appadurai 2002, 50, italics in the original), they forget that, for example, genera-tions and age-grades are not separate categories from migration and oppression. They are meant to describe "imagined worlds" in which "the individual actor is "the last locus of this perspectival set of land-scapes" (Appadurai, 51), in which the most determined part of any formation is *motion* (my emphasis). They therefore "characterize inter-national capital as deeply as they do international clothing styles" (50). But even if some credence is given to the possibility of subversion in these analytic domains, peoples, in the abstract, are still the passive recipients of global forces that run slipshod over traditional ways of thinking and being. In fact, these formulations start to sound very much like updated versions of core and periphery, where the core has become the abstraction of special configurations of capital, products, media, and ideas, and the periphery the undifferentiated peoples of the world subject to massive "scapable" and overwhelming forces. Given these circumstances, it is easy to conclude that an anthropology that depends on ethnography is dead, or at least unnecessary. But if this is to be the case, what can we say about the historical circumstances by which aboriginal peoples have rejected intrusions into their ways of being and their sense of place? What is the place of traditionalists and resisters in a world where modernizers and assimilationists have no choice but to go with the flow? What if, as Nash asks in her chapter, indigenous groups do not follow "an ideology that sees capitalist devel-opment as the pinnacle of healthy human progress?"

Conklin's essay, "Environmentalism, Global Community and the New Indigenism," illustrates how the new indigenism depends, first and foremost, on self-determination. Struggles for self-determination have been limited by national borders, particularly when policies put forward by indigenous groups have differed from those proffered by state managers, most notably in regard to land and its uses (see Conk-lin, Chapter 6, this volume). Sylvain (Chapter 7, this volume) takes this problem a step further in her discussion of San politics and definitions of indigenism, recounting how the Bushmen themselves, utilizing what Lee and Sylvain both refer to in their essays as a "strategic essential-ism," self-identify as organically linked to the land. In Sylvain's terms, the San are "not asserting ethnic or national identities in an effort to get their bearings, so much as they are mobilizing an idea of culture made available by globalization to secure resources and social, eco-nomic, and cultural rights."

The Bushmen have long had to contend with stereotypes and assumptions about their behavior and the nature of their very existence. Their identity has been manipulated to explain away violence, exploitation, and poverty. Sylvain's chapter documents a manufactured confusion derived from the needs of the state and an endemic corruption that has involved the San in their role as attractors of tourists as well as their place in increasingly politicized communities. The San themselves have often played the role of stereotyped pristine primordial hunter-gathers in an effort to reclaim their ancestral lands. This, as Sylvain explains, is a reaction to globalizing processes that present a stereotyped version of what constitutes culture. While local tourist agencies market "traditional" culture, the state and farmers both use these presentations to underpay San workers and ignore their class positions. By taking back the definition of their culture and using it to their own advantage, the San—who are the second largest group of farmworkers in the region—both appeal to a global understanding of indigenous rights while presenting a self-defined constituency. It is at the intersection of situated understandings of identity and place that the Bushmen carve out their demands for a share of the rewards of work and their rightful place in the economy.

The San have found ways of negotiating their position within a global framework by insisting on their inclusion in the state's definition of development. Development, as Nash tells us, involves ideologies that constantly evolve to justify investment and the extraction of profit that creates winners and losers on a worldwide basis. Investment is often simply colonialism under another name, and from the standpoint of capitalist managers, a benchmark of successful globalism is often the increasing differentiation of peoples within states, which creates new opportunities for internal colonization.

Development processes, as Nash's paper demonstrates, are products of ideologies and the rhetoric that rationalizes them. Nash identifies three stages of development in the twentieth century, the first consisting of the "stages of economic growth" discussed earlier (as promoted by Rustow and his followers), which rationalized both successful and failing capital-dependent economies and the strategies that accompanied them, from investments in capital-intensive agriculture to the burning of the Vietnamese forests that drove whole populations into urban areas. The second trend emerged in the 1980s as a result of the exhaustion of trade in primary products, and was led by international banking organizations that shifted debt from capital-intensive states and industries to low-income producers and taxpayers, bankrupting whole nations while capital flew into increasingly large industry banks.

The third stage, which we are currently witnessing, is one of neoliberal capitalist expansion that assumes the freedom of movement for capital, goods, services, and peoples, along with larger free-trade zones. Returning to the economics of Adam Smith's *The Wealth of Nations,* what neoliberalism requires for success is freedom from government intervention of any kind—indeed, the idea of government is inherently faulty; any regulations that pose the possibility of reducing profits needs to be deconstructed. Importantly, an ideology of neoliberalism upholds the individual as the primary vector of social responsibility, and the state's role becomes one of reducing itself rather than serving as a regulator of goods and services and a vehicle for governmentality. Hence, the crisis of the New Orleans hurricane strike and its aftermath in an age of neoliberalism becomes understandable. The appointment of incompetent managers to positions of major social responsibility is made predictable. If the ultimate goal is to diminish the role of government, then those marginally in charge of its institutions can use their positions to enable the growth of their own corporate connections without the responsibility of upholding past expectations of their agencies; their offices become playgrounds for their own entitled social networks. The Republican Party's Contract with America becomes one of the devolution of government controls and expected controls over government, rather than an idea of the public good and the defense of the nation and its communities.

Neoliberalism has not proceeded without resistance, however, and it is in the growth of civil society by way of nongovernmental organizations (NGOs), and other nongovernment-sponsored efforts that Nash argues indigenous people's have made gains in both recognition and claims of autonomy. If civil society, as Habermas (1991) would have it, is truly the alternative to the modern state, then the neoliberal state is the perfect place for its development and growth. Civil society has challenged the mechanisms of multilateral organizations and agreements in controlling debate and action. As governments have moved toward divorcing themselves from control over trade and expansion, they have also abdicated their central role in the global landscape. The weakening of states and the growth of civil society has given indigenous peoples an outlet for increasingly potent demands for inclusion in the distribution of goods as well as calls for autonomy from dominant social and cultural controls. Moreover, the growth of civil society has allowed, for the first time, a significant place for women and women's work in the definition of development, as indigenous peoples participate in regional and global congresses. While Castells warns us that the state and civil society are not as separate as Habermas would have us believe (in this words, "Civil society is where NGOs have their offices" [2003, 181]), clearly the expansion of this sector has led to a growth in opportunities and support for social movements and new forms of affiliation that have benefited previously excluded segments of the population. The struggles that continue, from the direct investment in indigenous areas for the commoditization of plants and human genes, to the contests over land claims and the natural resources they hold, will undoubtedly reverberate over the world stage as more indigenous groups integrate their concerns with like-minded communities and NGOs. As the primary labor force in the domestic economy, women will continue to act as forceful organizers in the defense of territory and culture (Nash, Chapter 4, this volume). Environmental movements in particular have recognized the importance of participating with indigenous groups in the defense of their communities and their resource claims. Nash notes that undercapitalized economies are being urged to develop commodity export strategies by multinational banking controls and development strategists without regard to internal consumption needs. The emphasis is still on what can be gained from ravaging local areas for the availability of cheap natural resources. But as all of the contributors to the section on "Development Theory and the New Indigenism" have noted, convincing indigenous groups to follow the rhetoric that would have them practice harmful strategies is no longer as trouble-free as earlier attempts would suggest.

IDENTITY, SOCIAL PLANNING, AND POLITICAL POWER

Identity has become an increasingly contested concept in anthropology, as it has in academia as a whole. Few would argue that the discussion is uniquely academic; the idea that identity does or does not exist normally has little place in public spheres where politics and the access to, and distribution of, resources are more noteworthy subjects. Nonetheless, the question of identity has become part of the postmodern debate, and has significantly engaged our analyses over the past twenty years, while influencing a whole generation of anthropologists.

The paper by Wolf that is included in this volume (Chapter 8) was given as the Edward Westermarck Memorial Lecture at the Westermarck Society of Finland in 1984. It was included because of its particular relevance to the issues addressed here. Although written in 1984, the concepts and explanations provoke important considerations that have been part of anthropology since its beginnings, and remain so in an era of increasing globalization. Wolf tells us that identity does not have a particular relevance without its connection to a larger whole, and he provides a brief definition of both incorporation and identity that will serve us well in this discussion. He writes:

> By processes of incorporation I mean the recruitment of people into particular modes of mobilizing and deploying social labor; processes of identity making and unmaking refer to the creation and abrogation of the cultural markers and culturally informed activities by which populations define themselves and are defined by others in the process of incorporation.

Incorporation and identity are therefore, as he continues, "'a process' because I believe that we cannot understand either incorporation or identity making as static phenomena; they must be seen as unfolding historically in time." Key to the understanding of identity, then, is the way in which peoples reproduce their social beings and the embodiment of mutual recognition among members of the group. Wolf goes on to comment that he sees these processes in objective rather than subjective terms. Culture content, for example, is subject to constant change and act as unreliable as markers of identity. Even received tradition is subject to change and interpretation. What is true about the modern world is that is has been shaped by capitalist relations of production, and it is therefore in this realm that we need to concentrate our discussions of how social order is maintained through the organization and reorganization of social relationships. Wolf points out that "distinctions of group identity may become strategic in securing or accumulating strategic resources," a point that every paper in this volume has demonstrated.

Postmodernists, on the other hand, posit that identity is not a viable category. Because individuals per se are merely the repositories of meaning as it is represented in language and text, identity can only serve to *essentialize* what would otherwise be fluid configurations of meaning and experience, which cannot be totally understood either by the reader or the author. In other words, describing the position of another can only result in the creation of "the other," a position that I have referred to elsewhere as the self-positioning of a "meta-identity," which defies description of oneself or others (Kirsch 2000). The position has relevance here because of the way that anthropologists have recently forgiven identity for the larger abstractions of time and space. For example, as James Clifford asks, "What does it mean, at the end of the twentieth century, to speak of … a 'native land?'" (quoted in Inda and Rosaldo, 68). In fact, conscientious postmodernists reject *all* categories as well as places; territories become reference points for metanarratives and definitions of community are rejected in favor of unstable boundaries (Kirsch, n.d.). The focus is on the individual, although it is rarely stated as such, for the category of individual, too, is unstable and undefinable.

For the anthropologist's project, this application of postmodern theory has indeed destabilized our methodologies and our narratives. Many seem no longer primarily interested in an ethnography that can tell about the goings-on of people on the ground, but rather are preoccupied with precepts and concepts that question basic anthropological knowledge. Gupta and Ferguson, who have played an influential role in this movement, have phrased their project this way:

> [The aim is] a critical exploration of the way received ideas about space and place have shaped and continue to shape anthropological common sense. In particular, we wish to explore how the renewed interest in theorizing space in postmodernist and feminist theory … —embodied in such notions as surveillance, panopticism, simulacra, deterritorialization, postmodern hyperspace, borderlands, and marginality—forces us to reevaluate such central analytic concepts in anthropology as that of "culture" and, by extension, the idea of "cultural difference" (2002, 65).

These concepts and approaches are attempts to understand and to restate a rapidly changing world and its consequences. The authors are worried that anthropological concepts do not adequately describe changes in world social organization by totalizing particular events and experiences, creating generalizations that do not stand up to closer scrutiny. But as the papers in the present volume show, one need not dismiss the strengths that are the hallmarks of anthropology—fieldwork, participation, and comparison—and by extension geographic space, culture, and oppression, in order to understand both specific cultures and general processes. Bridget O'Laughlin foresaw the problems with the impetus to redefine the description of society as early as 1975, when she wrote that "a 'vulgar' universalism is not the same as a general theory through which to interpret social representations and organization" (1975, 348).

I have argued (2000, 2006) that these propositions closely mirror the relations of production in late capitalism (cf. Mandel 1972). The late capitalism in which globalism has become a defining characteristic places the organization of social life in the realm of the individual. Because it is the individual who sells his or her labor, it is the individual's ultimate responsibility to survive, and it is the individual who becomes or rejects the markings of social groups. Capitalism has produced the ideal of the individual as separate and self-sustaining, a position that enhances the role of the self in determining consciousness and action. This has become even more evident in an era of neoliberalism where the individual becomes the recognized object of analysis; individuals are in charge of their own fate. In Western culture, we are reproached for our failure to eke out a living, while celebrated for taking charge. This ideology, which produces an *ideal* for living, has contradictory consequences. The failure of most to achieve workable lifestyles often accompanies the need to apportion blame. This blame is typically focused on oneself and on other individuals or groups. It is rarely directed at corporations with bureaucratic structures, which allow for distance from individual concerns. A self-involvement unknown in precapitalist societies thus promotes the social and individual disease that characterizes modern society.

The object of capitalist relations is profit and the accumulation of capital; it meets those ends by finding the cheapest sources of labor, and it is therefore that women and lower-paid segments of the labor force are the primary targets of transnational corporations. Through movement, deskilling, the destruction of communities, and through forced labor, capitalist managers attempt to maximize their position. As we see in Mantz and Smith's work, the workers may not even be aware of their place in the global economy, but their individual fate is dependent on the social relations of production that move their product from one part of the world to another. It is easy to forget, for example, that deterritorialization often proves to be much more a category of political strategy than a descriptive formulation.

By promoting the *self* of the individual as an alternative to wider social interaction, postmodern and poststructuralist analyses have mirrored these relations. The deconstruction that is a characteristic methodology of postmodern and poststructuralist discourse disassembles the social ties that bind, and labor, class, the political, and importantly, place, are contested categories. This brings us back to Wolf's (1974) warning that social analyses reproduce the attributes of the wider social organization, just as his discussion of identity and incorporation is based on the wider social organization of the period.

Safa's paper (Chapter 9) builds on the construction of identity and social cohesion as part of historical circumstance and changing social relations of production. Examining racial and ethnic divisions in Latin America, she counterposes the official refusal to acknowledge race as a category by Latin American and Caribbean governments to the reality of discrimination against Afrodescendent groups, and the attempts by these groups to gain official recognition. Racial phenomena are depicted by phenotype, and there has long been a tradition of *blanqueamiento,* or whitening, generally through marriage into a higher social class (which symbolically whitens, and when marrying a white person, physically whitens the children), or by adopting the behavior and values of higher classes. Those who engage this practice of whitening are not only those from lower economic strata: it is a cultural act of mainstreaming with the hope of improving one's position at the table, encompassing a long-standing global ideology of whiteness as an advanced, and by definition more acceptable and higher status. Like governments the world over, the state in Latin America has grown increasingly neoliberal and thus officially distant from the concerns of its citizens in regard to practices of inclusion and exclusion. Of particular note for Safa is the increasing organization of Afrodescendent women in nongovernmental organizations that accuse mainstream feminist and black movements of obscuring their cause.

The struggle for inclusion by Afrodecendent women in Latin American political struggles that demand recognition by the state reminds us that the organization of social movements around the world closely reproduces wider cultural realities. Thus many have claimed in the United States, for example, that the social movements of the 1960s did not provide a voice for women and minorities. The organization of these movements incorporated the hierarchy of the dominant culture, reserving leadership positions for men and those of a higher social class. Ultimately, this led to a splintering of these social movements, which did not have solid programs that could tie stakeholders together. Safa's Afrodescendent women are excluded both as nonwhite and as lower class by the more mainstream social movements. They are also devalued as women. Like their past counterparts in the United States, they are discriminated against both by the culture-at-large and by racial and class biases within organizations. Their struggle to gain strategic resources is also hampered by state policies that were put into place as a result of older, successful movements, such as the indigenous movements in Colombia and Nicaragua, which have laws on the books backed by international recognition, thereby granting resources to indigenous groups and making it easier to gain access to government agencies and resources. The growth of neoliberal policies is resistant to the creation of new protections or to the enforcement of policies that already exist. The strategy of the Afrodescendent NGOs to these policies and lack of enforcement is the attempt to raise the consciousness of blackness in Latin American and Caribbean contexts. This recognition of blackness is now under the umbrella of human rights, broadly asserted as the right to have access to life-sustaining resources *and* the right to be different. The additional paradox of governmental denials of racism based on biology and the reality of the social construction of race as a basis for discrimination has placed Afrodescendent women in a precarious position. There is a strategic necessity of deconstructing the racial democracy paradigms adopted by Latin American and Caribbean governments, just at a time when social movements in other parts of the world are presenting struggles against the racialization of populations and the concomitant access to resources. But as Safa tells us, there need not be the disappearance of racial or ethnic identities to recognize a pluralism that includes collective rights.

Kirsch's paper shows that even in the complex web of legislative politics and policies directed from outside communities and regions, local organizations can and do have a substantial effect on the way that global managers are allowed to carry out their strategies and frame their action. In the Florida Everglades, where Kirsch has carried out his work, the combination of a large and powerful sugar industry, highly profitable real estate development, and the need to redirect natural resources to high density coastal areas has resulted in a complex web of interaction among community organizations, politicians, and global managers of capital. The site is home to the Comprehensive Everglades Restoration Plan (CERP), a $16 billion project designed to "restore" the Everglades while providing additional water to the heavily populated coastal area. Funded by both state and federal sources, the question of how CERP operates and even what CERP will provide is one that changes daily as promised funding shifts and CERP projects are approved or rejected without public notice. Kirsch tells us that the region operates on local, national, and global levels, and access to resources may be directed as much by offices in the halls of the U.S. Congress as the dykes that control the flow of water in and out of the communities and to and from the Florida coast, where the decisions are made concerning community infrastructure and labor practices. By law, the operation of CERP requires community input, yet few members of the communities that surround Lake Okeechobee are aware of how CERP functions or the parts of CERP to which they are entitled. This situation is created by what Kirsch refers to as "manufactured participation," an intended method of exclusion whereby the required community input is sought in meetings scheduled early in the morning in cities as far as seventy miles away from the Everglades Agricultural Area (EAA). As might be expected, CERP is rife with politics, with scientific committees that disagree, with state political agendas simply disbanded, and development interests given priority in current planning. There is a real question as to whether CERP will happen at all, as early in the implementation a new biotech institute was given land for its development that is central to the successful restoration of the Everglades. Too, citizens and agencies alike now wonder whether any money will be available, given the war in Iraq, the destruction of New Orleans, and the stated priorities of providing water to new real estate developments. Lawsuits and secret planning abound, making it impossible for any individual or organization to fully understand what has occurred or what will be approved. Yet even under these circumstances, the citizens of Belle Glade have asserted themselves into the process, attending the meetings and closely following the purposefully complicated "explanations" that are presented by state and federal government agencies.

In Belle Glade, a community of 15,000 and the largest in the Everglades Agricultural Area, there are 192 community agencies and organizations, or one organization for every 152 citizens. The presence of the sugar industry and other agricultural interests and the long history of their labor practices has had a profound effect on the consciousness of the area's residents toward industry and politics, particularly as it affects community maintenance and daily living. The majority of these organizations are headed by African-American women, which is consistent with Nash's observation that as primary caretakers of families and communities, women tend to be more active in organizations meant to defend community life (Chapter 4, this volume). Up until recently, when much of the agricultural labor was mechanized as a result of lawsuits that challenged the inhuman working conditions present in the area and made real to the larger public by Edward R. Murrow's *Harvest of Shame* (1961), men were the primary workers in the sugar fields, migrating to other parts of the country when the crop in the EAA had been harvested. These days, agricultural workers are more likely to stay in the area year-round, living in the same migrant camps as they did forty years ago, but depending on far less work and with little or no access to even the most basic life-sustaining resources, such as health care and education. A recent essay by John Bowe in the *New Yorker*, titled "Nobodies," aptly asks if slavery exists in America. Using the same geographic area explored in Kirsch's paper, he concludes that it does. Even a representative of the U.S. Department of Justice refers to the area as "ground zero for modern slavery," (quoted in Bowe 2003, 121), and Bowe recalls some of the many stories of employer violence, hunger, sickness, and abuse that exist in the area.

While the receipts from fruit and vegetable sales has nearly doubled during the past two decades, the average wage of a farmworker in South Florida in 1998 was $6,574, lower than the national average of $7,500 (United States Department of Labor and the University of Florida surveys, quoted in Bowe 2003, 121). The corporations running the fruit and vegetable harvests are global: Pepsico, Coca-Cola, and Minute Maid to name a few; the fields are the *only* source of work for these migrants, as even fast food chains and movie theaters have shut down. The other source of employment in Belle Glade, prisons, is not available to these workers, who are often illegal. The result is the persistence of HIV transmission, domestic violence, and disease despite well-meaning intervention (cf. Stratford n.d.).

Belle Glade resembles a poor town in a newly independent county with few resources. Thirty miles east exists one of the symbols of international wealth and power: Palm Beach. The juxtaposition of these two small cities is a potent starting point for the analysis of internal colonialism in highly capitalized countries and the structural violence that accompanies it. The major industries, which in the past took at least a precursory interest in the town's infrastructure, are no longer playing that role. Like many towns and cities in the United States that have lost their primary employer, the town has been left without the resources or expertise to manage the infrastructure of daily living (cf. Kirsch 1998). But the citizens of the lake communities have not given up and continue to challenge the conditions under which they are meant to survive, and in small increments, they are able to move forward.

CONCLUSION: STRUCTURAL VIOLENCE AND STRUCTURAL POWER

The treatment of migrant workers that Kirsch describes, the conditions of the mines that Mantz and Smith document, the discrimination against Afrodescendent women that Safa discusses—indeed, the physical conditions of place that are remarked upon in all of the papers in the following pages have in common the position of workers, families, and communities in an era of rapid globalization. Endemic to that position is the structural violence that is present in the conditions under which these people live, and the structural power that creates it. Nancy Sheper-Hughes (Chapter 12) shows how violence has become a facet of everyday life. In both her case studies of Brazil and post-apartheid South Africa, violence is the unifying factor encountered by peoples of all groups and all age-groups. As this violence becomes a facet of everyday life, calls for the enforcement of human rights have been prominent on the world stage and have signified abuses that might otherwise have gone unnoticed. Sally Falk Moore's (Chapter 11) examples of human rights abuses in Burkina Faso and Kenya and the legal proceedings brought to counter these abuses have served to protect activists against the worst of government negligence or governmental participation in crimes against humanity. As a result of active NGO human rights networks, Moore tells us that legal sanctions have been imposed in almost every country in Africa, as they have in many countries around the world. As she tells us, "In Africa, the human rights movement has not only permeated the consciousness of elite educated Africans, but given the reach of the transistor radio, the idea of human rights, has sometimes touched the lives of ordinary, uneducated people." Further, she notes, "'human rights could be seen as one of the most globalized political values of our times'" (Wilson 1997, 1, quoted in Moore, this volume). The problem is enforcement, and the lack of power wielded by transnational tribunals and United Nations committees. Again, in her words,

> The International Criminal Tribunal for Rwanda (ICTR) set up by the U.N. Security Council is such an instance. The ICTR came into being in 1994 to find and prosecute those responsible for the Rwandan genocide, in which it is estimated that 800,000 Tutsi and some educated Hutu died. The International Tribunal arrested fifty-nine persons but has, to date, actually convicted only eight.

Even human rights NGOs regularly admit that the focus on rights rather than structural change runs the risk of masking the underlying principles that initiated the conditions that led to the abuse. Legal redress is difficult on both the local and the global levels, and in some cases, the focus on human rights has even strengthened neoliberal polices of nonintervention, which are backed by the economic ideals of free-market economies. While government agencies resist intervening in the name of neoliberal principles when it would seem necessary to do so, these same principles do not guarantee the calls for autonomy that are part of the struggles to gain access to or protect resources that have belonged to existing social groups for centuries. Often focusing on individual abuses rather than collective oppression, the discourse around human rights has occupied the space where discussions about collective interest, class-consciousness, and power were positioned. Too, as human rights NGOs are beginning to show, governmental bodies are experts at expounding the evils of human rights abuses in far-off places, while claiming that their own governments are abuse free. Calls for human rights protections and corrections by governments around the globe serve as definitional acts of their own practices, while human rights at home are assumed. There is a geography of human rights, one that assumes abuses in poorly developed economies while ignoring or recasting abuse in the highly capitalized states.

Derived from liberation theologians, structural violence is the situated place characterized by social inequality that is exerted systematically—"that is, indirectly—by everyone who belongs to a certain social order ... the concept of structural violence is intended to inform the study of the social machinery of oppression" (Farmer 2004). Scheper-Hughes and Bourgeois take the concept further by noting that it is "the violence of poverty, hunger, social exclusion and humiliation—[that] invariably translates into intimate and domestic violence" (Scheper Hughes and Bourgeois 2004, 1), and they make this part of their "violence continuum," which incorporates the "non-linear, productive, destructive, *and* reproductive" aspects of violence including the structural violence to which Farmer alludes (Scheper-Hughes and Bourgeois 2004, 1). Along with that violence and oppression, however, is the need to integrate the power that generates and maintains structural violence, and by which capitalist society is kept in operationally functional.

Wolf tells us that "power works differently in interpersonal relations, in institutional arenas and on the level of whole societies" (1999, 5). When we speak of structural violence, then, we need to identify the way in which structural power operates in order to obtain a full understanding of how it is generated and rationalized in social arenas. The structural power that maintains a capitalist mode of production is global, and it is those global relations or production that constrains or allows the parameters in which social fields operate. They, in turn, are conditioned by the circumstances that are confronted, whether through the nature of class struggle or the adamant demands for autonomy. Scheper-Hughes analyses of the operation of the death squads among the calls for democratization in Brazil and the Amy Biehl trial in South Africa, which reveal how ideation is created in the midst of crisis and its aftermath. All of the authors in this volume demonstrate the effects of power and advocate the need to empirically investigate how peoples deploy strategies of resistance in their demands for recognition and autonomy from sources of oppression. In short, what is called for is an anthropology of power that includes the analysis and reconstruction of events in localities around the world on scales that vary from the household to regional and continental organization.

Communication networks have made it possible for real-time witnessing of the violence that comes as a result of exclusion from the redistribution of resources. The uneven and combined development that can be the outcome of transnational interaction among social movements—and that has been realized in some areas, such as human rights—brings hope to those whose very lives are in danger and whose experience of violence is part of their families' and communities' daily survival.

Given the state of world politics, it is easy to become demoralized about the possibilities for change and the inclusion of all peoples in an equitable distribution of resources. Not only are we witnessing a rapid growth of extreme poverty, joblessness, and disease in both the developed and underdeveloped worlds, but even cultural production in the forms of literature, cinema, art, and science are increasingly bound by "commerce" and "market forces" and threatened with destruction (Bourdieu 1998, 122). Still, Bourdieu advocates "a reasoned utopia" against an "economic fatalism" that would have us believe that the world as it exists is as it should be. This reasoned utopia involves the rejection of the neoliberal society defined by banks and bankers and the documentation of the social costs of economic violence, while laying the foundation for *an economics of well-being* (Bourdieu 1998, 123). While he is referring specifically to the European context, his call forsakes wishful thinking for the creation of institutions and movements in redefining the social state and its functions. Anthropologists can play an important part in this reconceptualization of society by creating and evaluating the social indices that can lay the foundations for social movements and their adherents.

I conclude with statements by two of this volume's contributors, whose work has generated discussion concerning many of the trends covered in this introduction, and whose contributions to this volume build on their previous contributions to the discipline. Nancy Scheper-Hughes calls for an engaged anthropology that "witnesses" instead of "observes" (Scheper-Hughes 1995, 419), enabling description and involvement that can show the many ways in which people are exploited. One of the more insidious characteristics of structural violence, as Farmer (2004) points out, is the erasure of history and the machinery of suffering, and how suffering and poverty generate violence. Nash, in the first sentence of her ethnography of Mexican Maya, points out that "[a]nthropologists are privileged in the study of cultures with distinct worldviews since it allows us to explore alternatives to mainstream thought and action, and through this lens examine critically the assumptions that prevail in the centers of power (2000, 1). Both express a fundamental belief that we, as anthropologists today, must take political responsibility for our work and publications through a partnership with our subjects of study. All of the following papers advocate a moral philosophy of inclusion based on the rights and beliefs of peoples in their own surroundings. In a rapidly globalizing world, the movement of peoples from exclusion to inclusion will require fundamental changes in the way in which societies organize social reproduction and in particular, social labor. The lessons that can be learned from alternate ways of thinking and seeing provide a context for an anthropology that can make a difference.

REFERENCES

Appadurai, Arjun. 2002. "Disjuncture and Difference in the Global Cultural Economy." In *The Anthropology of Globalization*, ed., Xavier Inda and Renato Rosaldo, 46–64. Malden, MA: Blackwell.

Bourdieu, Pierre. 1998. "A Reasoned Utopia and Economic Fatalism." *New Left Review* 228:128–35.

Bourdieu, Pierre. 2005. *The Social Structures of the Economy*. Malden, MA: Polity Press.

Bowe, John. 2003. "Nobodies: Does Slavery Exist in America." *New Yorker*, April 21 & 28, 106–34,

Castells, Manuel. 1998. *The Rise of Network Society*. Malden, MA: Blackwell.

Castells, Manuel. 2003. *The Power of Identity*. Malden, MA: Blackwell Pub.

Edelman, Marc, and Angelique Haugerud, eds. 2004. *The Anthropology of Development and Globalization: From Classical Political Economy to Contemporary Neoliberalism*. Malden, MA: Blackwell Publishers.

Farmer, Paul. 2004. "The Anthropology of Structural Violence." *Current Anthropology* 45(3):305–25.

Goodhart, Michael. 2005. *Democracy as Human Rights: Freedom and Equality in Globalization*. New York: Routledge.

Gupta, Akhil and Ferguson, James, 2002. "Beyond Culture: Space, Identity and the Politics of Difference," in Xavier, Jonathan and Rosaldo, Rencto, eds. 2002, *The Anthology of Globalization*, Blackwell: Melden, MA.

Habermas Jurgen. 1991. *The Transformation of the Public Sphere*. Cambridge, MA: MIT Press.

Jacoby, Russell. 1999. *The End of Utopia: Politics and Culture in an Age of Apathy*. New York: Basic Books.

Kirsch, Max. 1998. *In the Wake of the Giant: Uneven Development and Multinational Restructuring in a New England Community*. Albany, NY: State University of New York Press.

Kirsch, Max. 2001. *Queer Theory and Social Change*. London: Routledge.

Kirsch, Max. 2006. "Queer Theory, Late Capitalism, and Internalized Homophobia." *Journal of Homosexuality* (spring); reprinted in *The Contested Terrain of LGBT Studies and Queer Theory*, ed. Karen Lovaas, John Elia, and Gust Yep. New York: The Haworth Press.

Kirsch, Max. N.d. "Community, Space, Place." Manuscript in preparation.

Lesser, Alexander. 1961. "Social Fields and the Evolution of Society." *Southwestern Journal of Anthropology* 17:40–48.

Lilla, Mark. 1998. "The Politics of Jacques Derrida." *New York Review of Books* (June 25), 45(11).

Mandel, Ernst. 1972. *Late Capitalism*. New York: New Left Books.

Murrow, Edward R. 1961. *Harvest of Shame*. CBS News Documentary. Film.

Mouffe, Chantal. 2005. *On the Political*. New York: Routledge.

Nash, June. 1981. "Ethnographic Aspects of the World Capitalist System." *Annual Reviews in Anthropology* 10:393–423

Nash, June. 2001. "Globalization and the Cultivation of Peripheral Vision." *Anthropology Today* 17:4, 15–22.

Nash, June. 2001b. *Mayan Visions*. New York: Routledge.

Nash, June. 2005. *Social Movements: A Reader*. Malden MA: Blackwell.

O'Laughlin, Bridget. 1975. "Marxist Approaches to Anthropology." *Annual Reviews in Anthropology*, 341–69.

Pecoud, Antoine, and Paul de Guchteneire. 2005. "Migration without Boarders: An Investigation into the Free Movement of People." *Global Migration Perspectives* 27 (April, whole issue).

Rostow, Walter Whitman. 1960. *The Stages of Economic Growth: A Non-Communist Manifesto*. Cambridge, UK: Cambridge University Press.

Sassen, Saskia. 1998. *Globalization and Its Discontents*. New York: New Press.

Sassen, Saskia. 2000. *Guests and Aliens*. New York: New Press.

Scheper-Hughes, Nancy and Philippe Bourgeois, eds. 2004. *Violence in War and Peace*. Malden, MA: Blackwell.

Scheper-Hughes, N. 1995. "The Primacy of the Ethnical: Propositions for a Militant Anthropology." Current Anthropology 36 (3): 409–40.

Scott, Joan. 1993. "The Evidence of Experience." In *The Lesbian and Gay Studies Reader*, ed. H. Abalove, M.A. Barale, and D. Halperin. New York: Routledge.

Stratford, Dale. N.d. "The Social Organization of Sexual-Economic Networks and the Persistence of HIV in a Rural Area," submitted manuscript, 2005.

Wolf, Eric. 1982. *Europe and the People without History*. Berkeley: University of California Press.

Wolf, Eric. 1999. *Envisioning Power: Ideologies of Dominance and Power*. Berkeley: University of California Press.

Wolf, Eric. 2001 (1969). "American Anthropologists and American Society." In *Pathways of Power*. Berkeley: University of California Press.

Xavier Inda and Renato Rosaldo, eds. 2002. *The Anthropology of Globalization*. Malden, MA: Blackwell.

I
World Systems Theory Revisited

1

GLOBALIZATION AND THE
DOMESTIC GROUP

Jack Goody

Globalization is often considered to be the process by which the world became the same or similar in certain aspects through the spread of Western, modern, ways. In this discussion I want to stress that it is not just a Western process, but that many similarities in social behavior, including those in the family, have long been present.

Globalization has become a prominent topic in recent years largely because of the extension of systems and modes of communication, to which I refer first to the media—the telegraph, the postal service, the newspaper, the radio, TV, e-mail and so forth—but also to transport, the fourteenth-century Chinese boats (junks), the improved sails of the smaller boats that took Vasco da Gama round the Cape to India and Columbus to the Americas. I want to insist this latter was not only a European process involving the so-called expansion of Europe, as important as that was; China, too, put out its feelers by land along the Silk Road to Europe, at least indirectly, and by sea into Southeast Asia and then to India and Africa, exporting manufactures (especially silk and ceramics) to the West long before the latter exported much to the East. Nevertheless, much of the later global framework was established as the result of the European voyages of the later fifteenth century onward and of the expansion of the media (initially printing) from the same period. Such activities were spurred on by commerce.

Let us remember that commerce, neither by land nor sea, was an invention of the West. The Semitic sailor-merchants of the Middle East, and here I refer to the Phoenicians and the Arabs generally as well as to the Jews, developed the trade route from the Suez area of Egypt down to western India, Gujerat, and Kerala.[1] There was an active seaborne trade in pepper and other spices, as well as other transportable luxuries from early in the modern era.[2] Indians were also coming to Africa and the Middle East. Indeed, it was Gujarat pilots (presumably Muslim since Hindus were more wary of the Five Seas) who directed Vasco da Gama's voyage from Malindi, a Muslim town on the east African coast, to Gujarat in western India. And in an eastward direction, the Portuguese Pires, and before him the Chinese, found many Indians inhabiting the entrepot of Malacca in present-day Malaysia.

This trade and commerce indeed brought about some interesting convergences, not only in consumption (of what was being traded). Whether over land or over sea, trade leads to developments, which while not inevitable, are encouraged or fostered. There was the organization of the voyage itself and the problem of the cargo (the dangers of losing it), which led to rather similar arrangements for the sharing of risk and for the distribution of profit; this developed into maritime insurance and the joint stock company. It led to communities of merchants, some rich, some less so, who developed similar cultural features in different parts of the world. For example, broadly similar artistic forms appeared in various urban communities. In the West, merchants encouraged the secular theater—Marlowe and Shakespeare in England especially in the city of London; in the East, in Tokyo (Edo), at roughly the same time, it was Kabuki. In China too, artistic activity flourished, not only at court, but especially in the merchant quarters. In port towns, members of different nations met, feasted together, and developed ways of cooking and preparing food that emerged out of these long-term encounters. Some convergence came from contact, even indirect, some from structural similarities in the situation, the fundamental requirements of parallel activities.

By structural similarities I mean that if you want to build a house or roof to keep out sun, rain, and other individuals, you can lean or bend the uprights together like a teepee, or you can curve the building blocks together as in an igloo or a mosque. If you want a flat roof, you need supporting posts or pillars and then long beams (only wood, traditionally), cross beams and slats, then a surface. You find ceilings or roofs of this kind in the LoDagaa compounds in northern Ghana and in dwellings in Spanish Wells in the Bahamas. There is no real question of borrowing or diffusion; similar problems require similar solutions. That is what I mean by structural similarities, leading to the widespread adoption of specific practices.

In both the case of contact and of structural similarities, there was a kind of globalization taking place. That is clear even in the Stone Age with hand axes, for example, which take similar shapes and have similar developmental sequences all over the globe. Archaeologists are accustomed to the notion of globalization in the sense that they find similar sequences of artifacts in many areas, from the Old to the Middle to the New Stone Age, and in some areas in the Chalcolithic (copper), to the Bronze and then the Iron Age.

Another phase of globalization began in the fifteenth and sixteenth centuries with the expansion not only of Europe, but of commerce more generally, and then again in the late eighteenth, nineteenth, and twentieth centuries with the spread of industrialization. These two processes are sometimes referred to under the rubric of the growth and advent of capitalism, or much more vaguely by the term *modernization* (generally Westernization). But it is better to separate the two periods, the first being marked by an intensification of mercantile activity (commercial as well as agricultural capitalism), which had long existed, plus the associated process of expansion and colonization, involving the extensive conquest (and sometimes settlement) of overseas territories. These new territories offered support to the metropolitan country by way of *privileged exchange* or what some have called "exploitation" (e.g., their trade with industrial Europe in foods, such as tea and sugar, and in textiles and raw materials), when that trade was not balanced or reciprocal.

Globalization, then, is often seen as the penetration and domination of the rest of the world by the West, but the process of globalization began long before. Similarities in human cultures were, as we have seen, due not only to external influence—to diffusion, as nineteenth-century anthropologists called it—but to parallel internal developments derived from what they also called the *unity of mankind* (man's common features), but also from common situations (structural) and from some process of common development, of social evolution, of changes arising out of the logic of the situation or its inherent potentialities. For example, if you were using Stone Age hand axes as the basic tool, one way you could progress was from flaked tools to polished ones—a change that roughly marked the shift from the Old to the New Stone Age, from Palaeolithic to Neolithic. Or the structure of the situation might work in a different way. Human reproduction requires the congress of man and woman, and the rearing of their vulnerable and unsocialized offspring, which implies some kind of a minimal structure that we can call a family. In this case there is no question of the similarities coming from an external force or mode, as we often think of when dealing with globalization.

There are some features of domestic relations that can be considered to have been global or globalized at an earlier time, but the tradition of many Western studies in history, demography, and the social sciences, embedded in the comparative advantage the political economy of Europe has displayed since the eighteenth century, has been to emphasize difference.

As Wolff (1994), Todorova (1993, 1997), and others have shown, the self-flattering viewpoint comparing a developed and progressive "West" with a backward and barbarous "East" came easily to Enlightenment intellectuals in western and central Europe, and left a residue of mental habits that weakened but did not disappear during the twentieth century. Twentieth-century revisions of this scheme have sometimes added to the West/East dichotomy a third region—the "Mediterranean" (cf. Mc Evedy and Jones 1978), and in some instances a fourth—"Central Europe" (Laslett 1983), "Northern Europe" (Coleman 1996: 4). Some of these clearly are categories to receive data, others to explain data patterns (Plakans 2001).

Some authors, especially Anglo-Saxon historians, have pursued an argument concerning the particularity of England as distinct from the rest of Europe, which they feel accounted for the emergence of the agricultural revolution and of industrial capitalism in that country. It is the island view—the Churchillian view—capitalism in one country.

Then there is the western European view adumbrated by Hajnal (among others) in a notable article on European marriage patterns (1965), where he tries to show how the differences in the general demographic trends in western European life (late age at marriage, accumulation of a dowry by working in towns, etc.); Flandrin (1979) stressed the psychological effects of *le marriage tardif*). Clearly this view is more acceptable to continental scholars, mindful of the not insignificant roles played by northern Italy, France, Spain, and Germany in the rise of the West—the uniqueness of the West. These are the views of Max Weber and Karl Marx, who were not as concerned about the peculiarities of the English as with the peculiarities of Protestantism or some forms of mercantilism.

In terms of earlier social formations, it is certainly the view of those scholars who have confined the distribution of feudal society to western Europe, and who, like Marx (until very late), have examined the non-European east in terms of quite different concepts, such as the

Asiatic mode of production, where a bureaucratic state imposed itself on so-called *primitive communities* or *primordial communalism*. The demographic transition in Europe is commonly viewed as a unique historical event, one quite distinct from the more recent decline in birth rates in various parts of the world, and associated with what is assumed to be another unique aspect of Europe—its development of capitalism.

Non-European countries were seen as unable to control their populations and, hence, as unable to adjust people to resources in order to produce the savings—the rational adjustment—that capitalism required. Such an argument was proposed by the famous historical demographer, Malthus, who saw Europe alone as having deliberate checks on its population, planning, in fact, where other countries (specifically China), had only the checks produced by natural forces such as famine, disease, and war. Thus Europe had deliberate internalized controls, planning, and restraint, where others were unrestrained except by external forces.

Lee and Wang have shown that this notion is quite incorrect with respect to China, which experienced a slow increase in population despite the earlier marriage, which Malthus and many subsequent demographers have seen as the critical factor: in Europe marriage occurred relatively late in life for both men and women, held back as people were by restraint.

The notion of restraint is very similar to that used by Norbert Elias (1978) in his work on what he calls, misleadingly in my opinion, the *civilizing process*. The internalization of prohibitions followed, he claims, the collapse of the feudal regimes with their reliance on external restraint, leading to the gradual shift to internal controls—a shift to modernization and to "civilization." Elias's notion has obvious affinities with Freud's view of the internalization of sexual drive and the restraints that civilized man exercises on his behavior in contrast to the uninhibited behavior of "savages" and children, who have not repressed their emotions.

In the same vein, Elias writes of the Africans he visited (he taught sociology for two years in Ghana, after his retirement in England) as *naturvolk*, people of nature, whose art forms (he collected African art) were less inhibited, freer, more natural, than those of modern man. These ideas were the common currency of much thinking about other cultures and earlier times and remain so today to a significant extent.

Until recently the demographic transition was viewed as a European phenomenon that was associated in some way (not always agreed upon), with modernization and the industrial revolution. Mortality rates dropped followed by a drop in birth rates, leading to smaller families. In developing countries in the 1960s and 1970s, mortality decreased but birth rates stubbornly refused to diminish, "no matter what the policies and practices of national and international relations" (Reher n.d., 2). There was a demographic explosion which was not at all discouraged by some African leaders, for example.

I have tried to show that from the standpoint of family, marriage, and indeed inheritance, which are closely linked, there are less differences between the East and West than those theories allow; the advanced societies on both continents display features of what I have called the *woman's property complex* in contradistinction to African societies. I see this difference as resulting from the difference between the advanced plough and irrigation systems of much of Eurasia and the hoe farming in Africa (Goody 1976). I argued that this difference would affect the speed of the demographic transition because the stratification and transmission systems of the former would require some greater calculation of the relationship of people to limited resources, whereas in the traditional societies of Africa, land was almost a free good.

However, one of the most striking aspects of the contemporary world and what has been called globalization is the remarkable convergence of aspects of familial relations; the focus on the small domestic group, including single parent households; and the increase in female-headed households, but above all the globalization of the demographic transition. My discussion is based on two recent studies, one by the East-West Center at Hawaii for Asia (Westley et al. 2002) and a more extensive enquiry by David Reher (n.d.).

Demographic transition is taking place throughout the continent of Asia. Death rates dropped first, birth rates remained high, and population was therefore greatly increased. But fifty or sixty years later, birth rates declined creating a relatively stable population, with a replacement rate of 2.1 (which allows for deaths, otherwise, of course, 2.0).

Over the past 50 years, many Asian countries have experienced a remarkable pace of economic development and social change. Modernization has progressed most quickly in the countries of East Asia. At 81 years, Japan now has the highest life expectancy in the world. In South Korea, the average annual income rose nearly ten-fold between 1960 and 1999. In the Philippines, more than three-fourths of girls now attend secondary school, and about one-third attend university. In India, fertility has dropped from about six to just over three children per woman (Westley et al. 2002, 1).

The change in eastern Asia has been more dramatic than anywhere else. In South Korea in 1950, a woman could expect to bear more than five children, in 2000 less than two. Over the same period, life expectancy in China has increased from 40 to 71 years. One result has been a very different life for women (especially the reduced time spent in childbearing) and a dramatic increase in the number of aged.

The change has been uneven, especially in southern, central, and Southeast Asia. Afghanistan has (at 46 years) one of the lowest life expectancies in the world. In Bangladesh, only 13 percent of girls attend secondary school. Women in several countries (e.g., Pakistan) have, on the average, more than five children each. Per capita income is low.

What has caused child mortality and other death rates in Asia to drop? The East-West Center credits new medical and public-health technology from Europe, especially vaccinations and pesticides (against malaria), that became available after World War II. The interesting point is that life expectancy increased in all the major regions of Asia, whatever the economic situation (though this, too, was improving throughout). The outcome has been a faster transition in Asia than in the West.

The transition involves the decline in birth rates that has occurred throughout Asia. It is argued that because child mortality has declined, fewer children are needed in any one family. As a result of education and changes in work patterns, children became a liability rather than an asset. Also the new economies compete for parents' time, which especially affects women and childbearing.

One other major result is that dependency ratios will change both for young and for old dependents. They will fall for the young and rise for the old. The temporary fall in ratios is known as a *demographic bonus*. If properly exploited, this change can lead to an opportunity for economic development.

Reher's data have the effect of generalizing this Asian picture to a global scale. He points out that from the perspective of the twenty-first century, the global nature of this transformation is hard to dispute. Within a period of 160 years, decisive demographic change has taken place throughout the world; decline in birth rates has commenced in all but 12 of the 145 nations used in his sample. This took place in two phases. From the latter part of the nineteenth century until about 1930, most European countries implemented conscious fertility control. During the second half of the century, the process spread throughout the world.

Reher argues that we should see the demographic transition as a "unified historical process," but there are differences, even among the forerunners. Birth rates were always considerably higher in the Americas than in Europe, both before and after the transition; for example, in the baby boom where rates approached 30 per thousand (which was close to the pretransition figure of 35). Growth rates in the Americas were therefore always much higher (15 to 18 per thousand) than in Europe (10 to 11 per thousand). Among those that followed the transition, mortality decline is first visible in the 1920s. Birth rates continue at 35 to 40 per thousand until the 1950s when they start a precipitous fall. Those countries Reder speaks of as the trailers had pretransition birth rates above 40 per thousand. Mortality transition started in the 1930s, birth rate decline in the 1970s. With respect to the latecomers, mortality began declining by the 1950s—the period for which we have data (possibly earlier if that were available). Birth rates declined in the 1980s, a feature that applied to Africa and parts of Asia. The general features in this process are that decreases in birth rates occur everywhere, proceeded by mortality decline—first for children, then for infants, then for adults. Reder sees this decline as beginning with the control of infectious diseases.

The interesting point is that this global shift has little to do with levels of wealth or with family-planning programs, but only with prior mortality. One great difference between the earlier transition and the later was that in the former, the gap between declines in mortality and birth rates was only five to ten years, whereas in the later it was thirty to forty years; this meant a huge increase in population, posing an enormous problem for development. Once it started, however, it was more rapid.

How should we account for this truly global change? "The original European mortality decline" (in the late nineteenth century) was mainly the result, argues Reher (n.d., 16), of "improved maternal education with respect to child bearing and child-rearing procedures, improving nutritional status and incipient public health measures spearheaded by government at the behest of the medical and scientific establishments." The decline in mortality rates depended on nutrition and education rather than intervention. But did practices really change so much in response to government pressures? And if so, what were the mechanisms?

I think we need to consider education in a more specific sense. Reher sees this change as due to "modernizing elements," which in Europe were basically "autochthonous." But in the rest of the world, it was due more to "the internalization of health care" even in the absence of profound social change.

Reher perceives this transition as taking place in Europe as the result of "a profound social transformation that involved the industrialization of society, the ascendance of salaried labour over inherited wealth, rapid urbanization, dramatic increase in educational levels, especially of women, massive overseas and rural to urban migration flows that helped stretch the strength of family ties, the increasing roles of public institutions, especially governments, for individual life, the emergence of powerful secular institutions (labor unions, for example) and, of course, the incipient democratization of public life" (n.d., 17).

Reher sees none of these forces as having much significance in most of the countries where a later decline set in, where although the response to mortality decline was delayed, it was much more rapid. That rapidity was partly due to the internationalization of reproductive behavior. The earlier transition (of the forerunners) took a shorter time to begin its adjustment, but a longer time to complete the process; currently, births no longer reach the replacement level (do not offset deaths).

The result is a severe labor shortage, extremely fast aging of the population, intense migratory pressure, and difficulties in maintaining pensions and other systems of social welfare. In advanced countries, the shortage of labor can be overcome by allowing immigration from the third world; pensions and social welfare can be partly covered because these are rich nations. What about Africa and the third world? Will this process cause births to fall below the replacement level producing similar problems for these countries, which will have no neighbors to provide labor and no accumulated resources to help the old? If so, the outlook for families in those areas may be bleak.

I want to refer to my experiences in West Africa for two reasons. First, because I predicted that the transition would be much slower than it has proved to be; I thought that profound economic changes would be necessary to enable people, where land was available, to realize this cost of growth. Second, because Africa was much less "developed" than most of Asia, much less ready for economic change, because in the precolonial period it still had hoe agriculture, fewer crafts, and virtually no written communication. So the most difficult task of all would be to explain (or even partly explain) the demographic transition there.

It has been largely a rural continent. As in India, urbanization could hardly be an adequate explanation of such a general phenomenon; nor could economic advances, since comparatively little has taken place. I suggest two factors were of great importance in the universal transition. The first is mobility. While little straightforward economic development had taken place, colonial and Western enterprises were heavily involved in exploiting primary resources such as mining, trading, the cultivation of cash crops, administration, all of which are activities that employed workers who had to leave their natal villages for long periods. Kith and kin had to be left behind, leading to an attenuation of such ties. In such families, the effects of migration on social life were enormous.

Both Asian and global studies concluded that medical and hygienic changes were important in reducing child mortality. While this factor was undoubtedly important, such changes have been uneven. I argue that we should pay more attention to education, which brought about its own more general changes. This has been significant throughout the world. There is scarcely a village anywhere since World War II that has not seen the advent of schools, of teachers, of pupils neatly dressed in shirts or blouses, in shorts or skirts. The authors of the East-West report remark upon this extraordinary growth of schools since Independence, when it has been one of the major changes promoted by new governments, by the United Nations, and by innumerable development agencies and religious bodies.

The effects of schooling have been staggering. I do not refer so much to the content of education as to other consequences, some of them unintended. That is clear from an autobiography of a close friend that I have just edited (Gandah n.d.). He was one of the first echelon of children to attend school in northwest Ghana and he describes in detail the almost obsessional discipline that was directed toward seeing that students' clothes and bodies were clean. These norms were internalized, reinforced by peer pressure, and affected even those village children who were not attending school. The schoolmaster took over a significant part of the parental role and provided an alternative focus of quasi-domestic authority for the growing child. Maintaining these standards involved considerable outlay on the parents' part. Not only did they have to give up claims on the children's labor, but they had to provide money for school uniforms, for food, and sometimes for books and materials. Parents were faced with the obvious calculus regarding the pros and cons of having more or fewer children. Not only did schools serve to reduce child mortality through hygiene, they also tended to reduce the numbers of births by increasing the burden on parents.

I have dealt very briefly with this important topic, but in this paper I have pointed to the universal phenomenon of demographic transition, unanticipated by many, and tried to indicate some equally important factors concerning its onset. Industrialization and urbanization seemed poor candidates; instead, I lean toward mobility and schooling as being more general, indeed, universal variables.

REFERENCES

Coleman, J. 1996. *Public Reading and the Reading Public in Late Medieval England and France*. Cambridge; New York: Cambridge University Press.

Elias, N. 1978. *The Civilizing Process*. Trans. Edmund Jephcott. New York: Urizen Books.

Flandrin, J-L. 1979. *Families in Former Times: Kinship, Household, and Sexuality*. Trans. Richard Southern. Cambridge; New York: Cambridge University Press.

Gandah, S. W. D. K. Forthcoming. *The Silent Rebel*. Institute of African Studies, Legon, Ghana.

Ghosh, Amitav. 1992. *In an Antique Land*. New Delhi: Ravi Dayal Publisher; Bangalore: Longman.

Goody, J. 1976. *Production and Reproduction*. Cambridge; New York: Cambridge University Press.

Hajnal, J. 1965. "European Marriage Patterns in Perspective." In *Population in History*, ed. D. V. Glass and D. E. C. Eversley. Chicago: Aldine.

Huntingford, G. W. B., ed. and trans. 1890. *The Periplus of the Erythraean Sea; with Some Extracts from Agatharkhidēs "On the Erythraean Sea."* London: Hakluyt Society.

Laslett, P. 1983. *The World We Have Lost: Further Explored*. London: Methuen.

Lee, J., and F. Wang. 1999. *One Quarter of Humanity: Malthusean Mythology and Chinese Realities 1700–2000*. Cambridge, MA: Harvard University Press.

McEvedy, C. (1978). *The Penguin Atlas of African History*. London Penguin.

Plakans, A. N.d.. "The Population of the Eastern European Region in the Second Millennium." IUSSP Conference, Florence, June 2001.

Reher, D. 2001. "The Demographic Transition Revisited as a Global Process." Paper presented at the IUSSP Conference, Florence, Italy, on The History of the World Population in the Second Millennium.

Todorova, M. N. 1993. *Balkan Family Structure and the European Pattern: Demographic Developments in Ottoman*. Washington, DC: American University Press.

Todorova. M. N. 1997. *Imagining the Balkans*. New York; Oxford, UK: Oxford University Press.

Westley, S. B., et al. 2002. *The Future of Population in Asia*. Hawaii:.

Wolff, L. 1994. *Inventing Eastern Europe: The Map of Civilization in the Mind*. Palo Alto, CA: Stanford University Press.

NOTES

1. For a popular account, see A. Ghosh, In an Antique Land. Otherwise, the works of Goitein on the Geniza manuscripts from tenth- to twelfth-century Cairo.

2. See G. W. B. Huntingford, ed., The Periplus of the Erythraean Sea.

2

THEORETICAL AND EMPIRICAL ELEMENTS IN THE STUDY OF GLOBALIZATION[1]

Saskia Sassen

This paper develops theoretical and methodological elements for studying and interpreting a variety of dynamics that are part of globalization but are often, perhaps typically, not thought of as such. Critical among these are questions of place and scale because the global is generally conceptualized as overriding or neutralizing place, and as operating at a self-evident global scale. I do this through a focus on three particular components—places, scales, and the meaning of the national today. Each of these entails a specific research and theorization practice.

In the first section I develop the question of place as central to many of the circuits constitutive of economic globalization. This opens up the conceptualization of the global economic system to the possibility that it is partly embedded in specific types of places and partly constituted through highly specialized cross-border circuits. The second section develops some of these issues by focusing on an extreme case of this combination of the global and place—the microenvironment with a global span, such as a financial services firm, but also the household of a global environmental activist. This, in turn, opens up our understanding of the local. These microenvironments may actually be oriented to other such microenvironments located far away, thereby destabilizing the notion of context, which is often imbricated with that of the local, and the notion that physical proximity is one of the attributes or markers of the local. The third section concerns the national as instantiated in national states and the consequences of the partial embeddedness of the global in the national, described in the first two sections. This opens up our understanding of the global to the possibility that it is in some way constituted through the partial denationalization of what has been constructed over the last century or more as *national* (in the sense of *national state*, not *national people*) territories and institutional domains.

PLACE IN A GLOBAL AND DIGITAL ECONOMY

One of the organizing themes in much of my work on globalization is that place is central to the multiple circuits through which economic globalization is constituted. One strategic type of place for these developments, and the one focused on here, is the city. Including cities in the analysis of economic globalization is not without conceptual consequences. Economic globalization has most often been conceptualized in terms of the duality *national-global,* where the latter gains at the expense of the former. And it has largely been conceptualized in terms of the internationalization of capital, and then only the upper circuits of capital. Introducing cities in an analysis of economic globalization allows us to reconceptualize processes of economic globalization as concrete economic complexes situated in specific places. A focus on cities decomposes the nation-state into a variety of subnational components, some profoundly articulated with the global economy and others not. It also signals the declining significance of the national economy as a unitary category in the global economy. And even if, to a large extent, this was a unitary category in large part constructed in political discourse and policy, it has become even less of a fact in the last fifteen years.

Why does it matter that we recover place in analyses of the global economy, particularly place as constituted in major cities? Because it allows us to see the multiplicity of economies and work cultures in which the global information economy is embedded. It also allows us to recover the concrete, localized processes through which globalization exists, and to argue that much of the multiculturalism in large cities is as much a part of globalization as is international finance. Finally, focusing on cities allows us to specify a geography of strategic places on a global scale, places bound to each other by the dynamics of economic globalization. I refer to this as a new geography of centrality, and one of the questions it engenders is whether this new transnational geography is also the space for the formation of new types of transnational political, social, cultural, and subjective dynamics. Insofar as my economic analysis of the global city recovers the broad array of jobs and work cultures that are part of the global economy, though typically not marked as such, it allows me to examine the possibility of these new formations.

The Material Practices of Globalization

I think of the mainstream account of economic globalization as a narrative of eviction (Sassen 1998, chapter 1). Key concepts in that account—globalization, information economy, and telematics—all suggest that place no longer matters and that the only type of worker that matters is the highly educated professional. It is an account that privileges the capability for global transmission over the material infrastructure that makes such transmission possible; information outputs over the workers producing those outputs, from specialists to secretaries; and the new transnational corporate culture over the multiplicity of work cultures, including immigrant cultures, within which many of the "other" jobs of the global information economy take place. In brief, the dominant narrative concerns itself with the upper circuits of capital, and particularly with the hypermobility of capital rather than with that which is place-bound.

Massive trends toward the spatial dispersal of economic activities at the metropolitan, national, and global levels are indeed all taking place, but they represent only half of what is happening. Alongside the well-documented spatial dispersal of economic activities, new forms of territorial centralization of top-level management and control operations have appeared. National and global markets, as well as globally integrated operations, require central places where the work of globalization gets done. Further, information industries require a vast physical infrastructure containing strategic nodes with sharp concentrations of a variety of facilities. Finally, even the most advanced information industries have a work process—that is, a complex of workers, machines, and buildings that are more place-bound than the imagery of information outputs suggests.

Centralized control and management over a geographically dispersed array of economic operations does not come about inevitably as part of a *world system*. It requires the production of a vast range of highly specialized services, telecommunications infrastructure, and industrial services. These are crucial for the valorization of what are today leading components of capital.

A focus on place and production produces an analysis that adds much unexpected empirical detail to the more typical focus on the power of large corporations over governments and economies, and the focus on the power of the new telecommunications. These are part of the story, but I argue there is also a story of work and place that is part of globalization. Work and place lead us to focus on the work and on the nonmobile structures necessary for the implementation and maintenance of a global network of factories, service operations, and markets (Persky and Wievel 1994; Peraldi and Perrin 1996; Allen et al. 1999; Marcuse and van Kempen 2000; Sum 1999). These are all processes only partly encompassed by the activities of transnational corporations and banks and by the new telecommunications.

One of the central concerns in my work has been to look at cities as production sites for the leading service industries of our time, and hence to recover the infrastructure of activities, firms, and jobs, that is necessary to run the advanced corporate economy. I want to focus on the *practice* of global control: the work of producing and reproducing the organization and management of a global production system and a global marketplace for finance, both under conditions of economic concentration. This allows me to focus on the infrastructure of jobs involved in this production, including low-wage, unskilled manual jobs typically not thought of as being part of advanced globalized sectors.

Global cities are centers for the *servicing* and *financing* of international trade, investment, and headquarters operations (Sassen 2001; Yeung 1996; Friedmann 1995). There are today about forty global cities with considerable ranking; they are a key set of networked spaces for the global operations of firms and markets (Taylor et al. 2002; Globalization and World Cities Study Group and Network [GaWC]). That is to say, the multiplicity of specialized activities present in global cities is crucial in the valorization, indeed overvalorization, of leading sectors of capital today. In this sense they are strategic production sites for today's leading economic sectors. This function is reflected in the ascendance of these activities in the economies of these cities. Elsewhere I have posited that what is specific about the shift to services is not merely the much noticed growth in service jobs but, most important, the growing service intensity in the organization of advanced economies: firms in all industries, from mining to wholesale, buy more accounting, legal, advertising, financial, and economic forecasting services today than they did twenty years ago (2001, chapter 5). Thus we see some of these trends also in cities that function as regional or national rather than global centers. Whether at the global or regional level, cities are adequate and often the best production sites for such specialized services. The rapid growth and disproportionate concentration of such services in cities signal that the latter have reemerged as significant production sites after losing this role in the period when mass manufacturing was the dominant sector of the economy.

The extremely high densities evident in the downtown districts of these cities are the spatial expression of this logic. The widely accepted notion that agglomeration has become obsolete when global telecommunication advances should allow for maximum dispersal is only partly correct. It is, I argue, precisely because of the territorial dispersal facilitated by telecommunication advances that agglomeration of centralizing activities has expanded immensely. This is not a mere continuation of old patterns of agglomeration but, one could posit, a new logic for agglomeration. Information technologies are yet another factor contributing to the new logic for agglomeration. These technologies make possible the geographic dispersal *and* simultaneous integration of many activities. But the distinct conditions under which such facilities are available have promoted centralization of the most advanced users in the most advanced telecommunications centers (Castells, 1996; Graham 2000; Orum and Chen 2002; Rutherford 2004).

A focus on the *work* behind command functions, on the actual *production process* in the finance and services complex, and on global market*places* has the effect of incorporating the material facilities underlying globalization and the whole infrastructure of jobs typically not marked as belonging to the corporate sector of the economy. An economic configuration very different from that suggested by the concept information economy emerges. We recover the material conditions, production sites, and place-boundedness that are also part of globalization and the information economy.

We also recover the broad range of types of firms, types of workers, types of work cultures, and types of residential milieus, which are also part of globalization processes, though never marked, recognized, or represented as such. Nor are they valorized as such. In this regard, the new urban economy is highly problematic. This is perhaps particularly evident in global cities and their regional counterparts. It sets in motion a whole series of new dynamics of inequality (Sassen 2001: chapters 8 and 9). The new growth sectors—specialized services and finance—contain capabilities for profit making vastly superior to those of more traditional economic sectors. The latter are essential to the operation of the urban economy and the daily needs of residents, but their survival is threatened in a situation where finance and specialized services can earn superprofits.[2]

New Geographies of Centrality and of Marginality

Sharp polarization in the profit-making capabilities of different sectors of the economy has always existed, but what we see happening today takes place on another order of magnitude and is engendering massive distortions in the operations of various markets, from housing to labor. We can see this, for example, in the retreat of many real estate developers from the low- and medium-income housing market in the wake of the rapidly expanding demand by the new highly paid professionals and the possibility for vast overpricing of this housing supply.

What we are seeing is a dynamic of valorization that has sharply increased the distance between high-profit-making sectors of the economy and medium- or low-profit-making sectors even when the latter are part of leading global industries. This devalorization of growing sectors of the economy has been embedded in a massive demographic transition toward a growing presence of women, African Americans, and third world immigrants in the urban workforce (Munger 2002; Ehrenreich and Hochschild 2003; Hondagneu-Sotelo 2003).

We see here an interesting correspondence between great concentrations of corporate power and large concentrations of "others." Large cities in the highly developed world are the terrain where multiple globalization processes assume concrete, localized forms. A focus on cities allows us to capture, further, not only the upper but also the lower circuits of globalization. These localized forms are, in good part, what globalization is about. We can then think of cities also as sites for the contradictions of the internationalization of capital (Amen et al. 2006). If we consider, further, that large cities also concentrate a growing share of disadvantaged populations—immigrants in Europe, the United States, and major cities in specific Asian countries, African-Americans and Latinos in the United States—then we can see that they have become a strategic terrain for a whole series of conflicts and contradictions (Sassen 1998; Cordero-Guzman et al. 2002; Drainville 2004; Dunn 1994).

The global economy materializes in a worldwide grid of strategic places, uppermost among which are major international business and financial centers. We can think of this global grid as constituting a new economic geography of centrality, one that cuts across national boundaries and across the old north–south divide. It signals the emergence of a parallel political geography, a transnational space for the formation of new claims by global capital.

This new economic geography of centrality partly reproduces existing inequalities but is also the outcome of a dynamic specific to the current forms of economic growth. It assumes many forms and operates in many terrains, from the distribution of telecommunications facilities to the structure of the economy and of employment. Global cities are sites for immense concentrations of economic power and command centers in a global economy, while cities that were once major manufacturing centers have suffered inordinate declines.

The most powerful of these new geographies of centrality at the interurban level binds the major international financial and business centers: New York, London, Tokyo, Paris, Frankfurt, Zurich, Amsterdam, Los Angeles, Sydney, Hong Kong, among others. But this geography now also includes cities such as Sao Paulo, Buenos Aires, Bangkok, Taipei, and Mexico City (see, e.g., Gugler 2004; Parnreiter 2002; Buchler 2002; Ciccolella and Mignaqui 2000). The intensity of transactions among these cities, particularly through the financial markets, transactions in services, and investment, has increased sharply, and so have the orders of magnitude involved. At the same time, there has been a sharpening inequality in the concentration of strategic resources and activities among these cities and others in the same country.

The pronounced orientation to the world markets evident in such cities raises questions about the articulation with their nation-states, their regions, and the larger economic and social structure in such cities. Cities have typically been deeply embedded in the economies of their region, indeed often reflecting the characteristics of the latter; and most still do. But cities that are strategic sites in the global economy tend, in part, to disconnect from their region. This conflicts with a key proposition in traditional scholarship about urban systems, namely, that these systems promote the territorial integration of regional and national economies. Alongside these new global and regional hierarchies of cities, is a vast territory that we need to specify or respecify theoretically and empirically.

But also inside global cities we see a new geography of centrality and marginality. The downtowns of cities and metropolitan business centers receive massive investments in real estate and telecommunications, while low-income city areas are starved for resources. Highly educated workers see their incomes rise to unusually high levels while low- or medium-skilled workers see theirs sink. Financial services produce superprofits, while industrial services barely survive. These trends are evident, with different levels of intensity, in a growing number of major cities in the developed world, and increasingly in some of the developing countries that have been integrated into the global economic system.

A New Transnational Politics of Place?

I have been particularly interested in the possibility of a new politics of traditionally disadvantaged actors operating in this new transnational economic geography. This is a politics that lies at the intersection of economic participation in the global economy and the politics of the disadvantaged, and in that sense would add an economic dimension, specifically through those who hold the other jobs in the global economy—from factory workers in export processing zones to cleaners on Wall Street.

The centrality of place in a context of global processes engenders a transnational economic and political opening in the formation of new claims, and hence in the constitution of entitlements, notably rights to place, and at the limit, in the constitution of *citizenship*. The city has indeed emerged as a site for new claims: by global capital, which uses the city as an *organizational commodity*, but also by disadvantaged sectors of the urban population, frequently as internationalized a presence in large cities as capital (Drainville 2004; King 1996; Machimura 1998; Dunn 1994; Eade 1996; Low 1999). The denationalizing of urban space and the formation of new claims centered in transnational actors and involving contestation, raise the question: Whose city is it?

I see this as a type of political opening that contains unifying capacities across national boundaries and sharpening conflicts within such boundaries. Global capital and the new immigrant workforce are two major instances of transnationalized categories that have unifying properties internally and find themselves in contestation with each other inside global cities. Global cities are sites for the overvalorization of corporate capital and the devalorization of disadvantaged workers. The leading sectors of corporate capital are now global, in their organization and operations. Many of the disadvantaged workers in global cities are women, immigrants, and people of color (Chang and Abramovitz 2000). Both find in the global city a strategic site for their economic and political operations.

Is there a transnational politics embedded in the centrality of place and in the new geography of strategic places, such as there is, for instance, in the new worldwide grid of global cities? This is a geography that cuts across national borders and the old north–south divide. Immigration, for instance, is one major process through which a new transnational political economy is being constituted (Samers 2002; Cordero-Guzman et al. 2002), one that is largely embedded in major cities insofar as most immigrants, whether in the United States, Japan, or Western Europe, are concentrated in major cities. It is, in my reading, one of the constitutive processes of globalization today, even though not recognized or represented as such in mainstream accounts of the global economy.

I ground my interpretation of the new politics made possible by globalization in a detailed understanding of the economics of globalization, and specifically in the centrality of place in a context where place is seen as neutralized by the available capacity for global communications and control. My assumption is that it is important to dissect the economics of globalization in order to understand whether a new transnational politics can be centered in the new transnational economic geography. Second, I think that dissecting the economics of place in the global economy allows us to recover noncorporate components of economic globalization and to inquire about the possibility of a new type of transnational politics.

SITED MATERIALITIES WITH GLOBAL SPAN

There is a specific kind of materiality underlying the leading economic sectors of our era, notwithstanding the fact that they take place partly in electronic space. Even the most digitalized, globalized, and dematerialized sector, notably global finance, hits the ground at some point in its operations. And when it does, it does so in vast concentrations of very material structures. These activities inhabit physical spaces, and they inhabit digital spaces. There are material and digital structures to be built, with very specific requirements—the need to incorporate the fact that a firm's activities are simultaneously partly deterritorialized and partly deeply territorialized, that they span the globe, and that they are highly concentrated in very specific places. This produces a strategic geography that cuts across borders and across spaces, yet also installs itself in specific cities.

There are three issues about locality and context that are illuminated by this configuration. One concerns the particular type of subeconomy this is: internally networked, partly digital, and mostly oriented to global markets, yet to a large extent operating out of multiple but specific sites around the world. The second is a more elusive and perhaps purely theoretical issue (though I do not think so) that has to do with the point of intersection between the physical and the digital spaces within which a firm, or more generally this subeconomy,

operates. Here my concern is to understand this point of intersection not as a line that separates two different, mutually exclusive entities, but as a border *zone*, with its own specific features. The third is the matter of contextuality—in the local, in the sited, in the contiguous. The particular characteristics of this networked subeconomy (in part, deeply centered in particular sites, partly deterritorialized and operating on a global digital span) would seem to unbundle established concepts of context, of the relation to the surroundings (whether social, visual, operational, rhetorical).

A Networked Subeconomy

To a large extent this sector is constituted through a large number of relatively small, highly specialized firms. Even if some of the financial services firms, especially given recent mergers, can mobilize enormous amounts of capital and control enormous assets, they are small firms in terms of employment and the actual physical space they occupy compared, for example, with large manufacturing firms. The latter are far more labor intensive, no matter how automated their production process might be, and require vastly larger amounts of physical space. Second, specialized service firms need and benefit from proximity to kindred specialized firms—financial services, legal services, accounting, economic forecasting, credit rating and other advisory services, computer specialists, public relations, and several other types of expertise in a broad range of fields. The production of a financial instrument requires a multiplicity of highly specialized inputs from this broad range of firms.

Physical proximity has clearly emerged as an advantage insofar as time is of the essence, and the complexity is such that direct transactions are often more efficient and cheaper than telecommunications (it would take enormous bandwidth and you would still not have the full array of acts of communications—the shorthand way in which enormous amounts of information can be exchanged among people in direct contact with each other). But, at the same time, this networked sector has global span and definitely operates partly in digital space, so it is networked also in a deterritorialized way, one not pivoting on physical proximity.[3]

The Intersection between Actual and Digital Space

There is a new topography of economic activity, sharply evident in this subeconomy. This topography weaves in and out between actual and digital space. There is today no fully virtualized firm or economic sector. Even finance, the most digitalized, dematerialized, and globalized of all activities has a topography that weaves back and forth between actual and digital space.[4] To different extents, in different types of sectors and different types of firms, a company's tasks are now distributed across these two kinds of spaces; further the actual configurations are subject to considerable transformation as tasks are computerized or standardized, markets are further globalized, and so forth. More generally, telematics and globalization have emerged as fundamental forces reshaping the organization of economic space (Graham 2004; Rutherford 2004; Allen et al. 1999). This reshaping ranges from the spatial virtualization of a growing number of economic activities to the reconfiguration of the geography of the built environment *for* economic activity. Whether in electronic space or in the geography of the built environment, this reshaping involves organizational and structural changes.

One question here is whether the point of intersection between these two kinds of spaces in a firm's or a dynamic's topography of activity, is one worth thinking about, theorizing, exploring. This intersection is unwittingly, perhaps, thought of as a line that divides two mutually exclusive zones. I would propose to open up this line into an *analytic borderland*, which demands its own empirical specification and theorization, and contains its own possibilities for shaping practices and organizational forms. The space of the computer screen, which one might posit is one version of the intersection, will not do, or is at most a partial enactment of this intersection.

Admittedly, the question of this intersection is one that I have been somewhat obsessed with, and toward which I have made only limited advances in its elaboration (Sassen 2002; Latham and Sassen 2005). It is, for me, one instantiation of a broader condition that I see as pervasive in the social sciences: the dividing line as the unproblematized way of relating and separating two different zones (whatever they might be—conceptual, theoretical, analytic, empirical, of meaning, of practice). What operations are brought in and what operations are evicted by putting a line there (Sassen 1998: chapter 1)? It is quite possible that these are analytic operations linked to the type of work I do and that they have little meaning for other types of inquiry and objects of study. They are certainly not an issue in conventional social science thinking.

What Does Contextuality Mean in This Setting?

A networked subeconomy that operates partly in actual space and partly in globe-spanning digital space cannot easily be contextualized in terms of its surroundings, nor can the individual firms. The orientation is simultaneously toward itself and toward the global. The intensity of its internal transactions is such that it overrides all considerations of the broader locality or region within which it exists. On another, larger scale, I have found in my research on global cities that they rather clearly develop a stronger orientation toward global markets than to those in their hinterlands. They thereby override a key proposition in the urban systems literature, to wit, that cities and urban systems integrate, articulate national territory. Cities may have had such a function during the period when mass manufacturing and mass consumption were the dominant growth machines in developed economies, and thrived on the possibility of a national scale for economic and political organization.

But this is not the case today with the ascendance of digitalized, globalized, dematerialized sectors, such as finance. The connections with other zones and sectors in its context are of a special sort—one that connects worlds that we think of as radically distinct. For instance, the informal economy in several immigrant communities in New York provides some of the low-wage workers for the "other" jobs on Wall Street, the capital of global finance. The same is happening in Paris, London, Frankfurt, and Zurich. Yet these other zones and other workers are not considered to be part of the context, the locality, of the networked subeconomy I have been speaking of—even if, in my reading, they are. On the other hand, the immediate physical surroundings of the financial business district may be marked by attempts to create the now much in vogue contextual architecture and urban design. Yet from the type of research and analysis I have done, this would be a way of veiling, of hiding the fact that the immediate physical surrounding is not a context for this networked subeconomy; there is, in fact, little if any direct connection.

What then is the context, the local, here? The new networked subeconomy occupies a strategic geography, partly deterritorialized, that cuts across borders and connects a variety of points on the globe. It occupies only a fraction of its "local" setting, its boundaries are not those of the city where it is partly located, nor those of the neighborhood. This subeconomy contains within itself the intensity of the vast concentration of the very material resources it needs when it hits the ground, and the fact of its global span or cross-border geography. Its interlocutor is not the surroundings, the context, but the fact of the global. Yet is is embedded, at least in one moment of its dynamic, in a set of very specific and material built environments.

I am not sure what this simultaneous embeddedness in physical sites and tearing away of the context (which comes to be replaced by the global) mean theoretically, empirically, and operationally. The strategic operation is not the search for a connection with the surroundings, the context. It is, rather, installation in a strategic cross-border geography constituted through multiple locals. In the case of the economy, we can see that the old hierarchies of scale, typically shaped by some elementary criterion of size—local, regional, national, international—defined through specific national instantiations no longer hold for particular configurations exemplified by the networked subeconomy I have been discussing. Going to the next scale in terms of size is no longer how integration is achieved. The local now transacts directly with the global; the global installs itself in locals and the global is itself constituted through a multiplicity of locals.[5] In this sense, we see the forming of a geography that explodes the boundaries of contextuality and traditional hierarchies of scale.

DENATIONALIZED STATE AGENDAS
AND PRIVATIZED NORM MAKING

States today confront a new geography of power.[6] The changed condition of the state is often explained in terms of a decrease in regulatory capacities resulting from some of the basic policies associated with economic globalization: deregulation of a broad range of markets, economic sectors and national borders, and privatization of public sector firms.

But in my reading of the evidence, this new geography of power confronting states entails a far more differentiated process than notions of an overall decline in the significance of the state suggest. We are seeing a repositioning of the state in a broader field of power and a reconfiguring of the work of states. This broader field of power is constituted partly through the formation of a new private institutional order linked to the global economy, and partly through the growing importance of a variety of institutional orders engaged with various aspects of the common good broadly understood, such as the international network of NGOs (nongovernmental organizations) and the international human rights regime. This new geography of power also entails a more transformative process of the state than the notion of a simple loss of power suggests. The work of states or raison d'etat—the substantive rationality of the state—has had many incarnations over the centuries. Each of these transformations has had consequences. Today the conditionalities for, and the content of, specific components of the work of states have changed significantly compared to the immediately preceding period of the post–World War II decades. Some of these changes are typically captured with the image of the current neoliberal or competitive state as compared with the welfare state of the postwar era.

In the larger research project, I develop three arguments.[7] First, I posit that the marking features of this new, mostly but not exclusively, private institutional order in formation are its capacity to privatize what has been heretofore public and to denationalize what were once national authorities and policy agendas. This capacity to privatize and denationalize entails specific transformations of the national state, more precisely of some of its components. Further, I posit that this new institutional order also has normative authority—a new normativity that is not embedded in what has been, and to some extent remains the master normativity of modern times, raison d'etat. This new normativity comes from the world of private power, yet installs itself in the public realm and in so doing contributes to denationalizing what had historically been constructed as national state agendas.[8] Finally, I posit that particular institutional components of the national state begin to function as the institutional home for the operation of powerful dynamics constitutive of what we could describe as *global capital* and *global capital markets*. In so doing, these state institutions contribute to reorienting their particular policy work or, more broadly, state agendas, toward the requirements of the global economy. This, then, raises a question about what is "national" in these institutional components of states linked to the implementation and regulation of economic globalization.

Geared toward governing key aspects of the global economy, both the particular transformations inside the state and the new emergent privatized institutional order are partial and incipient but strategic. Both have the capacity to alter possibly crucial conditions for "liberal democracy" and for the organizational architecture of international law, its scope, and its exclusivity. In this sense, both have the capacity to alter the scope of state authority and the interstate system, the crucial institutional domains through which the rule of law is implemented. We are not seeing the end of states, but rather that states are not the only or the most important strategic agents in this new institutional order, and second, that states, including dominant states, have undergone profound transformations in some of their key institutional components. Both of these trends are likely to add to the democratic deficit and to further strengthen the legitimacy of certain types of claims and norms.

One of the roles of the state vis-à-vis economic internationalization has been to negotiate the intersection of national law with the activities of foreign economic actors—whether firms, markets, or supranational organizations—in its territory, as well as the activities of national economic actors overseas. This is not a new role, but it is a transformed and expanded one. In the case of the United States, the government has passed legislative measures, executive orders, and court decisions that have enabled foreign firms to operate in the United States and its markets to become international. Are there particular conditions that make execution of this role in the current phase distinctive and unlike what it may have occurred in earlier phases of the world economy?

While this is in many ways a question of interpretation, I argue that there is indeed something distinctive about the current period. We have, on the one hand, the existence of an enormously elaborate body of law, developed in good measure over the last hundred years, which secures the exclusive territorial authority of national states to an extent not seen in earlier centuries, and on the other, the considerable institutionalizing, especially in the 1990s, of the "rights" of non-national firms, the deregulation of cross-border transactions, and the growing influence and power of some of the supranational organizations. If securing these rights, options, and powers entailed an even partial relinquishing of components of state authority as constructed over the last century, then we can posit that this sets up the conditions for a transformation in the role of the state. It also signals a necessary engagement by national states in the process of globalization (Aman 1998).

The next question, then, would concern the nature of this engagement and how it will vary for different types of states.[9] Is the role of the state simply one of reducing its authority (e.g., as suggested with terms such as deregulation and privatization, and generally less government) or does it also require the production of new types of regulations, legislative items, court decisions—in brief, the production of a whole series of new legalities.[10]

Further, if it is in fact some states (i.e., the United States and the United Kingdom), which are producing the design for these new legalities (i.e., particular aspects derived from Anglo-American commercial law and accounting standards), and are hence imposing these on other states given the interdependencies at the heart of the current phase of globalization, then this creates and imposes a set of specific constraints on participating states.[11] Legislative items, executive orders, adherence to new technical standards, and so on, will have to be produced

18

through the particular institutional and political structures of each of these states.[12]

We generally use terms such as *deregulation*, financial and trade liberalization, and privatization, to describe the changed authority of the state when it comes to the economy. The problem with such terms is that they only capture the withdrawal of the state from regulating its economy. They do not register all the ways in which the state participates in setting up the new framework through which globalization is furthered, nor do they capture the associated transformations inside the state—precisely my two concerns.

Central banks are national institutions that address national matters. Yet over the last decade, they have become the institutional home within the national state for monetary policies that are necessary to further the development of a global capital market, and indeed, more generally, a global economic system. The new conditionality of the global economic system (the requirements that need to be met for a country to become integrated into the global capital market) contains, as one key element, the autonomy of central banks.[13] This facilitates the task of instituting a certain kind of monetary policy, for example, one privileging low inflation over job growth even when a president may have preferred it the other way around, particularly at reelection time. While securing central bank autonomy certainly cleaned up a lot of corruption, it has also been the vehicle for one set of accommodations on the part of national states to the requirements of the global capital market. A parallel analysis can be made of ministries of finance (or the treasury in the United States), which have had to impose certain kinds of fiscal policies as part of the new conditionalities of economic globalization.

At the level of theorization, it means capturing and conceptualizing a specific set of operations that take place within national institutional settings, but are geared to nonnational or transnational agendas where once they were geared to national agendas.

The accommodation of the interests of foreign firms and investors under conditions where most of a country's institutional domains have been constructed as national entails a negotiation.[14] The mode of this negotiation in the current phase has tended in a direction that I describe as a denationalizing of several highly specialized national institutional components.[15] My hypothesis here is that some components of national institutions, even though formally national, are not national in the sense in which state practice has constructed the meaning of that term since the emergence of the so-called regulatory state, particularly in the West. Though imperfectly implemented and often excluding national minorities, Keynesian policies aimed at strengthening the national economy, national consumption capacity, raising the educational level of national workforces, are good illustrations of this meaning of the *national*. There are, clearly, enormous variations among countries, both in terms of the extent to which such a national policy project existed and the actual period of time of its implementation.

Crucial to my analysis here is the fact that the emergent, often imposed, consensus in the community of states to further globalization is not merely a political decision: it entails specific types of *work* by a large number of distinct institutions in each of these countries. In this sense, that consensus partly shapes the actual work of states rather than being just a decision. Furthermore, this work of states has an ironic outcome insofar as it has the effect of destabilizing some aspects of state power. Thus the U.S. government, as the hegemonic power of this period, has led and forced other states to adopt these obligations toward global capital, and in so doing, has contributed to strengthening the forces that can challenge or destabilize what have historically been constructed as state powers.[16] In my reading, this holds both for the United States and for other countries. One of the ways in which this becomes evident is in the fact that while the state continues to play a crucial, though no longer exclusive, role in the production of legality around new forms of economic activity, at least some of this production of legalities increasingly feeds the power of a new emerging structure marked by denationalization in some of its components, and by privatization in other of its components.

In this case, the state can be seen as incorporating the global project of its own shrinking role in regulating economic transactions. The state here can be conceived of as representing a technical administrative capacity that cannot be replicated at this time by any other institutional arrangement; furthermore, this is a capacity backed by military power, with global power in the case of some states. Seen from the perspective of firms operating transnationally, the objective is to ensure the functions traditionally exercised by the state in the national realm of the economy, notably guaranteeing property rights and contracts. How this gets done may involve a range of options. To some extent, this work of guaranteeing is becoming privatized, as is signaled, for instance, by the growth of international commercial arbitration and by key elements of the new privatized institutional order.[17]

There is a set of strategic dynamics and institutional transformations at work here. They may incorporate a small number of state agencies and units within departments, a small number of legislative initiatives and of executive orders, and yet have the power to institute a new normativity at the heart of the state; this is especially so because these strategic sectors are operating in complex interactions with private, transnational, powerful actors. This is happening to varying degrees in a growing range of states, even as much of the institutional apparatus of states remains basically unchanged. (The inertia of bureaucratic organizations, which creates its own version of path dependence, makes an enormous contribution to continuity). I conceptualize this transformation as denationalization—more precisely, the incipient and partial denationalization of specific, typically highly specialized, state institutional orders and of state agendas. From the perspective of research, I have argued that this entails the need to decode what is national (as historically constructed) about these particular specialized institutional orders inside national states, notably certain specific activities and authorities inside central banks and ministries of finance.

The mode in which this participation by the state has evolved has been toward strengthening the power and legitimacy of privatized and denationalized state authorities. The outcome is an emergent new spatiotemporal order that has considerable governance capabilities and structural power. This institutional order contributes to strengthening the advantages of certain types of economic and political actors and to weaken those of others. It is extremely partial rather than universal, but strategic in that it has undue influence over wide areas of the broader institutional world and the world of lived experience, yet is not fully accountable to formal democratic political systems. While partially embedded in national institutional settings, it is distinct from these. Because it is partly installed in national settings, its identification requires a decoding of what is national in what has historically been constructed as the national.

In brief, my argument is that the *tension* between (1) the necessary, though partial, location of globalization in national territories and institutions, and (2) an elaborate system of law and administration that has constructed the exclusive national territorial authority of sovereign states, has (3) been partly negotiated through (a) processes of institutional denationalization inside the national state and national economy, and (b) the formation of privatized intermediary institutional arrangements that are only partly encompassed by the interstate system, and are, in fact, evolving into a parallel institutional world for the handling of cross-border operations.[18] In terms of research this means, among other tasks, establishing what are the new territorial and institutional conditionalities of national states.

CONCLUSION

This chapter focused on a set of instantiations of the global that are actually sited in what are usually represented or thought of as national institutional orders and dynamics. These range from forms of globality centered on localized struggles and actors that are part of cross-border networks, through formations such as global cities, to specific types of state work geared toward accommodating global actors and their interests. Cutting across these diverse processes and domains is a research and theorization agenda. I have developed this agenda by bringing together different strands of a rapidly growing scholarship in several different disciplines, some focused on self-evidently global processes and conditions and others on local or national processes and conditions.

This agenda is driven by at least some of the following major concerns. At the most general level, a first key concern is establishing novel or additional dimensions of the spatiality of the national and the global. Specific structurations of what we have represented as the global are actually located deep inside state institutions and national territories. In turn, what has been represented (and to some extent reified) as the scale of the national, contains a simultaneity of power relations, some pertaining to the national and others to the global.

A second major concern is with critical examinations of how we conceptualize the local and the subnational in ways that allow us to detect those instances—even when these might be a minority of all instances—that are, in fact, multiscalar even when represented and experienced as simply local. The multiscalar versions of the local I focused on have the effect of destabilizing the notion of context, often imbricated in that of the local, and the notion that physical proximity is one of the attributes or markers of the local. Further, a critical reconceptualization of the local along these lines entails an at least partial rejection of the notion that local scales are inevitably part of nested hierarchies of scale running from the local to the regional, the national, and the international. Localities or local practices can constitute multiscalar systems, operating across scales and not merely scaling upward because of new communication capabilities.

A third major concern is how to conceptualize the national, particularly the specific interactions between global dynamics and particular components of the national. The crucial conditionality here is the partial embeddedness of the global in the national, of which the global city is perhaps emblematic. My main argument here is that insofar as specific structurations of the global inhabit and constitute what has historically been constructed and institutionalized as national territory, this engenders a variety of negotiations. One set of outcomes evident today is what I describe as an incipient, highly specialized and partial denationalization of specific components of national states. This type of focus allows us to capture the enormous variability across countries in terms of the incorporation and negotiation and resistance of globalization because these are partly shaped by the specifics, both de facto and de jure, of each country. The understanding of globalization in this case would demand detailed studies of the particular ways in which different countries have handled and institutionalized this negotiation.

In all three instances, the question of scaling takes on very specific contents in that these are practices and dynamics that, I argue, pertain to the constituting of the global, yet are taking place at what has been historically constructed as the scale of the national or the subnational. One central task this raises is the need to decode particular aspects of what is still represented or experienced as national, which may in fact have shifted away from what had historically been considered or constituted as national. This type of analysis also suggests a different, though by no means incompatible, research strategy from that which calls for transnational analyses as a response to methodological nationalism. Transnational analysis in that case is a response to the fact that the nation as container category is inadequate given the proliferation of transboundary dynamics and formations. I think of this as a crucial part of our large collective research agenda, but I want to distinguish it from the particular focus of this paper—the fact of multiple and specific structurations of the global *inside* what has historically been constructed as national. This is yet another type of emphasis in the (shared) critique of methodological nationalism.

There are conceptual and methodological consequences to this particular emphasis. Most important, it incorporates the need for detailed study of national and subnational formations and processes and their recoding as instantiations of the global. This means that we can use many of the existing data and technologies for research, but need to situate the results in different conceptual architectures from those for which they were originally designed. We have some of these—transnational communities, global cities, postcolonial dynamics—but are they enough? I am not so sure. Further, because the national is highly institutionalized and is marked by sociocultural thickness, structurations of the global inside the national entail a partial, typically highly specialized and specific denationalization of particular components of the national: is the analytic vocabulary of transnationalism, postcoloniality, and hybridity adequate to map these types of formations and dynamics? Again, I am not so sure. There is much work to be done.

REFERENCES

Abu-Lughod, Janet Lippman, ed. 2000. *Sociology for the 21st Century.* Chicago, IL: University of Chicago Press.
Allen, John, Doreen Massey, and Michael Pryke, eds. 1999. *Unsettling Cities.* London: Routledge.
Aman, Alfred C., Jr. 1998. "The Globalizing State: A Future-Oriented Perspective on the Public/Private Distinction, Federalism, and Democracy.: *Vanderbilt Journal of Transnational Law* 31(4): 769–870.
Amen, Mark M., Kevin Archer, and M. Martin Bosman, eds. 2006. *Relocating Global Cities: From the Center to the Margins.* New York: Rowman & Littlefield.
Arrighi, Giovanni. 1994. *The Long Twentieth Century: Money, Power, and the Origins of Our Times.* London: Verso.
Buchler, Simone. 2002. "Women in the Informal Economy of Sao Paulo." Paper prepared for the National Academy of Sciences, forthcoming in *Background Papers. Panel on Cities.* Washington, DC: National Academy of Sciences.
Brenner, Neil. 2004. *State Spaces.* Oxford: Oxford University Press.
Calabrese, Andrew and Jean-Claude Burgelman. 1999. *Communication, Citizenship, and Social Policy. Rethinking the Limits of the Welfare State.* Lanham, MD: Rowman & Littlefield.
Castells, Manuel. 1996. *The Network Society.* Oxford: Blackwell.
Chang, Grace and Mimi Abramovitz. 2000. *Disposable Domestics: Immigrant Women Workers in the Global Economy.* Boston, MA: South End Press.
Ciccolella, P. and I. Mignaqui. 2000. "Buenos Aires." In *Cities and Their Crossboarder Networks,* ed. Saskia Sassen. Tokyo: UNU Press.
Cordero-Guzman, Hector R., Robert C. Smith, and Ramon Grosfoguel, eds. 2001. *Migration, Transnationalization, and Race in a Changing New York.* Philadelphia, PA: Temple University Press.
Cutler, Claire A., Virginia Haufler, and Tony Porter, eds. 1999. *Private Authority in International Affairs.* Sarasota Springs, NY: State University of New York Press.
Davis, Diana E., ed. 1999. *"Chaos and Governance": Political Power and Social Theory 13* (Part IV: Scholarly Controversy): 307–15. Stamford, CT: JAI Press.
Dezalay, Yves and Bryant Garth. 1996. *Dealing in Virtue. International Commercial Arbitration and the Construction of a Transnational Legal Order.* Chicago, IL: University of Chicago Press.

Drainville, André. 2004. *Contesting Globalization: Space and Place in the World Economy.* London: Routledge.

Dunn, Seamus, ed. 1994. *Managing Divided Cities.* Staffs, UK: Keele University Press.

Eade, John, ed. 1996. *Living the Global City: Globalization as a Local Process.* London: Routledge.

Ehrenreich, Barbara, and Arlie Hochschild, eds. 2003. *Global Woman.* New York: Metropolitan Books.

Friedmann, John. 1995. "Where We Stand: A Decade of World City Research." In *World Cities in a World System*, ed. Paul L. Knox and Peter J. Taylor, 21–47. Cambridge: Cambridge University Press.

GaWC (http://bll.epnet.com/citation.asp) Globalization and World Cities Study Group and Network). Available at http://www.lboro.ac.uk/departments/gy/research/gawc.html.

The Global Advance of Electronic Commerce: Reinventing Markets, Management and National Sovereignty. 1998. Washington, DC: The Aspen Institute, Communications and Society Program.

Graham, Stephen and Simon Marvin. 1999. *Telecommunications and the City: Electronic Spaces, Urban Spaces.* London: Routledge.

Graham, Stephen, ed. 2004. *The Cybercities Reader.* London: Routledge.

Gugler, Joseph. 2004. *World Cities beyond the West.* Cambridge: Cambridge University Press.

Hall, Rodney Bruce and Thomas J. Biersteker, eds. 2002. *Private Authority and Global Governance.* Cambridge: Cambridge University Press.

Hardt, Michael and Antonio Negri. 2000. *Empire.* Cambridge, MA: Harvard University Press.

Hobsbawm, Eric. 1994. *The Age of Extremes: A History of the World, 1914–1991.* New York: Vintage.

Hondagneu-Sotelo, Pierrette, ed. 2003. *Gender and U.S. Immigration: Contemporary Trends.* Berkeley: University of California Press.

Indiana Journal of Global Legal Studies. 1996. Special issue: "Feminism and Globalization: The Impact of The Global Economy on Women and Feminist Theory) 4(1).

_____. 2000. Special issue: The State of Citizenship 7(2).

Jessop, Robert. 1999. "Reflections on Globalization and Its Illogics." In *Globalization and the Asian Pacific: Contested Territories*, ed. Kris Olds et al., 19–38. London: Routledge.

King, A. D., ed. 1996. *Representing the City. Ethnicity, Capital and Culture in the 21st Century.* London: Macmillan.

Krause, Linda and Patrice Petro, eds. 2003. *Global Cities: Cinema, Architecture, and Urbanism in a Digital Age.* New Brunswick, NJ and London: Rutgers University Press.

Latham, Robert and Saskia Sassen. 2005. "Introduction: Digital Formations, Constructing an Object of Study." In *Digital Formations: IT and New Architectures in the Global Realm*, 1–34. Princeton, NJ: Princeton University Press.

Low, Setha M. 1999. "Theorizing the City." In *Theorizing the City*, ed. Setha M. Low, 1–33. New Brunswick, NJ: Rutgers University Press.

Machimura, Takashi. 1998. "Symbolic Use of Globalization in Urban Politics in Tokyo." *International Journal of Urban and Regional Research* 22(2): 183–194.

Marcuse, Peter and Ronald van Kempen. 2000. *Globalizing Cities: A New Spatial Order*. Oxford: Blackwell.

Mittelman, James, ed. 1996. *Globalization: Critical Reflections*. Boulder, CO: Lynne Rienner Publishers.

Munger, Frank, ed. 2002. *Laboring under the Line*. New York: Russell Sage Foundation.

Olds, Kris, Peter Dicken, Philip F. Kelly, Lilly Kong, and Henry Wai-Chung Yeung, eds. 1999. *Globalization and the Asian Pacific: Contested Territories*. London: Routledge.

Orum, Anthony and Xianming Chen. 2002. *Urban Places*. Malden, MA: Blackwell.

Parnreiter, Christof. 2002. "The Making of a Global City: Mexico City." In *Global Networks/Linked Cities*, ed. Saskia Sassen, 145–182. London: Routledge.

Peraldi, Michel and Evelyne Perrin, eds. 1996. *Reseaux Productifs et Territoires Urbains*. Toulouse: Presses Universitaires du Mirail.

Persky, Joseph and Wim Wievel. 1994. "The Growing Localness of the Global City." *Economic Geography* 70(2): 129–143.

Public Culture. 2000. Special Millennium Issue. 1(1).

Rutherford, Jonathan. 2004. *A Tale of Two Global Cities: Comparing the Territorialities of Telecommunications Developments in Paris and London*. Aldershot, UK and Burlington, VT: Ashgate.

Sack, Warren. 2005. "Discourse, Architecture, and Very Large-scale Conversation." In *Digital Formations: IT and New Architectures in the Global Realm*, ed. Robert Latham and Saskia Sassen, 242–82. Princeton, NJ: Princeton University Press.

Samers, Michael. 2002. "Immigration and the Global City Hypothesis: Towards and Alternative Research Agenda." *International Journal of Urban and Regional Research* 26(2, June): 389–402.

Sassen, Saskia. 1996. "Losing Control? Sovereignty in an Age of Globalization." *The 1995 Columbia University Leonard Hastings Schoff Memorial Lectures*. New York: Columbia University Press.

_____. 1998. *Globalization and Its Discontents*. New York: New Press.

_____. 2000. "Digital Networks and the State: Some Governance Question." *Theory, Culture and Society* 17(4): 19–33.

_____. 2001. *The Global City: New York, London, Tokyo.* (2nd ed., originally published in 1991). Princeton, NJ: Princeton University Press.

_____. 2002. "Towards a Sociology of Information Technology." *Current Sociology* 50(3): 365–388.

_____. 2006. *Territory, Authority, Rights: From Medieval to Global Assemblages.* Princeton, NJ: Princeton University Press.

Smith, David, Dorothy Solinger, and Steven Topik, eds. 1999. *States and Sovereignty in the Global Economy.* London: Routledge.

Sum, Ngai-Ling. 1999. "Rethinking Globalisation: Re-articulating the Spatial Scale and Temporal Horizons of Trans-border Spaces." In *Globalization and the Asian Pacific: Contested Territories,* ed. Kris Olds et al., 129–145. London: Routledge.

Tabak, Faruk and Michaeline A.Crichlow, eds. 2000. *Informalization: Process and Structure.* Baltimore, MD: Johns Hopkins Press.

Taylor, Peter J. 2000. "World Cities and Territorial States under Conditions of Contemporary Globalization." *Political Geography* 19(5): 5–32.

Taylor, Peter J., D. R. F. Walker, and J. V. Beaverstock. 2002. "Firms and Their Global Service Networks." In *Global Networks/Linked Cities,* ed. Saskia Sassen, 93–116. New York: Routledge.

Yeung, Yue-man. 2000. *Globalization and Networked Societies: Urban-Regional Change in Pacific Asia.* Honolulu: University of Hawaii Press.

_____. 1996. "An Asian Perspective on the Global City." *International Social Science Journal* 147(March): 25–32.

NOTES

1. This paper is based on a lecture delivered at the National Meeting of the American Anthropological Association (San Francisco 2003); I would like to thank the session organizers, sponsors, and discussants for their encouragement and participation.

2. I have also tried to show how these new inequalities in profit-making capacities of economic sectors, earnings capacities of households, and prices in upscale and downscale markets have contributed to the formation of informal economies in major cities of highly developed countries (Sassen 1998: chapter 5). These informal economies negotiate between these new economic trends and regulatory frameworks that were engendered in response to older economic conditions. See also, generally, for a historical perspective, Tabak and Crichlow 2000.

3. I examine some of these issues, particularly the future of financial centers given electronic trading and the new strategic alliances between the major financial centers, in Sassen 2001, chapter 7.

4. Another angle into these issues can be found in the Aspen Roundtable on Electronic Commerce (Aspen, Colorado), an annual event that brings together the CEOs of the main software and hardware firms as well as the key venture capitalists in the sector. The overall sense of these insiders was one of the limits to the medium and that it will not replace other types of markets, but rather complement them. See The Global Advance of Electronic Commerce: Reinventing Markets, Management and National Sovereignty, Washington, DC: Aspen Institute, Communications and Society Program, 1998.

5. I also see this in the political realm, particularly the kind of global politics attributed to the Internet. I think of it rather as a multiplicity of localized operations, but with a difference—they are part of the global network that is the Internet. This produces a "knowing" that re-marks the local. See my "Digital Networks and the State" in Theory, Culture and Society (Sassen 2000), (Krause and Petro 2003), and Sack (2005) on the making of public digital spaces for further information.

6. Many scholars coming at the subject from a variety of angles would agree, even as they might use other vocabularies. See, for example, Hobsbawm 1994; Jessop 1999; Hardt and Negri 2000. See also various chapters in each of the following collections to get a cross-section of perspectives: Mittelman 1996, Olds et al. 1999, Smith et al. 1999, Hall and Biersteker 2002, and Calabrese and Burgelman 1999 just to cite English language literature.

7. For a full treatment of these issues as well as a whole set of other governance questions linked to the sphere of human rights, citizenship, and immigration, please refer to Sassen (2006).

8. I have developed this at greater length in Sassen 1996; 2006, Part 2. I should clarify that when I first developed the construct denationalization in the 1995 Memorial Schoff Lectures (1996), I intended it to denote a specific dynamic. I did not intend it as some general notion that can be used interchangeably with postnational, global, or other such terms. In this regard, see Indiana Journal of Global Legal Studies (2000) and the Special Millennium Issue of Public Culture (2000).

9. Even as I confine this discussion to what are described as states effectively functioning under the rule of law, we must allow for considerable differences in the power of these states. As has been said many times, the government of the United States can aim at imposing conditions on global markets and on participating states that the government of Argentina, for instance, cannot.

10. I use this term to distinguish this type of production from that involved in making law or jurisprudence (Sassen 1996, chapter 1).

11. This dominance assumes many forms and does not only affect poorer and weaker countries. France, for instance, ranks among the top

providers of information services and industrial engineering services in Europe, and has a strong, though not outstanding, position in financial and insurance services. But it has found itself at an increasing disadvantage in legal and accounting services because Anglo-American law and standards dominate in international transactions. Anglo-American firms with offices in Paris provide the legal needs of firms, whether French or foreign, operating out of France. Similarly, Anglo-American law is increasingly dominant in international commercial arbitration, an institution grounded in continental traditions of jurisprudence, particularly French and Swiss.

12. While it is well known, it is worth remembering that this guarantee of the rights of capital is embedded in a certain type of state, a certain conception of the rights of capital, and a certain type of international legal regime: it is largely embedded in the state of the most developed and most powerful countries in the world, in Western notions of contract and property rights, and in new legal regimes aimed at furthering economic globalization (e.g., the push to get countries to support copyright law).

13. While we take this autonomy for granted in the United States or in most European Union countries (though not all; thus France's central bank, before the formation of the European Central Bank, was not considered as quite autonomous from the executive), in many countries the executive or local oligarchies have long had undue influence on central banks—incidentally not necessarily always to the disadvantage of the disadvantaged.

14. In terms of research and theorization, this is a vast uncharted terrain: it would mean examining how that production takes place and gets legitimated. This signals the possibility of cross-national variations (which then would need to be established, measured, and interpreted).

15. The question for research becomes: What is actually national (as in national state, not as in national people) in some of the institutional components of states linked to the implementation and regulation of economic globalization? The social sciences are not well equipped for this task given a strong state-centric approach to theory and research. (For a critical examination of the state-centric bent in the social sciences see, e.g., Taylor 2000; Hardt and Negri 2000; Brenner 2004; see also generally Abu-Lughod 2000.)

16. See the argument by Arrighi 1994; see also the debate in Davis 1999.

17. See Dezalay and Garth (1996) on international commercial arbitration; Cutler et al. (1999), and Hall and Biersteker (2002) on private authority.

18. There are parallels here with a totally different sphere of state activity and transnational processes: the role of national courts in implementing instruments of the international human rights regime and the incorporation in several new national constitutions of provisions that limit the national state's presumption to represent its entire people in international fora.

3

DO CELLULAR PHONES DREAM OF CIVIL WAR?
The Mystification of Production and the Consequences of Technology Fetishism in the Eastern Congo

James H. Smith and Jeffrey W. Mantz

This will be a city unrooted to any definite spot on the surface of the earth, shaped by connectivity and bandwidth constraints rather than by accessibility and land values, largely asynchronous in its operation, and inhabited by disembodied and fragmented subjects who exist as collections of aliases and agents. Its places will be constructed virtually by software instead of physically from stones and timbers, and they will be connected by logical linkages rather than by doors, passageways and streets. How shall we shape it? Who shall be our Hippodamos?

William J. Mitchell,
City of Bits: Space, Place and the Infobahn

Throughout history cities have served regions of towns, villages, homesteads. They have had links with other cities of the same size and larger ones. They have been part of networks... Does one perhaps need a new name for a new kind of city: isolated by disintegration of the national state administrative and economic network? Maintained by the economic activity of foreign relief agencies, militias, and peace keepers? At risk to a wide variety of natural and technological hazards because of the deterioration of managerial capacity, economic viability, and infrastructure? Sarajevo? Kandahar? Mogadishu? Now: Goma?

Ben Wisner, in reference to the volcanic eruption that destroyed the city of Goma in the eastern Democratic Republic of the Congo in 2002

INTRODUCTION: CITIES OF BITS VERSUS CITIES IN BITS: COLTAN AND THE DIGITAL DIVIDE

How is it possible for two social observers, writing at roughly the same moment in history, to make such radically opposed pronouncements about the state of the world, of the nature of being in it, and of the capacity of humans to change it? One answer is that they are writing about very different things: Mitchell about the Internet as a new kind of urban sphere, and Wisner about the besieged, war- and volcano-ravaged city of Goma on the northern shores of Lake Kivu in the militia-occupied eastern region of the Democratic Republic of the Congo (DRC). The perspective that informs this research is that they are writing about two sides of the same coin, that these cities are very concretely, though invisibly, dependent on one another, and that social science needs to direct its attention to systematically unpacking connections such as these. In fact, the radical separateness of these places, and the very idea of the City of Bits as a transcendent futuristic beacon, is the outcome of a particular nexus of relations and forces of production centered in and around Goma.

In Mitchell's now commonplace argument about the globally integrative functionality of digital technology, social life is said to have been unleashed from materiality, and human experience made to float seductively, if not mockingly, above and beyond pedestrian stones and timbers. Here all of the optimism of the Enlightenment, and the attendant enthusiasm for civil society, open forums, transcendent reason, technological progress, and the realization of an ancient promise of freedom and democracy[1] is fused with the sense of contingent indeterminacy, ambiguity, and impending collective mutation that are hallmarks of postmodernism. Motivating all of this is the familiar, modernist belief that technology is enabling the evolution of a new kind of person whose immanent nature will eventually become a telos for the entire world. This inchoate subject is not, strictly speaking, a biological or material entity, and is not one but many, fragmented and disembodied in a way at once empowering and alienating. A person who, without necessarily realizing that anything has happened, annihilates such parochial stumbling blocks as national borders, inconvenient airport checks, the body, and gridlock, rendering them superfluous, and herself sublime (if also difficult to identify).

The city of Goma is the setting for a starkly opposite rendition of the human struggle. For one, the so-called *thereness* of Goma is not open to doubt, despite the fact that these days, there really is very little there (which, as we will see, gives a dark twist to the currently popular notion that nonplaces have become one of the primary products of globalization [Ritzer 2004]).[3] Let us briefly rehearse what should be, but is not, a very familiar story: Beginning in the mid-1990s, this DRC city of 500,000 on the shores of Lake Kivu devolved from a playground resort for the kleptocratic President Mobutu Sese Seko, to a breeding ground for genocide in Rwanda and the eastern Congo. In 1994, after the Tutsi-backed rebel group, the Rwandan Patriotic Front (RPF), returned to Rwanda through Uganda with a view to ending the extermination of the Tutsis in that country, Hutu power militias and ordinary Hutu citizens fled across the border to the DRC (then called Zaire) in terror, where the Hutu genocidaires ended up in refugee camps sponsored and maintained by the international aid community. There they planned their return home, while waging war on the Tutsis in the Congo until Lawrence Kabila and the AFDL came, with the backing of the Rwandan and Ugandan governments, to oust Mobutu. The refugee camps in Goma were terrorized by Hutu and Tutsi militias and, to make matters worse, everyone's effluvia combined with the dead bodies thrown into the lake during the genocide to turn the waters of Lake Kivu, on which Goma rests, into a poisonous breeding ground for cholera. This disease killed 30,000 people in three weeks in late 1994. And Goma became one of the principal starting points of the first African World War, a conflict that has involved nine African countries, that has so far cost the lives of nearly four million people, and that has fragmented the eastern DRC into diffuse enclaves controlled by indigenous and foreign militias and occupying forces.

Since 2002, Goma has been occupied by the Rally for Congolese Democracy (now RCD-Goma), a front for the Rwandan government, recently in collaboration with a much diminished central government in the DRC capital city of Kinshasa. All of this has happened with most of the West being largely unaware of a crisis whose scale and scope the world has not seen since World War II. Around the outskirts of Goma, the now fragmented RCD has fought for years against government forces, Ugandan backed militias, Rwandan Hutus, Ugandan and Congolese pastoralists who are misrepresented as Rwandan Hutus, and the indigenous militias collectively known as Mai Mai. Most of these groups have drawn their ranks principally from the conscription of children. Indeed, in a bizarre twist to the global reach of the digital age, the home page of the Mai Mai's website (http://www.congo-mai-mai.net/) features a photograph of an adolescent Général Padiri swimming in his oversized military dress.

The Congolese residents of Goma often say that God became angry with the city's inhabitants for housing Mobutu and the Hutu genocidaires, and later for allowing Rwandan foreigners to run the town and expropriate its wealth, and so decided to just be done with the place: in 2002, the nearby volcano erupted, destroying the town and burying it in molten lava. What is most interesting for our purposes is that in Goma, there has been little freedom (indeed, more often than not, there has been slavery) from exactly the same moment that Mitchell's new world—the city of bits inaugurated by the digital age—blossomed into being. This is not a coincidence, for what ties the city of Goma and the city of bits together is columbite-tantalite, known in the eastern Congo region as coltan. This silicate (from which the heat-resistant powder tantalum is extracted) is at present the most effective current conductor in existence, and a crucial component of the microchips found in all digital technology (cell phones, laptops, pagers, Sony PlayStation, iPods, etc.) as well as a host of other electronic devices, including hearing aids and pacemakers. It is estimated that the eastern region of the DRC is home to 80 percent of the world's reserves of coltan (Moyroud & Katunga 2002, 159). Despite some clamoring on the part of environmental NGOs (nongovernmental organizations), and even some Hollywood celebrities (Leonardo DiCaprio, Lucy Liu) concerned with the impact of mining on wildlife (though seldom with the loss of human life), DRC coltan appears to be the predominant variety traded in an elaborately layered and unregulated transnational market.

Coltan is bought by middlemen frequently operating under the auspices of one or another local militias, who in turn typically sell to Belgian and other expatriate traders, often in the Rwandan capital of Kigali. Those intermediaries then sell to buyers in the United States, Japan, and Europe, who will extract the tantalum powder from the ore and refine and process it for the construction of digital devices (processing is conducted in diverse parts of the world, including the United States, Europe, and Asia, but these days much of this work seems to be done in former uranium processing plants in Kazakhstan, for eventual sale in China [IPIS 2002, 8]). It is in the city of Goma that we came to know the coltan middleman, whom we will refer to here as Bwana Mkapa, while conducting fieldwork in the summer of 2003. We met in Kigali, where he had just concluded a hotel meeting with a Belgian businessman. Mkapa was forced to explain to the Belgian that he did not have the coltan that the latter wanted to buy from him, and then resell in Japan, because the lava from the volcano in Goma had incinerated the money Mkapa needed to buy the product. Until that point, Mkapa had been running a brisk trade in coltan, peaking in late 2000 when Sony did not have enough of the mineral to meet the Christmas season demand for its Playstation 2, causing the price of this commodity to skyrocket tenfold nearly overnight. At one point, Citibank and other multinationals were negotiating directly with the RCD, the Rwandan-backed army that was ruthlessly occupying that part of the Congo, plundering villages, and forcing their residents into slave labor camps to acquire this substance. At that point, Mkapa was making a great deal of money from coltan, which he bought, sometimes from independent miners and sometimes from the RCD. However, since the region was occupied by militias, Mkapa felt that he could not trust the banks or risk having his income known, so he hid his money (approximately $5,000) in burlap sacks in his house.

Mkapa was in Rwanda when the volcano erupted, engulfing Goma, and simultaneously torching his house and the bag of money hidden under his bed. Clearly, the story of Mkapa's incinerated cash perfectly captures the paradoxical fact that global disintegration has developed in pace with global integration. In particular, Mkapa was involved in a global trade in a commodity generative of computerization and the Internet, phenomena that epitomize global integration, but his fictive nation had disintegrated to such an extent that he could not move from one town to another, except by air or waterway, could not depend on the banks, and lived in a constant state of anxiety in a city that could not protect itself from volcanic eruption. All things considered, though, Mkapa was a pretty optimistic fellow, and he insisted that he be accompanied from Kigali to Goma and then to Bukavu by Lake Kivu, the only means of transport available. Mkapa promised to introduce every aspect of the coltan business, and if we were so inclined, investment opportunities either in coltan or gold. When the nature of social research was explained to him, and that what we wanted was to do a bottom-up analysis of the world system through coltan, rather than a financial assessment of a potential business venture, Mkapa eventually said that he understood. The problem, he warned in his broken

Swahili, was that it might find be to do this kind of research on a non-thing: "None of the miners know what this coltan is for," he quipped.

What made this so ironic was the fact that the extremely dense and heavy silicate that Mkapa bought and sold is the material bedrock on which the entire digital age, and everything associated with it, is founded. The promise of an interconnected world, of fluid identities— indeed the possibility of postmodern thought, and the notion that we live today in a postmodern world—arguably has as its precondition this commodity and its particular qualities (of density and relative accessibility, for example), as well as the labor relations, trade conditions, and internal fragmentation that have made this commodity available to the world at an affordable price. Clearly, the globally shared experiences of deterritorialization, multiplicity, and simulacrality are fueled by computerization, as Mitchell points out in his elaboration of the existential issues that emerge from the experience of being online. The fact that most of the world's supply of coltan is located in the Congo also means that the cultural dispositions associated with postmodernism (the emphasis on subjectivity, ambiguity, flexibility, multivocality, and the generative power of consumption as a form of agency and politics) are dependent on genocide, ecocide, incarceration, and perhaps most important for those seeking an antidote to the overriding focus on consumption in contemporary thought, production in the Congo.

This suggests a very different way of conceptualizing the relationship between postmodern thought and material processes than other social theorists, such as David Harvey (1990), have so far offered: postmodernism is not simply an ideological refraction of post-Fordist flexible accumulation (the notion that the economy is increasingly flexible, expansive, rapid, indeterminate, and shifting, and so thought follows suit); rather, postmodernism is a philosophical point of view that makes sense to people in the north because they are accustomed to directly engaging the fetish forms produced by a systematically *invisibilized* system of production based on instability, slavery, and terror. (This is similar to Frederic Jameson's argument in *Postmodernism, or, the Cultural Logic of Late Capitalism* [1991].) This system of production is abetted by the fetish nature of technology, which appears to live and evolve by virtue of its own characteristics, inviting people to live in a world that appears uprooted from anything material (virtual worlds like Everquest[4] or the ubiquitous chat room are perfect examples); this system is also undergirded by the Africa synonymous with excess and irrationality, which is imagined to exist in a dimension separate from the north. David Graeber (2001) has claimed that anthropology's preoccupation with the creative potential of consumptive practices has obscured the productive processes and political struggles that underlay them. We contend similarly that the contemporary Western consumer's detachment from the social life of things is enabled by the fact that these things are systematically stripped of all social referents, and hence of meaning.

Despite the concrete specificity of Goma, there was something postmodern about it, for there we encountered a populous, bustling city operating, as if by magic, in absentia—in particular, with very little infrastructure. Yet there were people everywhere, all quite intent on going somewhere, despite the fact that at the time it didn't look as if there were much of anything to go to. Many were decked out in jewelry, much of it gold; these people had returned from Rwanda because they did not want to lose access to the lucrative mineral trade. Many stores were empty, but the real business was located behind the shops: there young men sat sifting through coltan and gold, cleaning and separating the stones, then loading them into gunnysacks for transport to Rwanda. These men were from the mines in the forests, where they had worked under the strict supervision of the RCD army, supplying the soldiers with coltan in exchange for a small portion of what they mined. These people were among the luckier ones: at the height of the coltan boom, men and women were often forced to work together, starving and naked, at the barrel of a gun. There was still quite a bit of this kind of terror. Once, when trying to leave the town of Bukavu with Mkapa to visit a nearby coltan mine, we were forced to turn around: two brothers and their wives had been buried in the ground up to their necks by RCD soldiers when they refused the soldiers' demands of $200 from each of them. The soldiers had then ransacked their houses and fields and were due to return while the living disembodied made up their minds; no one in the bus was willing to risk helping these immobilized people who, it was tempting to interpret, were apt icons of the underbelly of this age of fluidity, openness, and possibility. Everywhere we went, Mkapa's prophecy was vindicated, for few could tell us what coltan was used for. We did find a number of people willing to discuss the effects, both positive and negative, of the trade—including various new ways of organizing production (the miner-militia complex being only one among many that have emerged from the coltan trade in Congo), the destruction of the forests and the gorillas that lived there, and (most galling for locals) the continued presence of an uncivil and uncontrolled occupying force in their backyard. We also found a pseudostate operating in perfect simulacrum: fake visas that no RCD official would accept once we left the town in which they were issued, fake money (mostly American, as Congolese money was banned, and

American money is used to facilitate the international mineral trade), and oceans of bureaucracy whose only purpose seemed to be to drive home, to the "citizens," the fundamental good sense of cutting through this mess by ultimately bribing "state" officials.

GLOBAL ACCOUNTING

This project is not only about locating the productive foundation of the digital age, neoliberalism, and postmodernism. Part of what we are arguing here is that in order to understand the world today we need to find ways of drawing conceptual connections between disconnected parts of that world, and one way to do this is to follow in the footsteps of Sidney Mintz (1985), who traced the connection between production and consumption through a particular object (sugar), showing how tastes, ideas, sentiments, and material processes (such as class and state formation) in Europe were rooted in productive processes elsewhere. We seek to do for coltan and postmodernity what Mintz did for sugar and modernity, and we believe that the commodity coltan is perfect for thinking through the postmodern moment because, far from overflowing sumptuously with meaning (like sugar), it is comparatively meaningless, undistinguished, and invisible. More accurately, coltan is systematically rendered meaningless and invisible by the production process and by the network of political and corporate bodies that control its distribution. What we are calling for, then, is not simply a new way of looking at the world as interconnected, but for a whole new field of study devoted to understanding it. Following on a host of others, we refer to this as global accounting, an emergent field of inquiry that combines political economy and cultural geography with classical anthropology and sociology.

We use the term global accounting to underscore the importance of making explicit and intelligible commodity flows that post-Fordist philosophy and everyday life have rendered spectral. We take our cue from Marx, who in *Capital* (1976 [1867]) sought to unravel the "mystical nature of the commodity" by thoroughly accounting the processes of production, distribution, and consumption in which objects were engaged.

THE POLITICAL AND CULTURAL ECONOMY OF COLTAN

In recent years, there has been a small explosion of writing on the "social life of things," much of which is indebted to Arjun Appadurai's (1986) edited volume of the same name. To cite but a few examples, anthropologists and social geographers have followed glass, paper, and beans (Cohen 1997), cod (Kurlansky 1997), maize husks (Long and Villareal 2000), tobacco (Gately 2001), bluefish tuna (Bestor 2001), potatoes (Zuckerman 1998), salt (Kurlansky 2002), coal (Freese 2003), and bananas (Striffler and Moberg 2003; Raynolds 2003), all with a view to showing how the world is interconnected through commodities (see also Ridgeway 2004). Clearly, as Bridge and Smith have portentously surmised, "the commodity is back" (2003, 257)—though, it often seems, without teeth. In addition, the very notion of the field site has been changing for some time, away from a focus on physical locations and toward more conceptual terrains (see Gupta and Ferguson 1997, Marcus 1995). Academic interest in the relationship between culture and globalization is largely dominated by Appadurai's (1990) ubiquitously cited essay on the "flows" of things, people, and ideas over tumultuous but meaningfully constituted "scapes" (for Appadurai, ethnoscapes, mediascapes, technoscapes, finanscapes, and ideoscapes are some example). Some have even suggested that the *scape* be used to explain a range of other transnational processes and flows, as with Brennan's "sexscapes," a concept she uses to make sense of the sex tourism industry in the Dominican Republic (Brennan 2004). Our approach fuses the contemporary focus on unbounded field sites with economic anthropology's commitment to conducting dogged fieldwork in productive sites of the global economy (Harvey 1990), while at the same time recognizing the limitations of privileging production over consumption (Castree 2001).

Thus far, two very different approaches have dominated the academic study of global flows of commodities. One group of scholars traces their interest in the relationship between globalization and culture to the "commodity biographies" approach of Igor Kopytoff (1986), published in *The Social Life of Things*. Many of these studies have focused on the influence of consumer culture on non-Western societies (e.g., Appadurai 1986; Fine and Leopold 1993; Miller 1998), and some have stressed the liberating promise of consumption as a mode of agency (see, for example, Miller's 1998 study of shopping). Much of this literature is conceptually indebted to Georg Simmel's work on the social and psychological impact of exchange, and represents a transformation of the more classic economic anthropology focus on productive cycles. In contrast, and often in reaction, to this cultural studies approach to the commodity, scholars writing in a Marxist vein have tended to focus on how production determines the meaning of commodities. Commodity studies of sugar (Mintz 1985), coffee (Roseberry, Gudmundson & Kutschbach 1995; Weiss 2003), cotton (Farnie 1979; Lemire 1991), and more recently of bananas (Stiffler and Moberg 2003) exemplify the trend. However, these two traditions, the productivist and the consumptionist, need not be mutually exclusive. Indeed, many political economists have called for an "ethnography of mediation" to understand the complex relationship between transnational global and cultural flows (e.g., Trouillot 1988; Mantz 2003). The emphasis in such studies is on interrogating the consequences of the fact that various global and local actors are interconnected at different levels of the commodity chain. Thus, the meaning or symbolic value of any particular commodity emerges from complexly interlaced processes of production, exchange, and consumption, which must first be unraveled and then reassembled before they can be understood.

Furthermore, the meanings of commodities cannot be understood solely in terms of their positions in a global economy, but must be analyzed in relation to localized systems of meaning, which change over time. Thus, the meaning of coltan for Congolese is partly derived from the fact that mining coltan is symbolically and practically opposed to agriculture, and is associated as well with the destruction of local forests. It is tied up in the meaning of the city, and of connection to the world community because coltan mining has transformed Congolese cities into food-producing areas for the countryside. In this way, the meaning of coltan also impinges on the meaning of trees and food, which are in turn invested in larger structures that change over time. And for many Congolese, coltan embodies an epic hope following upon a long decline (see Bloch 1986 and discussion by Miyazaki 2004), and in this way the coltan boom has picked up where the declining Zambian copper belt (and Africa's "industrial revolution") left off (Ferguson 1999). Clearly, the meanings of commodities are diffuse and shifting, and must be situated within a larger historical, cultural, and geographic context (Cook and Crang 1996; Cooper 2001; Dicken et. al 2001; Law and Hetherington 1999; Leslie and Reimer 1999; Weiss 2002; Whatmore and Thorne 1997). This perspective owes much to the work of Brad Weiss (2003), who shows how the meaning of coffee for Haya people has always been determined by its relationship to other meaningful things and activities, and has changed in response to larger structural transformations.

In many ways there is nothing particularly special about coltan, in that it is not essentially different from all of the other resources that have historically been expropriated from the Congo, such as gold, copper, and rubber; indeed, a transnational system of extraction and violence has shaped the region for generations, and would seem to override the meaning of any single commodity (see, for example, Hochschild 1998). Coltan is just one part of a tapestry of violence that is extremely complex, and which is epitomized by the widespread cases of rape and cannibalism committed on indigenous Congolese, non-Congolese Africans, and United Nations personnel—phenomena that have their own symbolic economies. However, coltan does have some unique properties, in that it has been more vulnerable than other Congolese commodities to market fluctuations; moreover, Congolese violence, and the restructuring of labor relations, has been directly related to the rapid upswings and downswings in the price of coltan (Jackson 2002). In addition, the relative accessibility and prevalence of this ore makes its production most difficult for any single governing authority to control, and thus helps to generate political fragmentation, a situation from which corporate buyers benefit. Even so, choosing coltan as an entry point is largely a methodological choice, which makes sense because of the centrality of this commodity to the digital age and the promise of open possibility and fluidity; its resistance to being traced, and its consequent invisibility; and its relative newness as a valuable commodity.

CULTURAL ECONOMIES OF WAR

The Democratic Republic of the Congo has long been dominated by what social scientists have typically referred to as an underground, informal, or second economy (MacGaffey 1988, 1991; Vwakyanakazi 1991; De Boeck 1999). However, such conventional dichotomies as formal and informal (Hart 1974) only obscure the Congolese case. One reason for this is that the so-called informal or illegal economy has long been the dominant one. Following Mobuto Sese Seko's injunction to all Congolese that they learn to survive by any means necessary (called "Debrouillez-vous" or "fend for yourselves;" see Jackson 2002, 520–521), "informal" ventures became the rule (De Boeck 1996; Jackson 2001; 2002; 2003a; 2003b). Though coltan mining has grown in scale and involves corporate entities, this process has done nothing to formalize the trade; rather, the conflict and violence that surround coltan functions to keep costs low and obscures the connections between producers and buyers. Clearly, the apparent chaos in the Congo can be understood as a kind of order that makes sense only when one considers its function in the larger world system. This perspective shares much in common with recent work on the criminalization of the state in Africa, and the functional utility of "disorder" (Bayart 1993; Bayart, Ellis, and Hibou 1999; Chabal and Daloz 1999; MacGaffey 1986, 1991; MacGaffey and Bazenguissa-Ganga 2000, Vwakyanakazi 1991). All of this makes coltan, and the DRC, perfect methodological vehicles for forging an anthropology that moves beyond the "persistently parochial and regional" (Ballard and Banks 2003, 287; see also Knapp and Pigott

1999), an orientation that plagued earlier studies of resource extraction. As Ballard and Banks have argued, the "monolithic entities of community, state, and corporation" (Ballard & Banks 2003, 289) need to be relativized and contextualized if we are to grasp the increasingly "transnational nature of the industry" (287).

Others have examined how the frenetic coltan and tantalum market flourished by undermining state structures or encouraging pseudopolities and clique confederacies bolstered by criminality and corruption (Jackson 2001, 2002, 2003a, 2003b; Koyame & Clark 2002; Montague 2002; Moyroud & Katunga 2002). Indeed, most of these studies have sought to go "beyond a simplistic post–Cold War analysis of conflict based upon tribalism, primitiveness, and chaos" (Montague 2002, 104), to provide an explanation of the relationship between the war and the economic exploitation of the eastern Congo's mineral resources (not only coltan, but diamonds, gold, tin, copper, and cobalt as well). Stephen Jackson has suggested, quite correctly, that the "economy of war" (citing Le Billon 2000) in the Congo has become "economised" through coltan production as "profits increasingly motivate the violence, and violence increasingly makes profits possible for all belligerents" (Jackson 2002, 517). However, the economy of coltan is not entirely determined by exogenous forces, in part because new, scarcely understood, relations of production have grown up around it, and coltan mining arguably has the capacity to empower certain communities and groups of people.

Our project will also enhance global understanding of the many transformations that are taking place on the African continent, with a specific focus on the rewriting of historically entrenched social and territorial boundaries, a process fueled by the simultaneous deterritorialization and relocalization of power in Africa. The names and numbers of the parties involved in the war are virtually impossible for an outsider to follow, and even Congolese speculate constantly about the true origins and backers of various militias and splinter groups said to be the false creations of foreign leaders who manufacture them to justify the continued presence of their occupying armies. The Congolese case thus epitomizes the processes of fragmentation and reconsolidation that are taking place in Africa in response to instability and the global circulation of things. The boundaries of the new territories that are being forged throughout the continent often bear no relation to the nation-state, and the categories state and nation have thus lost their former meaning and analytical function. As Achille Mbembe has written of Congo-Kinshasa:

Against a background of armed violence and severe depreciation of currencies, alliances are constantly made and unmade.
Ephemeral coalitions are formed on the regional scale. But no
force accumulates enough power to dominate all the others in
an enduring way. Everywhere, lines emerge and vanish. Structural instability makes Congo-Kinshasa the perfect example of
… the delocalization of boundaries. (2001, 48)

As Mbembe points out, in this context, apparently autochthonous
rebellions and social movements are often merely the face of foreign
armies squaring off against each other, and nation-states and multinational corporations combine to instigate and exacerbate fragmentation
at all levels of social organization, all the way down to lineage dynamics. In the process, humanitarianism and imperialism become indis-
tinguishable, as the United States funds and supplies the Rwandan
army, which in turn consolidates its position over the eastern Congo,
and expropriates vital resources from the region. Refugee camps managed by international aid organizations become military recruitment
training grounds, which in turn articulate with the new networks of
commodity production and distribution (as when Citibank negoti-
ates directly with the RCD). Meanwhile, fragmentation is paralleled
by new forms of consolidation and empire: most conspicuously, China's demand for mineral resources, including coltan, tin, and gold, has
led the country to developing an extractive imperial relationship with
many African countries that have been involved in the Congolese war,
including Zimbabwe. All of this is very mysterious, even to people on
the ground, as no one truly understands the multiple ways in which
local, regional, and global players are interconnected. In a context like
this, where there is no clarity, and where private interests benefit from
the murk, the analyst has to locate and follow something concrete—or
in this case an object which, ironically, is embedded in mud.

A number of related questions run through this project. For example, given that the Congo has long been the object of imperial extraction, and given that Congolese people have been consistently forced
into expropriative mining and commercial agriculture since the end of
the nineteenth century (Hochschild 1998), what is new about the current social and political organization of extraction? On the one hand,
events in the Congo have to be situated within the long history of copper and gold mining and deforestation (Marchal & Armah 2003). Yet
the conflicts there can only be understood in light of the crises affecting Congo-Kinshasa's neighboring states, especially Rwanda, Uganda,
and Burundi, which have sought to strengthen their own readjusted

economies by penetrating this region, and "blurring its sovereignty over major parts of its territory" (Mbembe 2000: 280). Moreover, fragmentation and imperial encroachment throughout the region emerged directly from global events, such as the fall of the Soviet Union, which caused Mobutu's Zaire to lose its status as a strategic bulwark against the global spread of communism. As anthropologists, we are interested in understanding the role of African agency in all of this, given that most analysts have made it clear that the region's events are the product of exogenous forces, such as the infiltration of foreign capital and the collapse of the state. We also seek to develop a better insight into the various forms of labor, artistic production, and patron-clientage that are developing alongside the trade. The vacuum of power in the region has opened up new opportunities for the reinvention of identity and the dismantling of old systems of exploitation, at the same time as it has portended unprecedented crises. For example, Koen Vlassenroot (n.d.) argues that Mai Mai militias, which use ritual and religious practice and symbolism to forge a new political order, are in part a local revolt against senior chiefs, and the system of resource expropriation that dates back to colonial times. Jackson has similarly warned against viewing the eastern Congo as merely a victimized site of highly exploitative extraction by enterprising Rwandan- or Ugandan-backed "foreign bandits" (Jackson 2002, 522–523). And many have argued that coltan mining could be the saving grace of the region, if local players could harness control over its production and distribution (see also Vlassenroot & Raeymaekers 2004).

THE CULTURAL DIMENSIONS OF COLTAN

All of which brings us to the issue of cultural change, for coltan is at the center of a multitude of social and political transformations that are by no means fully understood. There have been some very excellent reconstructions of the basic model of coltan production and exchange, of the impact of mining on food availability, and of how the trade has inverted economic relations between urban and rural areas (most notably, Stephen Jackson 2001, 2002, 2003a, 2003b). However, Jackson himself has argued that there has been very little work concerning the new social and cultural formations that have emerged around coltan mining and exchange. The central question is to what extent, and in what ways, are Congolese framing the changes wrought by civil war and economic devastation in such a way as to forge meaningful social ties? How, for example, has coltan mining and trade affected local forms of social organization, and are new forms of community emerging among miners in the forest, and among families who have long depended on these now absent male laborers? To what extent are people in the mines, and in the communities that depend on coltan mining, able to reproduce kin and community structures, and how have certain institutions, such as marriage and bridewealth, changed as a result? What are the lines of gender, generational, and class change, and how are different social groups taking advantage of the opportunity afforded by coltan and other forms of mining to change their position in society? A focused ethnographic analysis of miners and the home communities that depend on them is the only way to truly answer these questions.

The regions affected by coltan mining are also places of profound religious change, and many of the new forms of polity that have emerged in the wake of state collapse are interpreted by locals as deeply meaningful, for better or for worse, and thus represent far more than the fragmentation of the social order. Indeed, throughout the DRC, new religious movements have emerged in response to the collapse of the state; Renaat Devisch (1995, 1998) has argued persuasively that charismatic healing churches in Kinshasa represent new forms of polity, and are also sites where formerly marginalized groups build new forms of community and self-empowerment. Filip De Boeck's (1996, 1999, 2000, 2002, 2004) work has focused on how diamond mining in the western DRC has exacerbated generational conflict, which plays out in numerous terrains; most striking is the common accusation, among seniors, that their relatively empowered lineage juniors are witches. This has created a population of alleged child sorcerers who, after having been expelled from their homes, form itinerant gangs on the streets of Kinshasa. These displaced youths thus forge bonds of community based on perpetuating the mythology of their occult powers. Again, with regard to the eastern Congo areas affected by coltan mining, Koen Vlassenroot (n.d.) has argued that the Mai Mai movement must be understood as a revolt of youth against seniors, as well as "traditional" authorities that were formerly connected to the state; this revolt is total in the sense that it involves a complete overhaul of the social order, and is articulated in registers that are at once political and religious. And yet the positively transformative potential of coltan mining does not alter the current position of the Congo, and of Congolese coltan mining, vis à vis the global community in this digitalized age.

CONCLUSION

In the film *The Matrix*, the protagonist, Neo, discovers that the world in which he lives is a computer-generated mirage, that the physical world beyond this simulacrum is an all too real nightmare, where humans are allowed to exist because they are the only remaining natural resource, and where a truly human existence (in the Enlightenment or any other sense) is impossible, in part because the natural and authentic no longer exist: there are no trees, no food, no sunlight, no freedom to choose anything, no sex (except in simulation). This matrix world and society is a semblance of physical reality, pieced together by machines whose understanding of the social is more indebted to Nietzsche than Durkheim. They manufacture the virtual realities in which humans live, coupling their Machiavellian social engineering with their collected memories of human experience (which accounts for why, in this world, everything tastes like chicken). In fact, the energy for the program in which people's imaginations live, while their bodies are harvested elsewhere, is the product of a kind of cannibalism, where people within the Matrix exist by virtue of the fact that they are being slowly eaten by themselves, other humans, and machines that live on them for energy.

The truth of our times is that we are living in this Matrix now: (1) we are increasingly dependent on virtual realities, as Mitchell suggests, (2) these virtual realities are grounded in real human terror, slavery, incarceration, and world destruction somewhere, and (3) the rootedness of these virtual worlds in production and cannibalism (both in a metaphoric and a literal sense: for instance, reports of Mai Mai cannibalism as a form of counter-state production in the DRC) is systematically concealed from us, partly by virtue of the fetish form in which technology presents itself as a sui generis world-historic force. Any social theory that proceeds from virtual worlds as existing realities of their own accord (an analysis of the social-psychological, and even economic, implications of the online game and world Everquest, for example), detached from materiality and production, is choosing the Matrix as its reality, its home, and its sustenance. Doing so ignores the increasingly obvious fact that this virtual reality proceeds from work that is—in its current organization—rapidly bringing the underside of the matrix (dehumanization, implosion of the state, and ecocide) into being as objective global reality.

We envision a multisited ethnography that, at a later stage in this ongoing research project, we will focus our attention on the middlemen distributors and processors of coltan in Europe and Asia, where we will investigate the factories that manufacture cell phones and microchips in Kazakhstan and elsewhere. The final stage of our research is likely to focus on the information technology boom in the Silicon Valley during the 1990s, a period that paralleled the beginnings of the war in the Congo. This research will consist primarily of interviews with people who were involved in this industry, and will be aimed at drawing a relationship between the transformation of life in San Jose, and of peoples' understandings of work, business, and leisure, and the processes that were occurring simultaneously in the eastern Congo. We also intend to do comparative research on the culture of youth in Congo and California, focusing on the phenomena of child soldiers and cyberpunks, respectively.

REFERENCES

Appadurai, Arjun. 1986. "Introduction: Commodities and the Politics of Value." In *The Social Life of Things: Commodities in Cultural Perspective*, ed. Arjun Appadurai, 3–63. Cambridge: Cambridge University Press.

_____. 1990. "Disjuncture and Difference in the Global Cultural Economy." *Public Culture* 2(2):1–24.

Ballard, Chris & Glenn Banks. 2003. "Resource Wars: The Anthropology of Mining." Annual Review of Anthropology 32:287–313.

Bayart, Jean-François. 1993. *The State in Africa: The Politics of the Belly*. London: Longman.

Bayart, Jean-François, Stephen Ellis, and Béatrice Hibou. 1999. *The Criminalization of the State in Africa*. Oxford: James Currey.

Bestor, Theodore C. 2001. "Supply-Side Sushi: Commodity, Market and the Global City." *American Anthropologist* 103(1):76–95.

Bloch, Ernst. 1986. *The Principle of Hope*. Trans. Neville Plaice, Stephe Plaice, and Paul Knight. Cambridge, MA: MIT Press.

Brennan, Denise. 2004. *What's Love Got to Do With It?: Transnational Desires and Sex Tourism in the Dominican Republic*. Durham, NC: Duke University Press. Bridge, Gavin and Adian Smith. 2003. "Intimate Encounters: Culture—Economy—Commodity." *Environment and Planning D: Society and Space* 21:257–268.

Callaghy, Thomas M. 1984. *The State-Society Struggle: Zaire in Comparative Perspective*. New York: Columbia University Press.

Castree, Noel, 2001. "Commodity Fetishism, Geographical Imaginations and Imaginative Geographies." *Environment and Planning A* 33:1519–1525

Castronova, Edward. 2001. "Virtual Worlds: A First-Hand Account of Market and Society on the Cyberian Frontier." CESifo Working Paper No. 618.

Chabal, Patrick and Jean-Pascal Daloz 1999. *Africa Works: Disorder as Political Instrument*. Bloomington: Indiana University Press.

Clark, John Frank, ed. 2002. *The African Stakes of the Congo War.* New York: Palgrave Macmillan.

_____. 2002. "Introduction: Causes and Consequences of the Congo War." In *The African Stakes of the Congo War,* ed. John F. Clark. New York: Palgrave Macmillan.

Cook, Ian and Philip Crang. 1996. "The World on a Plate: Culinary Culture, Displacement and Geographical Knowledges." *Journal of Material Culture* 1(2):131–53.

Cohen, Leah Hager. 1997. *Glass, Paper, Beans: Revelations on the Nature and Value of Ordinary Things.* New York: Doubleday Books.

Cooper, Frederick, 2001. "What is the Concept of Globalization Good For? An African Historian's Perspective." *African Affairs* 100:189–213.

Cross, Tiare S. 2005. "The Challenge of War Economies to Peace Building: A Case Study of Coltan in the Democratic Republic of the Congo (DRC)." MA thesis, George Mason University.

De Boeck, Filip and Alcinda Honwana, eds. 2005. *Makers and Breakers, Made and Broken: Children and Youngsters as Emerging Categories in Postcolonial Africa.* Oxford: James Currey.

De Boeck, Filip and Marie-Françoise Plissart. 2004. *Kinshasa. Tales of the Invisible City.* Ghent: Ludion.

De Boeck, Filip. 1996. "Postcolonialism, Power and Identity: Local and Global Perspectives from Zaire." In *Postcolonial Identities in Africa,* ed. Richard Werbner and Terence Ranger. London: Zed Books.

_____. 1999. "Domesticating Diamonds and Dollars: Identity, Expenditure and Sharing in Southwestern Zaire (1984–1997)." In *Globalization and Identity: Dialectics of Flow and Closure,* ed. Birgit Meyer and Peter Geschiere. Oxford: Blackwells Publishers.

_____. 2000. "Le 'deuxième monde' et les 'enfants-sorciers' en République Démocratique du Congo." *Politique Africaine* 80:32–57.

_____. 2002. "Kinshasa: Tales of the 'Invisible City' and the 'Second World.'" In *Under Siege: Four African Cities Freetown, Johannesburg, Kinshasa, Lagos,* ed. Okwui Enwezor, et. al., 243–285. Kassel: Hatje Cantz Publishers.

_____. 2004. "On Being Shege in Kinshasa: Children, the Occult and the Street." In *Reinventing Order in the Congo: How People Respond to State Failure in Kinshasa,* ed. T. Trefon, 155–173. London: Zed Books.

Devisch, R. 1995. "Frenzy, Violence, and Ethical Renewal in Kinshasa." *Public Culture* 7:593–629.

_____. 1998. "La violence à Kinshasa, ou l'institution en négatif," *Cahiers d'études africaines* 38(2–4), nos. 150–52:441–69.

Dicken, Peter, Philip Kelly, Kris Olds, and Henry Wai-Chung Yeung. 2001. "Chains and Networks, Territories and Scales: Towards a Relational Framework for Analysing the Global Economy." *Global Networks* 1(2):89–112.

Farnie, D.A. 1979. *The English Cotton Industry and the World Market: 1815–1896*. Oxford: Oxford University Press.

Ferguson, James. 1999. *Expectations of Modernity: Myths and Meanings of Urban Life on the Zambian Copperbelt*. Berkeley: University of California Press.

Fine, Ben and Ellen Leopold. 1993. *The World of Consumption*. New York: Routledge.

Foster, Robert J. Forthcoming. "Tracking Globalization: Commodities and Value in Motion." In *The Handbook of Material Culture*, ed. C. Tilley et al. London: Sage.

Freese, Barbara. 2003. *Coal: A Human History*. Cambridge, MA: Perseus Publishing.

Freidberg, Susanne. 2004. *French Beans and Food Scares: Culture and Commerce in an Anxious Age*. New York: Oxford University Press.

Gately, Ian. 2001. *Tobacco: A Cultural History of How an Exotic Plant Seduced Civilization*. New York: Grove Press.

Golub, Alex. 2004. "Culture's Open Sources: Copyright and Taboo." *Anthropology Quarterly* 77(3):521–530.

Graeber, David. 2001. *Toward an Anthropological Theory of Value: The False Coin of Our Own Dreams*. New York: Palgrave.

Gupta, Akhil and James Ferguson, eds. 1997. *Anthropological Locations: Boundaries and Grounds of a Field Science*. Berkeley: University of California Press.

Hart, Keith. 1973. "Informal Income Opportunities and Urban Employment in Ghana." *Journal of Modern African Studies* 11(1):61–89.

Harvey, David. 1990. *Between Space and Time: Reflections on the Geographical Imagination*. Annals of the Association of American Geographers 80(3):418–434.

Hochschild, Adam. 1998. *King Leopold's Ghost: A Story of Greed, Terror, and Heroism in Colonial Africa*. Boston, MA: Houghton Mifflin.

IPIS. 2002. "Supporting the War Economy in the DRC: European Companies and the Coltan Trade." An IPIS Report. http://129.194.252.80/cat-files/2343.pdf

Jackson, Stephen. 2001. "Nos Richesses Sont Pillées: Economies de Guerre et Rumeurs de Crime dans les Kivus, République Démocratique du Congo." *Politique Africaine* 84:117–35.

_____. 2002. "Making a Killing: Criminality and Coping in the Kivu War Economy." *Review of African Political Economy* 93/94:517–36.

_____. 2003a. "War Making: Uncertainty, Improvisation and Involution in the Kivu Provinces, DR Congo, 1997–2002." PhD diss., Princeton University.

_____. 2003b. "Fortunes of Ear: The Coltan Trade in the Kivus." In *Power, Livelihoods and Conflict: Case Studies in Political Economy Analysis for Humanitarian Action*. ODI Humanitarian Policy Group Report 13, ed. Sarah Collinson, 21–36. London: Overseas Development Institute (ODI).

Jameson, Frederic. 1991. *Postmodernism: The Cultural Logic of Late Capitalism*. Durham, NC: Duke University Press.

Kopytoff, Igor. 1986. "The Cultural Biography of Things: Commoditization as Process." In *The Social Life of Things: Commodities in Cultural Perspective*, ed. A. Appadurai, 64–91. Cambridge: Cambridge University Press.

Koyame, Mungbalemwe and John F. Clark. 2002. "The Economic Impact of the Congo War." In *The African Stakes of the Congo War*, ed. John F. Clark. New York: Palgrave Macmillan.

Kurlansky, Mark. 1997. *Cod: A Biography of the Fish That Changed the World*. New York: Walker Publishing;

_____. 2002. *Salt: A World History*. New York: Walker Publishing.

Law, John and Kevin Hetherington. 1999. "Materialities, Spatialities, Globalities." Published by the Department of Sociology, Lancaster University. http://www.comp.lancs.ac.uk/sociology/soc029jl.html

Le Billon, Phillipe. 2000. *The Political Economy of War: What Relief Agencies Need to Know*. London: Humanitarian Practice Network Paper 33, Overseas Development Institute (ODI).

Lemire, Beverly. 1991. *Fashion's Favourite: Cotton and the Consumer in Britain, 1660–1800*. Oxford: Oxford University Press.

Leslie, Deborah and Suzanne Reimer. 1999. "Spatializing Commodity Chains." *Progress in Human Geography* 23(3):401–420.

Long, Norman and Magdalena Villareal. 2000. "Small Product, Big Issues: Value Contestations and Cultural Identities in Cross-border Commodity Networks." *Development and Change* 29:725–50.

MacGaffey, Janet. 1988. *Entrepreneurs and Parasites: The Struggle for Indigenous Capitalism in Zaïre*. Cambridge: Cambridge University Press.

_____. 1991. *The Real Economy of Zaire: The Contribution of Smuggling and Other Unofficial Activities to the National Wealth*. Philadelphia, PA: University of Pennsylvania Press.

MacGaffey, Janet and Rémy Bazenguissa-Ganga. 2000. *Congo-Paris: Transnational Traders on the Margins of the Law*. Bloomington, IN: Indiana University Press.

Mantz, Jeffrey W. 2003. "Lost in the Fire, Gained in the Ash: Moral Economies of Exchange in Dominica." PhD diss., University of Chicago, Illinois.

Marchal, Jules and Ayi Kwei Armah. 2003. *Forced Labor in the Gold and Copper Mines: A History of Congo under Belgian Rule, 1910–1945*. Senegal: Per Ankh Publishers.

Marcus, George E. 1995. "Ethnography in/of the World System: The Emergence of Multi-sited Ethnography." *Annual Review of Anthropology* 24:95–117.

Marx, Karl. 1976 [1867]. *Capital: A Critique of Political Economy*, Volume I. Trans. B. Fowkes. New York: Penguin Books.

Mbembe, Achille. 2000. "At the Edge of the World: Boundaries, Territoriality, and Sovereignty in Africa." *Public Culture* 12(2):259–84.

_____. 2001. *On the Postcolony*. Berkeley: University of California Press.

Miller, Daniel. 1998. *A Theory of Shopping*. Ithaca, NY: Cornell University Press.

Mintz, Sidney W. 1985. *Sweetness and Power: The Place of Sugar in Modern History*. New York: Penguin.

Mitchell, William J. 1998. *City of Bits: Space, Place and the Infobahn*. Cambridge, MA: MIT Press.

Miyazaki, Hirokazu. 2004. *The Method of Hope: Anthropology, Philosophy, and Fijian Knowledge*. Stanford, CA: Stanford University Press.

Montague, Dena. 2002. "Stolen Goods: Coltan and Conflict in the Democratic Republic of the Congo." SAIS Review XXII (1):103–118.

Moyroud, Celine and John Katunga. 2002. "Coltan Exploitation in the Eastern Democratic Republic of the Congo." In *Scarcity and Surfeit: The Ecology of Africa's Conflicts*, ed. Jeremy Kind and Kathryn Sturman. Pretoria: Institute for Security Studies.

Raynolds. Laura T. 2003. "The Global Banana Trade." In *Banana Wars: Power, Production and History in the Americas*, ed. Steve Striffler and Mark Moberg, 23–47. Durham, NC: Duke University Press.

Ridgeway, James. 2004. *It's All for Sale: The Control of Global Resources*. Durham, NC: Duke University Press.

Ritzer, George. 2004. *The Globalization of Nothing*. Thousand Oaks, CA: Pine Forge Press.

Roseberry, William, Lowell Gudmundson, and Mario Samper Kutschbach, eds. 1995. *Coffee, Society, and Power in Latin America*. Baltimore, MD: Johns Hopkins University Press

Simmel, Georg. 1978. *The Philosophy of Money*. Trans. Tom Bottomore and David Frisby. London: Routledge & Kegan Paul.

Striffler, Steve and Mark Moberg, eds. 2003. *Banana Wars: Power, Production and History in the Americas*. Durham, NC: Duke University Press.

Trouillot, Michel-Rolph. 1988. *Peasants and Capital: Dominica in the World Economy*. Baltimore, MD: Johns Hopkins University Press.

Vlassenroot, Koen. N.d. "Conflict and Militia Formation in Eastern Congo: The Role of Magico-Religious Systems of Reproduction." Unpublished paper.

Vlassenroot, Koen and Timothy Raeymaekers. 2004. "Introduction." In *Conflict and Social Transformation in Eastern DR Congo.* Gent: Academia Press Scientific Publishers.

Vwakyanakazi, Mukohya. 1991. "Import and Export in the Second Economy of North Kivu." In *The Real Economy of Zaire: The Contribution of Smuggling and Other Unofficial Activities to National Wealth,* ed. Janet MacGaffey. Philadelphia, PA: University of Pennsylvania Press.

Weiss, Brad. 2002. "Thug Realism: Inhabiting Fantasy in Urban Tanzania." Cultural Anthropology 17(1): 93–124.

_____. 2003. *Sacred Trees, Bitter Harvests: Globalizing Coffee in Northwest Tanzania.* Portsmouth, NH: Heinemann.

Whatmore, Sarah and Lorraine Thorne. 1997. "Nourishing Networks: Alternative Geographies of Food." In *Globalising Food: Agrarian Questions and Global Restructuring,* ed. D. Goodman and M. Watts, 287–304. New York: Routledge.

Zuckerman, Larry. 1998. *The Potato: How the Humble Spud Rescued the Western World.* Boston: Faber and Faber.

NOTES

1. Here dating back to Hippodamos, credited by many with being the first urban planner, and the originator of the classical Greek city. Not mentioned by Mitchell is the telling fact that Hippodamos was also credited, by Aristotle, with dividing the Greek city by social class.
2. Deleted.
3. We do not mean to suggest here that the tentacles of the digital age have reached Africa only in purely extractive ways; indeed, the African consumptive landscape has been very much impacted by technologies such as cellular phones, computers, and many other products.
4. Everquest is a massive multiplayer online game (MMOG) set in the virtual world of Norrath. According to Alex Golub, Edward Castronova discovered that 20 percent of all respondents consider themselves denizens of Everquest who merely "visit" Earth. Thirty percent spent more time in Norrath than they did working at their jobs (Castronova 2001).... The fact that There.com lists "shopping" as the second most important activity that can be undertaken in its game world is telling.... Powerful magic items such as magic swords and armor are highly sought after in games such as Everquest for the abilities they give to the players who possess them.... Many of these virtual items are sold on sites such as Ebay for real world dollars and then, as a result of the contract, transferred to their owner's online personas. The size of the market is breathtaking—shadow pricing of the marketing of in-game objects reveals that the value of the booty accumulated during play is significant. The average player of Everquest earns an hourly "wage" of US$3.42

and has an annual income of over US$12,000 and a per capita GNP of US$2,366 (Castronova 2001). Castronova has estimated that Everquest has an economy roughly the size of Russia. In comparison, Papua New Guinea has a per capita GNP of US$580" (Golub 2004, 526).

II

Development Theory, Social Cohesion, and the New Indigenism

4

DEVELOPMENT STRATEGIES, THE EXCLUSION OF WOMEN, AND INDIGENOUS ALTERNATIVES

June Nash

Development processes, like the imperial and colonial processes that preceded them, involve both an ideology and a practice to justify investment and the extraction of profit on a worldwide basis. In order to overcome the growing wealth gap between the winners and losers in the process, we have to go beyond analyzing and exposing the discourse that promotes inequalities. Ideologies that defend the processes grow like hydraheaded monsters, tangled in the rhetoric of those who would oppose the injustice of unequal exchange. With each inroad made by capital ventures in the remaining *semisubsistence* areas of the world, a new ideological format is invented to justify the capitalist premises for reproduction on a global basis. These include the unequal exchange between the developed and undeveloped world, dependency and the subversion of democracy in the periphery, and the shifting of risk to the primary producers. The penetration of capitalist enterprises seeking new sources of oil, minerals, and genetic diversity is destroying environments that were the reserves of indigenous people.

I will critique three major trends over time in development economics and assess how some theoreticians have provided the ideological rationales for each of them. In the early decades after World War II, development models assumed a *unilineal* evolution toward industrial capitalist expansion as the unique journey to progress. Investments in capital-intensive agriculture and assembly operations proliferated in less developed countries. This trend provided high profit margins to investors in the core industrial countries at the same time that less developed countries experienced a decline in the terms of trade for primary products. The growing dependency of developing countries on global financial and food markets reached a crisis in the 1980s when the second trend in development economics emerged. In this phase, development agencies and the institutional supports provided by the International Monetary Fund and the World Bank promoted restructuring programs that shifted the burden of debt to low-income producers and service suppliers in the developing economies and to taxpayers in metropolitan centers. We are entering a third phase in which neoliberal capitalist expansion appears to be the uncontested force in global development. In this third phase, theoreticians of development, who were ignored in the past, and new advocates are beginning to take the priorities of indigenous peoples into account. I shall argue that the course of autonomous development in this third phase not only enhances the life opportunities of indigenous families and communities, but will ensure the future of the environments that they have preserved since primordial times. This can only be achieved in the context of indigenous autonomy within the nation-states in which they are situated, and with cooperation from transnational NGOs (nongovernmental organizations) and a democratic civil society.

Development programs planned from above alienated indigenous people from their lifeways and environment, often destroying household subsistence practices that ensure the survival of families and life itself. I will bring this critique into perspectives raised by programs that indigenous peoples themselves generate. As custodians, indigenous peoples have proven their knowledge and skill in their continuous residence in environments that are havens for a rich diversity of faunal and floral organisms. This knowledge, and even the genetic diversity that women and men have preserved in the environment, are becoming commoditized as drug companies, geologists, and agronomists try to exploit them to their advantage. Aware of the violence and depredation of earlier penetration of capitalist enterprises, indigenous peoples, particularly women, are contesting capitalist development programs such as Plan Puebla Panama as the unique course. Paradoxically, the successful integration of indigenous peoples into the global system will depend on their ties with transnational civil society and the communications networks put in place by globalization processes.

DEVELOPMENT FOR WHOM?

Development economics began shortly after World War II. In 1957 when I was a graduate student at the University of Chicago, I was hired by Bert Hoselitz and Richard Woll as a research assistant in one of the first large-scale study projects to look at development investments in third world countries. Bert made the mistake of going to MIT and bragging about what they were doing, and when he returned and recounted what a great hit he had been in Cambridge, I remember Dick jumping on top of a desk and raging "Bert, you just gave away a half million dollars." He was only half-right, because MIT got in a proposal for a million dollars just before the Chicago proposal was finalized and sent to Washington. Chicago did get a few hundred thousand to start their research and to launch their journal, *Economic Development and Cultural Change*.

Development economics became a lucrative pursuit in its first decade from 1950 to the mid-1960s, as academics invented the ideological base for promoting capitalist development throughout the world. The discourse of modernization presumed that third world countries—those not aligned with the superpowers in the Cold War—would, with the right combination of investment and disengagement from traditional pursuits, evolve in the same way as "advanced" capitalist countries. The objective was phrased as a benefit to countries in need of growth, never the need for new sites of investment to maintain the level of return to capital, or the urgency of seeking new consumers and cheap labor for industries in the metropolis. Buttressed with the rhetoric of the Cold War against communism, no alternatives to capitalist enterprise were admitted. The needs and interests of the countries to be developed were irrelevant. Progress was defined unilaterally as industrialization in capital-intensive enterprises measured in gross national product (GNP). This meant that only products that reached the market were accounted for, since GNP did not measure the domestic production of goods and services for subsistence. As a result, women's work for their families was devalued, and women who persisted in household production of goods and services for their families with limited exchanges were categorized as unemployed. Measurement of growth in development economics was uniquely related to market sales, and unless products reached a market and were exchanged for money, they were not counted. This kind of thinking did not take into account improvements in the human conditions. In Mexico, for example, when President Lázaro Cárdenas implemented the land reform act of the 1917 constitution in the 1930s, it was often treated as a failure because overall production in the country dropped. The fact that peasants ate more and had more leisure time (because they did not have to sell their labor on the plantations) was not taken into consideration by most development experts.[1]

Walter W. Rostow set the pace for overseas development in the 1960s with his book *Stages of Economic Growth, a Non-Communist Manifesto* (1960). Inspired by the Cold War with Russia, it brooked no alternatives to capitalist development. Self-sufficient household production was not even a reference point for progress because it was assumed that it would collapse of its own inertia. During this decade, capitalist expansion into agroindustrial enterprises began to threaten the household production of food for autoconsumption, as petrochemical inputs in fertilizers, pesticides, and herbicides were used to increase outputs in the so-called *green revolution*. In Asia, food supplies increased, but not all of the benefits went to poor families. As Joan Mencher (1978) and other feminist critics of development showed, the net negative impact was greatest on women, who constituted the major work force on small-scale farms. Their jobs were replaced with technology—huge gas-guzzling tractors, cultivators, and reapers that drove out most small-scale producers and led to a concentration of land ownership. In Latin America, the green revolution was delayed by land reform programs that were enacted in several countries. Mexico began to promote capital-intensive agricultural production in the 1970s when Pemex, the national oil company, developed petrochemical production. The government then promoted the use of pesticides, fertilizers, and herbicides by offering low-interest credit to campesinos. It took more than two decades for the small plot cultivators to realize the long-term destruction of soils and the environment caused by chemical fertilizers. By that time, the balanced traditional rural subsistence cultivation and artisan production was upset, and self-sufficiency in food production of third world countries was seriously undermined.

It was also during the 1960s that the era of globalization was fueled by OPEC's (Organization of Petroleum Exporting Countries) control over oil supplies and increases in energy costs. A dual discourse about development was initiated, with conservationists warning the major consumers of energy that sources of nonrenewable resources were limited, while financial advisers promoted direct export investment. The rapid movement of goods and people around the globe intensified as investors sought low-wage producers in countries with low tax rates and no environmental protection laws. Ecological issues became part of the discourse, if not the practice, of governments that still thought in terms of national advantages rather than global urgency.

In subsequent decades, two measurements—direct foreign investment and the terms of trade between core centers and the periphery—which were devised to show global integration, also showed the deterioration of third world economies. The former—direct foreign investments from core developed economies, were increasing exponentially, while the latter—terms of trade, were declining in third world countries for the primary products they sold on the world market. For women who were trying to feed their families on the diminishing cash returns for their surpluses, the impact became a matter of life and death.

Theodore Schultz was one of the few mainstream dissidents in economics to challenge development from above, and to reevaluate semisubsistence household production. Drawing from Sol Tax's careful demonstration of the rational allocation of productive efforts by Guatemalan indigenous farmers in his book, *Penny Capitalism* (1950), Schultz (1964) advocated their incorporation into modernization programs on their own terms. The need for a dialogue with the population being developed was ignored because of priorities that promoted U.S. enterprises in the world market. I recall one U.S. AID (Agency for International Development) official who was fired from his job in Guatemala in the 1960s when he succeeded in developing a native grain that substituted for the costly American grains required for highly bred pigs.

Despite the caveats of these farsighted development critics, direct foreign investments (DFI) in highly capitalized enterprises, such as hydroelectric dams and superhighways, multiplied exponentially as OPEC dollars washed up on the shores of developed capitalist centers. In contrast to earlier development cycles, accumulation of capital increasingly derived from this low-wage sector in assembly operations. Because women constituted a major proportion of the labor force drawn into these operations, feminist scholarship became crucial in understanding the new arenas of capital accumulation. I will say more on that below.

FAILURE OF TRICKLE-DOWN EFFECT AND THE CRITIQUE OF DEVELOPMENT IN THE 1970S AND 1980S

The development euphoria of the 1960s began to fade in the following decades as the assumptions based on the trickle-down effect of capitalist accumulation proved inadequate to explain the persistent impoverishment of third world countries in countries that were experiencing "development" as measured by the GNP. This led to the second phase of development theory and practice in the 1970s, which began with the growing problems in those countries targeted for development, and surged with the feminist critique of development studies.

Ever more sophisticated rationales of the same inadequate database held that a highly unequal income distribution is necessary to facilitate investment. Economic development "experts," who consistently left women and their domestic concerns out of the picture, advocated a big push with high capital investments in modernizing sectors to ignite backward sectors of the economy. Despite their advantageous position in seeing how development projects affected local economies, anthropologists were on the low end of the development expertise hierarchy in academic as well as United Nations circles, perhaps because they harped on the inadvertent consequences of development for the people who were being developed. I remember back in 1971, when I served on the Social Science Research Council's Committee on Latin America, I was shocked to find myself the lone woman in a session for planning long-range research guidelines. In our opening meeting, I attacked the entire spectrum of social science models, including Marxism, dependency theory, modernity theory, and developmentalism for their failure to include women's perspectives in their schema. Not a single response came from the thirty or more men assembled in the meeting room of the Barbados Hotel.[2] In a subsequent grant proposal session, I felt completely alone in trying to block funding for a study of the economic feasibility of shipping polluting branches of the steel industry abroad, holding that the industry was just seeking legitimization of the project and therefore ought to fund it themselves. Albert Hirschman, who served as director of the research committee at the time, questioned why I was wasting the committee's time holding out against such a modest proposal of only $5,000. He later wrote a book extolling the virtues of high investment projects because the very expenditure of capital ensured continuity of projects that bore high risks (Hirschman 1967).

Frustrated with the lack of collegial support, I drafted a proposal for the SSRC (Social Science Research Council) to fund a conference on feminine perspectives. With a grant of $27,000, I worked with Helen Safa and Elsa Chaney to contact researchers for the first conference on Latin American gender issues. We intended to hold the conference in Santiago, Chile, in 1973, but the Pinochet coup intervened and made critical discourse of any kind impossible. Finally, the diTello Center in Buenos Aires agreed to sponsor the program, which was held in February 1974. The sixteen scholars, including two men, presented papers in which some attacked stereotypes of women's passivity in the development sphere; others presented ethnographic cases showing women's real contribution to the economy that was excluded in calculations of GNP;

and still others derided religious and political archetypes that denied a place for women in public life. Many of the participants have become leading contributors advancing scholarship on women in subsequent decades, providing the basis for the observations I summarize below.

In the 1970s it took the persistence of a detective agent to elicit the contributions of women in most Latin American countries. There were almost no national databases that included gender breakdowns. In the following decade, female contributions to national economies were assessed in careful political economic studies by Deere and Leon de Leal (1981) in Colombia; Aguiar (1986) and Saffioti (1978) in Brazil; Arizpe (1977), and Beneria and Sen (1981) in Mexico; Bourque and Warren in Peru (1981); Safa (1986) in Puerto Rico; and Safa (1981), Fernandez-Kelly (1983), and Nash and Fernandez-Kelly (1983) in export processing sites. By elaborating ethnographic observations of women's work, these studies exposed the specious argument that the value added by women's work could not be measured.

Feminist research proceeded to destroy the assumptions that income was shared equally among members of the household, which proved as illusory as the assumption that a rise in the GNP would benefit all families, leading to new policies of credit and family assistance in international agencies. The failure of development agencies to explain or mitigate persistent poverty was shown to result from their failure to take women into account in providing access to education, or credit, or other resources made available to men in developing countries. In 1978, Neuma Aguiar organized a conference in Rio de Janeiro on women in the labor force and the problem of assessing the contribution of women to development. Many of the papers presented at that meeting demonstrated the failure of censuses in all Latin American countries to assess women's contribution to GNP and to household welfare. Aguiar (1986) argued that women's economic activities are underestimated first because of patriarchal premises that attribute the product of joint male and female activities to the male, and second because women are principally employed in noncapitalist institutions. She concludes that, as a result, national and international change agents consistently failed to promote development projects that would improve the life chances of women and children. Some attacked the assumption that the head of the family, always considered to be the man, would turn over his paycheck to his wife, who was presumably sitting at home doing nothing on her own to maintain the family.

In this new regime of capital accumulation related to increasing direct foreign investment, women were the principal sector drawn into the global workforce to produce the surplus value expanding profits. This was realized directly in assembly line productions (Safa 1982, Fernandez-Kelly 1983, Nash and Fernandez Kelly 1983), or it was realized in the informal economy where women maintained low subsistence costs for workers in supplying fresh produce, meats, and fish while earning remarkably low profit margins. "From fields to cooking pots," the political slogan that Florence Babb (1989) found in Lima's urban markets, provided the key for understanding women's contributions to global exchange.

Feminist scholarship in these first two decades enhanced our awareness of women's economic contributions and rewards, establishing them as a target sector in development planning. Feminist critiques promoted some advances in United Nations census gathering techniques. The Gini Index, and the Morris Physical Quality of Life Index, which takes into account life expectancy, infant mortality, and literacy, were introduced in the late 1970s and early 1980s. These tools enabled policy makers to assess who was getting the bigger share of the cake at home and in the world market, and how it could best be distributed for the common welfare. This became ever more pressing in the subsequent debt crisis as the errors of past development processes began to devastate third world economies.

THE DEBT CRISIS AND WOMEN'S ROLES IN SURVIVAL ECONOMICS

During this second phase of development policies, two contradictory patterns emerged: (1) women became the targeted labor force in development programs based on assembly plant industrialization, and (2) out of the same urgent necessity to maintain their families, women invented a whole new economy as petty sellers and market venders in what came to be called the informal economy. As the most intensively exploited part of the global workforce, women provided the basis for primitive capitalist accumulation. As maquila workers in assembly production, they enabled the newly industrializing countries to attract investments, and as cultivators and market sellers, they subsidized biological reproduction during the Latin American debt crisis. Their voices began to be heard for the first time as anthropologists and sociologists perceived the quiet revolution going on (Babb 1989, Bunster and Cheney 1987, Fernandez-Kelly 1983, Deere and Leon de Leal 1981, Lim 1986, Nash and Fernandez-Kelly 1983, Safa 1982). Mariarosa Dalla Costa developed an argument that even the most orthodox Marxists were able to appreciate, noting that women's unpaid labor in the household lowered the costs of producing a labor force, and hence qualified as exploited labor in the class struggle. Picking up on this point, feminist sociologist Morris Blackman told Brazilian aid technicians that they could raise the GNP of Brazil by a simple method: take women's domestic labor into account.

Jamaica was the first country hit by development gone awry and the conditions set by the IMF (International Monetary Fund) for repayment of the country's debt, which skyrocketed during the decade of miracle growth in the 1960s. Lynn Bolles (1986) was carrying out fieldwork in the 1970s when the crisis hit Jamaica. She analyzes the crunch between industrial production and social reproduction, as women who had become dependent on wage work in assembly factories lost their jobs. Investors in footloose export processing firms, who had been attracted by low wages and taxes, withdrew their capital because of inflation and fear of worker takeovers during Michael Manley's term of office as a socialist prime minister. The IMF proceeded to devalue the currency, reduce import conditions, and set controls on credit. Women's recourse to the informal economy in the face of violent fluctuations in the export sector became a repeated pattern in the 1980s as economies collapsed in the face of indebtedness and violent fluctuations in the circulation of money.

As market vendors or producers in the informal economy, women provide, at low cost, the basic foods, clothing, and medicines for the urban barrios of Latin American cities. In her careful ethnography of market women during the political and economic crisis of the 1980s in Lima, Peru, Florence Babb (l989, 2) described, "picture card figures with full skirts, broad-rimmed hats, and long braids, who in fact underwrite the Peruvian national economy." What Babb and other ethnographers were discovering was the new informal economy generated by the crises of the 1970s and 1980s, which sustained the societies and economies in the traumatic adjustment and reconstruction caused by the development policies themselves. Cultivators and pastoralists, pushed out of the rural economy, were flocking to the cities where the women brought their domestic activities into the market sphere. Processing and cooking foods, knitting and weaving clothing and tourist novelties—women found in petty selling and marketing the kind of flexible schedules and arenas (where children were tolerated) that were unavailable in domestic service, which was once their unique way of earning a living (Babb 1989, Buechler 1986, Jelin 1977, Arizpe 1977). Some women in the Andes managed the crisis by turning their domestic pursuits into public enterprises, opening up collective kitchens and badgering government officials to provide basic water and health services. I was visiting one of these kitchens high up in the *barriadas* of Lima, chatting with the women and marveling over what they had accomplished in feeding hundreds of people daily, when the conversation suddenly stopped. The women later told me that one of the members of Senderos Luminosos had passed near the kitchen, and it was only a short time before that they had killed one of the leading women in the collective kitchens movement. Both populist and Maoist political movements realized the popularity of these survival practices and were trying to either capture their political potential or eliminate the leaders (Blondet 1988). As the women developed these self-help programs, they were overcoming the dependency at home and in public spheres that had crippled their autonomy in the past (Nash 1977).

It took more than a decade for the informal economy to be admitted into development studies and become validated for funding. In the decade of the 1990s, international NGOs, especially those organized by feminists appealing to humanitarian funding institutions, opened up spaces for the new cohort of female waged workers and those functioning in the informal economy to speak out. As anthropologists and sociologists amplified the voices of these third world women, advocates for alternative development processes began to listen, and some of their work even became incorporated into the work of mainstream economists.

What these scholars were making clear was that primitive accumulation for capitalist ventures in third world countries derived from work in the domestic or informal economy where women maintained low subsistence costs for the workforce by supplying fresh produce, meats, and fish while earning remarkably low profit margins. "From fields to cooking pots," the political slogan that Florence Babb (1989) found in Lima's urban markets, provided the key to her understanding of their contribution to women's processing as well as marketing foods that became the basis for their rising consciousness. The accumulation process was accelerated when direct foreign investment in assembly operations employing young women expanded in the 1980s.

Despite evidence showing the deteriorating local economy, neoliberal policies grew more formidable in the decade of crisis in the 1980s and were not even scuttled when entire countries, such as Bolivia, went into bankruptcy. I was in Bolivia in 1985 when Jeffrey Sachs arrived from Harvard as the boy wonder advocating International Monetary Fund conditions for repayment of the debt that had been run up by the military under Hugo Banzer in the 1970s. It was the first country—following Jamaica—to be hard-hit by restructuring, and the consequences were immediate and far-reaching. Victor Paz Estenssoro, the president who had nationalized the tin mines in 1952 and brought land reform to the countryside, was reelected that summer and quickly responded to IMF conditions for a loan by privatizing the mines. I was living with a family of miners when they voted for *el chivo* (the goat, a term of affection but also recognition of the man's foibles) because they gave him credit for the construction of low-cost individual homes that miners could buy.

Populist leaders who had survived the vicissitudes of the 1950s and 1960s revolutions, like Paz Estenssoro, were called in to carry out the "reconstruction" of countries hit by the financial disorder of the 1980s in Latin America. The ignominy of Paz Estenssoro ending his long political career in service to the neoliberal economy struck me even more cruelly when I returned the following year in July 1996. Paz Estenssoro had proceeded to reverse those populist victories by privatizing the nationalized mines and firing the union workers who had brought him to the presidency with the victory in the 1952 Bolivian Revolution. I remember walking with laid off miners and members of the housewives association in the 1986 March for Peace and Life with the intent of persuading Paz Estenssoro to keep the mines. During the stopovers in peasant communities on the one-hundred-mile route, nuns and lay sisters attended the marchers, giving food and medical care. As I watched them wash the feet of the marchers as they arrived in each way station with blisters, thoughts of the moral economy still espoused by the church now made more sense than ever. At our last stopover in Calamarca, Paz Estenssoro sent out a heavily armed regiment to surround the marchers and prevent them from completing the twenty-five kilometers to La Paz, where the marchers expected to be the following day. Women from the mining community, one of whom was my comadre, stood at the edge of a Bolivian flag laid out on the highway before the line of soldiers with M1 rifles issued by the U.S. government. Young men and women joined them, and as the sun rose they sang songs and played their guitars. The confrontation ended in the late afternoon. The miners returned to their encampment when the army brought in public busses rather than army vehicles to conduct them back to their communities late in the afternoon. Some chose to go down into the mineshafts that were already filled with the poisonous vapors that accumulate when the ventilators are not in operation. Others began hunger strikes in the church, radio station, and union hall. The closing of the mines spelled the end of a way of life, and many wanted to end their lives there.

The following year I visited the great mining center of Siglo XX to find a nearly devastated community. Mothers and their children, left behind by men who had migrated to the recently opened iron mines in Brazil or to Argentina, were begging in the streets of the miners' compound. I shall never forget the day I visited a parish where a foreign priest was presenting a homily to a crowd of about fifty women with their children, waiting for the distribution of milk and food. The priest asked the women to consider the nucleus of the Christian family and what it consisted of. When there was little response except for the crying of infants and children, he enlightened the mothers, saying: "It is based on the Father, the Son, and the Holy Ghost!" One young woman with a baby on her back broke in at that moment, "Excuse me, Padre, it is hard for us to attend to this while our children are crying of hunger."

The attack on the domestic economy carried out in the name of neoliberalism persisted as other Latin American countries were hit by the debt crisis in the mid-1980s (Nash 1990). Carlos Salinas de Gortari served a similar role in Mexico to that of Paz Estenssoro in Bolivia following his election in 1988. He opened up *ejido* communal plots to private enterprises in 1992, effectively ending the Agrarian Reform Act, which was the principle achievement of the revolution (1910–17), and signed into law the North American Free Trade Agreement (NAFTA), which was to go into effect in 1994. Both these acts precipitated the Zapatista uprising. Priests, and even some bishops, who began to espouse the cause of those struggling for survival were responding to the crisis with intervention measures through Caridad, but politicians persisted on a collision course with peasants, industrial workers, and increasingly, indigenous peoples.

ENDOGENOUS DEVELOPMENT WITH WOMEN AS LEADERS IN THE NEW REVOLUTION

We are now in the third phase of what seemed to be the inexorable advance of predatory capitalist expansion. This was initiated when cracks in the global system began to show in the 1980s, with whole nations going into bankruptcy. Institutions such as the International Monetary Fund and the World Bank, which were fashioned at Bretton Woods to balance the competing demands of nations in the world arena, were called upon to play the role of bailing out multinational firms and the politicians who served them. The burden of payment for the debt incurred was cast on peasants, workers, housewives, and their families in the underdeveloped areas of the world through currency depreciation and debased terms of exchange for their primary products. The new frontiers of capital advance in tropical forest areas, which for centuries have been exploited sporadically for rubber, chickle, minerals (including gold), wood, and exotic resources of the fauna and flora, is now claimed by cattle ranchers, oil explorers, and genetic biodiversity engineers.

This advance differs from past incursions, not because the predators ignore the prior rights of hunters and gatherers who had preserved the forest as a habitat, but because they are now threatening the habitat itself. In the 1980s, cattle ranchers burned much of the Amazonian forest cover and herded the inhabitants in reservations far from their traditional homes. This incursion, vividly described by Simonian in her thesis (1993), disrupted the populations of entire villages; people were packed into nonpressurized cargo planes and dumped in remote parts of the forest where many died from the consequences of the traumatic trip or from their lack of familiarity with strange territory. Jungles are now criss-crossed with paved roads to facilitate the passage of oil drilling machines and the armies that accompany them. Birds and beasts are commodities valued for their feathers and fur, but not their presence in the world, and the settlements that grew up along the highways bear the names of extinct populations that once lived there.

At the turn of the millennium, indigenous people are becoming the protagonists of alternative development programs that measure progress in relation to advances in human welfare, and seek collective, not individual, enrichment. They have emerged from a tumultuous half century, beginning with United Nations declarations on cultural rights and the mobilization for the 1992 Celebration of 500 Years of Conquest in the Western Hemisphere, which culminated with the charter of the indigenous Tribal Peoples of the Tropical Forests adopted at the Rio de Janeiro conference on ecology. Along with the nongovernmental organizations that support the indigenous peoples' right to speak and provide the arenas for their message to be heard, the original people or first nations are providing alternative paths to progress. Their distinctive voices are remarkable for the poetry of their expression and the message it conveys of the need for balance in the cosmos and at home. Women have, for the first time in modern history, emerged as central protagonists defining the values of indigenous people in national and hemispheric congresses. At the Beijing Women's Tribunal in 1995, indigenous women defined their relation to global change in these terms:

The Earth is our Mother: From her we get our life, and our ability to live. It is our responsibility to care for our Mother and in caring for our Mother, we care for ourselves. Women, all females, are manifestations of Mother Earth in human form.

This inspired what some of my colleagues considers an essentializing piece of rhetoric when I was writing my book, *Mayan Visions: The Quest for Autonomy in an Age of Globalization*:

> Women, as caretakers for young and old, are central actors in the emergent social movements of indigenous peoples precisely because of their connectedness to the issues of the survival of past traditions and future generations in their own lives. The concurrent rise of women's stature in global settings with their subordination in patriarchal families and communities has intensified gender conflict. The call for action expressed in the United Nations Convention in Geneva in 1993 and the resolution in 1995 to give further protection and promote the dignity and human rights of women and girls provide the direction for changing gender relations. So long as women lack a voice in public arenas, their particular concerns in survival and care for dependents will be ignored or marginalized. (Nash 2001)

Rereading this, I cannot disclaim the essentialist formulation of the problem, nor would I want to because it stems directly from women's experience. As I had discovered in my own experience in becoming aware of women's exclusion from social science planning sessions, my own self-awareness was the beginning of consciousness as a class of differentially treated people. Third world women are beginning to arrive at a distinct awareness of their problems, one that sees their sex as fundamentally committed to survival and regeneration of their traditional culture. For hundreds of years after the conquest of indigenous peoples of the Western Hemisphere, women have withdrawn, and sometimes been forced to withdraw, from the central arenas of public life. Indigenous men who were forced to undertake wage labor in distant plantations or fight in wars not of their own making, often made a collective decision that women should take primary responsibility for the protection of their culture and traditions. Now that indigenous people foresee the imminent destruction of these retreats, it is the women who take the lead in challenging the right of the invaders to dominate. I have seen the colonizers of Patiwitz in the Lacandón rainforest refuse much needed gifts of food offered by the army as appeasement on Mother's Day, four months after their invasion. I have also seen videos of women pushing soldiers out of their towns and linking their arms with other women to prevent tanks from rolling into their villages. It takes courage to reject these young soldiers cut off from their own families and communities and trying to find their manhood by brandishing powerful automatic rifles, especially on the day that Mexicans nearly sanctify motherhood. By taking a stand against the quintessentially male military institution in their midst, and by rejecting the gifts of food and medicine thrown at them by government agents, women are resisting the government co-optation that has demoralized the caciques—indigenous leaders— in traditional communities.

Yet in the postmodern, deconstructive mode now fashionable in anthropology, the very category of women is decried as essentialist.[3] This reductionist view of third world women, as people with "'needs' and 'problems' but no freedom to act" (Chandra Mohanty, cited in Escobar 1995, 8) certainly merits criticism, but the critique should not end with this. Said's barbed attack on the orientalizing tendencies noted in the Europeans' categorization of the East as they reduced its complexity to an essentialized category has transmuted into a decon-struction of indigenous peoples' attempts to present a common front in their resistance movements. We must go beyond deconstruction of the rhetoric to discover the structural factors deriving from neoliberal policies that reduce social welfare and expand military budgets. The task, then, is to discover and act on the alternatives posed by indig-enous people themselves.

AUTONOMOUS DEVELOPMENT AS AN ALTERNATIVE TO NEOLIBERALISM

We men and women, united and free, are aware that the war we declare is an extreme but just act. The dictators are applying an undeclared genocidal war against our pueblos for many years, for which we ask your determined participation in support of this plan of the Mexican pueblo that is fighting for work, land, shelter, food, health, education, independence, liberty, democ-racy, justice and peace. We declare that we will not stop fighting until we succeed in fulfilling these basic demands of our pueblo, forming a government of our free and democratic country.

Flier distributed by the Zapatista Army of National Liberation on New Year's Eve, 1994

On New Year's Eve 1994, a clandestine group of indigenous men and women seized the town offices of four cities in Chiapas, Mexico, and declared an end to their marginalization by the Mexican govern-ment. It was the eve of the implementation of the North American

Free Trade Agreement, which opened the Mexican market to imports from abroad and spelled an official end to government support for small plot cultivators. In their statement of ten basic demands—roofs over our heads, food, education, medical services, justice, the right to vote, independence, peace or justice, and so forth—the group that became known as the Zapatista Army of National Liberation (EZLN) had not yet formulated the underlying roots of their uprising. This was the desire for autonomy in cultural expressions, governance, and the management of their economic programs. Of the 15,000 soldiers in the EZLN, 40 percent are women. As the movement spread to the highland communities of Chiapas and lighted a spark among indigenous people of Guerrero, Oaxaca, and the other states with large indigenous populations in Mexico, the demand for autonomy subsumed all the other basic needs neglected by the nation.

The meaning of autonomy in Zapatista communities goes beyond the meaning of liberty or autonomy in Western society. It does not mean being free of any constraints by the society in which one is embedded, but to accept the collective will as one's own following intensive discussion in autonomous councils. Nor does it mean unlimited privileges, but rather to earn the rights of belonging through responsible participation. The demand for autonomy became ever more prominent in the conventions and congresses mobilized by the EZLN in the years right after the uprising. The demand was congruent with a growing awareness as to whom or what was their nemesis. A flier distributed at the 1996 Intercontinental Encounter against Neoliberalism and for Humanity sums it up in the phrase: "Neoliberalism Spells Death for Everyone!" In her welcoming speech to participants, who came from all over the world, Commander Ana Maria spoke at the encounter in these words:

As for the power, known worldwide as "neoliberalism," we do not count, we do not produce, we do not buy, we do not sell. We are useless in the accounts of big capital. And so we went to the mountain to seek relief from our pain at being forgotten stones and plants. Here in the mountains of southeast Mexico our dead live. Our dead who live in the mountains know many things. They speak to us of their death and we listen. The talking boxes told us another history that comes from yesterday and aims at tomorrow. The mountain spoke to us, the *macehualob* who are common and ordinary people. (Author's translation of speech delivered in Oventic, by Nash.)

Ana Maria captures the inner reality of being part of simple reproduction of noncapitalist society coexisting with expanded reproduction, which was central to Rosa Luxemburg's critique of capitalism in the early twentieth century. Some contemporary critics[4] are rereading Luxemburg and Lenin in search of an answer for the question raised by Marx as to why capitalist nations must look beyond national borders to maintain or raise profits. A superficial reading is that by drawing new consumers into the trading nexus, the crisis of overproduction of goods caused by the underconsumption by low paid workers is solved. But Luxemburg went beyond her contemporaries to show that capitalists had "to undermine the independence of social units," which she called the *natural economy*, "in order to gain possession of their means of production and labour power and to convert them into commodity buyers." This method of gaining compliance with the new system, she goes on to say, "is invariably accompanied by a growing military, whose importance will be demonstrated below" (Luxemburg 1971 [1913], 92). She predicted that if capitalism were to succeed in this—that is, undermining the independent subsistence sector—they would bring about their own demise.

Ana Maria reflects Luxemburg's premises about the relentless drive for new markets by capitalist producers when she states that the Zapatistas are of little account in the new economy developing in Mexico and in the world because they neither sell their labor or their products, nor do they buy from the world market. In order to break down that independence, the nation must deprive them of the land that they have settled, particularly because an ocean of oil has been discovered beneath the forest cover in the Lacandón. Luxemburg's prediction that it will require military force to break the independence of people in the natural economy is being fulfilled: on February 9, 1995 President Zedillo ordered the invasion of 60,000 federal troops into the Lacandón rainforest in the heartland of Zapatista territory. The Zapatistas had not violated the terms of the ceasefire agreed upon shortly after the uprising. Their mistake was to insist on the autonomy that has inspired the 500 years of resistance of many indigenous people throughout the hemisphere, as well as a share of the resources found in their territories.[5]

Civil society in Mexico has mobilized strong protests against the militarization of the Lacandón, rallying repeatedly in Mexico City's zocalo and joining peace brigades to ensure the safety of the Zapatistas in the Lacandón. Peace activists sent busloads of food and medicines to the conflict area, even though the army often confiscated these supplies. Mexican peace supporters were joined by delegations of human rights activists from many Latin American countries, Europe, Canada, and the United States, who conducted tours of the conflict area and protested the violations they observed. The growing pressure forced the government to concede to the Zapatista demand for autonomy in the regions where indigenous people were a majority, and President Zedillo signed the San Andrés Accord on February 16, 1996. It has never been enacted, and 60,000 armed forces remain quartered in the jungle. Nonetheless, indigenous communities are engaged in the practice of autonomy in the regions they control, and they are seeking the institutional bases to ensure the economic and political base for their distinct culture. They are now confronting a major threat in the form of a development project, Plan Puebla Panama, which might end their control over their dwindling land base, as I discuss below.

PLAN PUEBLA PANAMA AND THE INVASION OF OAXACA AND LACANDÓN JUNGLES

During his first year in office, Vicente Fox's government launched a major hemispheric development scheme, called Plan Puebla Panama, designed to promote modernity in the southern sector of Mexico and Central America. It projects a new vision of Mexico's place in the hemisphere by directing attention to the southern border with its Central American neighbors and away from the increasingly menacing northern border. Unlike earlier development programs, Plan Pueblo Panama is much more forthright in pointing to the dangers of the growing inequality between rich and poor in the area. Recognizing the growing wealth gap between the southern states and those of the central plateau and north, the plan intends to address the human needs of the people in the macroregion of southern Mexico and Central America, and to specifically promote development in indigenous communities of the southern states of Mexico, in a fight against poverty (Plan Puebla Panama 2001, 3). The scheme would promote education, the integration of sectors in the basic infrastructure of the state, and the growth of productive activities. Sustainable growth and protection of the environment are the key elements in the new development plans, terms learned from the critique by NGOs of past development. Assets are the abundant labor supply available at "competitive costs in the global level," a privileged geographic position, political democracy, and the commercial agreements already in place. The plan refers to the abundant natural resources, tourist attractions, and "biological richness" available. Infrastructure construction of roads and improvement of port facilities on both the Gulf and the Pacific coasts are highlighted.

The plan touches on all the buzzwords of the new development perspectives: the objectives of human and social advancement, the participation of society in planning, structural change to promote equality, productive careers and investments, sustainable growth, and environmental responsibility, occasionally slipping into retro terms like institutional modernization. The plan uses the rhetoric of consulting the pueblo, but does nothing to address the mechanisms for implementing the San Andrés accords as an institutional base for achieving a changed relationship with the state. The "wealth of traditions" and "rich multiculturalism" promise to contribute to a lucrative tourist industry, but little is said of the conflicts that must be solved for this to be realized in a cooperative venture in which the carriers of the culture benefit from their own commercialization.

The advantages of the plan lie in its turn away from centralization of government attention in the Federal District and the northern border with the United States, and its promotion of growth in the most backward sectors of the republic. Recognizing that this area demonstrates the growing wealth gap deriving from past development processes, the plan promises to bring it up to the level of development of the rest of the nation. By reaching out to its southern neighbors and engaging in trade and development projects with the Central American market, it has the possibility of lessening dependency on the United States. Indeed, the "privileged" geographic position of the region, located midway between the three great commercial blocks of North America, Europe, and Asia, Mexico could be in a position to deal directly with new trading partners in Europe and Asia.

The plan, however, now being discussed in Zapatista circles, denies the central concerns of this new revolutionary movement. Zapatistas have called for endogenous development for the advancement of human subjects who are agents of their own enterprises. The ultimate objectives of the plan, however, are the promotion of direct foreign investment in enterprises exploiting the rich resources of the region including oil, hydroelectric power, and biodiversity of fauna and flora—including the multicultural population as tourist attractions. The planners intend to facilitate trade and commerce to distant markets of North America, Europe, and Central America. In their statement (Plan Puebla Panama: Resumen y Gráficos; Análisis Crítico de Carlos Fazio, Declaración de Tapachula, May 2001) the government planners devote pages to the improvement of roads, communications, and port facilities, encompassing the highway, rail, and canal developments already undertaken that will parallel the Panama Canal through the Isthmus of Tehuantepec. Yet nothing is said of the institutional means to draw indigenous people into the planning process.

The Plan Puebla Panama is not without its critics in Mexico, and it is refreshing to see that their remarks are incorporated in the publications of the plan. Carlos Fazio points out that it is a plan developed "by a government of entrepreneurs for the entrepreneurs," and that the Mexican government is prepared to grant legality and security for private investments, both national and foreign (Plan Puebla Panama, July 29, 2001). He finds it ominous that there will be no restriction on remissions of profits to the country of origin of capital. The validity of his criticism is clear if we keep in mind that the miracle of the Asian Newly Industrialized Countries was achieved by governments carrying out precisely those restrictions that are considered anathema to IMF or neoliberal trading agreements. Based on the history of foreign capital investments on the northern border, we can expect that Fox's commitments to foreign companies will extend to labor practices, fiscal regulations, and environmental considerations, allowing foreign investors to take advantage of a cheap labor force, polluting practices, and health and safety requirements.

Even more significant is the opposition mounting in the region against the plan. Four of the eight countries in the Plan Pueblo Panama area (Mexico, Guatemala, Berlice, El Salvador, Honduras, Nicaragua, Costa Rica, and Panama) have formed coalitions to resist the plan. Civil society organizations have formed conferences "in search of a plural, full, and democratic multisectorial space" where the people can formulate alternatives. (Marco Fonseca@utoronto.ca, e-mail to Marc Edelman, transmitted to author). The coordination of organizations throughout the Central American region may portend a transnational organization uniting peasant sectors along three lines Marc Edelman (2001) has demonstrated.

The "new empire" that Fazio and others criticize in Plan Pueblo Panama is based on a model of exogenous capitalist accumulation. The reinvigorated formula for the concentration of wealth is one in which the titular leaders of client states, preferably elected by democratic voting procedures to satisfy international human rights observers, will yield strategic sectors of its economy to foreign investors in production, whether extraction of oil and lumber or in assembly production, with a trickle-down going to local elites. The new imperialism differs from empires of the nineteenth century in that there are no sectors of the domestic economy in which capitalist transactions are forbidden. The British established reserves in their African colonies where women and children maintained small plots for food production for themselves, and where aging workers withdrew when they could no longer serve in the mines and commercial ventures. The Dutch promoted a culture system that maintained a subsistence sector of cultivators that could sustain the population when the prices for primary products broke down, and where workers in the commercialized sector could withdraw when they were laid off. The current Thai king draws on the historical precedents in a country that had never succumbed to imperialism because the monarchy ensured rice cultivation for its subjects.

In contrast, neoliberal regimes offer no safety nets for semisubsistence cultivators drawn into global markets. After years of belt tightening in the 1980s, and violently fluctuating returns for the cash crops that governments encouraged campesinos to raise only to abandon them when the market collapsed on the world stock exchange, the domestic economy of rural Chiapas is in tatters. Women are suspicious of a plan that talks about invigorating the local economy but intends to send off the men to distant areas where they work on constructing the infrastructure for bigger and more costly enterprises. They have heard bulletins about the existing assembly plants in Central America, and are not enthusiastic about having their "underutilized labor" allocated to working ten to twelve hours a day with no time left to tend their families. Campesinos of Oaxaca are concerned that their lands will be seized by eminent domain, and that the archeological zone will be affected. The highway between Mitla and Oaxaca runs through the sacred Zapotec valley, which may have generated the religious discourse that was the founding nucleus of Mesoamerican civilization. As they see it, these new enterprises are shredding the fabric of society.

Some of these misgivings were expressed in a meeting held in Tapachula, Chiapas, on May 12, 2001, attended by NGOs, grassroots organizations, cooperatives, church groups, and women's groups. Those who attended the meeting called for representation from below and expressed their reservations about the outcome in polarization and exclusion that would violate the sovereignty of the pueblos of the Central American isthmus. In their demands, the group called for a moratorium on the "bioprospectors" and the importation of genetically altered foods. In the spring of 2002, the restriction on immigration in the south, heralded as a key element in the government's control of the area, began. Dozens of Chiapas campesinos were apprehended as illegal Guatemalan or Central American immigrants.

Based on past experience in the Grijalva River dam project, where cultivable lands were seized from campesinos with little compensation, the indigenous people object to the megaprojects that are imposed on them without their consent. The Angostura dam construction in the township of Venustiano Carranza is a case in point: built in the years from 1969 to 1974, the dam flooded over 5,000 hectares of rich arable land for which campesinos of the area have not yet been fully compensated. When communal lands are restituted on the basis of claims for usurped communal lands, the PRI government frequently returned the land to campesinos whose claims were contested by other groups. This stirs up endogenous conflicts, justifying the government sending in troops and further repressing indigenous people.

In the present contest for control over the Lacondon forest, the struggle for land now pits Zapatista rebels against ecologists (Tim Weiner, *New York Times*, December 8, 2002). Rebels blame the devastating fires in the spring of 1998 as attempts by the army to clear the forest and allow unimpeded views of their settlements, and facilitate the movement of armored vehicles, while the army blamed them on the slash and burn cultivation techniques of the colonizers. The fact that in the thirty years of increasing colonization of the jungle there was never such destruction, while major fires continue to plague the area since massive military invasions from 1995 on is cited by Zapatistas and their supporters to buttress their position. As the reserve areas of biological diversity, the dwindling forests, such as the Lacandon, are the front lines for the contest over development alternatives.

WHERE DO WE GO FROM HERE?

Because women are the principal labor force for the domestic economy, they have become the principal activists in opposing the current advance of capitalist enterprises in the tropical forest areas of the world. What were once the arenas of class struggle in plantations and factories during the nineteenth century are now displaced to the homes and communities of impoverished populations of the world. Women have a more poignant sense of the diminishing resources and territorial base because they accept the primary responsibility of sustaining themselves and their families. It is they who have to listen to the children cry. As their children lose their sense of belonging to the world, they become prey to drug addiction, prostitution, and paramilitary bands. More than any revolutionaries of the past who drew lines between ethnic, religious, and class groups, women are aware that the enemy lies within these spheres. Their sons and mates rank among those who are unofficial warriors in the new conflicts provoked by multinational enterprises. Unemployed youths high on drugs and equipped with weapons by the Mexican armed forces were neighbors

and relatives of the victims in the Acteal rampage. When their husbands threaten and beat them if they attend meetings of their cooperatives, as still happens in the Lacandón, and when neighbors and
relatives yield to corrupt local officials and carry out massacres against
them, as in Acteal where all but 9 of the 45 victims were women, children, and 4 uncounted fetuses, women realize the need for a new kind
revolution that does not use weapons of war or pretend to rally the
forces of good against the forces of evil. The Zapatistas use their anti-
quated firearms and sticks as symbolic reminders that they are prepared to die for their cause. They must fight their own wars against
alcoholism and corruption in order to reaffirm the sense of their own
cultural roots.

In the colonized areas of the Lacandón rainforest and in the Christian Base Communities of the highlands of Chiapas, women in the
Zapatista movement are seeking a new way of relating to their families and communities. In their cooperatives and collective work groups
they try to promote egalitarian relations, which deny the hierarchical
order based on gender and wealth that was their destiny in the plantations from which they came or the traditional order from which they
withdrew when they became committed to liberation theology. In my
limited stays in the rainforest I have seen remarkable transformations
in gender relations. Men often engage in child care and cooking, just
as women participate in public arenas. In their national appearances,
the Zapatistas always maintain an equal number of men and women.
We observed this as the caravan congregated in the cathedral plaza
in February 2001, and found it affirmed in the hearings in the federal
congress in March 2001. The Zapatistas seek ways of overcoming any
cult of personality by featuring new speakers, both female and male.
These are the conditions they want to replicate in any development
enterprises, just as that they are putting them into practice in their
daily lives.

The story I have told about the Chiapas rainforest echoes in other
indigenous retreat zones throughout the hemisphere. Government
agents and even environmental experts often treat these areas as unin-
habited zones to be exploited according to the whim of the administrators. Where oil or minerals are discovered, existing populations
are soon removed by force or persuasion.[6] The projects that pretend to
promote sustainable growth areas often fail in the planning stages or
are interrupted by contradictory projects that disorient the indigenous
populations. This was the case with Plan Pilota Forestal, a "community based silviculture project" initiated by the Mexican-German alliance dedicated to the "Rational Utilization of the Forest" in Quintano

Roo, Mexico in 1954. It was also true of the Plan de Acción de la Selva Tropical promoted by the World Bank and the Food and Agricultural Organization for the regrowth of forests (Nigh and Rodriguez 1995, 94–95), and it is an ongoing battle in the Chimalapas rainforest of Oaxaca (Doane 2001). The only projects that achieve sustainable regrowth are those that initiate pilot programs and turn them over to local populations to administer the funds made available, such as the Acuerdo Mexicano-Aleman para la Utilización Racional de los Bosques Tropicales (Nigh and Rodriguez 1995, 95). Brazilian and Venezuelan projects that pretended to conserve the ecosystem of jungles from 1987 to 1991, ended up as a typical commercial venture, overcutting the forest and replacing it with fast-growing trees, such as eucalyptus, that suck up the moisture and eradicate indigenous plant life in the area. Ronald Nigh and Nemesio Rodríguez (1995, 89–90) summarize the international project, Plan de Acción de la Selva Tropical (PAST) with the following cogent statement:

The overpopulation, the poverty and the destruction of the forests are the result of the same underlying principle: the pyramidal model of growth that favors, at the expense of inequality in the distribution of riches and the restriction of local participation, predetermined interests, those of large scale industry with an excessive bureaucracy. The history of such development projects originating from outside the target area and promoted by a political and financial elite shows that the ultimate effect is one of environmental destruction and eradication of the indigenous population.

Indigenous people are aware that the only way to break the cycle of poverty induced by development projects planned from above is to create their own opportunities independently of the experts. They are also aware that when development plans are on the agenda, they will succeed only when the entire local population has input into the decisions. As Duncan Earle and Jeanne Simonelli (n.d.) remark on the practices of autonomy in the Lacandon villages in which they did research, the term *self-development* is defined by the Zapatistas as the amount of autonomy social groupings can muster in order to control their lives. This contrasts with development done by others and the attendant threats to the survival of the local population.

CONCLUDING REMARKS

The unique advantage of the human species in evolution is the plasticity we have shown in adapting to new conditions in our physical and social environments. We are now on a trajectory that threatens to eliminate the variety of plant and animal species in our biosphere and even alternative responses in our policy making. More concern is expressed in international arenas on the loss of genetic variety in plants and animals than in people. Indigenous peoples still maintain distinct visions of their relationship to the cosmos and to other living organisms, which promote distinct responses from those advocated by dominant institutions in the global ecumene. They are the best custodians for the fragile environments now being invaded by development agents. Policy makers in the developed countries are still a decade late in responding to the protests from those subjected to development, yet there is a growing theoretical critique of development focused on gross national product and profit levels. Significantly, Amaryta Sen was given the Nobel Prize in Economics in 1998 for his views on development appraised in a new light: the impact on people, not GNP, and the impact on social welfare of the people inhabiting an area, not the infrastructural capacity to transfer the benefits of resources to other countries. Amaryta Sen is one of the few development economists of his time to seek a real measure of growth in life expectancy and reduction in infant mortality rates. Writing in the 1970s when China represented a Cold War threat instead of a preferred field for investment, Sen pointed out that in 1980 Brazil, with a $2,050 per capita GNP had a life expectancy of 30, China with a $290 per capita growth rate had a life expectancy of 64, and Sri Lanka with $270 per capita GNP had a life expectancy of 66. Back then, he called for better measurements and guarantees of entitlements based on the commodity bundles that a person could command in a society. His views of economic development as "a process of expanding the capabilities of people"are beginning to permeate development economics and to change the statistical tools to measure it.

Other contemporaries of Amaryta Sen, such as P. T. Bauer (1981) are now being reintegrated into mainstream economics (Griffith and McKinley 1994) and positively evaluated by scholars concerned with current trends (Dorn, Hanke, and Walters 1998). The issues of subsistence are now linked in moral commitments to adequate nutrition as never before (Seavoy 2000, viii). Even more significantly the World Bank, which serves as the fountain of development statistics, is now concerned with evaluating poverty indices more seriously as an indicator of economic stability or disruption (World Bank 2000). Joseph Stiglitz (2000, viii), chief economist of the World Bank, demonstrates the increasing concern with social dislocations caused by the need for reducing poverty.

These late millennial reflections on the external shocks, financial crises, and poverty of what some might consider mainstream economists, all seem familiar to me. I have been reading about them for three decades in feminist literature on development, which documented the fragmentation of the household economy in the 1970s, 1980s, and 1990s. Living with the myopic frame of their disciplines, economists saw no evil in the world of direct foreign investment. Even when the bubble of euphoria burst and workers and peasants who had lost their own savings had to assume the burden of speculative debts, what Peter Bauer (1981) calls the "disregard of reality" persisted. This is no longer possible when pickets denounce the disgrace of global inequality in the summit meetings of those who are its gatekeepers.

In the new global regime of accumulation, the moral economy that sustained the minimal guarantees of food sufficiency in nineteenth-century imperialism is discredited as public enterprises that will often maintain employees in cyclical downturns are taken over by "more efficient private producers." Bolivia was a testing ground for the conditions for restructuring a debt-encumbered country in 1985. It was also a testing ground for democracy because the military regimes put in place by military dictators, such as Rios Montt in Guatemala, Hugo Banzer in Bolivia, Pinochet in Chile, were evoking harsh criticism and protest from an increasingly active civil society in Latin America. One model for achieving acceptance of unpopular decrees is that of recycling populist leaders of the past, such as Paz Estenssoro, who came back from exile to serve the new interests of global capitalism in Bolivia in 1985. Another model is that of the PRI hegemony in Mexico, which served the United States and other global powers through the waning days of the second millennium. The meltdown of Argentina's economy, despite the government's adhering to IMF conditions for debt repayment, is embolding the new populists such as President Chavez of Venezuela and President-elect Lulu of Brazil to challenge U.S. hegemony in the southern hemisphere.

What seemed irrefutable in the mid-twentieth century is now open to critique. With whole economies going into bankruptcy as a result of neoliberal trading policies, the assumptions of progress, and even the indices claiming to measure advancement, are cast in doubt. Trading in the debts run up in the *periphery*—no longer called the third world after the collapse of the Berlin wall—became a major part of the exchanges in the developing countries in the 1980s and 1990s. We are in a phase where the global economy geared to accumulation on a world scale rejects most subsistence-oriented projects, which are nonfundable or noneconomic by definition. National economies are urged, or even ordered, to orient their production to export sales (as in Mexico after the debt crisis of 1995), and they respond by dismantling food production systems and turning to the production of coffee for export, which may lead their countries to the brink of starvation when the price for primary commodities declines (as in Nicaragua). Clearly the planners are not thinking of the consumption needs of the people when they measure the success or failure of their projects.

Economists who were once the principle ideologues of development now express misgivings as they reflect that capitalism may have become too successful in absorbing self-reliant agricultural communities. Anthropologists who were early critics of development in the post–World War II euphoria are now absorbed in the discourse connecting the diversity of cultures with the apparent monolithic power of globalization. Escobar (1995) and Ferguson (1990) provide devastating critiques of the development discourse, but are less adept at providing us with alternative perspectives. Florence Babb suggests an alternative strategy drawn from her study of predominantly feminine activists in Nicaragua (Babb 2001). These women bring the gendered body as an "originating point of discourse, community, and action" (Babb 2001, 179).

By returning to our ethnographic base, we can rediscover the sense of what people who experience the rigors of developmental breakdown are formulating as they fight for survival. Only when we attend to their case can we appreciate how their alternatives might ensure the survival of the human species.

REFERENCES

Aguiar, Neuma. 1986. "How to Study Women's Work in Latin America." In *Women and Change in Latin America*, ed. J. Nash and H. I. Safa, 22–33. South Hadley, MA: Bergin and Garvey Press.

Arizpe, Lourdes. 1977. *Indigenas en la ciudad de Mexico, El caso de las Marias*. Mexico: Sep Setent.

Babb, Florence. 1989. *Between Field and Cooking Pot: The Political Economy of Marketwomen in Peru*. Austin: University of Texas Press.

———. 2001. *After Revolution: Mapping Gender and Cultural Politics in Neoliberal Nicaragua*. Austin: University of Texas Press.

Bauer, Peter. 1981. *Equality, the Third World and Economic Development*. Cambridge: Harvard University Press.

Beneria, Lourdes. 1986. "The Mexican Debt Crisis: Restructuring the Economy and the Household." *Gender and Society* 4(3, September): 338–53.

Beneria, Lourdes and Gita Sen. 1981. "Accumulation, Reproduction and Women's Role in Economic Development: Boserup Revisited." *Signs* 7(2):279–299.

Blondet, Cecilia. 1988. "Pobladoras, dirigentes y ciudadantas: El caso de las mujeres populares de Lima." Paper presented at the Latin American Studies Association, New Orleans, March 1988.

Bolles, A. Lynn. 1986. "Economic Crisis and Female-Headed Households in Urban Jamaica." In *Women and Change in Latin America*, ed. J. Nash and H. I. Safa, 65–82. South Hadley, MA: Bergin and Garvey Press.

Bourque, Susan and Kay B. Warren. 1981. *Women of the Andes*. Ann Arbor, MI: University of Michigan Press.

Buechler, Judith-Maria. 1986. "Women in Petty Commodity Production in La Paz, Bolivia." In *Women and Change in Latin America*, ed. J. Nash and H. I. Safa, 165–189. South Hadley, MA: Bergin and Garvey Press.

Bunster, Ximena and Elsa Cheney. 1987. *Sellers and Servants: Working Women in Lima, Peru*. New York: Praeger.

Dalla Costa, Mariarosa and Selma James. 1972. "Women and the Subversion of the Community." In *The Power of Women and the Subversion of Community*. Bristol, UK: Falling Wall Press.

Deere, Carmen Diana. 1986. "Rural Women and Agrarian Reform in Peru, Chile, and Cuba." In *Women and Change in Latin America*, ed. J. Nash and H. I. Safa, xx. South Hadley, MA: Bergin and Garvey Press.

Deere, Carmen Diana and Magdalena Leon de Leal. 1981. *Women in Andean Agriculture: Peasant Production and Rural Wage Employment in Colombia and Peru*. Washington, DC: International Labor Office.

Doane, Molly. 2005. "The Resilience of Nationalism in a Global Era: Megaprojects in Mexico's South." In *Social Movements: An Anthropological Reader*, ed June Nash. Medford, MA: Blackwell.

Earle, Duncan and Jeanne Simonelli. N.d. "Tenemos Que Hablar: Autonomy, Development, and 'Informed Permission' in Chiapas." Unpublished paper.

Edelman, Marc. 2001. "Social Movements: Changing Paradigms and Forms of Politics." *Annual Reviews* 30:285–317.

Elmendorf, Mary. 1977. *Sociocultural Aspects of Extreta Disposal*. Washington, DC: World Bank.

Escobar, Arturo. 1995. *Encountering Development: The Making and Unmaking of the Third World*. Princeton, NJ: Princeton University Press.

Ferguson, James. 1990. *The Anti-Politics Machine: "Development," Depoliticization, and Bureaucratic Power in Lesotho*. New York: Cambridge University Press.

Griffin, K. and T. McKinley. 1994. *Implementing a Human Development Strategy*. New York: St. Martins Press.

Hardt, Michael and Antonio Negri. 2000. *Empire*. London and Cambridge, MA: Harvard University Press.

Harrison, Fay V. 1988. "Women in Jamaica's Urban Informal Economy: Insights from a Kingston Slum." *New West Indian Guide* 62(3–4):103–128.

_____. 1997. "The Gendered Politics and Violence of Structural Adjustment: A View from Jamaica." In *Situated Lives: Gender and Culture in Everyday Life*, ed. Louise Lamphere, Helen Ragonem, and Patricia Zavella, 451–68. New York: Routledge.

Hirschman, A.O. 1967. *Development Projects Observed*. Washington, DC: Brookings Institute.

Jelin, Elizabeth. 1977. "Migration and Labor Force Participation of Latin American Women: The Domestic Servants in the Cities." *Signs* 3(l):129–14l.

La Duke, Winono. 1996. "Keynote Address." In *Look at the World through Women's Eyes: Plenary Speeches from the NGO Forum on Women*, Bejing, 1995, ed. Eva Friendlander. New York: Women's Ink.

Lim, Cynda, Y. C. 1983. "Capitalism, Imperialism, and Patriarchy: The Dilemma of Third World Women Workers in Multinational Factories." In *Women, Men, and the International Division of Labor*, ed. June Nash and M. Patricia Fernandez-Kelly, 70–92. Albany: State University of New York Press.

Luxemberg, Rosa. 1971. *The Accumulation of Capital*. New York: Monthly Review Press.

Mencher, Joan. "Why Grow More Food? An Analysis of Some of the Contradictions in the Green Revolution in Kerala." *Economic and Political Weekly* (Bombay) 23–30:A98–A104.

Nash, June. 1977. "Women in Development: Dependency and Exploitation." *Development and Change*:161–82.

_____. 1990. "Latin American Women in the World Capitalist Crisis." *Gender and Society* 4(3): 338–353

_____. 2001. *Mayan Visions: The Quest for Autonomy in an Age of Globalization*. New York: Routledge.

Nash, June and M. Patricia Fernandez-Kelly, eds. 1983. *Women, Men and the International Division of Labor*. Albany: State University of New York Press.

Nigh, Ronald and Nemesio J. Rodríguez. 1995. *Territorios violados: Indios, Medio Ambiente, y Desarrollo en América Latina*. México, D.F.: Instituto Nacional Indigenista.

Oman, Charles P. and Ganechan Wignaraja. 1991. *The Postwar Evolution of Development Thinking*. New York: St. Martin's Press.

Plan Puebla Panama. 2001. "Plan Puebla Panama: Resumen y Graficos; Anal-
isis Critico de Carlos Fazio, Declaracion de Tapachula May 2001." San
Cristobal de Las Casas, Chiapas.

Rostow, W. W. 1960. *Stages of Economic Growth, A Non-Communist Manifesto.* Cambridge: Cambridge University Press.

Safa, Helen. 1974. *The Urban Poor of Puerto Rico.* New York: Holt, Rinehart
and Winston.

_____. 1981. "Runaway Shops and Female Employment: The Search for
Cheap Labor." *Signs* 7(2):418–433.

_____. 1986. "Female Employment in the Puerto Rican Working Class." In
Women and Change in Latin America, ed. J. Nash and H. I. Safa, 84–
106. South Hadley MA: Bergin and Garvey.

Saffioti, Heleieth E. 1978. *Women in Class Society.* New York: Monthly
Review Press.

Said, Edouard. 1978. *Orientalism.* New York: Pantheon.

Schultz, Theodore. 1964. *Transforming Traditional Agriculture.* New Haven,
CT: Yale University Press.

Seavoy, Ronald E. 2000. *Subsistence and Economic Development.* Westport,
CT: Praeger.

Sen, Amaryta. 1988. "Development: Which Way Now?" In *Resources, Values
and Development*, 485–508. Cambridge, MA: Harvard University Press.

Simonian, Ligia. 1993. "This Bloodshed Must Stop: Land Claims on Guarita
and Urueuwau-wau Reservations, Brazil." PhD thesis for the Department of Anthropology, Graduate Center, City University of New York.

Sinclair, Minor. 1993. *The Politics of Survival: Grassroots Movements in Central America.* New York: Monthly Review Press.

Stiglitz, Joseph E. 2000. *Global Economic Prospects and the Developing Countries.* Washington, DC: International Bank for Reconstruction and
Development/The World Bank.

Tax, Sol. 1950. *Penny Capitalism.* Washington, DC: Smithsonian Institution.

NOTES

1. Among the many critiques of development are those of Arturo Escobar
(1995), David Ferguson 1990, Charles P. Oman, and Ganeshan Wiug-
naraja (1991), which deal directly with the production of ideology justifying the predominant trends in development practice.

2. Many years later, Elsa Chaney sent me a note commenting that Robert Myers, then working for the Ford Foundation, said that there was a
tempest of memos caused by this first proposal on women and gender
to come to their attention.

3. Micaela di Leonardo (1985) reviews some of the literature critiquing
feminist theory on maternal morality and militarism.

4. Michael Hardt and Antonio Negri, Empire (2000) draw on Luxemburg's work to emphasize the need for consumers to reinvigorate capitalist enterprises, but miss the persistent tensions between natural and capitalist economies. I have found in Luxemburg's mode of analysis of the "natural economy" a parallel for what Zapatistas express in their commitment to a moral economy. That is, the need for an alternative, coexisting but autonomous base of production dedicated to the needs of people rather than the unique drive for profits (Nash 2001, 5–6).

5. Few of the Zapatista communities have titles for ejido land under the Land Reform Act of the 1917 Constitution. Thus the "Reform" of the Land Reform Act allowing for privatization of existing ejidos and declaring an end to further entitlements was a greater threat to them because it ended their hopes for communal control of the lands they colonized. The threat to Mexican campesinos evokes the concerns of family farms in Wyoming where the Bush government has discovered that their claims based on the Homestead Act that promoted the westward migration a century ago are in jeopardy since the act stated only that they had only usufruct rights and no claim to the resources found beneath the soil. Quite possibly, Vice President Cheney and his energy pals know that there is oil underneath those cornfields as well.

6. Colonizers of the Ixcan forest area just across the Mexican–Guatemala Border from the Lacandón were massacred in 1974 by the Guatemalan army shortly after oil was discovered.

5

INDIGENISM AND ITS DISCONTENTS

Richard B. Lee

The current prominence of indigenous social movements indicates not only the coming to political consciousness of marginalized peoples, but also a new global acceptance of these peoples and the legitimacy of their claims. Paradoxically anthropologists, long the primary advocates for the indigenous, may be out of synch with this new consciousness. Drawing on case material from southern Africa, the essay maps the complex terrain on which indigenous peoples, governments, publics, and anthropologists find themselves. Given the many social problems indigenous people face, can the indigenous movement make the most of this new political space, and what role, if any, can anthropologists play in fostering positive outcomes?

In July 1997, the Conference on Khoisan Identities and Cultural Heritage convened in Cape Town. It was the first time that this usually staid series of scholarly conferences of linguists, archaeologists, and ethnologists had actually met in Africa. In Cape Town the tenor and shape of the conference shifted radically. The final overthrow of apartheid in 1994 was recent enough to make the occasion quite celebratory, played out as a liberation of the spirit over the claustrophobic racism of the old regime. In addition to the scholars, Khoi and San people from over twenty communities were in attendance. Before the scientific portion of the meeting began, there were two days of public events attended by many hundreds. Colored Cape Town turned out in force. There were parades in the streets and a goat was sacrificed in the courtyard of the Museum of Culture History. But nothing prepared me for the ceremony that unfolded in the atrium of the South African Museum.

The founder of the Dutch colony at the Cape, Jan Van Riebeeck, is a cultural icon of Afrikanerdom and to the nonwhite people a symbol of their oppression. At the time of Van Riebeeck's arrival at the Cape in 1652, there were eleven Khoi clans present and recorded in his journals. Over the course of the next two centuries of predatory colonialism, all but two of these clans had been driven to extinction.

Yet in a solemn service conducted almost entirely in Afrikaans, these eleven Khoi clans were reconstituted. One by one, members of the audience were called to the podium where they donned a highly eclectic mix of regalia and announced to the assembly who they were, what clan they were representing, and what Khoi name they were adopting. The atmosphere was one of reverence and joy. Hobsbawm and Ranger would have had a field day.

I later learned that the ceremony had been the brainchild of a Mr. Joseph Little, prominent in Cape colored cultural circles and sometime city politician. The next day Mr. Little accompanied a group of scholars on a pilgrimage to Robben Island. But while most of us came to see Nelson Mandela's famous jail cell, Mr. Little had a different agenda. With documentary filmmakers in tow, he was there to consecrate the memory of an earlier political prisoner, Achimoa (Aushumato), a seventeenth-century Khoi chief imprisoned there by the Dutch. For Mr. Little and his allies in the colored community, Metissage, the celebration of hybridity, was not the need of the moment. Rather the two ceremonies were about recapturing history, casting off the persona of brown Europeans given them by apartheid, and reclaiming their identity as indigenous Africans (Bank 1998).

One might ask, what exactly does indigenous mean in this context? The concept, long an unproblematic staple in the anthropological vocabulary, is now beset by contradictory readings—a turmoil of voices, symptomatic of the broader currents and crosscurrents in our discipline today (cf. Beckett 1996). At the dawn of the new millennium the discipline of anthropology occupies a highly contested terrain, a battleground on which scientistic, humanistic, political-economic, and postmodern agendas are putting forth conflicting claims and vying for hegemony (Lee 1992b; 1998b). Most observers agree that the discipline is undergoing, in fact has undergone, a seachange in theory and subject matter, not the least in how anthropology has positioned indigenous peoples.

Forty or fifty years ago, the default first world anthropologist, white and male, trained as a Boasian or a Malinowskian, went overseas or onto Indian reserves to study, in the terminology of the day, bands, tribes, chiefdoms, or peasants from an unproblematically positivist perspective. Marshall Sahlins was writing books on cultural evolution (Sahlins and Service 1960), and even Clifford Geertz was writing about Javanese agrarian ecology (1956). Today their students and grand-students are deconstructing texts, reflecting on the politics of culture, unpacking the political economy of housing projects, homeless shelters, and HIV clinics, and sitting in the boardrooms of high-rolling biotech firms. And the composition of the profession has become more diverse in ethnicity and gender terms (cf. Lee 1998b).

Meanwhile the traditional subject matter of social and cultural anthropology, the smaller-scale unit cultures so central to the research agendas of Boasians and Malinowskians alike, appeared to be disappearing with the speed of light into the farms, factories, and favelas of the New World Order. The study of whole cultures on their own turf has slipped quietly but irrevocably into the twilight zone; like Kroeber's peasants, *all* societies are now part-societies with part-cultures (cf. Garcia Canclini 1995).

If former nonstate anthropological subjects are investigated, they are reconstituted as peasants or proletarians, victims of progress struggling in the coils of merchant or finance capital, manipulated by faceless bureaucracies, structurally adjusted by the IMF (International Monetary Fund), or deconstructed as objects of media (mis)representation.

Twenty-five years ago it was often assumed that with the apparent demise of what I like to call (following Russian usage), the (numerically) small peoples and their incorporation into regional, national, and global fields of force, anthropology as a discipline would disappear along with its subject. Happily, news of anthropology's demise has been greatly exaggerated. Anthropology's embrace of globalizing culture and the shift in its gaze from "exotic" others to the mean streets of "anthropology at home" has proved a lifesaver. The discipline thrives with new energy and continues to grow with the vast subject matters of the globalizing metropole now open to anthropological inquiry. To be sure, anthropology in the metropole is not an invention of the 1980s. Even in Kroeber's day, there were anthropologists working at home: Hortense Powdermaker in the Hollywood dream factory, Lloyd Warner in Yankee City, Anthony Wallace in the coal towns of Pennsylvania, and so on, but these sites were not at the discipline's center of gravity.

Now it is fair to say this *is* the discipline's center of gravity. Given this shift in focus, what is to become of the older anthropological gaze on the small peoples? In fact, the shift from periphery to metropole is far from complete. While many anthropologists have moved into the cities and settled there, others continue to work in the jungles of Central America, the highlands of Peru, and the plains of East Africa. But here the ground has shifted as well. It was one thing to live and work in these places when the subjects were nonliterate and politically disenfranchised. But how do we approach peoples in the year 2005 who are politically articulate and who in pressing their claims hold press conferences, hire lawyers, and operate websites?

Just as news of anthropology's demise has been greatly exaggerated, so has the demise of the small peoples. Instead of simply disappearing into the vast underclass of the capitalist periphery, many of these peoples—the Shuar, Kwakiutl, Ju/'hoansi, Kayapo, and so forth—have stood their ground, regrouped, and come to political consciousness.

In essence, the indigenous peoples have staked out new positions and claims on national and global political agendas. But in order to do this, the small peoples have had to reinvent themselves. Crucial in this redefinition of terrain has been the concept of the *indigenous* itself, a powerful concept whose capital has been steadily accruing (Niezen 2000).

Indigenous is not found in Raymond Williams's *Keywords* (1986), but it should be. The term, along with its equivalents, aboriginal, native, First Peoples, fourth world, and countless local variants, is marvelously polysemic. Whatever uneasiness anthropologists may have about the term, what it implies, and who it applies to, the fact remains that politically and socially, nationally and internationally, the concept of indigenous has become a powerful tool for good. After centuries of denigration, being recognized as indigenous has become an avenue for entitlement, enfranchisement, and empowerment. As such it has provided for formerly oppressed peoples, a proverbial seat at the table in negotiations with governments over land rights, compensation packages, and acknowledgement of past wrongs (Levin 1993; Niezen 2000).

This state of affairs did not materialize by magic. It was achieved after a long struggle, accompanied by the development of counterhegemonic discourse, which framed indigenous and nonindigenous relations in radically new ways (Maybury-Lewis 1997; Miller et. al. 1993; Neitschmann 1994; Dean and Levi 2003).

The term is increasingly recognized by the United Nations, the IMF, the World Bank, and other organs of the international order. It crops up in global fora in Rio, in Kyoto, at biodiversity conferences, and in a host of other contexts. Even Pope Jean Paul II on March 11, 2000, acknowledged to the world's native peoples the injustices committed upon them in the name of Church of Rome (along with mea culpas to Jews, women, and others).

But indigenism has a disturbing underside: for some it is a cloak for separatism, chauvinism, and reverse racism. And while indigenous leaders appear on the world's stage, many of the rank-and-file at home are grappling with alcohol, abuse, and suicide. Communities win key court battles and then dissipate their gains in ill-conceived business deals. Further, some indigenous peoples, even as they make their way in the world, are undergoing processes of internal differentiation, reproducing internally the inequities of the global order. And for small peoples the other side of the coin of indigenous identity is its opposite, the ever-present possibility of culture loss through ethnocide and assimilation into the far larger unmarked legions of the global underclass. These contradictions and ambiguities are among the discontents faced by the indigenous movement today.

INDIGENOUS DEFINED

One of its ambiguities is the wide range of usages. One often sees the term indigenous applied to the entire world population outside Europe (e.g., Slemon, March 14, 2000). Other definitions involve fine distinctions between majority and minority populations country by country (see also McIntosh 2000).

The 1993 UN Declaration of the Rights of Indigenous Peoples follows the famous Cobo definition, named for the rapporteur who led the original task force that drafted the UN Declaration. According to Cobo:

> Indigenous communities, peoples and nations are those which 1) having a historical continuity with pre-invasion and pre-colonial societies that developed on their territories, 2) consider themselves distinct from other sectors of the societies now prevailing in those territories or parts of them, 3) they form at present non-dominant sectors of society, and 4) are determined to preserve, develop, and transmit to future generations their ancestral territories, and their ethnic identity, as the basis of their continued existence as a people, 5) in accordance with their own cultural patterns, social institutions, and legal systems. (United Nations 1993 [1994])

In unpacking this definition one anomaly becomes quickly apparent: it works better in some world regions than in others. In settler societies such as Canada, the United States, and Australia, the question of indigenism is fairly straightforward because the line between indigenous and nonindigenous is at least theoretically clear. Because virtually all the nonaboriginal peoples of North America are post–1492 migrants, it is possible (in theory) to draw sharp boundaries around the concept of who can be considered indigenous. For similar reasons, Latin America has a long scholarly and political tradition of *indigenismo*. But who exactly should be considered indigenous in, for example, the South African context? As Murumbi (1994) has pointed out, the black peoples of Africa, whether hunter-gatherers, herders, farmers, or city dwellers, can all claim great antiquity on the continent. Thus any distinctions between indigenous and nonindigenous must necessarily be invidious ones. A case in point: the government of Botswana, home of over half of all the San peoples of Africa, refused to participate in the UN Decade of the Indigenous People (1993–2003), on the grounds that in their country *everyone* was indigenous (Mogwe 1992). Similar conundrums and paradoxes have faced the formation of indigenous policies and programs in Asia, especially southern, and Southeast Asia (Li 2000; McIntosh 2000).

The Botswana government's objections reveal a hidden subtext in the mainstream Western use of the term indigenous. It refers not just to people who have lived in place for a long time, but specifically to encapsulated minorities who are ethnically (and often linguistically) distinct from the surrounding population and who carry on an economic adaptation, invariably based on simpler technology, which further marginalizes them (cf. Perry 1996; Miller et. al 1993).

It is clear that the North American definition of indigenous will not work in all parts of the world. So as a way of clearing the ground for further inquiry, I propose that at a minimum, we need two definitions of indigenous:

- Indigenous One describes the Americas after 1492, Australia after 1788, and probably Siberia after 1600 in the period of Russian eastward expansion; small peoples facing Eurocolonial invasion and conquest. Native Americans, from the Arctic to Tierra del Fuego are the classic cases.
- Indigenous Two deals with the parts of the world where those claiming to be indigenous are encapsulated, not by European settler states, but by agrarian polities in which the dominant ethnicity situates itself in one or another of the great traditions from which the indigenes are excluded. Thus we have India and its scheduled tribes, Malaysia with its Orang Asli, and Indo-China and its Montagnards (cf. Mittal and Sharma 1998; Winzeler 1997).

(It may also be useful to add Indigenous Three for groups reclaiming lost identities such as the Neo-Khoisan discussed above.)

Some anthropologists have argued that the complexities and ambiguities of their origins make it difficult to differentiate so-called indigenous from other elements of the vast and variegated underclass. The indigenous, the argument runs, are really nothing more than encapsulated minorities, one more group in the long casualty list of those oppressed and victimized by capitalist or statist expansion. In what sense do they have any special claim in the setting of national priorities? Or as Jane Hill asked rhetorically in her 1999 AAA Presidential Address, "If they're not from the Stone Age, if they are just poor folks trying to get by, why should we care about them?" (Hill 1999, 5). Let them, the argument runs, take their turn with all the other legions of the poor and dispossessed. Their cause should be the universal cause of human rights, not the particularist cause of indigenous rights.

This critique does raise a serious question: Is indigenous simply another constructed label to describe poor and marginalized "others?" But like Hill, I would argue strongly against this view on the grounds that it does violence to the peoples' histories, their heritage, and aspirations, and not incidentally to our Boasian and Malinowskian heritage.

I would argue that both Indigenous One and Indigenous Two peoples have characteristics not shared with other fractions of the global underclass. First there is the mark of their otherness, presented in their music, art, folklore, and cultural traditions, a vast repository of cultural diversity of world historic importance. Then there is their way of life, particularly for band- and village-based societies, a way of life, small in scale and communally based, that speaks of spirituality, noncapitalist values, and harmony with nature, all of which are extremely attractive to many urbanites. But the most compelling feature that sets indigenous people apart is their sense of place. The vast majority of citizens in the countries of the metropole are migrants, removed from their ancestral homelands by ocean crossings or rural-to-urban migration, or both, and these urbanites often remain highly mobile within their own nation-states. This mobility and other permanent dislocations so characteristic of advanced capitalism in the era of flexible accumulation, reproduces chronic conditions of anomie and stress. What indigenous people appear to have is what migrants and the children of migrants (i.e., most of the rest of us) feel they lack: a sense of belonging, a sense of rootedness in place. It is this longing to belong that has become one of the most valued ideological commodities in the era of late capitalism. A corollary to their sense of place is the very practical legal consequence that their prior occupation of land, long denied by governments and elites, is now being accepted as legitimate juridical grounds for land claims and entitlements. For all these reasons, the indigenous is a category of importance that postmodern anthropology ignores at its peril.

THE TERRAIN OF THE INDIGENOUS

The above discussion renders more transparent the complex nature of the concept of the indigenous. It is a term of self-appellation, applied by people to describe themselves and their place in the world. At the same time it is a term that emerges in its present form at a certain stage in the evolution of planetary consciousness. The Ju/'hoansi have existed for millennia; the Inupiat have existed for millennia; the Arrente have existed for millennia—each in their own worlds and on their own terms. It is only in recent years that their collective conscience has congealed around the term indigenous. It is only in recent years that the term indigenous has been recognized in the world community as a signifier denoting entitlement and respect.

The point is that the discourse of indigenism in its contemporary sense must be understood as the outcome of interactions between the indigenes themselves, and other stakeholders. In the discourse of twenty-first-century indigenism at least five voices can be discerned:

1. First there are the indigenous peoples themselves; having arrived at their present status by a variety of pathways, product of diverse histories, and struggling to stay afloat. No one would suggest their's is a unitary voice. Most communities appear to be subdivided into at least two factions, modernizers and assimilationists on the one hand, and traditionalists and resisters on the other. Indigenous communities exist along a continuum of conscientization. Gender dynamics play an important and largely understudied role. The development of indigenous leadership and intelligentsia are important variables. (For examples of internal differentiation of indigenous groups, see Gose 1994, Li 2000, and Warren 1998).

2. Second, with the rise of the nation-state system, indigenous must imply the presence of a government, a state bureaucracy, granting or withholding indigenous status. For some states the indigenous presence may be a regrettable nuisance, while for others it is an iconic national symbol, a point of pride honored on postage stamps and tourist brochures (Saugestad 1998). In all states,

by their nature, the indigenous people are subject to the dividing practices of Foucauldian capillary power, giving rise to the important distinction, found in Latin America and elsewhere, between official indigenism and popular indigenism (see, e.g., Ramos 1996).

3. A third constituency includes the neighbors of the indigenous who live in proximity to them and who may covet their land or resources. These could be subdivided into old wealth and new, and big capitals and small. Ranchers in Brazil and Chiapas; multinational mining firms in Labrador and New Guinea; lowland peasantries to highland tribals in Kerala and Tamil Nadu. Their relation to the indigenes varies from tolerance and even respect to exploitation, racism, and ethnocide.

4. The fourth constituency includes the broader national and international publics and their discourses. Primitivism is a perennial staple of Western thought. Imaginaries of the exotic indigenous in the nineteenth century focused on themes of savagery, extreme alterity, and Social Darwinism, epitomized by the famous case of Sartie or Sarah Bartmann, the Hottentot Venus, the Khoi woman exhibited in London and Paris in the 1810s for the size of her buttocks (Gilman 1985; Gordon 1992; cf. Parsons 1988). In the twentieth and twenty-first centuries, public perceptions are more likely to draw upon discourses of sympathy and romantic engagement, represented iconically by the Bushman !Xau in the film *The Gods Must Be Crazy* (Davis 1996) and the writings of Sir Lawrence Van der Post (1958, 1961).

5. Anthropology constitutes a fifth constituency, in its formative years attracted to the indigenous by complex political, aesthetic, intellectual, or even spiritual motives, and in the late twentieth and early twenty-first centuries repelled for many of the same motives. We cannot claim to be disinterested parties (Hill 1999; Fabian 1983).

THE KHOISAN

The ground is now set to explore the issues of indigenous in the contemporary world. I want to draw on a region where I have been working for a number of years—southern Africa—to examine the fate and fortunes of two indigenous groups we met at the outset, the Khoi and the San. Their example is an interesting one for several reasons, first because southern Africa is a region in which Indigenism One and Indigenism Two coexist. Second because the persistence of indigenous identity has been paralleled by the processes of deracination and assimilation. And third because processes of reindigenization are also at work.

If you draw a line north to south from the Zambezi River to the Indian Ocean, bisecting the subcontinent into two equal portions, you will find that (both precolonially and today) 90 percent of the population lives in the *eastern* half of the subcontinent and only 10 percent in the western half. With the exception of Cape Town and its surrounding districts, the western half of southern Africa consists largely of the Karoo and the Kalahari, two vast, starkly beautiful, and sparsely populated semideserts. Precolonially, this same north–south line marked a major ethnocultural division: between the Bantu-speaking peoples in the eastern half, and the far less numerous Khoisan peoples in the west. The term *Khoisan* is itself a neologism coined in the twentieth century and used to describe two related peoples: the pastoral Khoi or Hottentots and the hunting and gathering San or Bushmen, both speaking unusual click languages.

Indigenous One peoples came into being when the Dutch colonized the Cape in 1652, encountering and brutalizing both Khoi and San. But long before 1652, Indigenous Two peoples were being created in the millennia-long interaction between the resident Khoisan and the more powerful and numerous in-migrating Bantu-speaking peoples who crossed the Limpopo River around the time of Christ or earlier.

There is a series of complex links between San and Khoi, but the focus here is on the links between the Khoisan and their Bantu neighbors, and between historic Khoisan and their twentieth-century descendants, the deracinated and proletarianized people called *coloreds* in South Africa's racial terminology.

Ancestral Khoisan peoples formerly occupied the whole of southern Africa, east *and* west. Their legacy can be found in the magnificent rock art, the length and breadth of the subcontinent (Lewis-Williams 1981, Dowson 1992). Sometime in the first millennium BC, some of these people obtained sheep, goats, and later cattle, while others continued to hunt and gather, the origin of the distinction between the pastoral Khoi and the foraging San.

With the entrance of Bantu-speaking peoples, the character of southern African populations changed further (Nurse and Jenkins 1977). In the east and southeast, Khoisan peoples formed a frontier with their Bantu neighbors, creating in the process an Indigenism Two situation. They coexisted, then intermarried, and were eventually assimilated to powerful Bantu-speaking chiefdoms, the descendents of which now form the bulk of South Africa's population. The standard explanation for the numerous click sounds found in modern Zulu, Swazi, and Xhosa is the linguistic influence of click speakers, assumed to be female, intermarrying with Bantu-speakers and passing on the clicks to their offspring.

But elsewhere the San people persisted. During the last two millennia the San have been the exclusive occupants of significant portions of southern Africa, in parts of the Karoo, the Kalahari, and the Namib Deserts (Solway and Lee 1990). San and Bantu present two distinct archaeological signatures, called Later Stone Age (LSA) for the San, and Iron Age for the Bantu. Relations between the two are complex. In some archaeological areas, the LSA presents as autonomous hunter-gatherers, in some areas LSA coexists with the Iron Age sites, and in some areas the archaeological evidence appears to support a view of LSA subordination to regional Iron Age power centers.

In this complex tapestry of migration, conflict, avoidance, and subordination, where and how does one draw the line between indigenous and nonindigenous? Disagreement about the nature of these relationships, between ancestral San and Bantu, is what underlies an intense controversy in the 1990s that became known as the Great Kalahari Debate (Barnard 1992a; Kuper 1992).

ON KALAHARI REVISIONISM

In the northern Kalahari, the Ju/'hoansi of the Nyae-Nyae/Dobe area were one of several San groups that had apparently maintained a hunting and gathering way of life into the twentieth century (Schapera 1930; Barnard 1992b, Tanaka 1989; Silberbauer 1981). A number of anthropologists had documented the hunting and gathering way of life of the Ju/'hoansi, a people who, though by no means isolated, lived largely independently on their wild food resources into the 1960s (Marshall 1976; Wiessner 1993; Lee 1965, 1979). It was not until the 1920s or even later that the process of their subordination to outsiders began (Biesele and Weinberg 1990). E. Wilmsen (1989) disagreed with this view and put forward the argument that their status as hunter-gatherers was an illusion. Instead he portrayed them as devolved pastoralists, long dominated precolonially by regional African centers of power. One line of evidence was the presence on LSA archaeological sites of small quantities of iron and pottery, presumably the result of trade with their Iron Age neighbors. With the nineteenth century arrival of the colonial frontier, the revisionists further argued, the impact of merchant capital was early and devastating, further transforming the Ju/'hoansi, who having lost their cattle became hunter-gatherers only in the 1890s

(Wilmsen 1979, 1989; Wilmsen and Denbow 1990; cf. Schrire 1984). This revisionist view struck a chord in the emerging postmodern intellectual climate, and became highly influential.

While the theoretical underpinnings of the revisionist argument have been critiqued (Lee 1992b; Kuper 1992) the main problem with the revisionist view is that neither ethnographic, documentary historical, oral historical, nor archaeological evidence supports it. As has been set out at length elsewhere; the Ju/'hoansi themselves had a strongly articulated sense of their own precolonial autonomy, and this view is supported by nineteenth-century explorers' accounts (Schinz 1891; Müller 1912; Passarge 1904, 1907; Szalay 1979; Solway and Lee 1990; Lee 1992a, 1998a, Lee 2004; Lee and Guenther 1991, 1993, 1995; Lee and Hitchcock 1998; Smith and Lee 1997).

In his 1907 monograph Siegfried Passarge, for example, rejected the idea that Bushmen were nonhunting subordinates of outside powers. He insisted that the Buschmännreich of mid-nineteenth-century Ghanzi was an independent polity based entirely on hunting. He wrote:

> They were a hunting people par excellence. All social and political relations, all rights and laws, their entire political organization was based on the hunt (1907, 119).

> The honor of the chief was hereditary in those days and the Bushmen were totally independent. The Batuana did not dare set foot into their region and the Hottentots only entered it on raids (1907, 115).

Accounts by Ju/'hoan elders correspond closely. Letting the subaltern speak is presumably a prime directive of the postcolonial agenda espoused by the Kalahari revisionists. Had they listened to Ju voices, they would have found in area after area, Ju/'hoan oral traditions telling of a long history of autonomous hunting and gathering without agriculture or domesticated animals. Elders insist neither blacks nor whites appeared in the interior until the latter part of the nineteenth century.

Between 1986 and 1997, I conducted a series of in-depth interviews on the question of their ancestor's prior practices of herding and farming, pottery and iron (Lee 1998a, 2004). Two elders, both named /Ti!kay from !Goshe, Botswana presented views that were representative of oral histories collected from a dozen different informants.

"Certain Europeans in Gaborone," I began, referring to the revisionists, "argue that long ago you Ju/'hoansi, [that is] your fathers' fathers' fathers' fathers had cattle. Do you agree?"

"No! Not a bit!" was the younger /Ti!kai's emphatic answer. "Long ago our fathers' fathers' fathers' fathers, the only meat they had was what they could shoot with arrows. We only got cows from the Tswana [in my father's lifetime]."

I persisted. "But when you dig holes deep down beneath where you live you find pieces of pottery. Where did they come from?"

"Oh those pots were our own work!" replied the elder /Ti!kai. "Our ancestors made them. They would put them on the fire and cook with them. But since we got iron pots from you Europeans we lost the knowledge of pottery making."

Shifting topic I asked, "What about iron?

"We got that from the Mbukushu [a Bantu people about 125 km away]," said /Ti!kai the younger. "But we learned how to work it ourselves.... We did it ourselves. We saw how they did it and we learned from them."

Shifting topic again I asked, "Long long ago, did your fathers' fathers' fathers' fathers practice //hara [agriculture]?"

"No, we didn't," the younger /Ti!kay replied. "We just ate the food that we collected from the bush."

The older /Ti!kai added, "When I was a boy we learned about //hara from the Tswanas. They showed us how [to do it]" (Lee 1998a).

When we turn to archaeology, the evidence for *contact* between so-called Iron-Age and so-called Stone Age peoples is good, but much weaker when one tries to show *domination* of Later Stone Age by Iron Age peoples. Current research attests that *coexistence* might be a better word. Archaeological studies by Yellen and Brooks (1988, 1990), and more recently by Karim Sadr of the University of Botswana and Andrew Smith at the University of Cape Town corroborate what the Ju themselves maintain: that whatever may have been the fate of some San people, the Dobe Ju/'hoansi lived on their own in the interior without cattle until the end of the nineteenth century (Lee 1998a, in press; Smith and Lee 1997, Guenther 1993/94, 1986; Sadr 1997).

Underlying the revisionist position is the view that all contact must result in domination of one group by another. Because the burden of the evidence suggests otherwise, that San autonomy is not a figment of the anthropological imagination, in what, then, lies the attraction of revisionism to a generation of scholars? The answer to this question is one of indigenism's discontents: the curious rejection among some anthropologists of even the possibility of autonomous others.

The revisionist debate broke in anthropology precisely at the time when anthropology was undergoing its aforementioned seachange. Under the largely positive influence of Eric Wolf's *Europe and the*

People without History (1982), small-scale societies, formerly treated as more or less autonomous, came to be regarded as bound up into larger systems of power. The change in anthropological perspective mirrored the changes that were going on in the globalizing world of the 1980s and 1990s.

While numerically larger and already more integrated, peoples like the Bemba, the Kikuyu, and the Minankabau were rapidly forging national (rather than tribal) identities and becoming economic players within their respective nation-states, the smaller-scale peoples like the Ju/'hoansi were recast as subalterns in agrarian states and proletarians in emerging fields of commodity production. Given the rapidity of these changes and the apparent omnipresence of the World System in the twentieth century, it was an easy step to universalize the present and project its image back in time, attributing the same power and reach to precolonial polities in the sixteenth, twelfth, and tenth centuries, or even earlier. If the world was so interconnected, it seemed implausible to imagine even the possibility of autonomous societies in recent history.

It is important to challenge the pervasiveness of this view in contemporary anthropology. I will argue, along with Sahlins (1994, 412–413), that despite the tremendous importance and lasting value of Wolf's *Europe and the People without History*, its impact has in subtle ways undermined anthropology's understanding of indigenous peoples and made it more difficult for us to make common cause with them. In the case of the Ju/'hoansi, the evidence points to the maintenance of autonomy and a process of subordination that is much more recent than the revisionists would allow. Yet even in the cases where early subordination is supported by the evidence, is the indigenous groups' domination by outsiders really the only thing or even the most salient thing we want to know about them?

An older generation of anthropologists has been rightly criticized for assuming that the indigenous group in question was pristine until just before the anthropologist's arrival, but isn't the opposite tendency—attributing omnipotence to the colonial order or to precolonial power holders—equally distorting in its own way? Jackie Solway and I (1990) have labeled this position the "coke-bottle-in-the-Kalahari" school, because in Davis's film *The Gods Must be Crazy*, the mere appearance of the coke bottle thrown from a passing plane, threatens to destroy the calm equilibrium of San society. But surely there is a middle ground between these two positions, one that does justice to the complex contact histories of indigenous peoples while still valorizing their continuing survival based on alternative ways of being.

THE KHOISAN STORY

If anthropologists are seeking constructed identities and complex histories, there is no lack of examples on offer. A second of indigenism's discontents flows from the example I opened with: the remarkable ceremony marking the reinvention and reaffirmation of their Khoisan heritage on the part of colored South Africans.

After Jan Van Riebeeck's arrival at the Cape of Good Hope, the San and the Khoi fought tenaciously to preserve their land in the face of European expansion (Wright 1971; Marks 1972; Elphick 1977; Marais 1957; Wilson and Thompson 1970; Thompson 1985; Theal 1888–1893, 1915–1926). In a long century of conflict that exceeded in brutality, even the American westward expansion, the Boer settlers pushed their frontier north and east from the Cape, smashing resistance valley by valley with the notorious commando raids. By the late nineteenth century, all but two of the Khoi clans had been driven to extinction within South Africa, and the San people had become largely a question of memory overlain with a thickening accretion of myth (Penn 1996).

Many thousands of Khoi and San perished in the conflict. Survivors of both groups were absorbed into a deracinated underclass, first as slaves and then after the 1830s as farm laborers, townsmen, artisans, and domestic workers, diverse categories of people that later became known as the Cape colored (Szalay 1995; Goldin 1992).

Both Khoi and San peoples did survive *outside* the boundaries of modern South Africa. But here their stories diverge. The Namaqua Khoi, now mounted and organized into predatory bands, fought their way from the Cape north, crossing the Orange River and settling in modern day Namibia, in the process giving the country and its desert their name. But when they reached Namibia, there were San and other Khoi already there. Some became subordinated to the Nama, others remained distinct. So we have further layers of complexity: first an indigenous people migrating and colonizing and undergoing a process of nativization; second, others assimilating to indigenous (not colonial) power holders; and third, still others resisting incorporation and maintaining autonomous timelines that are much deeper (Ross 1976, 1993; Kent 1996; Guenther 1986; Hitchcock 1987, 1996). Groups formed by all of these processes share the rubric indigenous in contemporary Africa, a theme taken up elsewhere by Gerald Sider in his pathbreaking studies of the Lumbee Indians of North Carolina, whose roots are in a complex amalgam of black, white, and Native American (1993).

Successful indigenous movements are usually accompanied by the formation of an indigenous intelligentsia. Colored intellectuals, in reasserting their Khoisan roots, found valuable allies among anthropologists and historians. One of the key figures of the movement is Professor Henry Bredekamp who conceived the idea of the 1997 Cape Town conference when he attended an earlier conference on Khoisan Studies in Germany in July 1994. Bredekamp, a historian from the former colored University of the Western Cape, rose to address the 1994 assembly with deep conviction:

> This meeting has a great deal of significance for me … because I am person of Khoisan heritage. There are millions of South Africans like me who trace their ancestry back to the Khoi and the San peoples. These are *our* histories *our* languages you are discussing. Under Apartheid we lost much of our culture. Now we want to work closely with you in recovering our past and our traditions.

Bredekamp's intervention energized the meeting, and before it dispersed, it was agreed to hold the next Khoisan studies meeting in Cape Town. Thus news of the Khoisan renaissance reached the ears of the anthropologists.

Looking back still further, the genealogy of the origins of this renaissance can be traced to the Black Consciousness Movement (BCM) of the 1970s, associated with the name of the South African revolutionary Steve Biko. What is less well known is that the much of the theoretical underpinnings of the BCM came from colored and black student intellectuals in Cape Town. The very choice of the word *black* in black consciousness represented an important symbolic step for the colored students. It was by this step that they reidentified themselves with their African roots and with the millions of their countrywomen and men fighting oppression (Biko 1978, 1979; Pityana et al. 1992).

In the struggle that led to the defeat of apartheid, there was at first an uneasy standoff between the BCM focus on the politics of identity and the ANC's long established commitment to class-based politics of the old school. But then there was a rapprochement. Observers of recent South African history agree that the key to the eventual overthrow of apartheid came only when the ANC and its internal allies combined their formidable mass organizational skills with the cultural politics of the Black Consciousness Movement.

In July 1997 the long-awaited conference, "Khoisan Identities and Cultural Heritage," convened in Cape Town. Here, academics and policy makers were outnumbered by members of the existing Khoisan communities and many representatives of the Cape Town nonwhite intelligentsia. Present were Griquas from the eastern Cape, Damaras from central Namibia, Basarwa students from the University of Botswana, as well as representatives of a dozen remote Kalahari communities brought together by WIMSA, the Workgroup for Indigenous Minorities of Southern Africa, based in Windhoek.

In addition to the ceremonies investing the eleven members of colored communities as chiefs of the rejuvenated Khoi clans, poetry written for the occasion was recited, such as this offering from Cape Town's Plakkekamp (Squatters' Camp) Poetry Collective:

Khoisan, rise from the vast valleys of Africa,
Khoisan, this was once in your hand,
This could be, once more, your promised land.

Throughout the proceedings the media focus was on the Khoi chiefs, and the many choirs from colored communities, most singing in Afrikaans, the language of the colonial oppressor.

The conference revealed important differences in the composition of the indigenous movement between the Black Consciousness-inspired Khoisan revivalists, and a very different constituency, the leadership of the largely upcountry rural San. The San presence was far less visible at the conference. Not having the educational opportunities enjoyed by the Khoi delegates or the ability to articulate their histories, the San people from Botswana and Namibia gave far less polished presentations. Their subject matter was focused, not on heritage and identity, but on land, hunting and grazing rights, and the ongoing discrimination they experience at the hands of their fellow citizens in Botswana and Namibia. One group was seeking to recapture a lost linguistic and cultural heritage. The other group was still very much in possession of its cultural capital, but did not know quite what to do with it.

By the end of the conference it was clear that there were two quite different kinds of stakeholders represented. One group, largely San with some Khoi, had claims to cultural legitimacy that were impeccable, but were weak in the areas of political leverage and media savvy. The other, largely Khoi (and Neo-Khoi) had political and media clout, but by reason of land and language loss, had claims to legitimacy that were far more tenuous.

Each of these constituencies has, in effect, what the other lacks. Yet their's was a dialogue of two solitudes. Hopes of the organizers, myself included, that the two would combine their strengths and make common cause, may have been premature, given the vast differences in the historical experiences between, say, colored communities in the postapartheid Cape, and San peoples scattered though northern Namibia and Botswana integrated into the regional political economy far more recently (Bank 1998).

What is the larger context in which to place these events and developments? One might start with the revolutionary philosopher, Amilcar Cabral, who fifty years ago, in his famous essay, "The Weapon of Theory," wrote that the task before the African people was not only achieving independence from colonialism but also recapturing history, a history taken from the African peoples by the colonialists (1974). Cabral's views became a foundational text in a movement whose origins could be found even earlier in the writings of W. E. B. DuBois, C. L. R. James, or Franz Fanon. It is a movement that spread elsewhere in Africa, and through the black diaspora to the Caribbean and the Americas, and from there to Europe, Oceania, and Asia.

The indigenous movement thus needs to be seen as part of a much broader social movement of the twentieth and twenty-first centuries (Hitchcock 1993, 1994; Wilmer 1993). Everywhere, it seems, minority peoples are rediscovering long-suppressed aspects of themselves. Recapturing history has become a major movement in literature, history, and anthropology: the study of colonial discourse, postcoloniality, and the attempts by subaltern peoples to liberate their consciousness from it (for the South African context see, for example, K. Smith 1988).

As in southern Africa, anthropologists have played an important role in these movements and debates. Kay Warren's important work, *Indigenous Social Movements and Their Critics* (1998) on the Mayan intelligentsia, is representative of a range of excellent work on the subject. But I wonder if the very topicality of this and its articulation with current debates on social construction, reflexivity, and the analysis of discourse, have led anthropologists to focus overmuch on issues of the politics of identity, and less on the more grounded issues of land, work, and livelihood. In other words, by focusing more on the social construction of current indigenous realities, have anthros neglected indigenous peoples' still precarious position in the political economy and class politics of their respective nation states?

Identity politics and grand notions of recapturing history were certainly in the foreground at the Khoisan Conference, but what about the people from remote San villages whose central concerns were more prosaic: getting the first member of their community into high school, securing title to a small tract of land from a local land board, maintaining the health of their community in the time of AIDS when all the educational materials are in languages few understand and fewer can read, or trying to build community leadership and cohesive organization against the grain of a long tradition of personal autonomy and absence of centralized authority—and trying to accomplish all this in an atmosphere of too few jobs and too much alcohol.

INDIGENISM TODAY

We have looked at some of the strengths and weaknesses of the indigenist movement and its allies at the millennium. After centuries of struggle and terrible losses, the indigenous peoples have won some important victories. Through determination and persistence, the movement has arrived at a period of unprecedented opportunity when conjunct forces have opened up an expanded political space for indigenous peoples. Can the movement seize the opportunities provided to secure permanent gains and right historic wrongs? And can anthropologists play or continue to play constructive roles? Among the impediments to these goals are the dilemmas and discontents we have been discussing. Among these we can consider:

1. Official versus popular indigenism. While governmental and international legitimacy for indigenous people has never been higher, the danger of co-optation is always present. When leaders lose touch with their home constituencies, the results can be painful for both sides. Also there is the still open question of the contradiction between indigenous rights and citizenship, and the backlash of nonindigenous neighbors who see indigenous rights as a threat to their own rights as citizens. These range from rednecks in the United States and Canada protesting gains by aboriginal people to vigilante rancheros massacring innocents in Chiapas and Guatemala.

2. Factionalism and differentiation. For peoples long used to individual autonomy, relinquishing that to a single spokesperson designated to speak to power on behalf of the group is a difficult step. Fields of authority in these societies are shifting and unstable. The independence of spirit so admired by outsiders is also a serious obstacle to unity. The widespread persistence of divided and conflict-habituated communities is one of the outcomes. Also well documented is the differentiation in some groups between the educated minority, who are wise in the ways of the wider world and can work the levers of power, and the

majority whose world is more circumscribed, and to borrow an image from the Canadian north, are still out on the trap line. Will these two constituencies within indigenous communities retain a commonality of purpose?

3. Dysfunction and violence. In the colonial and postcolonial era, indigenous people have presented contradictory personae to the outside world: fierce independence and adherence to lifeways the world finds exemplary, but also a tragic underside of family violence, alcohol, and despair. Increasing gender disparities and violence against women and children is common in some, but by no means all, indigenous communities. These manifestations give insight into the terrible costs of survival; through what North American observers have called the American Indian Holocaust. The one side speaks of nobility and harmony with nature, the other side pain and rage.

4. Bugbear of authenticity. While public receptivity to the message of the indigenous world has never been higher, that same public demands of the "native" a persona that contains an ineffable quality of authenticity, whatever that means, and is put off when the so-called native fails, in their eyes, to deliver. The Philippine Tasaday, beloved by the National Geographic and subject of TV specials, provide the classic example of public anger and disillusion when the extravagant claims made by their backers proved to be a hoax (Berreman 1999). The year of their exposure (1986) provided a media feeding frenzy about inauthentic "primitives" and the failings of anthropology to find and produce the "real thing." Public perceptions may coalesce along similar lines for the Yanomami with the publication of the controversial book, *Darkness in El Dorado* (Tierney 2000).

5. Meaningful work. National and international recognition of their rights is only the first step to long-term indigenous viability. In some areas traditional subsistence, miraculously, still provides a livelihood. In many others, indigenous groups are at odds with conservationists who see their subsistence practices as destructive of wildlife and habitat. Welfare provides the economic base in affluent countries such as Canada, the United States, Australia, and surprisingly, Botswana. In other areas, indigenous people continue to provide forest products to urban markets. But in many areas, indigenous status confers no privileges and the people eke out a precarious livelihood as craft producers and field hands in the plantations of the countries of the south.

Though there are no easy answers to these discontents, specific examples abound within the indigenous movement, of solutions, where obstacles are being faced and overcome. In countering official indigenism, many groups bring a refreshing in-your-face quality to their dialogues with power. Increasingly, indigenous groups are setting their own agendas in ways that discomfit elites and make them squirm in the glare of unfavorable publicity—what Niezen has labeled "the politics of embarrassment." Land invasions, road blocks, and guerrilla theater, such as setting up an aboriginal tent camp on the lawn of the Australian parliament, send messages that official spin doctors find difficult to counter; the most eloquent of these being the ongoing Zapatista rebellion in Chiapas. Continuing media and human rights scrutiny makes the costs of state suppression unacceptably high. Media workers, human rights activists, and like-minded anthropologists thus play the important role of bearing witness.

In countering the bugbear of authenticity, indigenous groups have made excellent use of what has been aptly named *strategic essentialism*, reinventing themselves as First Nations or First Peoples. Here arises a serious point of conflict between anthros and "natives." While anthropologists critique the discourse of primitivism that orientalizes and distances indigenous peoples, the people themselves may be saying: "don't take that away from us. We can use it to our advantage!" Seen in this light, essentialism is here to stay, so we better get used to it (cf. Conklin 1997).

In healing the wounds suffered by dominated and colonized peoples and expressed in social dysfunction, there are several initiatives from within aboriginal communities that involve breaking the cycle of pain through spiritual awakening. Dr. Cynthia Wesley-Esquimaux, a professor of aboriginal studies at Toronto, with years of experience in running workshops for abuse victims, has adopted the concept of generational grief from Bettleheim and others and pioneered its application in workshops and healing circles for the treatment of trauma in aboriginal communities. (Wesley-Esquimaux 2004; see also Waldram 1998).

On meaningful work, there is no substitute for the winning of land rights as a way of conferring dignity and self-reliance. Income-generation projects are urgently needed, hopefully better ones than running casinos. NGOs have an important role to play here, and I would like to think that anthropologists have something to offer to indigenous groups in finding ways of fitting into the commodified world. Artists and craftspeople are producing art of aesthetic value and can be useful to communities if exploitative middlemen are bypassed: witness the northwest coast artists, and the central desert and Arnhem land art traditions in aboriginal Australia. And what is so bad about ecotourism? In the Dobe area of Botswana, the Thlabololo Development Trust and the Tocadi Development Trust, aided by the Kalahari Peoples Fund are funneling resources to the Ju/'hoansi in the form of wildlife management projects for tourism and the encouragement of high quality crafts (Hitchcock 1987, 1992, 1996). Trading on your culture may not be the best possible outcome, but it is a lot better than remaining day laborers or welfare recipients in peri-urban slums.

Perhaps the least heralded weapon in the arsenal of the indigenous, and a key to their survival, is the use of humor. The indigenous groups I am most familiar with, aboriginal peoples in Canada and Ju/'hoansi in Botswana and Namibia, use deadpan humor as a tension releaser and when necessary as a devastating weapon. Ever since I was taken in by the elaborate scam of the Christmas Ox, written up in "Eating Christmas in the Kalahari," I have a healthy respect for the wit and irony of Ju and their compatriots in the indigenous world (Lee 1969). *The Dead Dog Cafe* is a series by native author Tom King showcasing aboriginal humor on national Canadian radio that did a brilliantly satirical weekly send-up of most of the issues discussed here (Canadian Broadcasting Company 2001).

CONCLUSION: INDIGENES AND ANTHROS

Finally what about the anthropologists? There are signs of a dangerous disjuncture between anthros' views and those of indigenous people. Currently some anthros seem to be more interested in the constructedness of indigenous histories and identities, at the expense of focusing on their hopes and aspirations.

In a widely discussed article, Adam Kuper (2003, 2004) questioned the reality of the term, and asserted that *indigenous* is an empty category: poverty and marginality are the defining characteristics of being indigenous, not primordial ethnicity. To label them as indigenous is to commit the error of essentialism, a cardinal sin in postmodern discourse. Going further he asserted that to invoke ethnicity in any political argument is to flirt with reactionary and even protofascist political rhetoric.

Ranged on the other side of the debate are those who see the assertion of the rights of people to be indigenous as acts of restitution and reinclusion, completely at odds with the exclusionary politics of right-wing ethnic chauvinism (e.g., Ramos 2003; Kenrick and Lewis 2004a, 2004b; Asch and Samson 2004; Saugestad 2004; Turner 2004). These observers argue the case that indigenous histories include elements of political autonomy, linguistic distinctiveness, and long-term land occupation, though in varying degrees from case to case. While acknowledging that the modern nation-state (cf. Benedict Anderson) may be an imagined community, and that all ethnicities are to a degree fictional, they would argue that there is a world of difference between the reclaiming and restitution of rights by dispossessed San people in South Africa and the assertion of a greater German (or American) national destiny. To conflate the two is to erase critical differences between oppressor and oppressed.

In the current conjuncture, the people themselves self-identify as indigenous by employing a complex amalgam of their articulated histories (backed by scholarly evidence) and an emerging capacity for self-promotion. As noted above, this may involve a process of reinvention, as an indigenous group recasts its identity in terms dictated by the politics and legal discourses of the nation-state. The term *strategic essentialism* has been applied to this political process, and supporters see this as a legitimate weapon of the weak—a means of redressing genuine grievances in courts of public opinion in a language the wider public can understand.

Identity politics is a theme that pervades many current anthropological contributions to the indigenous debate. The late Susan Kent (2002) edited a collection of papers that assessed the degree of autonomy and subordination of hunting and gathering peoples in the recent past. Contributors tended to support the indigenist position. This theme is developed further in the book *At the Risk of Being Heard* (2003), edited by Bart Dean and Jerome Levy. Susan Lobo and Steve Talbot (2001) and Marie Battiste (2000) have assembled excellent collections emphasizing the voices of indigenous peoples in the Americas. Ronald Niezen (2003) has written a masterful overview of the politics of indigenism in the late twentieth century, while Kirk Dombrowski (2002) and Renee Sylvain (2003) present informative case studies that critically assess both the indigenist and the revisionist positions.

Another theme addressed by recent anthropological work is the fostering of land and civil rights. Alison Brysk's *From Tribal Village to Global Village: Indian Rights and International Relations in Latin America* (2000) and Curtis Cook's and Juan Lindau's, *Aboriginal Rights and Self-Government: The Canadian and Mexican Experience in North America* (2000) are recent collections surveying this topic. Schweitzer, Biesele, and Hitchcock (2000) explore these themes in an edited collection based on an earlier Conference on Hunting and Gathering Societies. Thomas Widlok and Tadesse Wolde (2004) have edited a major two-volume edition surveying property rights of peoples on the margins of capitalism, including many case studies of former foragers in Africa, Asia, Alaska, and Australia.

Studies of governmentality address the issue of how foraging peoples articulate with their nation-states in ways that acknowledge their difference and preserve a semblance of political space. Recent studies include *In the Way of Development: Indigenous Peoples, Life Projects and Globalization* (Blaser, Feit, and McRae, 2004), and Paul Nadasdy's (2003) *Hunters and Bureaucrats: Power, Knowledge, and Aboriginal-State Relations in the Southwest Yuko*, as well as Colin Scott's (2001) *Aboriginal Autonomy and Development in Northern Quebec and Labrador.* Sidsel Saugestad's *The Inconvenient Indigenous (2001)* is a valuable study of the San peoples' relations with the Botswana state.

Any study of anthropologists and indigenous peoples must acknowledge two groups. The International Work Group for Indigenous Affairs (IWGIA), based in Copenhagen, and Cultural Survival International, based in Cambridge, Massachusetts, have been extremely effective advocates for the rights of indigenous peoples in international forums and public arenas.

A theme common to many of these recent studies is an acknowledgement of the beauty and utility of strategic essentialism as a tool in the arsenal of indigenous peoples' struggles. Of course the origins of many groups claiming the mantle *indigenous*—the Cherokee, the Mashpee, and many others—were forged in the traumas of the colonial period, but these recent studies challenge the unfortunate tendency among anthros to see that as their most salient feature. In our sophisticated critiques of the illusion of authenticity, are we losing sight of the bigger picture (cf. Sider 1993)?

To summarize, what are the lessons to be learned from indigenous people in the twenty-first century? For me, the main story is how indigenous people are connected to the land; how indigenous people are living in cultures that are profoundly noncapitalist, and how their ongoing existence bears witness that even in this hard-bitten age of realpolitik and globalization, other ways of being, other ways of living in the world are possible.

Marshall Sahlins summarized these themes in his 1999 article reviewing the state of anthropological enlightenment at the end of the twentieth century. His abstract advocates:

> A broad reflection on some of the major surprises to anthropological theory occasioned by the history, and in a number of instances the tenacity, of indigenous cultures in the twentieth century. We are not leaving the century with the same ideas that

got us there. Contrary to the inherited notions of progressive development, whether of the political left or right, the surviving victims of imperial capitalism neither became all alike nor just like us. Contrary to the "despondency theory" of mid-century, the logical and historical precursor of dependency theory, surviving indigenous peoples aim to take cultural responsibility for what has been done to them. Across large parts of northern North America, even hunters and gatherers live, largely by hunting and gathering. The Eskimo are still there, and they are still Eskimo. Around the world the peoples give the lie to received theoretical oppositions between tradition and change, indigenous culture and modernity, townsmen and tribesmen, and other cliches of the received anthropological wisdom. Reports of the death of indigenous cultures—as of the demise of anthropology—have been exaggerated. (Sahlins 1999)

A conjunct circumstance has brought indigenism forward as a major item on political agendas around the world. If governments claiming legitimacy are going to pay more than lip service to democracy, they will have to acknowledge indigenous claims. Right of prior occupation is a powerful judicial principle that lies at the heart of capitalist land tenure. Thus indigenous people's presence provides a point-of-purchase for critiques of capitalism and oppositional mobilization. In the emerging twenty-first-century civil society, I see indigenous people as an essential component of the coalition of progressive forces fighting globalization, a mix that includes environmentalists, anti-WTOers, feminists, health reformers, spiritual pilgrims, liberation theologists, and all others who support the Party of Humanity in its historic struggle against the Party of Order.

REFERENCES

Asch, Michael and Colin Samson. 2004. "On the Return of the Native." *Current Anthropology* 45(2):261–262.

Bank, Andrew, ed. 1998. *Proceedings of the Khoisan Identities and Cultural Heritage Conference.* Belleville, South Africa. Institute for Historical Research: University of the Western Cape.

Barnard, Alan. 1992a. "The Kalahari Debate: A Bibliographical Essay." Centre of African Studies, University of Edinburgh, Occasional Papers No. 35.

Barnard, Alan. 1992b. *Hunters and Herders of Southern Africa: A Comparative Ethnography of the Khoisan Peoples.* Cambridge: Cambridge University Press.

Battiste, Marie A. 2000. *Reclaiming Indigenous Voice and Vision*. Vancouver: UBC Press.

Beckett, Jeremy. 1996. "Contested Images: Perspectives on the Indigenous Terrain in the Late 20th Century." *Identities* 3:1–13.

Biesele, Megan and Paul Weinberg. 1990. *Shaken Roots: The Bushmen of Namibia*. Marshalltown, South Africa, EDA Publications.

Biko, Steve. 1978. *Black Consciousness in South Africa*. New York: Random House.

———. 1979. *I Write What I Like*. London: Heinemann.

Blaser, Mario, Harvey A. Feit, and Glenn McRae, eds. 2004. *In the Way of Development: Indigenous Peoples, Life Projects and Globalization*. London, New York, Ottawa: Zed Books and the Canadian International Development Research Centre.

Brysk, A. 2000. *From Tribal Village to Global Village: Indian Rights and International Relations in Latin America*. Stanford, CA: Stanford University Press.

Cabral, Amilcar. 1974. *Return to the Source: Selected Speeches*. New York: Monthly Review Press.

Conklin, Beth. 1997. "Body Paint Feathers and VCRs: Aesthetics and Authenticity in Amazonian Activism." *American Ethnologist* 24(4):711–737.

Cook, C. and J. D. Lindau, eds. 2000. *Aboriginal Rights and Self-government: The Canadian and Mexican Experience in North America*. Montreal: McGill-Queen's University Press.

Davis, Peter. 1996. *In Darkest Hollywood: Exploring the Jungles of Cinema's South Africa*. Johannesburg: Ravan Press, and Athens, OH: Ohio University Press.

Dean, Bart and Jerome Levi, eds. 2003. *At the Risk of Being Heard: Identity, Indigenous Rights and Post-Colonial States*. Ann Arbor: University of Michigan Press.

Dombrowski, Kirk. 2004. "The Praxis of Indigenism and Alaska Native Timber Politics." *American Anthropologist* 104(4):1062–1073.

Dowson, Thomas A. 1992. *Rock Engravings of South Africa*. Johannesburg: Witwatersrand University Press.

Elphick, Richard 1977. *Kraal and Castle: The Birth of South African Society*. New Haven: Yale University Press.

Fabian, Johannes. 1983. *Time and the Other: How Anthropology Makes Its Object*. New York: Columbia University Press.

Garcia Canclini, Nestor. 1995. *Hybrid Cultures: Strategies for Entering and Leaving Modernity*. Minneapolis: University of Minnesota Press.

Geertz, Clifford. 1956. *Agricultural Involution: The Process of Ecological Change in Indonesia*. Berkeley: University of California Press.

Gilman, Sander L. 1985. *Difference and Pathology: Stereotypes of Sexuality, Race, and Madness*. Ithaca: Cornell University Press

Goldin, Ian. 1992. "Coloured Identity and Coloured Politics in the Western Cape Region of South Africa." *Journal of Southern African Studies* 20:241–254.

Gordon, Robert. 1992. *The Bushman Myth: The Making of a Namibian Underclass.* Boulder: Westview Press.

Gose, Peter. 1994. *Deathly Waters and Hungry Mountains: Agrarian Ritual and Class Formation in an Andean Town.* Toronto: University of Toronto Press.

Guenther, M. 1986. *The Nharo Bushmen of Botswana: Tradition and Change.* Hamburg: Helmut Buske Verlag.

_____. 1993, 1994. "'Independent, fearless and rather bold'": A Historical Narrative on the Ghanzi Bushmen of Botswana." *Journal of the Namibia Scientific Society* 44:25–40.

Hill, Jane. 1999. "Anthropology: Just in Time for the 21st Century?" Presidential Address presented at the 98th Annual Meetings of the American Anthropological Association, Chicago, IL, November 20, 1999.

Hitchcock, Robert K. 1987. "Socioeconomic Change among the Basarwa in Botswana: An Ethnohistorical Analysis." *Ethnohistory* 34(3):219–255.

_____.1993. "Africa and Discovery: Human Rights, Environment, and Development." *American Indian Culture and Research Journal* 17(1):129–152.

_____. 1994. "International Human Rights, the Environment, and Indigenous Peoples." *Colorado Journal of International Environmental Law and Policy* 5(1):1–22.

_____. 1996. *Kalahari Communities: Indigenous Peoples, Politics, and the Environment in Southern Africa.* Copenhagen, Denmark: International Work Group for Indigenous Affairs.

Kenrick, Justin and Jerome Lewis. 2004a. "Indigenous People's Rights and the Politics of the Term 'Indigenous.'" *Anthropology Today* 20(2):4–9.

_____. 2004b. "On the Return of the Native." *Current Anthropology* 45(2):263.

Kent, Susan, ed. 1996. *Cultural Diversity among Twentieth Century Foragers: An African Perspective.* Cambridge, England: Cambridge University Press.

_____. 2002. *Ethnicity and Hunter-Gatherers: Association or Assimilation?* Washington: Smithsonian Institution Press.

Kuper, Adam, 1992. "Postmodernism, Cambridge and the Great Kalahari Debate." *Social Anthropology* 1:57–71.

_____. 2003. "The Return of the Native." *Current Anthropology* 44(3):389–411.

_____. 2004. "Reply." *Current Anthropology* 45(2):265–266.

Lee, Richard B. 1965. "Subsistence Ecology of !Kung Bushmen." Doctoral diss., University of California, Berkeley.

_____. 1969. "Eating Christmas in the Kalahari." *Natural History* 14–22 (December):60–63.

_____. 1979. "The !Kung San: Men, Women and Work in a Foraging Society." Cambridge and New York: Cambridge University Press.

_____. 1992a. "The !Kung in Question: Evidence and Context in the Kalahari Debate." *Michigan Discussions in Anthropology* 10:9–16.

_____. 1992b. "Art, Science, or Politics: The Crisis in Hunter-Gatherer Studies." *American Anthropologist* 90:14–34.

_____. 1998a. "Gumi kwara: e ba n//a basi o win si !kwana: Oral Histories from Nyae Nyae-Dobe and the Khoisan Renaissance." In *Proceedings of the Khoisan Identities and Cultural Heritage Conference*, ed. Andrew Bank, 67–73. Institute for Historical Research, University of the Western Cape.

_____. 1998b. "Anthropology at the Crossroads: From the Age of Ethnography to the Age of World Systems." *Social Dynamics* 24:34–65.

_____. 2002. "Solitude or Servitude? Ju/'hoan Images of the Colonial Encounter." In *Ethnicity and Hunter-Gatherers: Association or Assimilation?*, ed. Susan Kent, Washington, DC: Smithsonian Institution Press.

Lee, R. and R. H. Daly, eds. 1999. *The Cambridge Encyclopedia of Hunters and Gatherers*. Cambridge: Cambridge University Press.

Lee, R. and M. Guenther. 1991. "Oxen or Onions? The Search for Trade (and Truth) in the Kalahari." *Current Anthropology* 32:592–601.

_____. 1993. "Problems in Kalahari Historical Ethnography and the Tolerance of Error." *History in Africa* 20:185–235.

_____. 1995. "Errors Corrected or Compounded? A Reply to Wilmsen." *Current Anthropology* 36:298–305.

Lee, R. and R. Hitchcock. 1998. "African Hunter-gatherers: History and the Politics of Ethnicity." In *Transformations in Africa: Essays on Africa's Later Past*, ed. Graham Connah, 14–45. London: Cassels.

Levin, Michael, ed. 1993. *Ethnicity and Aboriginality: Case Studies in Ethnonationalism*. Toronto: University of Toronto Press.

Lewis-Williams, David. 1981. *Believing and Seeing: Symbolic Meanings in Southern San Rock Paintings*. London: Academic Press.

Li, Tania Murray. 2000. "Constituting Tribal Space: Indigenous Identity and Resource Politics in Indonesia." *Comparative Studies in Society and History* 42(1):149–179.

Lobo, Susan and Steve Talbot. 2001. *Native American Voices: A Reader*. 2nd. edition. Upper Saddle River, NJ: Prentice-Hall.

Marais, J. S. 1957. *The Cape Coloured People: 1652–1937*. Johannesburg: Witwatersrand University Press.

Marks, Shula. 1972. "Khoisan Resistance to the Dutch in the Seventeenth and Eighteenth Centuries." *Journal of African History* 8:55–80.

Marshall, John and Clare Ritchie. 1984. *Where Are the Ju/wasi of Nyae Nyae? Changes in a Bushman Society: 1958–1981*. Centre for African Studies: University of Cape Town, Communication No. 9.

Marshall, Lorna. 1976. *The !Kung of Nyae Nyae*. Cambridge: Harvard University Press.

Maybury-Lewis, David. 1999. *Indigenous Peoples, Ethnic Groups and the State*. Boston: Addison-Wesley.

McIntosh, Ian. 2000. "Are There Indigenous Peoples in Asia?" *Cultural Survival Quarterly* 24:4–7.

Mittal, A. C. and J. B. Sharma. 1998. *Tribal Movements, Politics and Religions in India*. New Delhi: Radha Publishers.

Mogwe, Alice. 1992. "Who Was (T)here First? An Assessment of the Human Rights Situation of Basarwa in Selected Communities in the Gantsi District." Occasional Paper No. 10. Gaborone, Botswana: Botswana Christian Council (BCC).

Miller, M. and the staff of Cultural Survival. 1993. *State of the Peoples: A Global Human Rights Report on Societies in Danger*. Boston, MA: Beacon Press.

Müller, H. 1912. "Ein Erkundungsritt in das Kaukau-veld." *Deutsches Kolonialblatt* 23:530–541.

Murumbi, D. 1994. "Concept of Indigenous Peoples in Africa." *Indigenous Affairs* 1/94:51–57.

Nadasdy, Paul. 2003. *Hunters and Bureaucrats: Power, Knowledge, and Aboriginal-State Relations in the Southwest Yukon*. Vancouver: UBC Press.

Neitschmann, Bernard. 1994. "The Fourth World: Nations Versus States." In *Reordering the World: Geopolitical Perspectives on the 21st Century*, ed. George J. Demko and William B. Wood, 225–242. Boulder, CO: Westview Press.

Niezen, Ronald. 2000. "Recognizing Indigenism: Canadian Unity and the International Movement of Indigenous Peoples." *Comparative Studies in Society and History* 42(1):119–148.

_____. 2003. *The Origins of Indigenism: Human Rights and the Politics of Identity*. Berkeley: University of California Press.

Nurse, G. T. and T. Jenkins. 1977. *Health and the Hunter-Gatherer: Biomedical Studies on the Hunting and Gathering Populations of Southern Africa*. Basel: S. Karger.

Parsons, Neil. 1988. "Frantz or Klikko, the Wild Dancing Bushman: A Case Study of Khoisan Stereotyping." *Botswana Notes and Records* 20:71–76.

Passarge, S. 1904. *Die Kalahari*. Berlin: Dietrich Reimer Verlag.

_____. 1907. *Die Buschmänner der Kalahari*. Berlin: Dietrich Reimer Verlag.

Penn, Nigel. 1996. "Fated to Perish: The Destruction of the Cape San." In *Miscast: Negotiating the Presence of the Bushmen*. Pippa Skotnes ed., 80–91. Cape Town: University of Cape Town Press.

Perry, Richard. 1996. *From Time Immemorial: Indigenous Peoples and State Systems*. Austin: University of Texas Press.

Pityana, Barney, Mamphela Ramphele, Malusi Mpumlwana, and Lindy Wilson, eds. 1992. *Bounds of Possibility: The Legacy of Steve Biko and Black Consciousness.* London: Zed Press.

Ramos, Alcida, Rita. 1996. *Indigenism: Ethnic Politics in Brazil.* Madison: University of Wisconsin Press.

_____. 2003. "Comment." *Current Anthropology* 44(3):407–408.

Ross, Robert. 1976. *Adam Kok's Griquas: A Study in the Development of Stratification in South Africa.* Cambridge: Cambridge University Press.

_____. 1993. *Beyond the Pale: Essays on the History of Colonial South Africa.* Hanover, NH: Wesleyan University Press.

Sadr, Karim. 1997. "Kalahari Archaeology and the Bushman Debate." *Current Anthropology* 38:104–112.

Sahlins, M. 1994. "Cosmologies of Capitalism: The Trans-Pacific Sector of the World System." In *Culture/Power/History: A Reader in Contemporary Social Theory*, ed. N. Dirks, G. Eley, and S. Ortner, 412–55. Princeton, NJ: Princeton University Press.

Sahlins, M. and E. Service. 1960. *Evolution and Culture.* Ann Arbor: University of Michigan Press.

Saugestad, Sidsel, 2001. *The Inconvenient Indigenous: Remote Area Development in Botswana, Donor Assistance and the First Peoples of the Kalahari.* Uppsala: Nordic Africa Institute.

_____. 2004. "On the Return of the Native." *Current Anthropology* 45(2):263–264.

Schapera, I. 1930. *The Khoisan Peoples of South Africa: Bushmen and Hottentots.* London: Routledge and Kegan Paul.

Schinz, H. 1891. *Deutsch-Südwest Afrika: Forschungreisen durch die deutschen Schutzgebiete, Gross-Nama-und Hereroland, nach dem Kunene, dem Ngami-See und der Kalahari, 1884–1887.* Oldenberg: Schulzescher Hof.

Schrire, Carmel, ed. 1984. *Past and Present in Hunter-gatherer Studies.* Orlando: Academic Press.

Schweitzer, P., M. Biesele, and R. Hitchcock, eds. 2000. *Hunter-gatherers in the Modern World: Conflict, Resistance and Self-Determination.* New York and Oxford: Berghahn.

Scott, Colin, ed. 2001. *Aboriginal Autonomy and Development in Northern Quebec and Labrador.* Vancouver: University of British Columbia Press.

Sider, Gerald M. 1993. *Lumbee Indian Histories.* Cambridge: Cambridge University Press.

Silberbauer, George B. 1981. *Hunter and Habitat in the Central Kalahari Desert.* Cambridge: Cambridge University Press.

Slemon, Stephen 2000. "Post-Colonialism: The New Face of Imperialism." *Toronto Star* March 14, 18.

Smith, Andrew and Richard Lee. 1997. "Cho/ana: Archaeological and Ethno-historical Evidence for Recent Hunter-Gatherer/Agro-Pastoralist Contact in Northern Bushmanland." *South African Archaeological Bulletin* 52:52–58.

Smith, Ken. 1988. *The Changing Past: Trends in South African Historical Writing.* Athens, OH: Ohio University Press.

Solway, J. and R. Lee 1990. "Foragers Genuine or Spurious? Situating the Kalahari San in History." *Current Anthropology* 31(2):109–146.

Stow, J. M. 1905. *The Native Races of South Africa.* London: Swan and Sonnenschein.

Sylvain, Renee. 2002. "Land, Water and Truth: San Identity and Global Indigenism." *American Anthropologist* 104:1074–1085.

Szalay, M. 1979. "Die ethnographische Südwestafrika-Sammlung Hans Schinz 1884–86." Special issue of *Ethnologische Zeitschrift Zürich*, 1.

_____. 1995. *The San and the Colonization of the Cape: 1770–1879. Research in Khoisan Studies*, Band 11. Köln: Rüdiger Köppe Verlag.

Tanaka, Jiro. 1989. *The San, Hunter-Gatherers of the Kalahari: A Study in Human Ecology.* Tokyo: University of Tokyo Press.

Theal, George McCall. 1888–93. *A History of South Africa*, vols. 1–5. London: Sonnenschein.

_____. 1915–26. *A History of South Africa*, vols. 6–9. London: Allen and Unwin.

Thompson, Leonard. 1985. *The Political Mythology of Apartheid.* New Haven, CT: Yale University Press.

Tierney, Patrick. 2000. *Darkness in El Dorado: How Scientists and Journalists Devastated the Amazon.* New York: W. W. Norton.

Turner, Terry. 2004. "On the Return of the Native." *Current Anthropology* 45(2):264–265.

United Nations. 1993[1994]. Draft United Nations Declarations on the Rights of Indigenous Peoples. United Nations, E/CN.4/1995/2, 105–117.

van der Post, Laurens. 1958. *The Lost World of the Kalahari.* Harmondsworth: Penguin.

_____. 1961. *The Heart of the Hunter.* Harmondsworth: Penguin.

Waldram, James. 1998. *The Way of the Pipe: Aboriginal Spirituality and Symbolic Healing in Canada's Prisons.* Peterborough, Ontario: Broadview Press.

Warren, Kay. 1996. *Indigenous Movements and Their Critics: Pan-Maya Activism in Guatemala.* Princeton, NJ: Princeton University Press.

Widlok, Thomas and Tadesse Wolde, eds. 2004. *Property and Equality. Vol. 1. Ritualization, Sharing, Egalitarianism. Vol. 2. Encapsulization, Commercialization, Discrimination.* Oxford and New York: Berghahn.

Wiessner, P. 1993. "Hxaro." In *Im Spiegel der Anderen: Aus Lebenswerk des Verhaltenforschers Iraenaus Eibl-Eibesfeldt.* Munchen: Realis

Williams, Raymond. 1986. *Keywords: A Vocabulary of Culture and Society,* rev. ed. London: Oxford University Press.

Wilmer, F. 1993. *The Indigenous Voice in World Politics.* Newbury Park, CA: Sage.

Wilmsen, E. 1979. "Prehistoric and Historic Antecedents of a Contemporary Ngamiland Community." *Botswana Notes and Records* 10:5–18.

_____. 1988a. "Antecedents of Contemporary Pastoralism in Western Ngamiland." *Botswana Notes and Records* 20:29–37.

_____. 1988b. "Comment on Yellen and Brooks, 'The Late Stone Age Archaeology of the !Kangwa and /Xai /Xai Valleys.'" *Botswana Notes and Records* 20:37–39.

_____. 1989. *Land Filled with Flies: A Political Economy of the Kalahari.* Chicago: University of Chicago Press.

_____. 1993. "On the Search for (Truth) and Authority: A Reply to Lee and Guenther." *Current Anthropology* 34:715–721.

Wilmsen, E. and J. Denbow. 1990. "Paradigmatic History of San-speaking Peoples and Current Attempts at Revision." *Current Anthropology* 31(5):489–524.

Wilson, Monica and Leonard Thompson, eds. 1968. *The Oxford History of South Africa*, Vol. 1, Oxford: Oxford University Press.

Winzeler, Robert L. 1997. *Indigenous Peoples and the State: Politics Land and Ethnicity in the Malaysian Peninsula and Borneo.* New Haven, CT: Yale University Southeast Asian Studies.

Wolf, E. 1982. *Europe and the People without History.* Berkeley and Los Angeles: University of California Press.

Wright, J. 1971. *Bushman Raiders of the Drakensburg 1840–1870.* Pietermaritzburg: University of Natal Press.

Yellen, John E. and Alison S. Brooks. 1988. "The Late Stone Age Archaeology of the !Kangwa-/Xai/Xai Valleys, Ngamiland." *Botswana Notes and Records* 20:5–28.

_____. 1990. "The Late Stone Age Archaeology in the /Xai /Xai Region: A Response to Wilmsen." *Botswana Notes and Records* 22:17–19.

6

ENVIRONMENTALISM, GLOBAL COMMUNITY, AND THE NEW INDIGENISM

Beth A. Conklin

The decade of the 1990s was the tipping point for a major shift in the position of indigenous peoples in the world system. In international affairs and in many national societies, native people who in the past had been marginalized, excluded, and disempowered experienced new kinds of attention, respect, and inclusion in certain political and cultural arenas.

The global spread of common ideas, vocabularies, symbols, and transnational organizational networks offered new resources to reconceptualize and renegotiate indigenous peoples' position in contemporary society. Linking local struggles over land, resources, and cultural rights to international issues and organizations, native activists and their allies have been on the cutting edge of trends to "think locally, act globally" (Varese 1991), mobilizing transnational resources and universalist ideas to strengthen local struggles.

"Think globally, act locally," was the watchword of 1970s environmentalism. That slogan was coined by the visionary microbiologist Rene Dubos when he served as an adviser to the first United Nations conference on the environment in 1972. Although Dubos died in 1982, when the transformation and transnationalization of indigenous politics was in its early stages, he almost certainly would have approved of how his slogan came to be turned on its head in indigenous political activism. Dubos (1965, xvii) developed the ecological definition of health, which defines health not as the absence of disease or stress, but as the organism's ability to respond and adapt to changing circumstances. This ecological understanding underpins environmentalism's emphasis on protecting biodiversity: maintaining the variety of species and ecological niches is essential for the health of the planet. Contemporary indigenist politics make similar claims for cultural diversity, asserting that protecting indigenous peoples' distinctive ways of living and thinking is essential for the health of society and of the planet itself.

At the center of this new indigenism is an emphasis on what June Nash (in this volume) calls "indigenous autonomous development"— the right (and necessity) for native communities to define their own goals and forge their own paths to make a living and govern themselves. Rejecting dependency and paternalism in relations with outsiders, such movements emphasize partnership and collaboration. They recognize that indigenous people have the capacity to represent themselves and their interests, to speak on their own behalf and participate in decision making about issues that affect them.

This differs markedly from two approaches that, historically, have dominated the treatment of native communities. Colonial and neo-colonial policies aimed to do away with indigenous cultures, or with indigenous people themselves, by forcing or allowing them to disappear through extermination, relocation, or assimilation. In the twentieth century, more humane policies emphasized physical protection and the extension of basic human rights and government services such as education and health care. The ultimate vision, however, was to turn indigenous people into culturally homogenized citizens of the nation, based in assumptions about their backwardness and incapacity to survive modernity's onslaught. In education, for example, when national governments provided schooling for indigenous children, they were almost always taught in the national language and often forbidden (under pain of physical punishment) to speak their own native language. Indoctrinating students in the superiority of the national culture and the need to divest themselves of their backward native heritage, indigenous education promoted the goals of "state-sponsored monoculturalism" (Niezen 2003).

The new indigenism, in contrast, asserts that native peoples are full citizens in the global community of twenty-first-century modernity. This goes beyond basic human rights: indigenous people do not belong in the global community despite their cultural differences but in part because of them. A key idea is that the survival of distinctive indigenous cultures has value for humanity as a whole; that the fate of indigenous people affects others as well. Safeguarding indigenous land rights and cultural integrity is important to the well-being of the larger society.

The bottom-line justification, the linchpin in arguments for indigenous autonomous development, has been the idea that promoting indigenous peoples' control of their lands and natural resources benefits the environment. Environmental arguments for indigenous rights have been most prominent in regions where native territories are on the frontiers of capitalist expansion, particularly in the world's tropical forests where native rights are under assault by logging, mineral, and petroleum enterprises. In South America, Indonesia, and elsewhere, national economic development schemes promoting agricultural colonization, ranching, and road-building have sparked massive migration into tropical forest regions inhabited by native peoples and coveted by states, corporations, migrants, and entrepreneurs. The ecological damage and social disruption wreaked by these invasions makes natural allies of environmentalism and indigenous rights.

The link with environmentalism that has developed since the 1980s greatly expanded the terrain for indigenous rights advocacy, which formerly had been based mostly on human rights arguments. It connected native causes to the much larger, well-funded networks of international environmental NGOs (nongovernmental organizations) and set indigenous claims apart from the claims of other impoverished people and ethnic groups with their own histories of oppression and suffering. Environmental discourses offered native activists new language to communicate the value of their peoples' beliefs and practices, find common ground with outsiders, and affirm the value of their traditions and pride in being indigenous. But embracing environmentalism as a dominant frame for indigenous rights struggles brings limitations and liabilities as well.

This chapter examines one of the earliest cases in which linkages to environmentalism transformed indigenous advocacy movements, in Amazonian rainforest activism in Brazil, where I have worked with native people for the past two decades. Since the late 1980s, Amazonia has been a kind of testing-ground for optimistic visions of how globalization can facilitate new forms of community, ethical engagement, and local empowerment. Amazonian rainforest activism is a case study in how a more technologically connected world offers marginalized peoples new political venues and resources. It is also a case study in how environmentalism and science can be powerful resources to challenge oppressive state and corporate policies.

The solidarity that developed around rainforest activism highlights the promise, and also some of the problems and tensions, in environmentally focused transnational collaboration and community building. Indigenous experiences suggest that the ecological principle of diversity as a prerequisite for health may apply in transnational collaborations as well: overdependence on environmentalism as a monocultural frame for indigenous rights claims can jeopardize native communities' political viability.

ENVIRONMENTALISM AND GLOBALIZATION

Optimistic theorists of globalization see it as a democratizing force that can foster new forms of transnational community and cooperation (Croucher 2004, 28–29). In a more connected world of rapid communication and intensified flows of information, new forms of collaboration and community may arise, based on new possibilities for people to recognize common interests and identify with others distant from themselves. In the process that John Tomlinson (1999) calls "complex connectivity," global communication systems create possibilities for more direct moral engagement that transcends national boundaries, as the Internet, television, and video bring information, images, and ideas about distant people close to home. Groups that have difficulty leveraging political support at the local and national levels may find ways to use transnational communications to establish political presence and exert political and cultural leverage (Brysk 2000, 286; Wriston 1992, 170, 176).

In such a world of global connectivity, new forms of solidarity may coalesce around new notions of shared identity. Environmentalism, some theorists have suggested, offers one of the most promising conceptual bases for new forms of transnational community. Indeed, it is difficult to imagine a more inclusive framework. Every human on the planet is a citizen of Earth; every individual has some relation to place, to biological interconnections, and to the environment. As an issue around which people from diverse backgrounds may find common interests, environmentalism has obvious power. Threats like global warming potentially affect everyone on Earth. Planetary community is the largest possible community, the most comprehensive arena for belonging and identity open to every human (and nonhuman) being. Environmentalism offers a positive alternative to (and critique of) the only other form of global identity and belonging promoted with the spread of global capitalism: cosmopolitan consumerism.

Interconnectedness is the key concept in ecological awareness: environmentalism is about recognizing linkages, interactivity, interdependence. An ecological worldview is consistent with subjectivities shaped by transnationalism and global information media. Heightened awareness of interdependence resonates with subjective experiences of intensifying flows of ideas, images, people, things, and influences across local and national boundaries. Globalization and the technologies propelling it are transforming concepts and experiences of time, space, and social relations in ways consistent with the ecological cosmology.

For indigenous intellectuals, environmentalism has offered a host of fertile ideas and perspectives that resonate with many aspects of native cosmologies and the primacy native people place on land, territorial autonomy, and traditional ways of life intimately connected to plants, animals, and environmental processes (cf. Macas 2003). In contrast to traditional human rights discourses, which focus mostly on the individual, environmentalism tends to treat people in more collective terms, as communities, which resonates with indigenous cultural emphases on sociality, kinship, and community.

The localism of environmentalism is another of its strengths. Environmental thinking offers a comprehensive universalism, but by definition this is a universalism shot through with deep veins of attention to locality and local conditions. Ecological concerns are place-based, sensitive to specific locales and the biological interrelations of plants, animals, air, water, and life-sustaining processes. In connecting the local and the global, environmentalism recognizes the value of diversity—not just biological diversity, but also the diversity of cultural practices adapted to local conditions. Identifying with environmentalism reinforces both cosmopolitan and local identifications simultaneously, emphasizing connection, belonging, and community at multiple levels that are not mutually exclusive. In this way, environmentalism encompasses both poles of globalization's pull—the twin, apparently opposing, cultural trends toward deterritorialization and reterritorialization, toward affirming translocal affiliations and reinforcing local identities and resistance (see Nash 2005).

Beyond the attractions of this combination of universalism and localism, several other aspects of environmentalism give it special force as a unifying basis for new forms of community and collaboration that can empower marginalized groups. These include environmentalism's legitimation in Western science, its usefulness in cultural critique, and the appeal of its pragmatic ethics and possibilities for concrete individual actions to express identity and agency.

SCIENTIFIC LEGITIMACY AND TRANS-NATIONAL EMPATHY

One of environmentalism's major strengths is its grounding in science, a system of knowledge with claims to authority acknowledged by a large portion of the world's public and the institutions of nation-states and global capitalism. As both a knowledge system and a political force, science has many advantages, including its goal of seeking empirical truths, its ability to change and adapt as new information comes to light, and its partial independence from political structures and state institutions.

For opposition movements in the developing world, environmentalism's base in hard Western science makes it a powerful tool. Anna Tsing (2005,8) observes that in Indonesia, "The universalism of environmental politics articulated widespread desires for knowledge free from state regulation and for ties with the heritage of Western Europe. Freedom and science augmented each other's universal claims."

Ecological science is especially useful for local groups critical of state and corporate policies because it is concerned with place-based ecosystem processes and often validates local cultural knowledge and environmental resource management practices. Scientific knowledge has become a powerful tool for local groups attempting to resist top-down development schemes and outsiders' claims on local natural resources.

In the Brazilian Amazon in the 1980s, early environmental mobilization grew out of a conjunction of advances in scientific knowledge and failures in orthodox economic development policies. Massive government-sponsored schemes based on orthodox development policy approaches paved roads and promoted new agricultural and ranching enterprises in the interior of the country, sparking massive uncontrolled migration, clear-cutting and deforestation, large-scale erosion, crop failures, and a host of social problems. These policy failures highlighted the limits of existing Western scientific understanding of rainforest soils and agronomy at a time when new research in ethnobiology and cultural ecology had begun to reveal the sophistication and productivity of local native peoples' knowledge systems and sustainable resource management practices. This new research had great impact among policy makers and the educated public. For environmentalists, the new scientific findings legitimized the twin goals of preserving the biodiversity of rainforest flora and fauna and ensuring native communities' control of natural resources. The idea of protecting the forest became attached to the idea of protecting indigenous peoples' knowledge of forest resources and, by extension, the idea of protecting indigenous peoples themselves. In a rapid about-face from earlier views of native people as backward obstacles to progress and economic development, Amazonian Indians suddenly were hailed—at least in transnational environmentalist circles—as natural conservationists, guardians of the forest (Conklin and Graham 1995, 698). Ecological science thus brought the value of native cultural practices and land rights to the attention of a global public and convinced concerned citizens that they have a stake in the fate of indigenous communities.

CULTURAL CRITIQUE AND MORAL IDENTITY

The holistic ecological science in which environmentalism is grounded documents interactions among biotic systems and demonstrates connections between local and global processes, creating powerful information resources for local resistance movements. In Amazonia, ecological research has been a key factor in validating local cultural knowledge and documenting the sustainability (and in some cases, superior economic productivity) of traditional resource management practices of both native and nonnative small farmers and collectors of forest products. Scientific information is a key strategic resource for local movements in developing critiques and policy alternatives.

More broadly, ecology's emphasis on the interconnectedness of all life lends itself to spiritually oriented critiques of cultural trends based on individualism, inequality, unrestrained corporate capitalism, and consumerism. Every major world religion has discursive spaces for some critiques along these lines. The work of the Forum on Religion and Ecology at Harvard University, which was cosponsored by the United Nations Environment Programme, pulled together vast amounts of information about the bases for environmentalism in major world religions—a stunning testimony to the array of textual sources and spiritual traditions that can be framed and mobilized to promote environmentalism (see Tucker and Grim 2001 and http://environment.harvard.edu/religion/main.html). Even the World Bank has produced a major publication, Faith in Conservation (Palmer 2003), which highlights the enormous potential to further protection of biodiversity through cooperation with religious faiths whose beliefs, traditions, and institutional resources might be directed toward environmentally beneficial goals.

The ethical orientation of environmentalism makes it compatible with religious and spiritual concerns, and is a key component of its potential as a unifying framework for global community. Environmentalism highlights how pragmatic, everyday individual choices and behaviors, as well as larger societal patterns and policies, make concrete differences in the state of the world and the quality of life for individuals and communities. Identities, commitments, and communities are constructed through practice, in the performance of behaviors, rituals, and identifying markers. Environmentalism offers a host of practices for communicating individual values, identity, and affiliations with others. Every time someone in my hometown of Nashville makes a trip to the recycling center or decides to mow her lawn in early morning instead of during the heat of the day to reduce air pollution, this small individual action reinforces a personal identification with "green" civic morality. Similarly, each time men from Masali Island off the coast of East Africa decide to fish with nets instead of dynamite in obedience with their religious leaders' declaration that dynamite fishing is contrary to the Qur'an and Shariah law (Palmer 2003, 3–5), they mark a pious Muslim identity framed in terms that open common ground with environmentally concerned non-Muslims. In Amazonian rainforest advocacy, cultural practices such as consumers' receptivity to "green" products, such as Ben and Jerry's Rainforest Crunch ice cream and The Body Shop's cosmetics made with oils produced by the Kayapo in Brazil, were another ingredient in the cultural trends that gave rainforest causes unprecedented clout.

Environmentalism offers a language, concepts, and tangible forms of action to express cultural critique and assert moral agency and identity. Its ethical dimensions make it compatible with many other social movements concerned with human rights and social justice. In Amazonia and elsewhere, environmentalism brought a host of new philosophical, organizational, and technological defenses that empowered indigenous groups and their advocates to resist the destruction and assimilation of their ways of life (Varese 1996).

TENSIONS IN ECO-COMMUNITY

The early phase (from the mid-1980s to mid-1990s) of collaboration between environmental and indigenous rights organizations in Brazil was characterized by enormous enthusiasm and a sense of empowerment, along with a good deal of romanticism and sometimes-simplistic assumptions that native control of territory and resources would guarantee environmental preservation. Collaboration between indigenous Amazonian rights struggles and international environmentalism was productive and empowering for groups on both sides. In Brazil, media attention to environmental issues and collaboration and support from environmentally minded NGOs helped native activists win a series of key victories in their struggles for Constitutional rights and for the demarcation and protection of many indigenous territories. The flood of NGOs that poured into virtually every corner of the Brazilian Amazon in the 1990s brought new personnel, financial resources, and information to many formerly marginalized peoples. NGO support was a critical destabilizer of older power relations.

Relationships between NGOs and native peoples, however, proved to be fraught with tensions and complexities that few foresaw in the optimistic days of the early 1990s. From the perspective of indigenous rights activism, major limitations included the tensions between nationalism and transnationalism, the inherent power inequities between north and south, first world and fourth world participants, and outsiders' unrealistic stereotypes and expectations for indigenous people.

One lesson was that good global politics do not always make good domestic politics (Conklin and Graham 1995, 705). As political scientist Allison Brysk observes, "the very factors of identity politics that facilitate transnational appeals often complicate domestic alliances" (2000, 281). International criticism and political pressure collide with notions of national sovereignty, especially when economic resources are at stake, and nationalist discourses of citizenship and patriotism may conflict with universalist human rights discourses or the quasi-universalism of environmentalism. In Brazil, foreign criticism of national policies toward the rainforest and its native inhabitants fed a nationalist backlash that portrayed environmentalists as new "green" imperialists, using indigenous rights causes as a cover to justify interfering in Brazilian national affairs in order to get control of the country's natural resources. Transnational support for local native causes proved to be a double-edged sword that could be turned against indigenous interests, and native Brazilian activists have had to work to reposition themselves as patriotic guardians of the nation's biological patrimony (Conklin 2002).

Tensions between universalism and localism are a recurring issue in nonindigenous environmental politics as well. In Indonesia, for example, Tsing (2005, 233) describes how environmental activists rejected offers of financial support from transnational NGOs out of fear of a backlash against foreigners' involvement in national issues. The quandary these local activists faced may bedevil other forms of transnational community building. Transnational collaboration is forged by emphasizing the common ground shared by diverse groups, and framing local causes in the language and ideas of transnational environmentalism. Environmental values and concerns, however, may only partially overlap, or even conflict with, local communities' and national societies' values and priorities. Foreign frameworks can be an uneasy fit with local groups' own worldviews and priorities, and common ground is only a small part of the territory native people inhabit.

Outsiders' unrealistic expectations are another problem. Niezen (2003, 211) observes that, "as the weakest and most isolated of the world's nationalist entities, indigenous people rely more heavily than other 'minorities' upon public sympathy within nation-states and the lobbying efforts of international NGOs with their own ties to public fund-raising and support." For native people who live in remote areas like the Brazilian Amazon, face-to-face contacts with their urban supporters are rare, and limited mostly to the small number of native representatives who travel to conferences and media events. Beyond the local level, solidarity and support are generated by imaginative projection, through messages and images circulated by media and NGOs.

The imaginings through which the transnational Indian–environmentalist partnership has flourished proved to be both its strength and its weakness (Conklin and Graham 1995, 697). The power of ideas and images to cross national boundaries generated unprecedented political support and leverage for local indigenous struggles. Activists and NGOs were able to channel public empathy and idealized images of native people into concrete forms of political support that helped some Brazilian Indians win key battles for land rights and more favorable government policies. This was one of the most empowering developments in the history of Brazilian native rights struggles. However, the generic stereotype of native people as natural conservationists proved to be a treacherous foundation for indigenous rights advocacy because it represented native cultures in ways that did not match the realities of many native peoples' lives (cf. Langer 2003, xxv).

Popular images of "ecologically noble savages" who always act in harmony with the earth ignore the local realities of distance, discrimination, and disadvantage that force almost all native people into the market economy while often giving them few options for making a living (Redford 1990). Whereas environmentalists' first priority is to protect natural resources, many Brazilian Indian leaders prioritize self-determination. Self-determination means different things to different people; to many native Brazilians, it includes the right to use their lands' natural resources as they see fit. Some individuals and communities have pursued environmentally destructive paths, selling timber and minerals to commercial interests, and the contradictions between local actions and romantic transnational images of ecological nobility have provided hostile politicians and journalists with ammunition in their war against indigenous rights (Conklin 1997; Ramos 1994, 1998; Turner 1995; and cf. *Economist* 1993).

When native people's actions contradict outsiders' expectations, support for specific indigenous causes may be diluted or withdrawn (see Ramos 1998). Legitimacy is defined and policed largely on first world terms, by first world funders and organizations. Indigenous individuals and communities cannot possibly live up to the ideals of purity, harmony, and ecological balance that some of their most sympathetic supporters project onto them, but these expectations remain strong. Alcida Ramos (1994), who dubbed this idealized imagery "the hyperreal Indian," notes that many NGOs in Brazil seem to have a hard time dealing with flesh-and-blood Indians whose desires and demands for assistance often focus on things like chainsaws, tractors, trucks, and arranging contracts for commercial logging operations (see Graham 2002, 198–200).

Funding from NGOs and governments can depend on meeting outsiders' criteria of indigenous authenticity (Jackson 1995; Ramos 1998). When real native peoples' behavior contradicts their allies' hyperreal expectations, there is a risk: because environmental problems are so large, the global environment is so diverse, and the onslaught of information and crises is so overwhelming, communities and causes that do not fit dominant transnational fashions will fall out of favor, victims of the weakness of relations based heavily on images and symbols, and the realities of information overload and compassion fatigue.

The needs and priorities of indigenous communities go far beyond environmental protection, and sometimes conflict with environmental priorities. Indigenous communities around the globe are experiencing tensions similar to those that surfaced in Amazonian activism. Niezen, for example, describes the experience of the Cross Lake Cree community in Manitoba. In trying to communicate with the public, they first framed their grievances as human rights violations, but their story "fell largely on deaf ears. Poverty, relative to the rest of Canada, was not enough to command attention, not the kind of story that could compete with the human rights catastrophes happening in other parts of the world." The community then hired a lobbyist who recast the issue as an environmental catastrophe caused by hydroelectric development. This reframing brought extensive press coverage and support from a host of environmental organizations. In the focus on ecological destruction, little attention was given to the question of most concern to the Cross Lake people themselves—the question of how to survive economically. Niezen (2003, 181–182) writes:

Clearly the greatest—if not only—possibility for Cross Lake's economy lies in resource extraction from their territory, the timber and minerals coveted by outside 'developers.' ... Hopes and visions of the future ... take the form of jobs, houses, stores, expansion of the town.... Even though the Crees would probably be more environmentally careful with their own projects on their own territory than multinational corporations acting more or less alone, these are not the kind of visions the outside world wants to hear about.... The high—or one might say impossible—expectations of environmental stewardship applied to indigenous peoples have a tendency to intrude upon their rights and thus their ability to prosper.

Over the past decade, indigenous rights advocacy by NGOs has shown signs of maturing beyond ecofetishism toward a more grounded pragmatism that recognizes diversity within and among indigenous communities, and takes seriously the economic constraints under which native communities struggle and the economic aspirations of native individuals. Paternalistic attitudes and oppressive policies are far from disappearing, however. For many local native communities, little has changed in the conditions of poverty and marginality they experience in relation to the larger society. What has changed in many areas is the possibility of mobilizing new ideas and advocacy resources, especially at the global and national levels. Indigenous activists are insisting on taking new pride in being indigenous. They are claiming legitimacy and a place at the tables where decisions affecting their futures are made, and they expect to be heard.

AGAINST MONOCULTURALISM

One place where the distinctive voices of indigenous perspectives have been heard is in international environmentalism itself. In the 1980s, environmentalism focused mostly on preserving flora and fauna. By the mid-1990s, *sustainable development* had moved to the center of environmental discussions, research, and policy making. This came about partly as a result of the new perspectives to which environmentalists were exposed in their attempts to work with native peoples and others who make a living using the resources of the rainforest and other natural environments. Just as environmentalism changed the face of indigenous politics, indigenism has changed ecologists' understandings and priorities. Native activists who have learned to "act globally" are teaching their nonindigenous collaborators to "think locally" in cultural as well as ecological terms. Kay Warren (1998, 65), for example, describes the emergence in Guatemala of indigenous ecological discourses that approach environmental issues as one part of an interconnected dynamics comprised of Mayan cosmology, ritual practices, land rights, and social identity. Throughout the world, native communities and native activists are experimenting with "alternative modernities" (Knauft 2002), using innovative fusions of ideas, technologies, and cultural practices to forge new ways to be indigenous in contemporary society.

Recognition of indigenous communities' roles in environmental protection provided powerful scientific and moral legitimacy and political leverage for native rights claims. Overreliance on environmental rationales carries risks, however. If fidelity to sustainable ecological practices is the litmus test for inclusion in global support networks, then many indigenous people will be excluded. A monocultural focus on environmental dimensions of indigenous communities' problems devalues native peoples' other pressing concerns. It disenfranchises indigenous groups that have lost their land and been forced into degraded environments, or whose land is already ravaged. And it contradicts the principle of self-determination by denying the legitimacy of indigenous groups whose self-determined choice is to use their land and resources in nonsustainable ways. Self-determination will sometimes include viewpoints and practices that are not homologous with those of environmental NGOs and other supporters of indigenous rights.

Others who receive short shrift in the focus on indigenous environmentalism are nonindigenous small farmers and forest product collectors whose lifeways and resource management practices are similar to those of native people, but who lack the cachet of a distinctive ethnic identity and the environmentalist credentials so readily available to native people. Such individuals are at the rock bottom of the social hierarchy and receive far less attention from transnational NGOs and global media. Similarly, the many native people who live in urban areas are shortchanged by policies and politics that rely on relations to land as the justification for indigenous rights claims. For those whose ties to land have been broken or attenuated, the ecological emphasis in popular stereotypes of native identity is problematic. The "bugbear of authenticity" that Richard Lee describes (in this volume) rears its counterproductive head when indigenous legitimacy is defined by conformity to Western ideals of ecological balance.

One way forward may be to take seriously the parallels between biodiversity and cultural diversity as twin resources essential for a healthy global society. Environmental protection is a powerful reason to promote native communities' well-being and support their autonomous development, but it is not the only reason. Less easy to capture in sound bites, but equally valuable, are indigenous communities' roles in demonstrating time-tested possibilities for other ways of living and being in the world. Native peoples' distinctive social and spiritual practices are antidotes to the homogenizing monoculturalism of national and global consumer cultures. As indigenous communities carve out spaces for developing their own alternatives on their own terms, they preserve cultural diversity needed for a healthy global community.

REFERENCES

Brysk, Alison. 2000. *From Tribal Village to Global Village: Indian Rights and International Relations in Latin America.* Stanford, CA: Stanford University Press.

Conklin, Beth A. 1997. "Body Paint, Feathers, and Vcrs: Aesthetics and Authenticity in Amazonian Activism." *American Ethnologist* 24(4):711–737.

———. 2002. "Shamans versus Pirates in the Amazonian Treasure Chest." *American Anthropologist* 104(4):1050–1061.

Conklin, Beth A. and Laura R. Graham. 1995. "The Shifting Middle Ground: Brazilian Indians and Eco-politics." *American Anthropologist* 97(4):695–710.

Croucher, Sheila L. 2004. *Globalization and Belonging: The Politics of Identity in a Changing World.* New York: Rowan & Littlefield.

Dubos, René. 1965. *Man Adapting.* New Haven, CT: Yale University Press.

Economist. 1993. "The Savage Can Also Be Ignoble." *Economist* 327(7815):54.

Graham, Laura. 2002. "How Should an Indian Speak? Amazonian Indians and the Symbolic Politics of Language in the Global Public Sphere." In *Indigenous Movements, Self-Representation, and the State in Latin America*, ed. Kay B. Warren and Jean E. Jackson, 181–182. Austin: University of Texas Press.

Jackson, Jean E. 1995. "Culture, Genuine and Spurious: The Politics of Indianness in the Vaupés, Colombia." *American Ethnologist* 22(1):3–27.

Knauft, Bruce M. 2002. *Critically Modern: Alternatives, Alterities, Anthropologies.* Bloomington, IN: Indiana University Press.

Langer, Erick D., with Elena Munoz, eds. 2003. *Contemporary Indigenous Movements in Latin America.* Wilmington, DE: Scholarly Resources.

Macas, Luis. 2003. "Interview." In *Contemporary Indigenous Movements in Latin America*, ed. Erick Langer, 195–200. Wilmington, DE: Scholarly Resources.

Nash, June. 2005. "Defying Deterritorialization: Autonomy Movements against Globalization." In *Social Movements: An Anthropological Reader*, ed. June Nash, 177–186. Malden, MA: Blackwell.

Niezen, Ronald. 2003. *The Origins of Indigenism: Human Rights and the Politics of Identity*. Berkeley, CA: University of California Press.

_____. 2004. *A World beyond Difference: Cultural Identity in the Age of Globalization*. Malden, MA: Blackwell.

Palmer, Martin, with Victoria Finlay. 2003. *Faith in Conservation: New Approaches to Religion and the Environment*. Washington, DC: The World Bank.

Ramos, Alcida Rita. 1994. "The Hyperreal Indian." *Critique of Anthropology* 14:153–171.

_____. 1998. *Indigenism: Ethnic Politics in Brazil*. Madison: University of Wisconsin Press.

Redford, Kent H. 1990. "The Ecologically Noble Savage." *Orion Nature Quarterly* 9(3):25–29.

Tomlinson, John. 1999. *Globalization and Culture*. Chicago, IL: University of Chicago Press.

Tucker, Mary Evelyn and John Grim, eds. 2001. "Religion and Ecology: Can the Climate Change?" Special issue, *Daedalus* 130(4).

Tsing, Anna L. 2005. *Friction: An Ethnography of Global Connection*. Princeton, NJ: Princeton University Press.

Turner, Terence S. 1995. "An Indigenous People's Struggle for Socially Equitable and Environmentally Sustainable Production: The Kayapo Revolt against Extractivism." *Journal of Latin American Anthropology* 1(1):98–121.

Varese, Stefano. 1991. "Think Locally, Act Globally." NACLA Report on the Americas 15(3):13–17.

_____. 1996. "The New Environmentalist Movement of Latin American Indigenous People." In *Valuing Local Knowledge: Indigenous People and Intellectual Property Rights*, ed. Stephen B. Brush and Dorothy Stabinsky, 122–142. Washington, DC: Island Press.

Warren, Kay. 1998. *Indigenous Movements and Their Critics*. Princeton, NJ: Princeton University Press.

Wriston, Walter B. 1992. *Twilight of Sovereignty*. New York: Scribner's.

NOTES

An earlier version of this paper was presented at the Southern Anthropological Society meetings in Chattanooga, Tennessee, in March 2005, and will be published in the proceedings of those meetings. For support of research contributing to this article, I thank the Wenner-Gren Foundation for Anthropological Research, Vanderbilt University, and

Vanderbilt's Center for the Study of Religion and Culture. I am grateful to Betty Duggan, Steve Folmar, Max Kirsch, Mark Wollaeger, and David Wood for their generous readings and constructive comments.

7

DISORDERLY DEVELOPMENT
Globalization and the Idea of Culture in the Kalahari

Renee Sylvain

In postapartheid Namibia, the San (Bushmen) have been increasingly exposed to the effects of liberalizing trade markets, the global flows of capital and people associated with a booming tourism industry, and a massive proliferation of nongovernmental organization (NGO) activity.[1] Since Namibian independence from South African rule in 1990, the San have become engaged in rights-based activism as indigenous peoples. With the assistance of the Working Group of Indigenous Minorities in Southern Africa (WIMSA), San people throughout southern Africa now participate in international indigenous peoples' rights forums and are organizing as a vocal and sophisticated political community. The current integration of the San into the new global order introduces important opportunities for empowerment and "development," but is also fraught with contradictions and challenges inherent in local identity politics and global indigenous activism. One of the most puzzling features of postcolonial life for the San is that at the very moment they are beginning to travel the world, speak at international conferences, and keep in regular e-mail communication with interested parties overseas, primordialized and essentialized representations of primitive "Bushmen" are being vigorously reasserted in mainstream media and NGO rhetoric. These representations are often difficult to distinguish from colonial stereotypes.

In this article, I examine the environment for development that globalization is currently creating in the Kalahari and, more specifically, how globalization is influencing San struggles for rights, recognition, and resources. I first bring into focus one form of collusion between the processes of globalization and the indigenous peoples' movement that results in the promotion of a particular idea of culture—one that meshes uncomfortably with the idea of culture inherent in the anthropology of *separate development* in southern Africa. I then illustrate how this idea of culture is played out in the Omaheke Region of Namibia.

GLOBALIZATION AND CULTURE

The central problematic in most analyses of globalization is the relationship between global forces and responses at the local level. Specifically, scholars seek to address the apparent paradox between "the homogenizing tendencies which appear inherent to globalization" and the "continued or even intensified [cultural] heterogeneity" asserted on the local level (Meyer and Geschiere 1999, 1; see also Appadurai 2000). Many studies of the cultural aspects of globalization focus on how the content of global capitalist culture, global consumer culture, or global political culture influences the content of local cultures.

This focus on the interactions of global and local cultural content contributes to a picture that pits global homogenization against local resistance to it. With this view of globalization operating in the background, explanations of the ubiquity of ethnic assertions on the local level standardly resort to universalistic (and essentialist) assumptions about psychological needs. The uncertainty that globalization creates—the political, economic, and cultural shifts—results in ethnic movements that reflect "a search for fixed orientation points" (Meyer and Geschiere 1999, 2) or a search for "solid ground" (Hall 1997, 35–36); they are a means for people to "regain their bearings" (Wallerstein 1997, 104) or "fix the flow" (Meyer and Geschiere 1999, 7). Kloos, for example, explicitly resorts to speculative psychology when he claims that people's awareness of global forces beyond their control "results in feelings of insecurity and a quest for configurations people feel they can trust" (2000, 291).

These explanations, however, are unsatisfying for three reasons. First, such explanations are tautological: People fix ethnic boundaries because they feel the need to fix ethnic boundaries. Second, they tend to limit their characterization of local-level responses to parochial reactions against globalization—a mere circling of the wagons. Finally, this view also neglects the widespread phenomenon that Richard Falk describes as "globalization-from-below," which "consists in an array of transnational social forces [especially NGOs] … [dedicated to] the strengthening over time of the institutional forms and activities associated with global civil society" (1993, 39). One may be able to get around the apparent paradox between universalizing, homogenizing tendencies of globalization and the intensification of local, primordialized ethnic heterogeneity—and better understand why identity movements, particularly ethnic assertions, are such a common local response—if one asks what it is that is being globalized and homogenized. Stuart Hall addresses this question by claiming that globalization produces a "global mass culture" that entails a "homogenizing form of representation" (1997, 28). According to Hall, global mass culture recognizes and absorbs "differences within the larger, overarching framework of what is essentially an American conception of the world" (1997, 28). But one important component of a Western conception of the world is a Western idea of "culture." So I would put Hall's point differently and suggest that it is not, or not only, a U.S. or Western culture that is being globalized, but also a Western idea of what culture is—specifically, the idea that cultures are bounded, ahistorical "facts of nature." This is already implicit in Hall's claim that "forms of representation" are being homogenized; but we need to make explicit that among those forms of representation is a particular way of representing culture.

Rather than narrowly viewing identity politics as distress-driven attempts to impose order on an increasingly chaotic world, we should also consider the extent to which people on the ground are manipulating the idea of culture as a tool for securing political, economic, and development resources. The international indigenous peoples' movement is an important example of "globalization from below" (see also Appadurai 2000), and it is a good example of a global deployment of a particular Western idea of culture.

My picture at this point suggests that the proliferation of essentialist claims to identity is owed to a globalizing idea of culture that proves useful for generating income and securing recognition, particularly for indigenous peoples. The situation, however, is more complex. My case study shows how a globalized idea of culture, embodied in the identity expectations imposed by donor agencies and the tourism industry, converges with historical habits of racially based misrecognition operating within a context of local corruption and disorder. Ironically (but not paradoxically), this convergence both promotes essentialized and primordialized images of indigenous Bushmen and perpetuates their underclass status.

INDIGENOUS IDENTITIES IN SOUTHERN AFRICA

Indigenous peoples' activism arose largely in response to the disenfranchisement and dispossession that followed from development strategies dominated by megaprojects and imposed by states and multilateral agencies during a wave of developmentalism in the 1960s and 1970s (Bodley 1990; Wright 1988, 377). Establishing a basis for particular rights for indigenous peoples involves crafting a unique, locally grounded but globally recognizable indigenous identity, which would bear enough of a family resemblance to nationhood to be suitable for some form of self-determination. At the heart of indigeneity is an overt link between cultural, or "national," identity and a unique relationship with "the land" (see also Beckett 1996 and Muehlebach 2001). The idea of culture mobilized here is adapted from familiar nationalist rhetoric. As Niezen notes, indigenous identity developed within the institutional framework of successful nationalisms (2000, 121). But, Indigenous peoples come to represent the most natural of nations through what Liisa Malkki calls "sedentarist metaphysics," in which territorial—and familial—metaphors naturalize nations as discrete, territorially grounded and bounded entities (Malkki 1992, 32).[2] Alan Barnard evokes these naturalizing and territorializing metaphors in his description of (Khoi)San national identity: "Khoisan identity through 'blood' ... is only really meaningful as a sense of belonging conferred by the land" (1998, 54).[3]

Such territorial conceptions of national culture provide the basis for a "globalized aboriginality," which Maximilian Forte describes as "the embryonic creation of a worldwide indigenous macro-community seemingly with its own indigenous macro-culture" (1998). One need not doubt the utility of a concept of culture, or even that some groups see their identities as owing to a particular relationship to the land, to recognize that essentialist conceptions of national culture assume a discomfiting salience in postapartheid southern Africa, where conflated notions of culture and race have been politicized as natural, territorial national units more explicitly and consequentially than in most other areas of the world. The essentialized idea of culture mobilized by the global indigenous movement—particularly its "blood and soil" rhetoric and its perceived agenda of "ethnic separatism"—conjures up images of apartheid "homelands" (Muehlebach 2001, 439) and harks back to the Herderian Romanticism that so strongly influenced apartheid anthropology.[4]

One would be hard-pressed to find a more natural nation than the Bushmen, whose colonial designation explicitly signifies a land-linked, organic identity. The historical processes of Bushman iconography are too vast and complex to address here (but see Dubow 1995; Gordon and Douglas 2000; Guenther 1980; Wilmsen 1989). It is widely recognized, however, that the trope of the Bushmen as the ultimate African Ur-race figured prominently in the colonial formulation of a "civilized" white racial and national identity (see Gordon 1988, 43). Bushmen came to embody the original, primitive condition of humanity, generally, first as "brutal bandits" and later as "harmless people" or "noble savages" (see Guenther 1980). Mathias Guenther notes that "the motif of the noble Bushman ... consists of such themes as ecological sensitivity and responsibility, the innocent, the beauty, the humanness, and the harmony" (1980, 123).

Today, the San's activism as indigenous people is most positively received in public forums when they present themselves, in stereotypical terms, as Bushmen whose identity is organically linked to the land. For example, the South African ≠Khomani San won 65,000 hectares of land in and around the Kalahari Gemsbok National Park in March 1999, and as Steven Robbins notes, "Media representations of the San land claim comprised a series of stereotypical images of timeless and primordialist San 'tribes' reclaiming their ancestral land" (2001,833–834). Robbins also points out, however, that "the colonial stereotype of the pure and pristine bushman hunter gatherer" has also been "embraced 'from below'" (2001, 839). For example, Dawid Kruiper, the traditional leader of the ≠Khomani San community, has publicly promoted the image of primordial, hunting-and-gathering San by claiming that he is "an animal of nature" (White 1995, 19).

Although arguments have been made for the use of such "strategic essentialism" (see Lattas 1993), what is important here is that the San are not asserting ethnic or national identities in an effort to get their bearings, so much as they are mobilizing an idea of culture made available by globalization to secure resources and social, economic, and cultural rights. Rather than circling the wagons, the San are responding to identity expectations placed on them by the local mainstream society, the state, NGOs, and the international donor community, all of whom expect to find a bounded cultural entity to which rights can be attached and a discrete target group for development (see also Robbins 2001). Nevertheless, although the idea of culture may be a useful tool in the hands of some, it can also serve to obscure other groups of

San, whose living cultures and identities are, in the vernacular of globalization, of the hybrid variety.

TAMING THE "WILD" BUSHMEN

The Omaheke San, whose identity is owed to a confluence of race, class, and ethnic relations, is one such hybrid group. The San are the third largest ethnic group in the Omaheke Region (Central Statistics Office 1996, 19). The largest group is the Bantu-speaking Herero, who raise cattle in the former reserves—homelands, now known as the communal farming areas. Nama-Damaras are the second largest group, and they, along with the San, constitute the largest proportion of farmworkers in the region. A small minority of Bantu-speaking Tswanas raise cattle in the communal areas in the south of the Omaheke. The German and Afrikaner descendents of white settlers constitute only 8 percent of the population, but own 65 percent of the land in the Omaheke, where they operate approximately 900 cattle ranches in what is known as the "commercial farming block" (Suzman 1995, 4).

The 6,500 San in the Omaheke belong to three main language groups: Ju/'hoansi are found in the central and northeastern parts of the region; Nharo-speakers are concentrated in the east, along the Botswana border; and !Xûn-speakers live primarily in the south. These groups of San are not self-contained; because they are highly mobile, a great deal of intermarriage has occurred, not only among Ju/'hoansi, Nharo, and !Xûn, but also between these groups and Nama-Damaras. Ethnicity is often reckoned opportunistically, depending on employment opportunities and the proximity of kin who can provide support and assistance during periods of economic distress.

The class system in the Omaheke was shaped by deeply essentialist notions of bounded and territorially grounded cultural entities. Stereotypes of "feral" foragers—and the definition of the Bushmen as an ethnic group—did not, however, result from a straightforward imposition of colonial ideologies onto passively subaltern San (contra Gordon and Douglas 2000; Suzman 2000; and Wilmsen 1989). Rather, these stereotypes emerged out of struggles over land, labor, and political position as white settlers attempted to secure a livelihood in the Omaheke.

Large-scale white settlement began in the region in the 1920s, as poor whites moved in from South Africa and, especially, after a substantial number of Afrikaners from Angola were resettled in the Omaheke in 1928 and 1929 (van Rooyen and Reiner 1995:40).[5] Most new arrivals were poor bywoners (tenants) and were highly dependent on the colonial administration for subsidies and infrastructural inputs. The settlers required two things to establish viable farming ventures: land and cheap labor. Both were supplied by the dispossession of local Africans. Hereros and Tswanas were relegated to overcrowded reserves (later, ethnic homelands), whereas the San and Namas were eventually completely encapsulated as white farms overtook their traditional territories.

The San did not simply acquiesce to land dispossession. They retaliated by stealing and mutilating the intruders' livestock. Many farmers saw this behavior as evidence of the innate wildness of the Bushmen: Being beyond the bounds of civilization, Bushmen were unable to distinguish between game and domesticated animals, and so were seen as hunting the farmers' cattle out of ignorance. Other farmers interpreted the mutilation of their livestock as evidence of the innate cruelty and depravity of "brutal Bushman bandits" (see also Suzman 2000, 32–33). Although white settlers were concerned with protecting their livestock from "Bushman depredations," calls for tougher measures to deal with "the Bushman problem" were also demands to have recalcitrant natives pressed into service on the farms. Furthermore, efforts to pacify the Bushmen and acquire cheap labor were at the same time attempts by white settlers to assert greater political influence. For example, a 1923 letter to the newspaper *Swakopmund Zeitung* from farmers in Grootfontein (just north of the Omaheke) asked:

> Why is it not possible to enact a law empowering the Magistrate—or better still forcing him—to send idle natives or those who have offended against the laws requiring passes to some farm for a definite period where they would have the opportunity of getting used to hard work? Unfortunately nothing can be looked for in this respect so long as we have the infamous "One Man Government" and have no say ourselves. (National Archives of Namibia 1923)

White farmers and colonial administrators were not always likeminded when it came to defining the Bushman problem. In 1927, the native commissioner responded to complaints of stock theft in the following way: "As is well known, the Bushman by instinct is not a thief but changed circumstances are driving him to slaughter cattle when game and 'veldkos' [bush food] are not available" (National Archives of Namibia 1927). The existence of a few sympathetic explanations of San behavior reflects the divergent class interests and ethnic–national backgrounds that divided the white community. Whereas a few administrators—many of whom were British South Africans enjoying a more privileged social position—could afford to assume a benignly paternalistic stance toward the San, impoverished Afrikaners were struggling to secure a livelihood and gain a political voice.

Although land expropriation secured cheap labor by undermining traditional subsistence patterns, it failed to ensure a stable labor force, especially in the case of the San. Initially, San only selectively participated in the white economy, working on the farms during the dry season when veld food was scarce and returning to the veld to forage when the rains came. This dual subsistence strategy was a response to inadequate subsistence resources both on the farms, where workers were inadequately remunerated, and off the farms, where the diminishing and increasingly denuded veld was unable to sustain full-time foraging. Many in the white community, however, consistently interpreted the San's dual subsistence strategy as evidence of an innately feral nature. For example, in 1939, the magistrate of Grootfontein expressed an attitude that many white farmers hold today: "[The Bushman] is independable [sic] as, after the rains have fallen, he often cannot resist the call of the wilds and simply deserts from his master's service. For this reason farmers prefer more reliable native labour, although at a considerably higher wage" (National Archives of Namibia 1939).

By the 1930s, farmers were becoming increasingly aggressive in their attempts to bind San workers to the farms year-round. One method was to recruit San children for apprenticeships (often a euphemism for slavery in southern Africa [see Morton 1994]), which not only provided cheap and steady labor, but also ensured the "good behavior" of nearby "wild" Bushmen. Such coercive tactics were rationalized by an elaborate system of stereotypes centered on the distinction between *wild* and *tame* Bushmen. Initially, coercive forms of labor recruitment were justified on the grounds that taming the Bushmen required exposing them to the civilizing effects of hard work. After white settlement had reached its peak in the 1950s and the San were completely encapsulated within the white political economy, more nostalgic sensibilities prevailed: Exposing the Bushmen to civilization threatened to bring about the disappearance of these "children of nature." The discordant vocabulary that developed during the process of class formation served to rationalize the widespread exploitation and marginalization of the San.

THE OMAHEKE SAN TODAY

Today, the San in the Omaheke exist at the bottom of the local ethnic labor hierarchy as third- and fourth-generation farm laborers and domestic servants. On white farms, they are the first to be laid off when drought hits or when market conditions deteriorate; they face the greatest difficulties securing employment because white farmers generally prefer to hire non-San workers; and they are paid on average less than half the wages of non-San workers.[6] Remuneration for farm-work consists of a balance between monthly wages and weekly rations. The wages and rations are usually inadequate to support an entire household, and so the San are compelled to purchase food from the farmer on credit, leaving many San families tied to the farms through a system of debt bondage.

About one-third of the Omaheke San work on Herero or Tswana cattle posts in the communal areas. San men tend livestock and San women cook and do laundry. They receive some food or only home-made beer for their labor. San children, usually girls, are recruited by Hereros and "adopted" as servile household members.

After independence, jobs on white farms became scarce as farmers adapted to liberalizing markets, new labor legislation, and drought by retrenching large numbers of San workers. Life on Herero or Tswana cattle posts, however, is often one of extreme poverty and eventual alco-holism, and is therefore unattractive to many San. Thus, many San are on the road in a perpetual search for employment, traveling from farm to farm where they have friends or family who can provide food and shelter while they ask local farmers for jobs. These job hunters often must squat illegally because farmers discourage visitors. Many prefer to stay with friends or kin in the squatters' villages along the edges of urban centers and in government resettlement camps, which were established to resettle indigent people shortly after independence. The majority of the more permanent resettlement camp residents are San, many of them too old or too sick to work on the farms. In the camps, the San have access to sporadic supplies of drought-relief food, water, housing, small plots of land for kitchen gardens, and grazing land for those who have livestock. The major source of personal income is old-age pensions. Those not old enough to collect pensions gather cam-elthorn seeds and truffles (tsotso) to sell to local farmers or sign on for piecework when farmers come into the camps to fill their pickup trucks with seasonal, casual laborers. A few San men tend livestock for absentee Herero, Tswana, or Nama-Damara stock owners in return for milk and a small wage. Very often, however, the wages offered are never paid or are only paid after intervals of several months, during which time the San must get by without money. San women are able to get extra food by tending the gardens and doing the laundry of non-San camp residents. Given the alternatives—camp life or the cattle posts—most San prefer more steady work on white farms, where historically entrenched stereotypes continue to sustain their underclass status.

Today, white farmers frequently report that San workers will disappear without giving notice, only to return months or years later asking for their old jobs. The explanation usually given by the farmers is that Bushmen are incorrigibly—perhaps even innately—nomadic. Whereas farmers explain the San's "unreliability" in terms of their innate ethnic character, the San themselves provide class-based explanations for their disappearances. One former San farmworker explained the situation to me this way:

> It's about money. If you are on a farm and they [the farmers] are not very good and don't give enough money, then you have to go to another farm. If that farmer is not very good, he gives enough money, but the rations are not very good, then you leave for a different farm. If there is enough food and money, but he is cruel, then you leave and go to another farm.

Other justifications for lower pay continue to be underwritten by reference to "traditional" Bushman culture. Farmers claim that, just as San ancestors gorged themselves after a kill and then went hungry for long periods before the next successful hunt, the contemporary San spend all of their wages on payday, with no thought of saving for the days ahead. Many farmers are still unable to see the San in terms of their class position, and so they often miss an important part of how the San see themselves.

Many San I spoke to differentiated themselves from non-San—and especially white farmers—on the basis of moral behavior. San widely consider "stinginess" the most iniquitous vice (see Lee 1993) and often attribute it to white farmers and other non-San employers. By contrast, the San insist on high standards of generosity among themselves—and this expectation contributes to San self-definition as a community. The widely scattered farm San maintain community ties through elaborate networks of kinship and mutual support. Widespread visiting, child fostering, and generalized reciprocity sustain a dynamic moral community. San struggling with unemployment or cash shortages can count on kin and friends to supply food, money, and shelter as they are able, and few San, whether kin or not, are denied such assistance (which explains why the San are "unable to save money"). Generosity is a highly valued personality trait, not just because it is culturally prescribed, but also because it enables the San to cope with the hardship of their underclass condition. Their coherence as a community—the dynamics of cooperative conflicts that characterize their own forms of sociality—are shaped by the ways in which they are compelled to engage with others as Bushmen in their efforts to cope with their material conditions.[7]

Despite the existence of the class-shaped and dynamic cultural life of the Omaheke San, the general conviction that Bushman culture and character are innate was expressed by a phrase repeated to me by a number of Omaheke farmers: "You can take the Bushman out of the bush, but you can't take the bush out of the Bushman!" (see also Suzman 2000). Farmers with more romantic and nostalgic sensibilities lament that there are no "real" Bushmen in the Omaheke anymore—because the Omaheke San no longer hunt and gather, they are no longer "wild" and "authentic" Bushmen, but only detribalized workers dressed in tattered Western clothing. Thus, the Omaheke San must negotiate a complex and contradictory terrain at the intersection of class and cultural identity politics: Whereas their definition as Bushmen consists of a number of stereotypes that justify their exploitation as an underclass, their status as an underclass also disqualifies them from counting as "real" Bushmen.

The formation of the idea of the Bushmen was as disorderly and discordant as the process that turned various groups of San into an ethnic underclass. This process was characterized by hegemonic struggles within the white community; by genuine, if ideologically driven, misinterpretations of San strategies of resistance and survival; and by opportunistic stereotyping that continues to justify their exploitation. Although the nature of uncertainty and disorder has changed in the Omaheke since independence, the modes of ethnic differentiation and class exploitation developed during the colonial encounter are sustained and intensified.

DISORDER, CORRUPTION, AND CLASS CONSCIOUSNESS

The argument that assertions of primordial ethnic identities are defensive responses to forces of globalization suggests too tidy a picture. As the case of the Omaheke San demonstrates, identity is formed and negotiated in contexts of power asymmetries. An analysis of the politics of identity will need to include a consideration of local power struggles—unfolding in contexts of chaos, corruption, and class exploitation—and the role they play in promoting primordial expressions of identity.

Africanists have recently turned their attention to two trends associated with globalization and the decline of the state: on the one hand, the suggestion of democratization, associated with the increasingly important role that NGOs are assuming as agents of civil society; on the other hand, the escalation of disorder and conflict.[8] Patrick

Chabal and Jean-Pierre Daloz suggest that these trends derive from the "instrumentalization of political disorder," which is a "process by which political actors ... seek to maximize their returns on the state of confusion, uncertainty and sometimes even chaos" (1999, xviii). As I show in the following discussion, the "instrumentalization of political disorder" contributes to both the promotion of an essentialized definition of Bushmen identity and the exploitation of the San as an underclass.

In the Omaheke, liberalizing trade markets, contracting economies, and the decline of state resources have shifted the responsibility for economic and social advancement onto NGOs and private entrepreneurial ventures. Postcolonial Namibia, however, has also witnessed a general deterioration of human rights standards and an alarming increase in corruption (see Bauer 2001). This situation, combined with an explosion of uncoordinated NGO activities, has created new opportunities for the exploitation of the Omaheke San and for the exploitation of their popular image as pristine Bushmen.

When I first arrived in the Omaheke region in 1996, I met /In!gou, shortly after his cattle had been stolen by a group of local Hereros. As is common practice in the Omaheke, /In!gou was required to track the cattle thieves, locate his stolen cattle, and then report to the local police (who are also Herero). /In!gou located his cattle and went to the police with the names of the men who had stolen them. A few weeks later, /In!gou made the day-long journey to the police station to inquire about the status of his case. He was told his cattle had been recovered and that charges were pending; to get his cattle back, he need only sign the document the police put in front of him. /In!gou informed them that he could not read English, so the police explained that the document outlined the details of the case. He signed the document and returned to his home in a nearby resettlement camp. A few weeks later, he returned to the police station to inquire, again, about his stolen cattle. He was then told that he had already signed a document stating that his cattle had been returned and that he had dropped the charges.

While /In!gou was struggling to recover his cattle, the San people in the resettlement camp in which he lived were dealing with an even larger problem. The camp manager—who had gained her position through her connections with the ruling South-West African Peoples Organization—was withholding the monthly supplies of government drought-relief food. She gave some rations to San people who agreed to work for her. For instance, Gase, an elderly man with one leg, cut the grass in the area surrounding the manager's house, crawling on his belly with a pair of sheep shears, in return for mielie meal, a tin of fish, and some cooking oil. The San who worked for the camp manager received only a small portion of the drought-relief food; the rest the manager fed to her pigs.

Overt corruption is not always necessary to create conditions in which the San are vulnerable to exploitation—general disorder and ambiguity are often sufficient. For example, since my first visit in 1996, the number of areas set aside for indigent people in the Omaheke has grown from two resettlement camps (Skoonheid and Drimiopsis) to an indeterminate number. By June 2001, nobody was clear about how many such areas existed or which areas inhabited by indigent people counted as resettlement camps, government farms, squatters' areas, or simply well-populated cattle posts on abandoned farms. Most San refer to these ambiguous areas as reserves, falling back on the colonial term for land designated for nonwhites; most non-San refer to them as resettlement camps, even if their official status is not known. The distinction is important because resettlement camps fall under the jurisdiction of the Ministry of Land, Resettlement, and Rehabilitation, which is accountable for management practices and utilization of resources in the camps. Within the political and administrative vacuum in these areas, non-San designate any settlement area a resettlement camp, assume positions of power, and control the distribution of resources.

When I first visited one of these informally proclaimed resettlement camps near the border of Botswana, I was advised by the San residents to present myself to a Damara man who was described as the manager and ask him for permission to visit. When I enquired about the official status of the camp, the manager replied, "Well, I guess I could call this a resettlement camp." I later learned, from other San informants, that several other Damaras also claimed to be the camp manager. These various "managers" were not in competition with each other, but all claimed official power over the San in the camp. A number of Damara residents also formed a water committee, took control of the borehole, and charged the San N$10 per month for water. The San were not convinced that the water committee was legitimately empowered to impose these fees, but they were coerced into paying for water after Damaras placed guards at the communal borehole. Few San could afford to pay for the water, and so they were forced to sell their livestock and to seek work on nearby commercial farms or work for their Damara neighbors in return for food and a small wage.

Taking control of land and water, by assuming positions of power in unregulated areas off the farms, is one common method non-San use to keep the San in servitude. One enterprising group of Mbanderus (an ethnic group linguistically related to Hereros) found a more novel way to profit from the San's identity and labor by manipulating newly opened channels of development funding. In 1993, a group of Mbanderus in the northern Omaheke secured funding from the aid organization Terre des Hommes for what was ostensibly a San development project. They received development inputs, such as breeding cattle and infrastructural equipment, and relocated fifty San people onto a newly designated farm project. While the San labored on the new farm, the Mbanderus made all the decisions; they also limited San presence on the farm to three years (just long enough for the San to build the fences and drill the boreholes). In effect, the Mbanderu were simply building a new farm, financed by Terre des Hommes, and using unpaid San labor. The San Bushmen's image made them an attractive target for donor money, and their underclass status made them easily exploitable labor.

Experiences of corruption and exploitation convinced many San of the need for a San leader in the Omaheke. With the assistance of WIMSA, two chiefs-designate were elected by the San, who live in communities off the farms, and both now regularly attend leadership training workshops initiated by WIMSA. Of course, a leader must have a community to lead, and so WIMSA's activities are contributing to the formation of a self-consciously cultural community—locally referred to as a *nasie*, or a *nation*—among the widely scattered farm San. The formation of a self-conscious and increasingly politicized pan-San cultural community in the Omaheke, however, is not entirely a result of efforts to defend culture; it is also a result of the widely recognized need to address the twin problems of exploitation and corruption that keep the San in conditions of servitude and poverty.

MOVING TARGETS

Corruption and confusion are not the only factors that contribute to development difficulties in the Omaheke. The majority of San in the region are farmworkers who do not live on land they own or to which they have de facto rights. Also, as I have shown, the San's extreme economic vulnerability means that many are compelled to move almost constantly in search of employment. Those San who are able to maintain steady employment on a farm are isolated and largely inaccessible. Thus, the Omaheke San do not constitute a sedentary, fixed, and territorially contained community. Nevertheless, much mainstream development theory and practice is dominated by Malkki's "sedentarist metaphysics," and the combination of conventional development wisdom and indigenist agendas of ethnodevelopment encourage the

San to reinvent themselves as a culturally homogeneous, bounded, and territorially grounded ethnic community. The incongruity, however, between popular conceptions of indigeneity and the daily realities the Omaheke San must deal with creates problems for putting development models into practice.

The need to address the problems faced by the San, as a group stigmatized and exploited on the basis of their identity, suggests an approach to development that emphasizes empowerment along ethnic and cultural lines. Any development or advocacy work that addresses San issues will therefore also inevitably contribute to the creation of an identifiable and manageable San constituency (see also Garland 1999 and Robbins 2001). As Robbins notes, the "strong interest of international donors in the 'cultural survival' of vanishing cultures and languages" (2001, 849) contributes to the pressure put on indigenous communities to be recognizably indigenous, according to the terms of global indigenist discourse. As a result, the Omaheke San are, ironically, encouraged to conform to the very picture of pristine Bushmen that continues to justify their exploitation as an underclass.

These pressures also cause some difficulties for local NGOs, which must struggle with the contradictions inherent in their role as advocates for the San: On the one hand, they are committed to promoting the San's human rights, which involves challenging the stereotypes that denigrate and dehumanize them; on the other hand, securing funding and promoting cultural survival means that they are compelled to strategically adopt the very stereotypes they challenge. These difficulties become even greater when mainstream development wisdom and global indigenist agendas confront the untidy realities of San life on the ground. For although that culture brokering is inevitable and even necessary, the primacy placed on culturalist conceptions of indigenous identities and issues has important consequences for the definition of target groups in the NGO community and also for what development entails. The Omaheke San, as an underclass of indigenous people, therefore present important challenges to both third world development paradigms and to fourth world models of ethnodevelopment.

In 1998, WIMSA facilitated the establishment of the Omaheke San Trust (OST), an NGO concerned exclusively with the San people in the Omaheke. The OST and WIMSA have been instrumental in the establishment of culturally appropriate educational programs, building traditional leadership structures, and supplying development inputs for a range of projects. The aims and activities of the OST are commendable, but its strategies also reveal the implications of an almost exclusive emphasis on the cultural aspects of ethnodevelopment.

In its first report, the OST notes, "the San work as farm laborers for commercial farmers and wealthy communal farmers who often pay them the lowest wage" (Moore with Omaheke San Trust Board of Trustees 2000, 3). Yet the description of its target group reads as follows: "The majority of the population of the Omaheke lives on communal land or resettlement farms and it is in these areas that the San communities eke out a living" (Moore with Omaheke San Trust Board of Trustees 2000, 3). The OST recognizes twenty-six such communities: twenty-five are clusters of San people living in small pockets off the farms, many of them in conditions of servitude with non-San neighbors in resettlement camps. The remaining community—more than two-thirds of San residents in the Omaheke—consists of farmworkers and domestic servants scattered widely throughout the commercial farms and cattle posts in the communal areas. Each community is entitled to elect two representatives to attend OST meetings, vote, and exercise membership rights on behalf of their community (Omaheke San Trust 1999, 4). The result is that a minority of San who live off the farms have fifty representatives, whereas the majority of farm-dwelling San have two.[9] Many of the San in the twenty-five communities off the farms only live there part-time, compounding this representational imbalance. Many leave to look for employment when food runs out and return when government drought relief appears. The OST's definition of *community* remains true to both third world and fourth world development models, insofar as both assume sedentarism and territorial boundedness. Labor relations are largely beyond the scope of the OST's mandate, and so the majority of the Omaheke San remain invisible to the one NGO in the region that explicitly targets San people.

Although there are practical constraints to addressing class issues in the Omaheke—namely, the difficulties associated with accessing San living on the private property of farmers—class exploitation is also a common feature of San life off the farms, and so one could fairly say that ideological reasons exist for marginalizing class in the OST's mandate. Whereas indigenous discourse has politicized culture to great strategic advantage, class has become depoliticized, and to be recognized as indigenous people, the San are compelled to present themselves as largely uncorrupted by historical and political–economic contexts. As I have already suggested, one important component of this essentializing move has been to insist on a special relationship to the land. Thus, one finds that struggles over land rights are often couched in terms of retaining or regaining a traditional (primordial) cultural identity.[10] But, in the Omaheke, San calls for land also reflect

their self-consciousness as an underclass. ≠Oma described the problems of the Omaheke San this way:

> You must improve things or resettle. If you resettle then they
> [Damaras and Hereros] will steal your things. The government
> says we must develop things here, like a garden. But if you do it
> the other people will just destroy it. We should get a place of our
> own so that we know what we can do with it, so that the gov-
> ernment can work directly with the San.

N≠isa, a middle-aged San woman living in one of the communities
near the Botswana border, described the situation this way: "When we
stay together with the Damara people we are not free. When will we
get our freedom? That is the most difficult thing. Like now, we must
pay for the water. Where will we get the money? Now, we are asking
ourselves, 'Where will we have a place to stay?'" N≠isa is a respected
traditional healer, and on the same day she said these things to me, she
and other women from her community dressed themselves heavily in
beadwork and animal skins to perform what they described as a "traditional dance." But it is still class-consciousness that shines through
in her complaints. Whereas indigenist discourse emphasizes the relationship between indigenous peoples and the land, the Omaheke San
emphasize the relationship between themselves, the land, and non-San
peoples with whom they are in unequal relationships.

NGO networks in the Omaheke are quite new, and so NGO activity is still relatively chaotic and uncoordinated. Many of the directors
of local NGOs do not know each other, and they have no idea how
many or even which NGOs are working in the region. The San themselves are unfamiliar with NGOs and are not clear on the distinctions
among development projects, government or church-funded food-for-
work programs, drought-relief programs, and temporary employment
opportunities. All of these efforts are broadly described by the San as
"projects."[11] The San are, thus, vulnerable to exploitation as local Hereros, Tswanas, and Damaras approach unemployed San to initiate
what they describe as income-generating "projects." One fairly typical
such project used San women at a remote community to knit sweaters;
Herero women dropped off large quantities of wool, returned after a
couple of months to collect the sweaters, and sold them in town. The
San women were never paid. Other so-called projects—which draw
explicitly on the San's cultural image—enlist the San to perform their
traditional dances at local political events and tourism venues.

ETHNIC ENTREPRENEURS AND ETHNOTOURISM

The globalized idea of culture—specifically, the notion of a primordial indigenous culture—is also reinforced in a context of local disorder, in which identity-based entrepreneurial ventures, both formal and informal, take on development functions. Koba described how a Damara woman approached her and five other San women and offered them money to perform in various venues:

> The first dance we did was in Gobabis.... Then we went to dance at Buitepos [on the border of Botswana] when the [trans-Kalahari] road was opened.... The work was not good for me. If you dance there, you are not wearing any clothes. We are wearing the !gu, like we were wearing in the old time. [But] we didn't get any money [and no food].

//Aese, who lives on a cattle post in a communal area 250 kilometers (about 155 miles) south of Koba's camp, told me about his community's experiences performing for tourists at the behest of Hereros:

> They were there, the people from other countries.... The Hereros came and picked up the San people to dance—they said it was a concert. My son was also a performer. But he didn't get money in his hands. All the money goes to the Hereros—the money that comes from other hands [i.e., from the tourists].

In a village settlement approximately 200 kilometers (124 miles) northeast of Koba's camp, Tchi!o, a middle-aged San woman, described how a group of Hereros offered the women in her village an opportunity to earn money by performing at a cultural festival:

> The Hereros came and took us from here. When we got [to the town], they took off our clothes in front of many people. And they put a !gae [a leather apron] on us and they took off our doeks [head scarves] and tied them between our breasts. And our breasts were out. Hereros made us like that so that we could go and dance for them. They said, "You must come and play. You will be paid, and you will also get some food. Come and eat. You are suffering a lot." ... The women said, "Let's go and get food and money!" That's why all of us stood up and went— we were hungry. When we came back home, they gave us a small packet of tea and sugar and soup ... [but] no money! They

wasted us. They made us dance, and made us naked, and they left us with nothing.

In Tchi!o's story, the Hereros transformed their San recruits according to a familiar conception of what pristine primitives should be—naked dancers. The San who were recruited, most of whom were unemployed former farmworkers and domestic servants, clearly saw these ventures as income-earning opportunities, not as opportunities for cultural assertion.

Informal ethnic entrepreneurial activities represent an extreme form of cultural exploitation. The same dynamics, however, are often reproduced in formal-sector cultural marketing because the conditions for "acceptable" expressions of identity and the conditions sustaining class inequalities are often the same. The IMF now considers tourism a viable export strategy for debt-ridden countries, and industry members and states promote tourism as a means for achieving sustainable development (World Travel and Tourism Council 2001). Tourism is also one of the fastest growing industries in Namibia, with a projected growth rate of 10 percent per year (United Nations 1999).[12] Tourism is also one of the least-regulated industries in the world, and the Namibian farming sector—in which most commercialized ethnotourism ventures are initiated—is itself characterized by a lack of regulation, especially with respect to the enforcement of labor laws.

Many white farmers, feeling the pinch of liberalized trade markets and decreased government subsidies, have begun to diversify into the tourism sector, using the Bushmen to draw tourists to their newly established guest farms. A visitor to the Omaheke region can now find brochures marketing Bushmen as tourist attractions. For example, the brochure for San World invites tourists to "meet the last survivors of an ancient society ... living in close harmony with nature" and to "come and explore the secrets of the Bushmen." San World is a guest lodge owned and run by a local white farmer and had been, prior to 2001, a cattle ranch where San worked as farm laborers.

A recent brochure for Bona Safaris, a tour company based in Gobabis, provides the following description of the Omaheke San for potential customers:

Amid these desolate expanses [of the pristine Kalahari] the Bushman clans have wandered for thousands of years.... This race of people is ancient—as shown in their ability to store fat reserves in their buttocks, to be used when food is scarce. Bushmen live on game and wild fruit. They are still mainly hunters and gatherers.... They are unable to comprehend what happens beyond their world.

According to the itinerary, tourists will visit, not the pristine Kalahari, but a lion farm, a leopard farm, and an ostrich farm. This tour is careful to perpetuate a mythical image of the hunting-and-gathering Bushman, and this requires that the real San in the Omaheke—the farmworkers and domestic servants—remain invisible.

Unfortunately, the working conditions on many of the guest farms differ little from those on the cattle ranches. San I spoke to complained that they were not getting paid, their rations were inadequate, and the farmers kept the money that the tourists offered to the San roleplayers. Oba, an elderly man from /In!gou's resettlement camp, was recruited by the owners of the lion farm promoted by Bona Safaris. At the farm, they replaced his tattered clothing with a loincloth and put him to work showing tourists how to track animals and make arrows. He described his experience on the guest farm in the following way:

> I bought food [from the farmer] with the money I received from the government—my pension. I received nothing from [the farmer].... When [the tourists] came to see me, they were only interested in my weapons like my spear, the hunting equipment that I made; [we danced for them], but they gave me nothing ... they took pictures, but they gave us nothing.... When I refused to give [the farmer] my pension money, he stopped giving us food.

Oba worked on the guest farm for less than a year before returning to the resettlement camp, where at least he could get drought-relief food each month. By this time, the camp manager had ceased feeding drought-relief food to her pigs, so conditions in the camp had improved enough for Oba to believe that life there would be better than on the lion farm.

Other ventures capitalize on the recent trend toward ecologically and politically responsible tourism. In August 1998, members of the !Xûn community—a group of unemployed farmworkers in the southern Omaheke region—entered into a joint tourism venture with Intu Afrika Lodge (located outside of the Omaheke region). With the assistance of WIMSA, a contract was drawn up to ensure appropriate housing and remuneration for the San, and to secure a share in the returns from the venture (Working Group of Indigenous Minorities in South Africa 1998, 40). The lodge promotes itself to tourists by claiming, the Intu Afrika corporation has developed a project that it believes will provide a blueprint for the successful implementation of development projects with the Bushmen and other indigenous minority peoples... . The objective of the Intu Afrika Bushman project is to empower the community in order to regain their dignity and pride. This has been done by creating employment opportunities and giving the Bushmen scope to practice cultural activities that utilize traditional Bushman skills in order to generate income for the community. (Intu Afrika Game Lodge n.d.)

The only identity given scope for expression, however, is the one that is marketable; that is, the traditional foraging identity as it is defined largely by stereotypes feeding the demand for this kind of ethnotourism. The manager of Intu Afrika Lodge even contributed his own idea of authentic Bushmen behavior and required the men to rub the blood from a recent kill onto their legs while tourists watched.[13]

Problems plagued Intu Afrika almost as soon as it was opened. Before the lodge owner recruited the Omaheke !Xûn, he had tried to import Bushmen from the Schmidtsdrift army base in South Africa. These San had been relocated to Schmidtsdrift from the Caprivi strip in northern Namibia, where they had been recruited by the South African Defence Force to fight in covert operations units during Namibia's liberation struggle.[14] The lodge owner had inadvertently hired a motley crew of excombatants. Even worse, they were not the Bushmen of popular imagination, but the tall, dark Kxoe "river Bushmen." The irate lodge owner eventually sent the Kxoe back to Schmidtsdrfit because "they were not short and yellow" but were merely "ordinary folk" who "wore trousers, shirts and dresses" and "did not appreciate having to sport animal skins;" some drank too much and "refused to behave like 'genuine bushmen'" (*Mail and Guardian* 1995).

The lodge owner's concern to have "real" Bushmen working at his lodge was only in part a product of apartheid stereotypes: Market demand also imposes an authenticity imperative on such ventures. For example, shortly after the South African ≠Khomani San signed a historic land deal in 1999, the *Cape Times* uncovered the "Great Bushman Tourism Scam" (Robbins 2001, 839). According to the *Cape Times* exposé, "fake bushmen" were being marketed at the world-famous Bushman village at Kagga Kamma—the lodge's bogus Bushmen were at worst actually Coloured people and at best not "one hundred percent pure Bushmen" (Robbins 2001, 839).[15]

This was not the first time Kagga Kamma had been accused of marketing inauthentic Bushmen. In October 1997, an article entitled "The Search for Authenticity," published in the *Nation*, complained that the Bushmen at Kagga Kamma were wearing "Mets baseball caps and Nikes," and so were obviously not the "real thing." The author eventually found "real" Bushmen in Namibia:

> My search for authentic Bushmen finally took me to the northern extremity of the Kalahari Desert.... . I had hoped to make some contact with "the wild Bushmen in all of us"—the free spirit that once resided in all men and that all men still hanker for; the way we were, uncomplicated, uncluttered, at peace. I'd been told that the Ju/'wasi Bushmen in this desolate outpost were as close as I would get, and this turned out to be true.... . Any doubts I had about their authenticity were obliterated the day I went hunting with the village elder, a wiry man in his late 60s named Old Kaece.... . They say a true Bushman twangs with the bush and watching Old Kaece sniffing and twitching and sensing everything around him ... it was as if he was a part of the natural world himself. (Boynton 1997, 19.)

Complaints from those on the consumer side of the tourism industry (including journalists) consistently cite the failure of real San to conform to idealized images of "Bushman Noble Savages." The expectation of an organic link between the Bushmen and the land or nature—already imposed by donor behavior in the development industry—is now reinforced by market demand. Where Bushmen ethnotourism ventures—whether in the formal or informal sectors—are in the hands of non-San, the same disturbing pattern recurs. The very people who help to sustain the myth that the Omaheke San remain pristine foragers, in need of nothing but game and wild fruits, are the first to believe that myth when payday comes.

The San are themselves quite critical of others marketing their identity. One San man told me, "At the lodges—the places of the white people—they are just busy making money for themselves." A San woman I spoke to exclaimed, "Everybody likes to steal our traditions!" At the same time, the San recognize tourism as an opportunity to both make money and express cultural pride. The same woman who spoke out against tradition theft told me that she is hopeful that she and other San living at a small cattle post in the southern Omaheke will be successful in their own tourism scheme because "our culture is very good to us ... it is beautiful." When I asked Koba, the San woman who had been recruited by Damaras to perform traditional dances, if she was still interested in identity work, she said, "Yes, so that our traditions don't die out." Kxao Moses ≠Oma and Axel Thoma argue that ethnotourism can revitalize traditional culture, and that "the recent introduction of tourism-based undertakings among San communities has made the San aware that their culture is a valuable social and economic asset" (2002, 40).

Involvement with WIMSA and the OST has already produced a visible impact on the ways the San choose to present themselves to outsiders. During my fieldwork in 1996 and 1997—before WIMSA and the OST were operating in the Omaheke—when the San I visited learned that I had a camera, they often asked to be photographed. To prepare themselves, San living on the farms put on the best clothes they could borrow and posed with their most prized possessions—usually with radios or, if one was available, with a bicycle. Those who had no such symbols of affluence often asked to be photographed standing in front of, or leaning against, my truck. But now, in the communities in which the OST is active and development work has begun, an opportunity to be photographed sends the San residents to dress up in beadwork and animal skins. However inextricably class and culture are interwoven in the lives of the Omaheke San, their images are easily separated for the camera. For all that, the displays of the San in beadwork and animal skins were genuine expressions of cultural pride.

CONCLUSION

I suggested at the outset that one part of the explanation for intensified ethnic and cultural assertions in the face of globalization relates to the globalization of an increasingly essentialized idea of what culture is, and therefore ethnic and cultural assertion is often an expression of globalization rather than a reaction against it. In the confusion that follows in the wake of globalization, the idea of culture becomes an instrument in the struggle for resources and, in the processes by which it is instrumentalized, culture is also essentialized. The international indigenous peoples' movement, as a form of globalization from below, adds another layer of essentialism to the idea of culture by using it to provide a crucial part of the contrast between indigenous peoples and impoverished "ordinary folk." Predicating the survival or resurgence of an indigenous identity on a unique relationship to the land—itself an essentializing move—has proven a strategically useful tool in the struggle for resources. Furthermore, discrete and bounded communities make easy targets for donors and for ethnodevelopment projects.

Finally, a booming global industry in ethnotourism, which requires that indigenous culture be a suitable subject for photography, contributes a glossy finish to how a pristine culture looks in the global marketplace. The Omaheke San illustrate the consequences of these instrumentalizing and essentializing trends. When the idea of culture becomes instrumentalized in the struggle for resources, then in situations of extreme marginalization and class inequality, it easily becomes another instrument for continued exploitation. And, as the idea of culture becomes essentialized, the San's own distinctive but class-shaped culture—the lived patterns of practices and beliefs that make up their moral identity—goes unnoticed.

REFERENCES

Appadurai, Arjun. 2000[1990]. "Disjuncture and Difference in the Global Cultural Economy." In *The Globalization Reader*, ed. Frank Lechner and John Boli, 322–330. Malden, MA: Blackwell.

Barnard, Alan. 1998. "Problems in the Construction of Khoisan Ethnicities." In *Proceedings of the Khoisan Identities and Cultural Heritage Conference—Cape Town 12–16 July 1997*, ed. Andrew Bank, 51–68. Cape Town: Institute for Historical Research, University of Western Cape, and Infosource.

Bauer, Gretchen. 2001. "Namibia in the First Decade of Independence: How Democratic?" *Journal of Southern African Studies* 27(1):33–55.

Bayart, Jean-François, Stephen Ellis, and Béatrice Hibou. 1999. *The Criminalization of the State in Africa*. Trans. Stephen Ellis. Oxford: International African Institute and James Currey.

Beckett, Jeremy. 1996. "Contested Images: Perspectives on the Indigenous Terrain in the Late 20th Century." *Identities: Global Studies in Culture and Power* 3(1–2):1–3.

Bodley, John H. 1990. *Victims of Progress*. 3rd edition. Mountain View, CA: Mayfield.

Boynton, Graham. 1997. "The Search for Authenticity: On Destroying the Village in Order to Save It." *Nation* 265(10):18–19.

Central Statistics Office. 1996. *Living Conditions in Namibia: Basic Description with Highlights. 1993/1994 Namibia Household Income and Expenditure Survey, Main Report*. Windhoek, Namibia: Central Statistics Office and National Planning Commission.

Chabal, Patrick and Jean-Pascal Daloz. 1999. *Africa Works: Disorder as Political Instrument*. Oxford: International Africa Institute and James Currey.

Clifford, James. 1988. *The Predicament of Culture: Twentieth-Century Ethnography, Literature, and Art*. Cambridge, MA: Harvard University Press.

Devereux, S., V. Katjiuanjo and G. van Rooy. 1996. *The Living and Working Conditions of Farmworkers in Namibia*. Windhoek: Legal Assistance Centre, Farmworkers Project and Social Sciences Division, Multi-Disciplinary Research Centre, University of Namibia.

Dubow, Saul. 1995. *Illicit Union: Scientific Racism in Modern South Africa*. Cambridge: Cambridge University Press.

Falk, Richard. 1993. "The Making of Global Citizenship." In *Global Visions: Beyond the New World Order*, ed. Jeremy Brecher and John Brown Childs, 39–49. Boston, MA: South End Press.

Forte, Maximilian C. 1998. *Renewed Indigeneity in the Local-Global Continuum and the Political Economy of Tradition: The Case of Trinidad's Caribs and the Caribbean Organization of Indigenous People*. Electronic document, http://www.centrelink.org/renewed.html, accessed November 11, 2001.

Fuller, B. and D. Hubbard. 1996. *The Living and Working Conditions of Domestic Workers in Namibia*. Windhoek, Namibia: Legal Assistance Centre.

Garland, Elizabeth. 1999. "Developing the Bushmen: Building Civil(ized) Society in the Kalahari and Beyond." In *Civil Society and the Political Imagination in Africa: Critical Perspectives*, ed. John L. Comaroff and Jean Comaroff, 72–103. Chicago, IL: University of Chicago Press.

Gordon, Robert. 1988. "Apartheid's Anthropologists: On the Genealogy of Afrikaner Anthropology." *American Ethnologist* 15(3):535–553.

Gordon, Robert and Stuart Sholto Douglas. 2000. *The Bushmen Myth: The Making of a Namibian Underclass*. 2nd ed. Boulder, CO: Westview Press.

Guenther, Mathias. 1980. "From 'Brutal Savages' to 'Harmless People.'" *Paideuma* 26:123–140.

_____. 2002. "Ethno-Tourism and the Bushmen." In *Self- and Other-Images of Hunter-Gatherers*. Senri Ethnological Studies, 60, ed. Henry Stewart, Alan Barnard, and Keiichi Omura, 47–64. Osaka, Japan: National Museum of Ethnology.

Hall, Stuart. 1997. *The Local and the Global: Globalization and Ethnicity. In Culture, Globalization and the World-System: Contemporary Conditions for the Representation of Identity*, ed. Anthony D. King, 19–39. Minneapolis: University of Minnesota Press.

Intu Afrika Game Lodge. N.d. Intu Afrika Game Lodge. Electronic document, http://www.namibweb.com/intuafrica.html, accessed June 2003.

Kloos, Peter. 2000. "The Dialectics of Globalization and Localization." In *The Ends of Globalization: Bringing Society Back In*, ed. Don Kalb, Marco van der Land, Richard Staring, Bart van Steenbergen, and Nico Wilterdink, 281–297. Lanham, MD: Rowman and Littlefield.

Lattas, Andrew. 1993. "Essentialism, Memory and Resistance: Aboriginality and the Politics of Authenticity." *Oceania* 63(3):240–268.

Lee, Richard B. 1988. "The Gods Must Be Crazy but the State Has a Plan: Government Policies toward the San in Namibia." In *Namibia: 1884–1984: Readings on Namibian History and Society*, ed. Brian Wood, 181–190. London: Namibia Support Committee and United Nations Institute for Namibia.

———. 1993[1969]. "Eating Christmas in the Kalahari." In *The Dobe Ju/'hoansi*, 183–188. Fort Worth, TX: Harcourt Brace.

Mail and Guardian. 1995. Whose Land Is This. *Mail and Guardian* Online, February 17. Electronic document, http://www.sn.apc.org/wmail/issues/950217/wm950217-56.html, accessed October 5, 2001.

Malkki, Liisa. 1992. "National Geographic: The Rooting of Peoples and the Territorialization of National Identity among Scholars and Refugees." *Cultural Anthropology* 7(1):24–44.

Meyer, Birgit and Peter Geschiere. 1999. "Globalization and Identity: Dialectics of Flow and Closure: Introduction." In *Globalization and Identity: The Dialectics of Flow and Closure*, ed. Birgit Meyer and Peter Geschiere, 1–15. Oxford: Institute of Social Sciences and Blackwell.

Moore, Anna, with the Omaheke San Trust Board of Trustees. 2000. *Omaheke San Trust Annual Report, March 1999 to February 2000*. Windhoek, Namibia: Working Group for Indigenous Minorities in Southern Africa.

Morton, Fred. 1994. "Slavery and South African Historiography." In *Slavery in South Africa: Captive Labor on the Dutch Frontier*, ed. Elizabeth Eldredge and Fred Morton, 1–9. Boulder, CO: Westview Press; Pietermaritzburg: University of Natal Press.

Muehlebach, Andrea. 2001. "'Making Place' at the United Nations: Indigenous Cultural Politics at the U.N. Working Group on Indigenous Populations." *Cultural Anthropology* 16(3):415–448.

National Archives of Namibia. 1923. Draft of letter to administration, November 10, 1923. SWAA A521/3: Farm Labour, Desertions, 1928–1941. National Archives of Namibia, Windhoek.

———. 1927. Minutes from the Native Commissioner to the Magistrate of Gobabis, November 3, 1927. SWAA A50/67: Native Affairs, Bushmen, 1926–1947. National Archives of Namibia, Windhoek.

———. 1939. Memorandum, Magistrate of Grootfontein, February, 1939. SWAA A198/26: Ethnological Inquiry into Control of Bushmen, 1934–1947. National Archives of Namibia, Windhoek.

Niezen, Ronald. 2000. "Recognizing Indigenism: Canadian Unity and the International Movement of Indigenous Peoples." Comparative Studies in Society and History 42(1):119–148.

≠ Oma, Kxao Moses, and Axel Thoma. 2002. "Will Tourism Destroy San Cultures?" *Cultural Survival Quarterly* 26(1):39–41.

Omaheke San Trust. 1999. *Constitution of the Omaheke San Trust. Drawn up by the Board, 9/7/99.* Windhoek: Working Group for Indigenous Minorities in Southern Africa.

Robbins, Steven. 2001. "'Bushmen' and Double Vision: The ≠Khomani San Land Claim and the Cultural Politics of 'Community' and 'Development' in the Kalahari." *Journal of Southern African Studies* 27(4):833–853.

Suzman, James. 1995. *Poverty, Land and Power in the Omaheke Region.* Windhoek, Namibia: Oxfam.

——. 2000. *Things from the Bush: A Contemporary History of the Omaheke Bushmen.* Basel, Switzerland: P. Schlettwein.

Sylvain, Renée. 2001. "Bushmen, Boers and Baasskap: Patriarchy and Paternalism on Afrikaner Farms in the Omaheke Region, Namibia." *Journal of Southern African Studies* 27(4):717–737.

——. 2002 "'Land, Water, and Truth': San Identity and Global Indigenism." *American Anthropologist* 104(4):1074–1084.

United Nations. 1999. "Africa Recovery Online: Country Report." Electronic document, http://www.un.org/ecosocdev/geninfo/afrec/vol12no4/namibxs.htm, accessed November 2, 2001.

van Rooyen, P. H. and P. Reiner. 1995. *Gobabis: 1845–1895–1995.* Gobabis, Namibia: Municipality of Gobabis.

Wallerstein, Immanuel. 1997. "The National and the Universal: Can There Be Such a Thing as World Culture?" In *Culture, Globalization and the World-System: Contemporary Conditions for the Representation of Identity,* ed. Anthony D. King, 91–106. Minneapolis: University of Minnesota Press.

White, Hylton. 1995. *In the Tradition of the Forefathers: Bushman Traditionality at Kagga Kamma.* Cape Town: University of Cape Town Press.

Wilmsen, Edwin. 1989. *Land Filled with Flies: A Political Economy of the Kalahari.* Chicago: University of Chicago Press.

Working Group of Indigenous Minorities in Southern Africa. 1998. *Working Group of Indigenous Minorities in Southern Africa, Report on Activities, April 1998 to March 1999.* Windhoek, Namibia: Working Group of Indigenous Minorities in South Africa.

World Travel and Tourism Council. 2001. "World Travel and Tourism Council Forecast Places Tourism among Leading Economic and Employment Generators." Electronic document, http://www.wttc.org/resourceCentre/mediaCentre/releases/1010508Forecast2001.asp?, accessed November 15.

Wright, Robin. 1988. "Anthropological Presuppositions of Indigenous Advocacy." *Annual Review of Anthropology* 17:365–390.

NOTES

Research for this article was generously funded by the Social Sciences and Humanities Research Council of Canada and the Izaak Walton Killam Trust. I wish to thank Tania Li, Pauline Gardiner-Barber, and Deidre Rose for their thoughtful comments and suggestions as I was developing these ideas. Deepest gratitude goes to the San people of the Omaheke region for sharing their knowledge and insights with me, and to the members of WIMSA and the OST for their support and encouragement. As always, I am indebted to Rocky Jacobsen for his invaluable advice and assistance throughout all phases of my research.

1. From 1884 to 1915, Namibia (then South-West Africa) was a German colony. In 1920, South-West Africa was mandated by the League of Nations to South Africa as a trust territory. After a lengthy liberation struggle (1966 to 1989), led by the South-West Africa Peoples Organization (SWAPO), Namibia achieved independence on March 21, 1990.
2. James Clifford also notes that "the idea of culture comes with it an expectation of roots, of a stable, territorial existence" (1988, 38).
3. The term Khoi is often used to refer to Nama-speaking peoples, who are linguistically and culturally similar to San.
4. See Gordon (1988) for a detailed treatment of these influences.
5. The Angola Boers were the descendents of the Dorsland Trekkers who had passed through the Omaheke en route to Angola fifty years earlier and who returned in the late 1920s to constitute the largest single influx of settlers into the region.
6. On the farms I surveyed in 1996, the average wage for San male workers was N$82.00 per month (equivalent to US$20.50). This compares to an average monthly cash wage of N$166.12 for non-San farmworkers, or N$300 a month if payment was made in wages only (Devereux et al. 1996, x, 23). The average wage for San domestic servants was N$45.00 per month (US$11.25). Wages for non-San domestic servants reported by the Namibian Domestic and Allied Workers Union averaged N$221.90 per month (Fuller and Hubbard 1996, 114–115).
7. For details on the intersection of San class and culture, see Sylvain 2002. For a description of the intersections of race, class, and gender inequalities, see Sylvain 2001.
8. For recent work on disorder, corruption, and the "criminalization" of states in Africa, see Bayart et al. 1999 and Chabal and Daloz 1999.
9. The chief-designate of the northern Omaheke San suggested a remedy for this imbalance by pointing out that farm San could be counted as belonging to the community located closest to the farm on which they work.

10. This is also illustrated by the case of the ≠Khomani San in South Africa (see Robbins 2001).
11. This was the situation as of June 2001. WIMSA and the OST have been working tirelessly to raise awareness of their activities and to forge fruitful networks with other local development and advocacy organizations.
12. According to the World Travel and Tourism Council (2001), tourism contributed 7.8 percent to Namibia's GDP (gross domestic product) in 2001. The director of tourism at the Ministry of Environment and Tourism estimates that "tourism will be the largest contributor to the national GDP in six or seven years" (United Nations 1999).
13. For a detailed description of the touristic experience at Intu Afrika, see Guenther 2002.
14. In the mid-1970s, the South African army began recruiting Ju/'hoan and Kxoe as trackers and reconnaissance troops in covert operations units against SWAPO's (South-West Africa People's Organisation) armed wing, the Peoples' Liberation Army of Namibia (PLAN; see Gordon and Douglas 2000; Lee 1988).
15. In his study of the Kagga Kamma settlement in the western Cape, Hylton White (1995, 42) describes many of the same stereotypical justifications for low wages that I found in the Omaheke: Bushmen are too primitive to handle money, and besides, "real" Bushmen have no need for it anyway.

III

Identity, Social Planning, and Political Power

8

INCORPORATION AND IDENTITY IN THE MAKING OF THE MODERN WORLD

Eric Wolf

After I wrote *Europe and the People without History* (1982), I was invited by the Westermarck Society of Finland to give the Edward Westermarck Memorial Lecture. It was delivered in the resplendent House of Estates in Helsinki on May 11, 1984. In the lecture I sought to take a stand against the growing tendency in the human sciences to utilize an unanalyzed notion of "identity" to cover all cases of self-recognition by human groups. I argued, instead, that social and cultural identities, far from being self-evident, developed in the course of incorporation into larger systems, and were as manifold as these systems were diverse. Thus, the various phases of capitalist development in the modern world gave rise to widely different kinds of identities.

It is a singular honor to address you in the name of the great Finnish scholar whose work unites the social science traditions of Scandinavia with those of the English-speaking world and for whom the purpose of these sciences was "to explain … social phenomena, to find their causes, to show how and why they have come into existence" (Westermarck 1908, 24–25). I shall try to do justice to that purpose by speaking about incorporation and identity in the making of the modern world.

By processes of incorporation I mean the recruitment of people into particular modes of mobilizing and deploying social labor; processes of identity making and unmaking refer to the creation and abrogation of the cultural markers and culturally informed activities by which populations define themselves and are defined by others in the process of incorporation. I see the two sets of processes as relational and interdependent. The processes of incorporation arrange and rearrange people in terms of the governing social relations of production; the processes of identity making and unmaking represent responses on the part of particular populations to such arrangements. I emphasize the term *process* because I believe that we cannot understand either incorporation or identity making as static phenomena; they must be seen as unfolding historically, in time. Thus, to understand processes of incorporation, we need to know not only what new order is installed but how the installation of that new order dislocates and rearranges the preexisting relationships governing the deployment of social labor. To understand identity making, we must know how people reorganize preexisting cultural activities and markers in responding to the exigencies and pressures of the new.

I see identity making and unmaking, therefore, in objective terms and not purely as subjective processes, in the manner of Fredrik Barth. Barth contended that, in the formation of ethnic groups, "socially relevant factors alone become diagnostic for membership, not the overt 'objective' differences which are generated by other factors" (1969, 15). The deployment in social relations of the cultural activities and markers involved in identity-formation is quite as much an objective process as are technological practices or performances of ritual. What Barth wanted to say, I think, is that it is not culture, content, or tradition as such that defines groups and boundaries; but if that is so, then he was taking a very static view of culture and tradition. Tradition is not a corpus of objects, acts, and ideas handed down integrally from ancestors to descendents. Its components are more often invented, rearranged, and reorchestrated in transfers from generation to generation than fixed and immemorial.

In this perspective I also take issue with Clifford Geertz, when he argued that ideology comes to the fore when society frees itself from "the immediate governance of received tradition, from the direct and detailed guidance of religious or philosophical canons on the one hand and from the unreflective precepts of conventional moralism on the other" (1973, 219). I see received tradition as changing and changeable cultural activities that include the making and unmaking of ideologies, even if these activities are not embodied in specialized institutions but come embedded in relations of kinship, power, or religion. I do so because it has been my argument that the modern world has been shaped by the powerful impact of capitalist relations of production. Everywhere, populations have been constituted or have constituted themselves in a flow of events unleashed by the impact of these forces. Everywhere, these forces have generated responses. There are, thus, no cold societies, in Claude Levi-Strauss's terms, no "geschictslose Volker," no "people without history."

Geertz mentions religious and philosophical canons and precepts of morality in his discussion of tradition and ideology, and I would not discount such canons and precepts in the construction and deconstruction of identities. Yet I would also stress the significance of everyday activities in that construction. You can see such simple crystallizations of identity, for instance, in the gatherings of Indian plantation workers in Guyana described by Chandra Jayawardena (1963, 1968). Men meet to drink together, and in drinking together create and reinforce their fellowship as *matis* (mates). The term first came into use in the transportation of Indian indentured servants to the Caribbean, where men of different castes and ethnic origins were thrown together on board ship; strong ties of solidarity developed out of such shipboard contacts, to sustain friendships in the new land. Later, the concept of *mati* came to mean fellow being, associate, equal, pal; the tie, as Jayawardena says, "between persons who share the same kind of life and fate" (1968, 417).

Or, take as another example, the involvement of Mexicans and Mexican Americans in rotating credit associations (Velez-Ibanez 1983). These are informal, interpersonal networks that function as saving, lending, and borrowing associations. Members contribute weekly payments and are able to draw out, on a rotational basis, relatively large amounts of money or other valued resources. These scenarios of risk and indeterminacy are founded on a culturally expressed idiom of mutual trust. *Confianza* (trust) establishes indices of who can be relied on, as well as the limits of that reliance: Because *confianza* in *confianza*, trust in trust, depends on cultural standards of evaluation, however, it simultaneously reaffirms Mexican identity in the midst of environing and often competitive populations. Or, to use still another example: North American Indians of the plateaus and prairies to the south of the forest belt play a gambling game in which individuals or the representatives of bands and tribes alternately guess at the presence or absence of counters, such as bones, secreted in the hands of their opponents. Special songs are sung before, during, and after the game. During the period of nativist revival connected with the Ghost

Dance movement of the late nineteenth century, these games changed from gambling events into ritualized ceremonials, accompanied by dancing, feasting, visions, and smoke offerings, in which winning or losing became demonstrations of faith and spiritual power. In the context of forced assimilation the hand game became, as Alexander Lesser has pointed out, "a reassertion of ethnic identity" (1978).

Such humble assertions of identity may indeed escalate into more dramatic demonstrations. "Supporting mati" burgeoned into the mass strikes of Guyana sugar workers. The understandings that underlie *confianza* can become manifest in confrontations with political and legal agents of the powerful establishment; John Nichols has captured just such a transformation in his delightful novel *The Milagro Beanfield War* (1978). The handball game can serve as cultural form in the revindicationist demands for Red Power of the American Indian movement. Yet these shifts from muted assertion to open demonstration are greatly dependent on the arrival of political and economic conjunctures that allow for such openings or that foreclose them, and it would be false romanticism to accord recognition only to the taking of the Bastille or assaults on the Winter Palace.

What I have said here about identity making necessarily applies to the genesis and development of resistance. There has been a tendency recently to understand *culture* primarily as a manifestation of resistance. Resistance there may be, and even heroism and sacrifice; yet if we ground identity making in everyday life, we must comprehend resistance in the same terms. If we treat drinking on the job, malingering, absenteeism, desertion, sabotage, theft, or bargaining over the setting, sequencing, and intensity of work as forms of resistance, however, we will also recognize that in sociological terms, there is often a very fine line between resistance and delinquency. Yet Charles van Onselen was surely right when he wrote, about the Rhodesian mines, that such "less dramatic, silent, 'and unorganized responses … which occurred on a day-to-day basis … reveal most about the functioning of the system and formed the weft and warp of worker consciousness. Likewise it was the unarticulated, unorganized protest and resistance which the employers and the state found most difficult to detect or suppress." (1976, 227).

Just as it would be mistaken to see identities mushrooming overnight into collective resistance, so it would also be misleading to regard the construction of identities as inevitably generalizing and all encompassing. Playing the North American Indian hand game can become a marker of pan-Indian identity; it can also divide opponents along identity lines. Crow Indians who play it at intertribal gatherings (powwows) set off Pryor Mountain Crow—"the original, true Crow"—from River Crow; River Crow from Utah and Idaho Crow; all Crows from the Hidatsa (from whom Crow originally sprang), Kiowa, and Blood; all these related tribes from Chicanos, Blacks, and Breeds (*mestizos*); and all these from formerly hostile tribes like the Sioux, the Arapaho, and especially the Cheyenne; "You Cheyenne speaker" is the ultimate Mountain Crow insult. Cheyenne victory in a Crow–Cheyenne hand game became a factor in tribal negotiations with coal companies for exploitation of coal reserves on the reservations. When the Cheyenne, who had refused contract negotiations, won the game, the Crow, also previously hostile to contract talks, then reopened discussion (Cheska 1979). In a similar vein, tributary conquest states often incorporate the distinction between victors and vanquished into their organizational structure to rule and divide. And the division of the capitalist labor market into segments both creates and feeds on differentiations of identity by gender, ethnicity, and social race among the labor force.

Through these skeins of arguments runs still another: the controversy among American social historians over the extent to which the population at large is dominated by the hegemonic ideology of the ruling class or classes, and the extent to which they are capable of generating their own patterns of culture and resistance. The controversy has been most notable among historians of slavery. Eugene Genovese has upheld the power of hegemony; Herbert Gutman has stressed the importance of noting not only what was done to slaves, but also what slaves did for themselves. I cannot see this as an either/or proposition. It seems clear that the exercise of power and control of the means of violence by the planter class greatly circumscribed the opportunities and terrain within which slaves could generate their own patterns, and that many of these opportunities and terrains were limited or even mediated by hegemonic law, religion, and control over communication. At the same time, there were undoubtedly areas in which slaves built up their own cultural repertoires, most obvious in the development of black religious congregations, drawing energy from their identification with the oppressed children of Israel, and in the formation and maintenance of ties of kinship and quasi-kinship documented by Gutman (1976).

There is clearly a dialectic here between the armature of domination and the proliferation of autonomous subaltern patterns, a dialectic well expressed by Diane Austin in a study of working-class people in Kingston, Jamaica:

Subordinate classes do forge their own cultural practices, not simply in response to a material environment but also to provide identity and prestige in a milieu often denigrated by the rest of society. At the same time it is optimistic, even romantic, to suggest that these forms of creative response to a subordinate position can exist in the majority of cases unaffected by the ideologies of the powerful as propagated in the very institutions in which working-class people experience their subordination. (1983, 229)

The examples I have offered—drinking in Guyana, building relations of trust in credit networks, playing handball, "soldiering on the job," or shirking work in the Rhodesian mines—should also tell us, however, that we cannot come to comprehend these responses unless we see them in the wider context of the economic and political forces that shape the modern world. To understand incorporation and identity formation, therefore, we need to have a sense of the periodicities of European expansion, carried first by mercantile wealth and later by industrial capital. We also need to follow the sequential advances and retreats in the fate of states that strove to establish control of the new mercantile and industrial networks. In so doing, we will be able to define the historical and sociological sites and space in which new identities are created and defended.

Yet let us remember that we are dealing with moving phenomena, not static ones. New identities are created and abrogated within a field of ever-shifting political competitors, moving for and against changing economic linkages. Charles Tilly has pointed out that the Europe of 1500 included some 500 separate political entities; the Europe of 1900 about 25 (1975, 15). Even the initial 500 were the products of processes of aggregating and compounding diverse peoples such as the Gallo-Romans and Italian Greeks; of Rhaetians and Germanic tribes; of Celtic, Baltic, Slavic, and Finnish populations; of Vikings and Normans, Saracens and Moors, Turks and Mongols. On further inspection, moreover, these political entities are themselves not unitary but constitute shifting battlegrounds among ever-changing social strata, arenas in which classes and sections of classes negotiate and renegotiate their conflicts and coalitions. These conflicts and coalitions are not only internal to the state; they are external as well. To offer just one example: the growth of slavery in the cotton South of the United States was predicated on the expansion of textile manufacturing in England. To expand slavery and cotton growing, the cotton masters wanted to carry slavery into the American West and to annex northern Mexico to boot. The victory of the North not only resulted in the legal freeing of the slaves (one of the largest unremunerated expropriations of a dominant class in history), but opened the road to the importation of a new industrial working class from Europe.

Let me, then, sketch out the phases of European expansion. The first thrust was carried out by Spain and Portugal, followed closely by Holland, a former Spanish dependency. When I say Spain, I mean the coalition of king, licensed merchants, financiers from Castile, Genoa, and Bavaria, and military aristocrats in search of booty after the reconquest of Spain from the Moors. When I say Portugal, I mean the coalition of merchants and military lords grouped around the dynasty of Aviz. When I say Holland, I mean the federation of merchant oligarchies pivoted upon Amsterdam and represented in overseas trade by the armed joint-stock company of the Dutch East India Company.

The Spanish thrust was primarily into the Americas. Carried by sea, it aimed nevertheless primarily at the control of landmasses and of deposits of prestigious metals within those lands. The strongholds of Spanish power were the Spanish towns, sown strategically across the landscape; the motor of its economics were the silver mines, usually located in inhospitable regions peripheral to the key areas of pre-Hispanic horticulture. The polities of the Aztec, Chibcha, and Inca were dismantled; the native elites were stripped of strategic politywide political and economic functions. The Indian economy was reshaped to supply the towns and mines with foodstuffs, craft products, and labor; the Indian towns were charged with local governance, subject to the watchful and exploitative Spanish administrators. The outcome was territorial empire, built upon the shattered fragments of the pre-Hispanic polities.

Native resistance was inhibited by compartmentalizing and atomizing the population in their separate "republics of Indians." These communities then became the sites of native reintegration and affirmation. This was made possible through the coordination of three Hispanic forms—the town council, the *cofradia* (religious sodality in the service of a saint), and the *caja de comunidad* (communal treasury)—into one organization. This organization supported an annual round of rituals, which celebrated the worship of Catholic saints syncretized with native supernaturals and concepts. Participation in these rituals gave recognition to the more successful and affluent members of the communities denied them in the larger, Spanish-dominated society. It allowed them to build up a fund of credit and influence within the community through periodic redistributions of food and drink. It also gave people a sense of identity and autonomy apart from the larger society. At the same time, this remained a dependent autonomy in that the required expenditure for ritual goods tied celebrants to external markets, and the local ritual structures articulated communal hierarchies with those of the hegemonic church. Yet there was also an ambiguity and a hidden promise in much of that ritual. Under the integument of Christian religion, locally anchored pre-Hispanic beliefs and myths were preserved, which furnished markers of identity with their own points of reference, their own accents. It is an identity that is always potentially translatable into ethnic politics.

In contrast to the Spaniards, the Portuguese did not aim primarily at the control of landmasses. Portuguese ships first hugged the African coast and then sailed into Asian waters, erecting naval stations and commercial depots on the way, seeking not continental domination but profitable trade. In the Indian Ocean and South China Sea, they encountered a trade network as highly developed as that of Europe. Into this complex they inserted themselves by means of their armed merchantmen. Where the Spaniards began to rule their lands as lords of Indians, the Portuguese interacted with local populations primarily through commercial agents and through clerks and artisans of mixed Portuguese and native ancestry, emplaced in fortified but isolated coastal emporia of elite ostentation and ecclesiastical splendor. The Dutch adopted the same pattern. "All they wanted was a free-flowing trade based on contracts with local potentates." In this effort they effectively ousted the Portuguese, who complained that they had flushed the deer but that the Dutch would take them. The Dutch only moved to secure a foothold on land when forced to do so by conflict with England or with native states. In the Portuguese and Dutch naval empires, therefore, opposition and resistance to the intruders might take the form of religious opposition invocations of the varieties of Christendom, Islam, and Hinduism—but both the Portuguese and Dutch remained rajas among other rajas, though equipped with more powerful naval artillery.

The second cycle of expansion and incorporation revolved around the conflicts of England and France. By England I mean here a coalition of court, merchant companies, and commercially oriented agricultural gentry; by France, the absolutist king, supported by an administrative apparatus of military and bureaucratic nobility, as well as by merchant groups from the towns of the Atlantic fringe. In three successive wars fought during the seventeenth century, this England defeated Holland in Europe and Asia and induced Holland to join it in a war on France. The Treaty of Utrecht of 1713, won by England on the sea and by Holland on land, confirmed English dominance as a sea power and brought both Holland and Portugal into the English orbit as client states. Through Lisbon and through Caribbean contraband, England began to tap the poorly defended wealth of the Spanish-American dominions. At the same time, the Anglo-French wars in North America and in India drove the French back upon the continent of Europe; and the renewed wars of 1792 through 1815, ending in the defeat of Napoleon, also ended French plans for a continental empire in Europe. By 1803, France also lost Haiti to a massive insurrection of the Haitian slaves. Haitian coffee and sugar had accounted for two-thirds of French overseas trade, and Haiti had been the greatest single market for the European slave trade. At the same time, England moved toward control of India. Like the Portuguese and Dutch before them, the English had at first clung to isolated forts and depots on the periphery of the subcontinent; but as the Mogul power crumbled in the wars between French and English forces and their Indian allies, the road stood open to the annexation of the Mogul political heritage, region by region.

These wars between England and France were fought for political predominance in the global hierarchy of independencies and dependencies, but they also involved as prizes control or influence over the major theaters of economic activity. The first of these—founded in the sixteenth century, built up further in the seventeenth, but expanded to levels of barbaric and lucrative splendor in the eighteenth—were the sugar islands of the Caribbean. This source of wealth depended on the emplacement of quasi-industrial processing centers for sugarcane, the establishment of large plantations devoted in the main to the growing of cane, and the deployment of labor in organized gangs—labor obtained primarily through slaving and slave trading in Africa. That trade, already entered into by the Portuguese in the fifteenth century, reached its zenith in the eighteenth century, and declined gradually thereafter. Burgeoning demand for slaves, coupled with very high rates of slave mortality, moreover, demanded the continual importation of Africans to replace the already seasoned slaves with cohorts of *bozales*—Africans still close to their African roots.

The slaves that the Caribbean consumed were furnished by Africa, the second theater of economic significance in this international division of labor. To connect sources of supply with target areas of demand, the European and Euro-American slave traders entered into collaboration with African "fishers of men." The slaves had to be captured, transported to the coast, fed and guarded while awaiting transshipment, and ferried out to oceangoing ships in locally made skiffs. All of these tasks and their organization fell into African hands, mostly those of "kings, princes, and prime merchants," in the words of the French factor Jean Barbot. Equipped with large quantities of European-made muskets, many ecologically anchored polities became slave-hunting armies on the move. The formation of each new predatory state, in turn, had a domino effect on its neighbors, each slaving polity pushing on its neighbors to the east and each population of victims telegraphing the impulse farther eastward through the heart of Africa.

Documentary and oral historical investigations have combined recently to unveil, in rich detail, this forgotten history of the so-called Dark Continent. I will single out here only one example—the transformations of cultures and identities along the delta and course of the Cross River in eastern Nigeria. Here the slave trade contacted Ibibio-speaking fishermen and salt producers who had traded their products northward in exchange for yams. In the sixteenth and seventeenth centuries, segments of lineages originally located at Creek Town hived off to settle different towns. Together, these towns came to be known as Old Calabar, dominated by an elite called the Efik. From here, an estimated 250,000 slaves were exported between 1650 and 1841, in exchange for European metalware, firearms, and Indian fine cloth. Once slaving became big business, the patrilineages and their councils of lineage chiefs gave way to territorial wards, each centered upon an important trader and his slave, following and surrounded by extended families and lineage segments. Competition for European connections and credit resulted in an elite of successful traders, who underlined their status and solidarity through worship of a common tutelary deity, and enforced law and control over credit through their dominance in Ekpe, a secret society named after a forest spirit. Ekpe spread rapidly upriver, where enrollment in the society opened up Efik credit. Several European traders also joined the society. Most of the slaves traded by the Efik were sold to them by the Aro, a consortium of patrilineages of diverse origins, whose unity found expression in the oracle and pilgrimage center at Aro Chukwu. They obtained slaves through raiding and purchase, through advancing credit and enslaving the recipients in case of nonpayment, and through use of the oracle to administer justice and enslave the guilty parties. The basis of their power lay ultimately in their access to firearms, purchased in quantity in Calabar.

The establishment of plantation agriculture with African labor produced a double strain in the receiving areas: the need to maintain continuous control over coerced populations in the plantation belt, and the challenge of slave flight or marronage. The formations organized by runaway slaves—the free maroon villages of Jamaica, the *quilombos* of Brazil, the *palenques* of Cuba, the busch societies of Surinam—

constitute what Jean Casimir, writing about Haiti, has called "the counter-plantation" (1980). Here we see a third major arena of popular identity-making resistance, somewhat different in form from the attempts to develop autonomous communities hedged about by ritual in Indian America. An innovative theme in black plantation America is the rise of Afro-American religious cults. These not only preserve the identities of African deities under syncretized Christian nomenclatures and attributes, and keep adherents in touch with ancestral powers; they occasionally issue in political-military rebellions, as in Myal-Kumina curing and possession practices associated with the rebellion of the maroons in Jamaica and of Vodun in the slave resistance and rebellion of Haiti.

In North America, the incorporation first centered upon the drive to acquire valued furs and hides for European markets. This was an extension overseas of the European fur trade. In its North American sector, the advance depended strongly on relationships with kin-ordered Indian populations, involving both trade and alliance in warfare. European alliances with Indian groups were dictated by the continuation of their Old World quarrels in the New World. These rivalries soon shook out to confrontations between the French and the English, each seeking to attract auxiliaries. At the same time, the European traders needed native partners who were willing to exchange furs for European manufactures. The resulting ties between agents of the European powers and kin-ordered Amerind populations intensified warfare and mayhem, but they also generated such phenomena as the Algonkin florescence and the glories of the Iroquois, in which, for a time, the Amerind populations used European artifacts and patterns to construct wider alliances and new cultural identities.

The Iroquois offer a salient case of how an ethnic entity and identity were constructed and reconstructed in the midst of armed conflict and trading for prestigious furs. The Iroquois deserve special consideration if only because they served Lewis Henry Morgan as a type case of lower barbarism in his evolutionary schemes (1963 [1877]). The Iroquois appear to have long resided in the lake region to the south of the St. Lawrence River, and can be interpreted as a local reaction to the spread of the expansionist, Mississippi-based archaeological temple mound culture into the Northeast. It is possible that the constituent units of the Iroquois League had begun to confederate before the advent of the Europeans, although the legend of unification under the aegis of a non-Iroquois Algonkian prophet, Hiawatha-Dekanawida, points to a postcolonization date. The fur trade gave the various clusters an overriding converging interest in eliminating the control of their neighbors over fur grounds and trade links. They also came to play the role of an effective buffer between the advancing English and French. The prolonged absence of men in the hunt and on the warpath strengthened the role of women, including the right to adopt captives into the local matrilineages, a function that grew vital as the Iroquois sought replacements for men killed in warfare. By the last quarter of the seventeenth century, several of the constituent clusters of the league contained more non-Iroquois than Iroquois. The Jesuits even complained that just when they had learned Iroquois in order to preach in that language, they could no longer make themselves understood. Continued external recruitment and alliance making turned the league from a kinship-based alliance into an entity parallel to the European trading companies, which also combined economic and political functions.

Trading furs for European weapons and objects of manufacture made the league economically dependent on the Europeans, as did the acceptance of gifts and advances extended to cement political and military alliances. A notable example of this dependence is furnished by the expanded use of wampum, a case documented archaeologically and ethnohistorically by Lynn Ceci (1977, 1982). Wampum are beads made from white and purple shells found on the west coast of North America. The shells were cut and drilled by the European colonists and Indians working under their command, and traded to the Iroquois for beaver skins. The Iroquois endowed strings and belts of wampum with high symbolic value, using them in gifts to the dead, the spirits, and the living, to cement ties of kinship, friendship, and alliance. Wampum thus spread along with the fur trade and political alliance making, mediating monetary exchange and native reciprocities and connecting European markets with the North American interior. There was even a point in the seventeenth century when the European colonists, faced with a shortage of European currency, turned to wampum as their own form of money in what Ceci has called "New York's first fiscal crisis."

The glories of the Iroquois waned in the mid-eighteenth century, however, when the Europeans reduced their dependence on Indian trade partners and military allies. European-organized trading companies penetrated into the interior, in order to gain direct access to sources of beaver and buffalo. This reversal in Indian–white relationships was marked by Pontiac's rebellion of 1763. That revolt exemplifies a dialectic between incorporation and resistance that became repetitive in the relations of North American Indians and Euro-American intruders. French defeat opened the trans-Allegheny to intrusion; at the same time, the British superintendent of Indians put an end to the system of annual presents to Indian allies. Suddenly the seemingly symmetrical exchanges of European manufactured goods and Indian furs stood revealed as aspects of an asymmetrical relation of power. Commodities are not neutral. Embodied in each European commodity was the entire industrial capitalist power of the European realm. The call of the Delaware prophet Neolin to the Indians to forswear the white material culture and all the customs associated with it was the logical counterpart to his exhortation to make war upon the whites, "to suffer them not to dwell upon your lands." This sequence of incorporation into the network of exchange, growing dependence, and sudden risings in despair would mark the entire westward march of empire, until the only form of resistance left to the incorporated Indians was withdrawal into a forced and painful quietism.

The nineteenth century went forward under the double hegemony of Britain as the dominant world power and the workshop of the world. Economically, its forward thrust was now augmented with a vast leap in output produced by labor power purchased in expanding labor markets and harnessed to the steam-driven machines of the Industrial Revolution. Politically, Britain managed to defeat France across the globe and quickly compensated for the loss of the North American colonies with military and political advances in Africa and Asia. The conquest of India turned the subcontinent into an exporter of opium, cotton, rice, oil seeds, jute, tea, and wheat, and into an earner of major surpluses in Asia, especially in China. Thus Asia—especially India and China—became, as A. J. H. Latham has argued, "a vital integral part of the international system" (1978, 81).

What interests us in the present context is the enormous expansion, first under British aegis and then in the nineteenth century, through the active competition of new powers of industrial, plantation, and mining enterprises all over the globe. Mineral, vegetable, and animal products were collected, cultivated, and processed as commodities on an ever-expanding scale. Archipelagos of industrial and agrarian activity proliferated on five continents. Ever-increasing numbers of men and women were set in motion to turn the wheels of industry, to harvest sugarcane or coffee, to gather rubber, to build railroads, and to service port facilities. The movement of people to cities and industries, within political borders and across political boundaries, went on apace. Thus, the United States imported nearly its entire working class from abroad. Some four million people left Italy between 1861 and 1911 to settle in North America or South America; an estimated two million Indian contract laborers went to work in the islands of the

Caribbean, the Indian Ocean, or the Pacific; millions of Chinese went overseas in the so-called coolie trade. In the twentieth century, a vast labor reservoir has come to extend "in a broad band from India and Pakistan in the east across northern Africa and southernmost Europe all the way into the Caribbean and other portions of Latin America to the west. Indian, Pakistani, Turkish, Greek, Italian, African, Spanish, Portuguese, West Indian workers supplement the indigenous under-class in northern Europe and make up its lowest layers. In the United States, the same role is occupied by Puerto Rican, Mexican, and other Latin American workers, who have been added to the pool of lowest-paid labor which is made up chiefly of Blacks" (Braverman 1974, 385).

Under the aegis of the capitalist mode of production, such a labor reservoir is tapped through the sale and purchase of labor power offered in what economists call the labor market. Analytically power-ful as such notions are, however, they constitute abstractions or fic-tions summarizing complex human arrangements. *Labor power* is, after all, the capacity to work of human beings who are differentiated by gender, age, and marital status, by placement in social networks and class relations, as well as by language, cultural provenience, and reli-gion. In turn, the labor market upon which this labor power is thrown is differentiated by channels of access, location, concentration or dif-fuseness, entrepreneurial structure and capitalization, distinctions of skill and occupation, seasonal or conjunctural variability of demand, and degrees of openness in recruitment or closure. Offerings of labor power in a labor market therefore involve a complex interplay of people—employers and employees—with varying social and cultural ties, responding to the requirements of capitalist relations of produc-tion, but responding to these in a highly differentiated field. Capitalist enterprises maximize what has been called the Babbage principle (after Charles Babbage, 1832), which argues that labor costs are best saved when the labor process is divided into different segments for which labor can be recruited in precise quantities and remunerated accord-ing to the level of skill required for each segment. Labor markets, in turn, are segmented both by the demand of entrepreneurs for differ-ent skills and wage levels and by the differentiation of the workforce entering one or another segment. There is a dialectic at work in which entrepreneurs seek recruits in different labor pools for different seg-ments of production, and in which workers from different labor pools encounter differential opportunities for access to different segments and then try to fortify themselves in these segments, frequently to the exclusion of others. We thus find that the workings of the central class relation produce a multiple differentiation into culturally marked identity groups.

Examples come readily to hand. In the United States, the Immigration Commission of 1911 documented the process of ethnic replacement throughout the industrial structure of the country. Native Americans or older immigrants from the British Isles and northern Europe either moved into positions of management or skilled work or left industry altogether, while the unskilled jobs of common labor went to new immigrants from southern and eastern Europe. This was not merely a matter of occupational mobility; it was an outcome of the wholesale mechanization of industry that eliminated special skills in manufacturing in favor of simple, repetitive, and low-paid operations. Within this new matrix of unskilled jobs, Polish and Italian immigrants occupied special niches and developed new group identities. Caroline Golab has described this process for Polish immigrants, pointing out that they took their primary identity not from state or province, but from their village and parish (1977). When registering members of a Polish parish in America, it was usually the priest who supplied the name of the province, from a map kept for that purpose. Golab sums up: "The Poles seem not to have learned of their larger 'Polishness' until after their arrival in America; it was here they confronted the counter-reality of an Anglo-American macroculture and a multiplicity of nationalities."

A parallel process characterizes the movement of people into the industrial orbit of the central African copper belt. In the early 1950s, A. L. Epstein studied Luanshya in what is today Zambia (1958). He showed how work opportunities in the mines were divided among populations of different backgrounds: managerial positions were held by whites from Britain, South Africa, or Rhodesia; clerical jobs fell primarily to the so-called Nyasalanders, a cover term that included many smaller groups such as Henga, Tonga, and Tumbuka, who came from an area that had experienced an early dissemination of European literacy through missionary efforts; most of the labor force in the mines was made up of Bemba, a category that came to include Bemba, Lungy, Tabwa, eastern Lunda, and other tribes from the northern province; Nyakyusa and Luvale were accorded the lowest and lowest-paying positions. It should be remembered that the concept of tribal separateness and identity was, to a very large extent, a colonial invention, originally imposed—as Terence Ranger has shown (1981)—upon complicated and differentially interlocking social, political, and religious networks. The salience of the Bemba in the midst of these networks is due to the success in the early nineteenth century of a district chief of

Luba origin in gaining power over the trade in ivory and slaves with the Swahili coast. Being Bemba, therefore, carried a special connotation of military prowess, which came to be used as a marker of identity by many cognate Bemba-speaking mine laborers from the northern and western provinces and could be put into play against others—Ngoni, Lozi, Nyakyusa. Yet the assertion of these categorical identities in the mining towns, themselves new, was also at work within the exigencies of a new social field, where "the wage economy of the towns, the urban forms of local grouping and administration, and the increasing assimilation of European patterns of behaviour, give rise to new sets of relations and interests. Here 'tribalism' ceases to be a relevant category, and new forms of association, and new types of leadership, come into being to express the new sets of interests involved" (Epstein 1958, 239).

Ethnic categories reappear in contexts that structure differential access to resources, as in Bemba attempts to dominate the African Mine Workers Union. Put another way, distinctions of group identity may become strategic in securing or accumulating valued resources. The resources at stake include not only work, but also matters of housing, transportation, information, credit, education, health maintenance, protection of rights, and support in old age. Where these are provided by interpersonal networks, group identification permits access to them, against possible competitors. Where such services are provided by public authorities, the formation of identity groups and categories constitutes an important strategy in making claims on the state and in defending them against other claimants.

I have argued that we need to understand the social processes of identity making and identity unmaking as responses to historically unfolding processes. I discussed these processes as emanating primarily from the dynamics of labor mobilization, as well as from the closely connected consolidation of competitive political power. I emphasized that these processes need to be looked at in a global perspective, and I stressed the importance of visualizing the creation of culturally marked groups in relation to the global impact of economic and political forces. I offered examples of so-called primitive populations to show that their identities, too, were shaped in this global process; their cultural markings were constructed and reconstructed in the course of their engagement with external forces, much as is the case with people mobilized for labor in the enterprises of the twentieth century. Only if we can lay hold of the interplay of general processes and local response will we be able to do justice to Edward Westermarck's demand that we strive for causal explanation.

9

QUESTIONING *MESTIZAJE*
The Social Mobilization of Afrodescendent Women in Latin America

Helen I. Safa

Historically, Latin American states have feared racial and ethnic divisions, which hampered their quest for identity and nationhood in the region. Rather than excluding these subaltern populations, as in the United States (where nonwhite populations were much smaller), they were to be assimilated by a process of *mestizaje* or race mixture, which was seen as both biological and cultural. White immigration was stimulated along with the teaching of Spanish or Portuguese as the dominant (and often only) language and conversion to Catholicism. The drive to assimilate racially or ethnically distinct populations in order to forge a unified and homogeneous image persists today in the region. This helps explain the Latin American states' reluctance to recognize race or ethnic discrimination (Safa 1998). Hence the importance of the 2000 Santiago declaration[1] in which Latin American states explicitly recognized Afrodescendent populations as victims of racism, that had been denied rights to equal participation in the political, social, economic, and cultural life of the nation (Cimarronas 2001; Turner 2002)—they had been socially excluded.

The refusal to acknowledge race as a basis for social exclusion in Latin America and the Caribbean is facilitated by the fluid nature of racial classification in the region. Racial categories are socially constructed and based largely on social status and phenotype, where factors such as skin color, hair, and facial features figure prominently. Though indigenous and Afrodescendent populations in Latin America and the Caribbean have been portrayed as inferior both biologically and culturally, and are largely confined to the lower socioeconomic strata, individuals could modify their racial category through *blanqueamiento* or whitening. *Blanqueamiento* in Latin America is achieved primarily through upward mobility and intermarriage with whites, who, as in the United States, enjoyed the highest racial status. This bias toward whiteness is a major component of *mestizaje*, which Afrodescendent groups have attempted to combat. Their adoption of the term *Afrodescendent* to cover all nonwhite persons eliminates the invidious distinction between blacks and mulattoes, whereby the latter were considered closer to the white norm. Although the term Afrodescendent has its critics (as will be discussed later), it will be used in this paper interchangeably with black and other terms such as Afro-Latinos.

This paper addresses the efforts of Afrodescendent solidarity groups to combat *blanqueamiento*, focusing on three areas: (1) developing racial consciousness to overcome the feelings of inferiority induced by slavery and *blanqueamiento*; (2) promoting the well-being and upward mobility of the Afrodescendent population, which often suffers from social exclusion in employment, housing, and public services such as health and education; and (3) pressuring the state to address these grievances and give the Afrodescendent population greater cultural recognition.

The paper focuses on the social mobilization of Afrodescendent women in Latin America and the Caribbean, a topic that thus far has received little attention in the literature. It is likely that a gender perspective will gain prominence in the literature on social exclusion as Afrodescendent women become organized and make their voices heard. The increasing public presence of Afrodescendent women in the region has been influenced by the growth of the feminist movement in Latin America and the Caribbean, and the emergence of black women professionals and their organization into NGOs or nongovernmental organizations. Afrodescendent women accuse the mainstream feminist movement of neglecting their concerns and, like the state, adopting a culturally homogenous view of women that fails to do justice to their cause. Afrodescendent women have also had to negotiate a place within the larger black movement, traditionally led by men.

Afrodescendent women are clearly not the only contemporary group to challenge the state in Latin America, as the social movements by the indigenous, women, and human rights advocates demonstrate (cf. Safa 2005). Neoliberal policies designed to minimize the state in the name of free trade and a market economy have contributed in the 1980s and 1990s to increasing inequality and poverty in the region. Growing inequality increased the urgency of Afrodescendent and indigenous groups to legitimate their claim to resources from the state and to recognition of their cultural autonomy.

Afrodescendent women's organizations are now found in virtually every country in Latin America and the Caribbean, but this paper cannot cover them all. We shall focus on Brazil, where the movement is most advanced, and on the Atlantic coast of Central America, where people of African descent are in a clear minority in mestizo societies. Statistical data by race and gender is still lacking in all areas, even in Brazil, which is the best documented. This lack of data also demonstrates the state's unwillingness to deal with black people and their problems, which remain largely invisible. Nevertheless, Afrodescendent groups are beginning to challenge the old *mestizaje* paradigm based on *blanqueamiento* or whitening, as will become apparent in the following analysis.

DEVELOPMENT OF RACIAL AND GENDER CONSCIOUSNESS

Development of racial consciousness has long been a goal of the Afro-Brazilian movement, which dates back to the 1930s. However, despite the proliferation of Afro-Brazilian organizations and their emphasis on black pride, they have not yet achieved mass support among the Afrodescendent population, which is increasingly socially differentiated (Hasenbalg and Silva 1999). Black consciousness is also in opposition to dominant values of harmony and lack of racial confrontation, while black movements are manipulated by the state as a means of containing potential collective political protest. For example, the Brazilian state's promotion of black cultural representation does not necessarily translate into political mobilization (Hanchard 1994). As Wade (1993) and others have shown, there is a fear among Afrodescendents that to separate themselves out as a group may imply lack of allegiance to the nation, to which most are fiercely loyal. Thus, nationalism takes precedence over racial consciousness, as distinct from the situation in the United States (Walker 2002).

The very definition of who is black is a problem, and has led to severe undercounts, as in the Costa Rican census of 2000 or the Colombian census of 1993. Part of the undercount is due to Afrodescendents' reluctance to identify as black because of the negative stereotypes associated with it. In Brazil, since 1940 there has been a noticeable move in the national census away from the black to the mulatto or *pardo* category (Lovell and Wood 1998). The "mulatto escape hatch," as Degler (1971) termed it, helped lighter-skinned Afrodescendents escape some of the oppression of blackness by convincing them they were more like whites than blacks. However, Lovell and Wood (1998) have shown that nationwide, blacks and mulattoes face similar differences from whites on critical issues such as life expectancy, school enrollment, and occupational distribution. In Latin America, racial constructions depend heavily on social class, so that a rich black person is "whitened" and may be considered mulatto regardless of his or her skin color. This is one reason why almost all Afrodescendent organizations, both mixed and exclusively of women, have focused on raising black consciousness and propagating black culture (Morrison 2002, 19).

The need for a uniform standard and generic term has recently led to the adoption of the term Afrodescendent, coined by Brazilian leaders of the black movement, which would signify a change of emphasis from phenotype to descent in the Latin American definition of race. Afrodescendent also focuses on the African heritage among the great majority of blacks who are racially mixed, and thus avoids the whitening bias inherent in earlier notions of *mestizaje*. However, the term also has its critics because it brings Latin American racial constructs closer to the United States by adopting a bipolar dichotomy between Afrodescendents and whites, which many Latin American activists strongly reject. Despite the need for greater black solidarity, most Latin American activists fear the racial oppositions that exist in the United States. Although adopted by some academics outside of Brazil, the term Afrodescendent is still sparsely used in popular discourse.

The competition Afrodescendent NGOs face for funding and government support from other groups like the women's movement or indigenous NGOs, helps explain why black NGOs feel they need to maintain a solid front in dealing with the state and donor organizations. While we did not examine indigenous groups, it is clear there are tensions between them and Afrodescendents, particularly in Colombia and in ethnically charged areas like the Nicaraguan Atlantic coast. This is aggravated when, as in these cases, the two groups have disputing claims to land and other resources. But government actions have also served to reinforce these tensions, as the failure to fully implement Law 70 in Colombia and the Autonomy Law in Nicaragua show.

The indigenous movement, which is older, better organized, and better funded internationally, is often given priority.[2]

Given their precarious base, some of the male-led Afrodescendent NGOs have also been hostile to the formation of separate women's organizations. Many of the leaders of the existing black women's NGOs started out in mixed organizations. Among the Garifuna of Honduras, there is clear rivalry and tension between the two major organizations, OFRANEH, a grassroots support organization led by women, and ODECO, a nongovernmental organization led by a man, but largely staffed by women and serving a largely female constituency. As Eva Thorne (2004) demonstrates, both have been actively pressuring the Honduran government to recognize the land rights of the Garifuna population along the Atlantic coasts, which is now under threat from tourism development and *mestizo* colonization. By 2001, thirty-nine collective titles to land had been granted, totaling 32,000 hectares, but this land is limited to the residential centers and does not include the agricultural land and fishing rights on which the Garifuna traditionally depended for a livelihood. In 2004 a new law passed allowing foreigners to buy Honduran coastal property, which further threatens Garifuna land. ODECO advocates a developmentalist approach working within the Honduran state, while OFRANEH is more separatist and focused on indigenous identity. OFRANEH feels development will destroy Garifuna culture (cf. Brondo n.d.). When we met with ODECO staff and visited their community projects, there was no mention of OFRANEH.

The split within the Garifuna community in Honduras and their distance from other Afrodescendent groups such as the Afro-Creoles with whom they share much of the Atlantic coast, has seriously weakened Afrodescendent solidarity in Central America. In 1995 they formed a joint organization called CABO (Central American Black Organization), but their mutual disdain is evident. The Garifuna claim to have "autochthonous" status, based on their arrival in Honduras before the formation of the Honduran state (England 1999). They also claim never to have assimilated to European culture, and to be the only Afrodescendent group to retain their language (which is, however, dying out due to pressure from the Honduran state to teach only Spanish in schools, and also due to migration). In contrast, the Afro-Creoles pride themselves on their British heritage, which they brought with them from Jamaica and other West Indian islands. As Protestants and English speakers brought to Central America to build a railroad and work on banana plantations (Gordon 1998), they gained a higher status than the Garifuna, whom they treated with disrespect. Afro-Creoles are urbanized and wage earning, with a much higher educational level, especially among women. But like the Garifuna, their ethnic standing has diminished with mass male migration to the United States, and today the remaining populations are largely dependent on remittances, sent principally from the United States.

England (1999) argues that what is emerging among the Garifuna is a new ethnic identity as a Garifuna nation, tied by common language, culture, and history, but not bound by any territorial state. Both Garifuna and Afro-Creoles have settled in New York City, and to a lesser extent Miami and other coastal cities, reflecting men's expertise as seamen, which opened opportunities to emigrate (on cruise ships, etc.). But to press their land claims, the Garifuna must continue to legitimate their status as an autochthonous people tied to territorially bounded communities. Outside of this space, as England shows, their "authenticity and often the rights that go with it become questioned" (1999, xx).

In order to understand the experience Afrodescendent women have had in working within the wider black movement and within the feminist movement, the Inter-American Development Bank (for whom this research was originally conducted) distributed questionnaires to a select group of black women's NGOs with whom they worked. Afrodescendent women in Colombia and Central America spoke most clearly about opposition from men within the wider black movement. They still seem to be reluctant to challenge men on ethnic issues, which speaks to the vulnerability of the black movement in both regions. The relationship between consciousness of inequality by gender and by race and ethnicity still needs to be explored, because it is a problem in indigenous communities as well.

Participation in the wider women's movement undoubtedly contributed to raising the gender consciousness of Afrodescendent women. However, most of the black women's NGOs we met with are very critical of the wider women's movement because of its racial and class biases. Institutionalized women's NGOs in recent years have turned away from their grassroots constituencies in favor of focusing their attention on the state and lobbying (Alvarez et al. 2003, Lebon 1996). Afro-Brazilian women's NGOs are now heavily involved in policy, and form one-third of the National Council of Women's Rights in Brazil. While this has led to some success in terms of pressuring the government to implement affirmative action policies, and to disaggregate race and gender based data on health, education, wages, and so forth, lobbying also restricts their time and ability to communicate with grassroots constituents, who often feel neglected. This, in turn, weakens their political base of support, which may be one reason why implementation of racial and gender legislation has lagged so markedly in the Latin American region.

The viability of Afrodescendent women's NGOs varies widely in the region, as does their degree of gender consciousness. But even the most fragile Afrodescendent women's NGO focuses on dignity and cultural identity, which is often manifest in an interest in Afrodescendent history, culture, and language, long ignored in their countries, both on the popular and the academic level. This focus on racial consciousness is what distinguishes black women's NGOs from the mainstream white and *mestizo* organizations. The recognition of black identity is often phrased in terms of human rights, which is now understood, particularly by feminists, to encompass not only equality under the law, but the right to be different, and to have this difference be socially recognized (Jelin 1996, 178–179). In the hands of black feminists, such a conception of human rights takes on added racial significance.

PROMOTING THE WELFARE AND SOCIAL MOBILITY OF THE AFRODESCENDENT POPULATION

Afrodescendent women have taken a leadership position in the struggle for cultural autonomy, just as they have long stood at the forefront of material survival. In all the countries reviewed, Afrodescendent women have a high labor force participation rate that is partly the result of the high percentage of female heads of household. I have argued that Afrodescendent women do not share in the myth of the male breadwinner, which persuaded many white and *mestiza* women to rely on their husbands as economic providers (Safa 1995). The racial and class barriers faced by most Afrodescendent men reduce their capacity to be adequate breadwinners, and this is aggravated by decades of large-scale male emigration, particularly in areas like the Afro-Creole and Garifuna communities. At the same time, many Afrodescendent women have succeeded in significantly raising their educational levels, particularly in Brazil and to some extent in Colombia, while the Afro-Creole women in Nicaragua and Costa Rica have long enjoyed higher educational status than their neighbors on the Atlantic coast. Only Garifuna women are still plagued by low levels of schooling and jobs, and also maintain higher birth rates than their Afrodescendent sisters. The degree to which these factors help explain the level of gender and racial consciousness in these distinct Afrodescendent populations remains to be explored.

Considerable gains in promoting gender equality have been achieved in countries like Costa Rica and Brazil, where the women's movement is strong. In fact, it would appear that in Brazil, gender inequality has been addressed more than racial inequality. Overall, gender gaps in years of schooling and illiteracy have been done away with, but the educational differential between blacks and whites has remained virtually unchanged since the 1920s (Henriques 2001). This raises the issue of the degree to which the achievements of the women's movement in terms of education, jobs, and political power have been limited largely to white or *mestiza* women. Again, we are uncertain to what extent we are dealing with a racial or class issue, where these benefits have gone largely to white or *mestiza* middle- and upper-class women, and have not reached the poor, many of whom are black (Cf. Guimaraes 2000: 51; Lovell 1999). Recent efforts have been made by the wider feminist movement in Brazil to incorporate Afro-Brazilian women, but as Lebon (2001) points out, they continue to differ on policy, where the wider women's movement focuses on rights, while Afrodescendents are more concerned about socioeconomic conditions.

There are good reasons for this difference. Despite impressive educational gains, illiteracy is 22 percent for Afro-Brazilian women versus 10 percent for white women (Sant'Anna 2001, 19). Many of these poorly educated Afrodescendent women remain in the rural area, or the most impoverished region of the northeast, where the Afrodescendent population is still much higher than in other regions, despite large-scale emigration from their area since the 1960s. Many women work in the informal economy, chiefly as domestic servants, in which half of all employed black women worked in 1991 (Lovell 2000a, 284). Afro-Brazilian women have made greater educational gains than black men, and are entering the university at a proportionately faster rate than white women, though the racial gap between women remains (Sutherland 2002). Since the 1960s, Afro-Brazilian women have made the greatest gains in white-collar work, and while they still lag far behind white women, they are better represented than black men in professional and technical jobs (Lovell 2000b). They also continue to have a higher labor force participation rate than white women, which is associated with the high percentage of female-headed households, who are often the poorest of the poor (AMB [(Articulacao de Mulheres Braileiras] 2001, 18).

Despite their educational and occupational gains, Afro-Brazilian women continue to lag behind black men in wages, while both sexes earn less than white women and especially white men. In 1991 in Sao Paulo, the average monthly wage of Afro-Brazilians and women was roughly 60 percent the respective wage of whites and men (Lovell 2000b: 286). The racial wage gap actually increases with education for both Afro-Brazilian women and men, suggesting that better schooling and jobs cannot by themselves eliminate the racial and gender wage gaps (Lovell 2000b, 286; Arias et al. 2002). The gender wage gap shrunk at about 1 percent per year between 1987 and 1998, while the race-based wage gap has not budged (Soares 2000). This demonstrates that racial inequality is not solely a product of poverty and class differences in human capital, as earlier thoughts espousing a theory of racial democracy have claimed.

The discrimination faced by Afro-Brazilians in education, employment, and wages was made more difficult by structural adjustment programs that cut government jobs and budgets, on which Afrodescendents relied heavily. The growing Afrodescendent middle class took the imitative in creating NGOs to mobilize for affirmative action and other programs aimed at bridging this racial divide. Black women leaders struggle to improve themselves, prove their capacity, and become accepted and successful in diverse aspects of a competitive world whose cultural norms are those of white male professionals. And in this personal fight, they acquire a keen and accurate perception of racial discrimination, less available to their poorer sisters, locked in the struggle for everyday survival (Damaesceno 1999).

The Afro-Creole population on the Atlantic coast of Central America also has higher levels of education than neighboring ethnic groups, and once dominated this enclave. But their ability to resist *mestizo* encroachment is waning as increasing numbers migrate abroad, while the remaining Afro-Creole population is dependent on remittances. The Afro-Creole population in Costa Rica is making more progress because they receive more state support than in Nicaragua (Putnam 2002). A 1990 study of the Afro-Creole population of Limon by McIlwaine (1997) suggests that women are faring better than men, and are more competitive than mestiza women. Afro-Creole women have higher educational levels than *mestizas* and earn more. Afro-Creole women are also more likely to be employed in professional jobs such as nursing and teaching. Incomes within Afro-Creole households are higher, due to higher labor force participation by Afro-Creole women, and to remittances, especially from abroad (mainly the United States), which constituted 70 percent of unearned income (McIlwaine 1997, 7). As McIlwaine points out, paid employment has long been at the core of Afro-Creole women's identity, whereas *mestiza* women are more closely identified with the domestic domain, and face more male restrictions on working. Here we see again the consequences of different gender ideologies for Afrodescendent and *mestiza* women. However, Afro-Creole women remain virtually excluded from key decision-making positions occupied by *mestizo* men, even in health and education, where women predominate.

Afro-Creole men have been largely confined to manual, unionized jobs in the port and on the railway, which are now closing and/or being automated. Both men and women have been severely impacted by government budget cuts and now face large-scale unemployment. As in Nicaragua, this has contributed to massive emigration, estimated in the early l990s at 30 percent, primarily of men (McIlwaine 1997, 12).

Epsy Campbell, the former president of the Network of Afro-Caribbean and Afro–Latin American Women, was elected in 2002 as a congresswoman and in 2005 was elected president of her party, the PAC (Partido Accion Ciudadana). She has long been active in the struggle for gender and racial equality. In a recent meeting to which she was invited in Washington, DC, she noted that the early incorporation of Afrodescendent women into the labor force had made them more economically independent of their husbands, and made it easier for them to leave abusive relationships (Campbell). However, she decried the absence of women in the formal political realm, noting that there are less than forty Afrodescendent women in national-level politics in all of Latin America, and twenty-six of those are in Brazil. Despite the patriarchal political structure in Latin America, she urged Afrodescendent women to become more active as elected officials and in political parties. In her own PAC, gender equity is observed in all of its structures, but there are still only two Afrodescendent women leaders in the party.

Certainly greater political participation by Afrodescendent women would aid them in pressuring the state to redress racial and gender inequities, as we shall see in the next section.

PRESSURING THE STATE TO REDRESS INEQUITIES

The state, as Eva Thorne (2000) and others have noted, not only responds to race- and ethnic-based movements, but shapes them. This is particularly true in Latin America and the Caribbean, where all states, newly independent in the nineteenth and twentieth centuries, shared a goal of biological and cultural *mestizaje* designed to forge a homogeneous and unified nation out of a multiethnic and multiracial society. *Mestizaje* was designed to blur racial differences through a process of physical and cultural racial mixture, in which, however, *blanqueamiento* or whitening was still the goal. The failure to recognize distinct racial and ethnic groups as citizens of the nation with equal rights led to the social exclusion of indigenous and Afrodescendent groups. Their needs were not met, and their access to educational and occupational resources and other basic services were very limited. Most Latin American and Caribbean states still have not established separate categories for Afrodescendents and indigenous peoples in the national census, making it difficult to measure racial and ethnic inequalities. Lack of adequate statistical data make these groups invisible, and continues to hamper policies to address their poverty and neglect.

Latin American governments justify their denial of racial differences on scientific grounds, arguing that because race is no longer valid as a biological category, it should no longer be measured or differentiated through the census (Guimaraes 1999, 144). This contributed to the replacement of the word *race* by *ethnicity* in scientific texts and government documents for fifty years, starting in the postwar period, while skin color categories remained. Latin American governments argue that the denial of race or nonracialism implies rejection of racism, and in turn the possibility of racial discrimination. However, such a stance ignores the importance of the social construction of race, which is still used to differentiate and discriminate against the Afrodescendent population. In fact, several scholars contend that cultural or class criteria (which deem white European culture and civilization as supreme) have come to replace biological phenotype as the primary basis of discrimination in Latin America (Guimaraes 2001; de la Cadena 2001). To quote de la Cadena (2001, 16), "culture has been racialized."

However, as Lebon (2001) asserts, "the first roadblock to the dismantling of racial inequalities in Brazil" is overcoming the myth of racial democracy. Proponents of racial democracy argue that racial inequalities may be subsumed under class differences and are not due to racial discrimination. They also suggest that with economic development, and the improvement of educational and occupational opportunities among the Afrodescendent population, racial inequalities will diminish. The fallacies inherent in racial democracy were made apparent by the rise of an educated black middle class, which still suffers from discrimination in jobs, wages, and access to state services. In fact, competition may be greater among people of higher status, as we have seen in the case of the wider wage gaps between Afro-Brazilian and white professional women. A recent study by the Inter-American Development Bank demonstrates that at the top of the wage scale, blacks suffer greater disadvantages in terms of returns from education than in the lower ranks, while the opposite is true for mulattoes (Arias et al. 2002). So the theory that "money whitens" appears to be true for pardos or mulattos, although the bulk of racial earnings inequality is due to the advantages whites have accumulated in human capital. In the period of economic growth between 1960 and 1980, Lovell shows, labor market inequalities between whites and Afro-Brazilians (and between women and men) increased. Similarly, recent economic growth in Salvador, Brazil has not reduced the gap in unemployment rates by race (Castro and Guimaraes 1999).

Sharp regional differences in access to state resources persist in all these countries, in part a product of the colonial enclave economy that imported Afrodescendent laborers to its own advantage and later abandoned them. In Nicaragua, Afro-Creoles have been displaced by *mestizos*, who now constitute 72 percent of the Atlantic coast population, and are politically and economically dominant (CONPES, Consejo Nacional de Planificación Económica Social). The students in the newly established university on the Atlantic coast are predominantly mestiza women.

The Brazilian state has now begun to question racial democracy and to give some support to affirmative action policies to benefit the Afrodescendent population (Htun 2004). The Durban World Conference on Racism, where four hundred Brazilians—black and white, and women and men—formed the official delegation, played a major role in addressing racism and its consequences. Much support in preparing for this conference and for Afro-Brazilians generally was given by the Ford Foundation. In 2002, President Cardoso issued a National Affirmative Action Program charged with studying the feasibility of percentage goals for blacks, women, and the handicapped in public service. In that same year, Bahia's state university announced that 40 percent of spots in undergraduate and graduate programs would hereafter be reserved for Afro-Brazilians. Later some other state universities followed suit.

Such policies have been seriously questioned on the grounds that they will only benefit the black middle class and may reinforce racial identities (Guimaraes 2000), leading to racial dichotomies as exist in the United States. It is also argued that affirmative action is increasing racial tensions in working-class Brazilian communities, where traditionally the lowest level of racial discrimination was observed. At any rate, given the difficult financial situation in Brazil, affirmative action may remain largely symbolic, but certainly the issue of racism has been publicly discussed very differently from before.

The 2003 electoral success of the Workers Party, with strong black support and the installation of a labor union leader, Lula (Luis Ignacio da Silva), as president suggests that class-based interracial solidarity may be more important than strictly racial consciousness. This is not a return to class-based racial democracy, but an acknowledgement of the demographic fact that most Afrodescendents are poor, as are a near majority of white Brazilians (Guimaraes 2001). To underline the importance of class, Telles (1999) observes that race has never served as the basis for overt legal discrimination in Brazil, nor as the basis for marked residential segregation, but there are marked class residential differences.

However, relying on class-based institutions like political parties and labor unions for access to political power may disadvantage Afrodescendent women. Although they have always been very active at the community and family level and some are now organized in NGOs, this has not translated into political power. Brazil now has a 30 percent quota of women as candidates in political parties, but this has yet to be implemented (Lebon 2001). The same lack of access to political power has been noted among Afro-Creoles and Garifuna women in Central America. Opposition by Afrodescendent and *mestizo* men is undoubtedly a factor.

In conclusion, despite greater rhetorical support for racial and cultural pluralism and the efforts of Afrodescendent organizations to press their claims for greater cultural recognition and for more state resources to address the needs of the Afrodescendent population, whitening and assimilation through *mestizaje* is still the clear preference of most Latin American and Caribbean states. As a recent analysis of the stalemate in the Zapatista's quest for autonomy argues, the neoliberal state recognizes a plurality of indigenous (and Afrodescendent) identities, so long as "those identities do not become the basis for collective organization around substantive rights "(Stahler-Sholk 2005, 37). The emphasis on individualism within the neoliberal economy erodes solidarity and eventually destroys the basis for collective action.

Latin American states undoubtedly remain concerned that the social mobilization of Afrodescendent populations may promote internal dissent and fragmentation, but the Afro-Brazilian experiment suggests that this is not the case. It is possible for Afrodescendent groups to promote their own cultural identity and welfare, yet remain loyal to the larger nation-state, particularly if, as in Brazil, the state moves toward a more pluralistic framework. Where the state demands conformity to a rigid mestizo model of *blanqueamiento*, as in Nicaragua, then racial and ethnic minorities may become alienated and lose a sense of national allegiance.

Afrodescendent groups are not rejecting *mestizaje* per se, rather the bias toward *blanqueamiento* promoted in earlier Eurocentric versions. They wish to redefine *mestizaje* to have their own cultural identity valued on an equal footing with that of whites or *mestizos*, which would require access to the resources and services which many of the latter now enjoy. Reform would also replace racial democracy with racial pluralism, coupled with a recognition of the need for collective rights. Thus, social inclusion need not be based on homogenization, but on an appreciation of the existing racial and ethnic diversity in Latin American and the Caribbean. The roles that women play in these Afrodescendent movements argue for a greater concern for gender equality in the quest for greater social justice in the region.

REFERENCES

Alvarez, Sonia, Elizabeth Friedman, Ericka Beckman, Maylei Blackwell, Norma Stolz Chinchilla, Nathalie Lebon, Marysa Navarro, and Marcela Ríos Tobar. 2003. "Encountering Latin American and Caribbean Feminisms." *Signs* 28(2):537–580.

AMB (Articulacao de Mulheres Braileiras). 2001. *Mulheres negras: Um retrato da discriminacao racial no Brasil*. Brasilia: AMB

Arias, Omar, Gustavo Yamada, and Luis Tejerina. 2002. *Education, Family Background and Racial Earnings Inequality in Brazil*. Washington, DC: Inter-American Development Bank.

Brondo, Keri. N.d. "Of Earth and Women: Honduran Women's Activism in Honduras." Unpublished manuscript.

Campbell, Epsy. "Afro-descendant Women's Leadership on Gender and Race Policies in Latin America." Inter-American Dialogue, http://www.thedialogue.org/lack/eng/events/Afro-Latin American Women's Leadership.

Castro, Nadya and Antonio Sergio Guimaraes. 1999. "Racial Inequalities in the Labor Market and the Workplace." In *Race in Contemporary Brazil: From Indifference to Inequality*, ed. Rebecca Reichmann, 83–107. University Park: Pennsylvania State University Press.

Cimarronas. 2001. Boletín de la Red de Mujeres Afro-latinoamericanas y Afro-caribeñas, no. 11, April.

Damasceno, Caetana Maria. 1999. "Women Workers in Brazil: Laborious Interpretations of the Racial Condition." In *Race in Contemporary Brazil: From Indifference to Inequality*, ed. Rebecca Reichmann. University Park: Pennsylvania State University Press, 117–131.

Degler, Carl. 1971. *Neither Black nor White*. New York: Macmillan.

De la Cadena, Marisol. 2001. "Reconstructing Race: Racism, Culture, and Mestizaje in Latin America." *NACLA* (North American Congress on Latin America) 34(6):16–23.

England, Sarah. 1999. "Negotiating Race and Place in the Garifuna Diaspora: Identity Formation and Transnational Grassroots Politics in New York City and Honduras." *Identities* 6(1):5–54.

Gordon, Edmund T. 1998. *Disparate Diasporas: Identity and Politics in an African-Nicaraguan Community.* Austin: University of Texas Press.

Guimaraes, Antonio Sergio. 1999. "Measures to Combat Discrimination and Racial Inequality in Brazil." In Race in Contemporary Brazil: From Indifference to Inequality, ed. Rebecca Reichmann. University Park: Pennsylvania Stare University Press.

_____. 2000. "The Causes of Black Poverty in Brazil: A few reflections. In Race and Poverty: Interagency Consultation on Afro-Latin Americans." LCR Sustainable Development Working Paper No. 9. Inter-American Dialogue, Inter-American Development Bank, World Bank.

_____. 2000. "Race, Class and Color: Behind Brazil's Racial Democracy." *NACLA* 34(6).

Hanchard, Michael G. 1994. *Orpheus and Power: The Movimiento Negro of Rio de Janeiro and Sao Paulo, Brazil, 1945–1988.* Princeton, NJ: Princeton University Press.

Hasenbalg, Carlos and Nelson do Valle Silva. 1999. "Notes on Racial and Political Inequality at Work in Brazil." In Racial Politics in Contemporary Brazil, ed. Michael Hanchard, 154–178. Durham, NC: Duke University Press.

Henriques, Ricardo. 2001. *Desigualdade Racial no Brasil: Evolucao das Condicoes de Vida na Decada de 90.* Texto para Discusscao no 807. IPEA: Rio de Janeiro.

Htun, Mala. 2004. "From 'Racial Democracy' to Affirmative Action: Changing State Policy on Race in Brazil." *Latin American Research Review* 39(1):60–89.

Jelin, Elizabeth. 1996. "Women, Gender and Human Rights." In *Constructing Democracy: Human Rights, Citizenship and Society in Latin America,* ed. E. Jelin and E. Hershberg, 177–196. Boulder, CO: Westview Press..

Lebon, Nathalie. 1996. "Professionalization of Women's Health Groups in São Paulo: The Troublesome Road towards Organizational Diversity." *Organization* 3(4):588–609.

_____. 2001. "Beyond Confronting the Myth of Racial Democracy: The Role of Afro-Brazilian Women Scholars and Activists." Paper presented at Congress of LASA (Latin American Studies Association), Washington, DC.

Lovell, Peggy. 1999. "Development and the Persistence of Racial Inequality in Brazil: 1950–1991 " *Journal of Developing Areas* 33:395–418.

_____. 2000a. "Gender, Race, and the Struggle for Social Justice in Brazil." *Latin American Perspectives* 27(6): 85–103.

_____. 2000b. "Race, Gender and Regional Labor Market Inequalities in Brazil." *Review of Social Economy* 58(3):277–293.

Lovell, Peggy and Charles Wood. 1998. "Skin Color, Racial Identity, and Life Chances in Brazil." *Latin American Perspectives* 25(3):90–109.

McIlwaine, Cathy. 1997. "Vulnerable or Poor? A Study of Ethnic and Gender Disadvantage among Afro-Caribbeans in Limón, Costa Rica." *European Journal of Development Research* 9(2):35–61.

Morrison, Judith. 2002. "Cashing in on Afro-Latin Communities: Strategies for Promoting Grassroots Initiatives." In *Economic Development in Latin American Communities of African Descent: Presentations from the XXIII International Congress of the Latin American Studies Association*, 17–28. Washington, DC: Inter-American Foundation.

Putnam, Lara. 2002. *The Company They Kept: Migrants and the Politics of Gender in Caribbean Costa Rica, 1870–1960.* Chapel Hill: University of North Carolina Press.

Safa, Helen I. 1995. *The Myth of the Male Breadwinner: Women and Industrialization in the Caribbean.* Boulder, CO: Westview Press.

_____. 1998. "Introduction to Race and National Identity in the Americas." Special issue of *Latin American Perspectives* 25(3):3–20.

_____. 2002. "Challenging Social Exclusion: Afro-Descendent Women in Latin America and the Caribbean." Report presented to IADB with Nathalie Lebon and Kirin Asher.

_____. 2005. "Challenging Mestizaje: A Gender Perspective on Indigenous and Afrodescendant Movements in Latin America." *Critique of Anthropology* 25(3):307–330.

Sant'anna, Wania 2001. *Relacoes Racais no Brasil: Entre a Unianimidade e Paralisia. Perspectivas em Saude e Direitos Reproductivas. no. 4, ano 2.* Sao Paulo and Chicago: Macarthur Foundation.

Soares, Sergei Suarez Dillon. 2000. *O Perfil da Discriminacao no Mercado de Trabalho: Homens Negros, Mulheres Brancas e Mulheres Negras. Texto para discussao No 769.* Brazilia: IPEA.

Stahler-Sholk, Richard. 2005. "Time of the Snails: Autonomy and Resistance in Chiapas." *NACLA* 38(5):34–40.

Sutherland, Jeannette. 2002. "Economic Development vs. Social Exclusion: the Cost of Development in Brazil." In *Economic Development in Latin American Communities of African Descent: Presentations from the XXIII International Congress of the Latin American Studies Association.* Washington, DC: Inter-American Foundation, 138–155.

Telles, Edward. 1999. "Ethnic Boundaries and Political Mobilization among African Brazilians: Comparisons with the U.S. Case." In *Racial Politics in Contemporary Brazil*, ed. Michael Hanchard. Durham, NC: Duke University Press.

Thorne, Eva. 2000. *The Role of Civil Society in the Collection of Data on Race.* Washington, DC: Inter-American Development Bank. Reprinted in revised version in *Social Inclusion and Economic Development in Latin America*, ed. Mayra Buvinic and Jacqueline Mazza with Ruthanne Deutsch, 307–334. Inter-American Development Bank and Johns Hopkins University Press, 2004.

——. 2004. "Land Rights and Garifuna Identity." *NACLA* 38(2):21–25.

Turner, J. Michael. 2002. "The Road to Durban—and Back. *NACLA* 35(6):31–35.

Wade, P. 1993. *Blackness and Race Mixture: The Dynamics of Racial Identity in Colombia*. Baltimore and London: Johns Hopkins University Press.

Walker, Sheila. 2002. "Africanity vs. Blackness: Race, Class and Culture in Brazil." *NACLA* 35(6):16–20.

NOTES

1. Santiago was the site of the regional preparatory conference for the III United Nations World Conference against Racism, Racial Discrimination, Xenophobia and Related Intolerances, held in Durban South Africa in September 2001.
2. For a fuller comparison of Afrodescendent and indigenous movements, see Safa 2005.

10

THE POLITICS OF EXCLUSION
Place and the Legislation of the Environment in the Florida Everglades

Max Kirsch

Every time you go to a place
That has those animals on its face,
It makes you laugh and cheer
Because it's fun out here.
We love you Everglades!
We'll help to save the place!

Poem written by a group of six-graders on a bronze plaque at the Pay-Hay-Okee boardwalk overlook.

The Everglades has long been the site of culture wars over the future of environmental standards in the United States and in Florida. Environmental and development issues are continuing to generate increasing conflict in Everglades' communities, which are already under stress from rapid social change. The current restructuring of the agricultural industry and new environmental legislation have highlighted the differences in approaches to the maintenance of places that exist within Everglades communities and the proposals for development that are being presented by industries and governmental agencies. These differences are challenging communities to respond to changes initiated from outside their boundaries.

There has been a substantial effort on the part of community-based organizations to engage citizens in the decision-making process of legislative policies. The current threats to environmental justice make community involvement and education even more significant than past concerns about equity and participation in the formulation of environmental planning.

This paper will explore the position and interaction of Everglades' communities as they struggle to maintain a sense of place in an arena where the federal and Florida state governments have pledged to spend an estimated $16 billion dollars in restoration activities over the next ten to thirty years. It will do so within a framework that argues against attempts to analyze communities through the postmodern discussions of deterritorialization and flexibility of capital that now characterize much of the analyses of globalization. These abstractions fail to assess the conditions of community resistance to outside forces, as Nash (2001a, 2001b) so strongly notes. It proposes that what is needed are more localized descriptions and histories that influence global forces and help interpret their prominent role in local developments.

A BRIEF HISTORY OF THE EVERGLADES

The Florida Everglades is an unique environment that is characterized by a subtropical vegetation, wildlife, and hydrology. Created more than 6,000 years ago by changes in the Atlantic Ocean's water levels and characterized by heavy rainfall and a low-nutrient soil, it was taken over by subtropical plants and a river of grass that extended from the banks of Lake Okeechobee to the Florida Bay. The Everglades Agricultural Area (EAA) is now situated in an area of intense commercial and real estate development, managed by a complex interaction among local, state, federal, and private interests. The private investments are primarily in sugar production, although the increasing introduction of new vegetable crops and attempts at building a tourist industry have also greatly affected the current discussion.

The EEA is a drained swamp established by government decree in the mid-nineteenth century when twenty million wetland acres were handed over to Florida lawmakers, and reclamation became a statewide rallying cry (cf. Roberts 1999). Reclamation meant turning the land from swamp into palatable farmland that could support rice, cotton, citrus, and sugarcane. The land was restructured by the construction of canals that drained the swampy water into the Atlantic Ocean, thus exposing a mucky soil inhabited by saw grass. By the 1920s, development of the area was in full swing, with the population growing tenfold between 1900 and 1930 (Roberts 1999). By the end of the drainage project in the 1960s, over 18,000 square miles had been drained, utilizing 1,000 miles of canals, 720 miles of levies, and over 200 water control structures (Scully 2001, B13–14).

As David McCally tells us:

> The Engineering plan that was formulated in the 1940s ... effectively killed the Everglades. To be sure, wetlands did not totally disappear from peninsular Florida, but these remnants are decidedly not the Everglades, even though the name still appears on maps. Of the three traits that characterized the pre-drainage system in the Everglades—habitat heterogeneity, large spatial extent, and a distinctive hydrologic regime—the new water-control works most directly affected the last, but the destruction of the system's hydrologic regime led, inevitably, to a reduction in the size and biotic diversity of the wetlands (McCally 1999, quoted in Scully 2001, B13).

Despite the many obstacles that confronted the early farmers on what turned out to be a low-nutrient soil, sugar production in the area began to swell, particularly with the development of new strains of sugar crops that were more adaptive to the local environmental constraints. The area began to commercially thrive, but the real story began with the Cuban revolution and the consequent embargo on Cuban sugar. The impact of the revolution, and the United States response to it, drew more outsiders to the area, including former Cuban sugar producers. By the mid-1960s, sugar acreage had increased tenfold, making it a major industry in the state that rivaled citrus production and tourism. In the process, the folksy *Gladesmen* (Simmons 1998) and sugar producers that are portrayed in accounts such as *Big Sugar* (Wilkinson 1989), *Crackers in the Glade* (Storter 2000), *Totch, a Life in the Everglades* (Brown 1993), and *The Everglades: River of Grass* (Douglas 1947), have been replaced in the agricultural fields and communities of the EAA by the harsh realities of Alan Burn's *Maya in Exile* (1993), a tale of the migrant labor that fuels the production of cane and vegetables that are sold all over the world.

The sugar industry has manifested an overwhelming influence on state and federal regulations, and plays a large role in electoral politics. Sugar companies were a major contributor to the Clinton, George W. Bush, and Jeb Bush election campaigns. Bruce Babitt, the Clinton administration's environmental chief, managed to win over the support of the World Wildlife Fund, the National Wildlife Federation, the Nature Conservancy, and the Wilderness Society, despite the harm many environmental critics and local communities claimed the Clinton policies would produce. This was the same Bruce Babbitt who devised a market-oriented environmentalism that negotiated with environmental groups, ultimately convincing the Sierra Club to work with him to pass legislation that halved the old growth that remained in the Pacific Northwest.[1] The Sierra Club had initially taken a stand but did not actively oppose NAFTA, which by general agreement of environmental scientists and activists weakened existing environmental policies. All of these environmental organizations receive large corporate contributions, and positions that threaten corporate funding also threaten organizational viability.

The Clinton administration's plan for Everglades restoration bore an uncanny resemblance to a plan championed by the sugar industry. The plan calls for restoration to begin south of the sugar farms, and requires that Florida taxpayers pay half the $700 million cost for filtration marshes. In a highly politicized move, also initiated by Florida Crystals, the sugar industry was exempted from the NAFTA deregulation of industry until at least 2008, while its production continues to be subsidized. The arrangement defies free trade logic, while irking refiners and consumers (Barboza 2002, 1).

While the sugar industry does not have the magnitude of environmental pollutants as, for example, the electrical machine industry and its use of polychlorinated biphenyl (PCBs) (Nash and Kirsch 1986, 1994), the heavy use of phosphorus as a fertilizer has raised concerns about the area's flora and fauna. The sugar industry has poured millions of dollars into discrediting studies documenting the harmful effects of phosphorous, successfully directing the flow of information to the public through advertising and private research.

There has been almost no documentation of the effects of sugar burning on the area's residents, who report that there is an increase in rashes on children's legs during the burning season. There has also been little research concerning the rise of asthma, as one of the many health concerns voiced by citizen's groups. Without a doubt, there are other pollutants and health concerns that have gone unnoticed due to the immigration status of the area's workers, and the concern (and threats) about the possible loss of jobs. Thus, the conditions of work run counter to residents and their communities' engagement with the maintenance of land and resources (cf. Portes and Stepick 1985). As it is, prospects for agricultural work are worse than they were when Edward R. Murrow's *Harvest of Shame* was filmed in 1961. Belle Glade, the largest center on the lake, lacks even a movie theater but welcomes its visitors with the sign "Her Soil Is Her Fortune" (Longman November 23, 2001).

In recent years, farming co-ops have risen as an alternative to the major corporations, and many have been more engaged with environmental concerns and the health of their workers. A myriad of lawsuits involving sugar farmers and migrant workers has resulted in the mechanization of harvesting, and while housing and health care has improved for some, workers are mostly relegated to sugar planting and manual harvesting, forced to migrate to other areas for citrus production in the off-season (Resnick 1991, Jefferson 1993; United States Accounting Office, 1991).

The fate of the Everglades is now in the hands of a new administration in Washington closely tied to development interests in the state of Florida. In a 2000 editorial, the *New York Times* publicly worried about the fate of the restoration project, when Gale Norton, Bush's Secretary of the Interior, removed Michael Davis, the Clinton administration's point man on the Everglades (*New York Times*, November 23, 2001, A32). The possibility that what is left of the restoration may be derailed has been heightened by fear that the effects of the September 11 attack will curtail budgets and cast a large shadow over environmental efforts. As Robert P. King wrote in the *Palm Beach Post*:

> It's just one example of a chill that has settled on a variety of environmental causes in wartime America, where data on toxic chemicals have vanished from some government Web sites and activists have felt compelled to refrain from criticizing President Bush. (October 29, 2001)

Indeed, reporting on current negotiations about the restoration has taken a notable back seat to U.S. activities abroad, and there is concern that the U.S. Congress and the Florida Legislature will this year cut back on planned restoration funding.

GETTING THERE

The trip into the northern part of the Everglades invariably involves a superhighway, as any travel in central and south Florida now does. Coming from the south, there are three routes, but the most popular is I-95, the infamous stretch of highway that reaches down the east coast from Maine to Miami. In Florida, it becomes one of the most dangerous highways in the nation. The urban sprawl and growth of suburban enclaves, which has doubled Florida's growth several times in the past forty years, has created an infrastructure crisis: crowded highways, substandard schools, and overcrowded prisons among the most discussed. The other, overarching problem is water.

As you leave I-95, turning toward Palm Beach International Airport and through the new urbanism that has become the staple of Florida's development, you pass through various towns of strip malls and shopping centers, gated communities, and building developments. About twenty miles out, however, the landscape dramatically changes. Quite suddenly the speed limit changes to sixty-five miles per hour, and a vastness of sky appears, limited only by what appears on both sides of the two-lane highway: sugarcane. To the uninitiated, these fields appear somewhat like cornfields, their plant structure resembling the large hard-leafed stalks of maize or bamboo. We have entered the Everglades Agricultural Area, home of not only sugar but also tomatoes, beans, lettuce, sugar beets, tomatoes, watermelons, celery, leafy vegetables, cabbage, and Chinese vegetables. Citrus fruit is also prominent in the mix. Resembling the cultivated farmlands of the Midwest, the fact that this was once saw grass–filled marshes is difficult to imagine, and the language of globalism, for which the discussion of sugar is noted, seems even more abstract and disconnected to the site in view. In the Everglades, place is determined by the seasons and its crops, and the workers and farmers who populate the area. Like Sassen's (1998) discussion of the telecommunications industry in New York City, place is here determined by the necessity of geographic locale and by the product it supports. But beyond the importance of locale and product, there have been strong fluid communities long before the advent of agricultural conglomerates. The presence of African-American and American Indian populations, along with the newer Mayan-speaking Guatemalans, Caribbean immigrants, and white enclaves speak to the structures of community maintenance that exist beyond the realm of the production line. Kinship and family and the organizations that support them are the buffer between the local population and the changing hands of corporate multinationals and legislation that now dominate the headlines.

The principal destination from this road into the Everglades is Belle Glade, a city of 14,000 people and 2,862,000 acres of subtropical Everglades. Founded in 1928, the area was first inhabited by the Calusa Indians, and later by the Seminole Indians who gave Lake Okeechobee (Land of Big Water) its name. Today it houses farmers (those who stay in the area year round, and migrants (those who travel for agricultural work) and the auxiliary services needed to maintain their presence. Noticeable as one enters Belle Glade are the ramshackle houses and the number of churches of every denomination. Social agencies that service the area are prominent in number and diversity. Belle Glade is a town that has long experienced the need for supportive community organizations and social service agencies, both publicly and privately funded.

The stark transition between the growing developments of the east and the agricultural fields and towns of the Everglades symbolizes the contradictions inherent in Florida's development and the current strategies to address differing interest groups and communities. The politics that are played out in the media and the halls of government often obscure the current state of community participation in decision making, and the attempts by community-based organizations to maintain a sense of place and history in these processes.

LEVELS OF INTEGRATION
Global Forces

It is nearly impossible to find fresh produce in South Florida's grocery stores. Beyond the occasional roadside stand or individual truck selling watermelons in the more populated areas, most produce found in grocery stores comes from outside the area: berries and fruits from Chile, apples from New Zealand or the American Northwest, onions and root crops from the north. That one of the most productive agricultural areas in the country does not sell its crops to the local population speaks to the integration of the area in the global economy. Tardanico and Rosenberg (2000) show that processes of globalization, particularly in the name of the North American Free Trade Agreement (NAFTA) integrate both underdeveloped economies, such as those of southern Mexico, and the rich economies of the north, including the southern United States. The marginalization of indigenous and local groups feeds into the global and continental shifts that are "segmenting societies and linking up valuable functions, individuals, social groups, and territories, while excluding others" (Tardanico and

Rosenberg 2000, 4; Castells et al. 1995–1996, 53). They also point out that the southern United States does not fare well in comparison to the Northeast corridor. Differences in the New South are acute: telecommunications in North Carolina's Research Triangle do not compare with the poor agricultural areas of the Old South, which harbor far more migrant and poorly paid labor than the NAFTA documents would suggest (Tardanico and Rosenberg 2000, 4–5).

Accordingly, regions are not comparable simply by economic output. The time–space compression that Harvey (1990, 1998) refers to as the condition of late capitalism, is not clearly apparent in the vegetable and sugar fields of the Everglades, nor can it explain the mechanization of cultivation that has been introduced during the past decade. The postmodern discussions of deterritorialization and the inevitability of capital fluidity tend to naturalize the break between people and place, and fail to indicate the resistance to such exogenous forces by local communities (Nash 2001a, 2001b). In Appadurai's (1991) terms, "Deterritorialization," is where "money, commodities and persons unendingly chase each other around the world that the group imagination of the modern world find their fractured and fragmented counterpart"[2] Grounding this view in the realm of migration, Inda and Rosaldo tell us that:

> as a result of all this back and forth movement, from the West to the rest and vice versa, the familiar lines between "here" and "there," center and periphery and vice versa, West and non-West have to some extent become blurred. That is to say, insofar as the Third World is the First and the First World is the Third, it has become difficult to specify with any certitude where one entity begins and the other one ends…. Where, for example, does one draw the boundaries of Mexico when many of "its people" live in the U.S.? Or where does one draw the boundaries of the U.S. when "its capital" has such a strong presence in Mexico? (Inda and Rosaldo 2002, 22)

Both Nash (2001a, 2001b), and Mintz (1998) warn that this fascination with deterritorialization and deculturalization focuses analyses on the abstraction of capital accumulation, including its control over the movement of people, leading to the conceptual loss of agency in communities and regions disaffected by organizational changes in production. Current debates over deterritorialization and capital fluidity are not exceptionally different from the contested analyses of the 1970s and 1980s that characterized Wallerstein's *The Modern World*

System (1974), which posited *core* and *periphery* as primary units of analysis, often forgetting the periphery had much to do with how the core countries organized their intrusions into uncolonized, and later colonized, regions of the world. The argument has evolved so that the core is now described as ethnoscapes, technoscapes, and financescapes (Appaduari 1986, 1990) and the periphery as the world at large.

The creation of a binary between space as fluid and place as decentered has taken the role of the social scientist outside the community and into the world of power as an abstraction. The people who inhabit these spaces are easily identified as spokes in the global wheel, reacting solely to the forces of capital surrounding them rather than to their own histories, religions, families, and beliefs. What is forgotten is the increasing fragmentation of regions and communities and often the violence that accompanies the attempt to recapture identity through the political maize of global politics. As the personnel involved in these new descriptions of capital flows constitute a kind of global network entrenched in a narrow cosmopolitanism, we run the risk of creating a novel, class-based centrism that focuses on the managers of capital rather than the communities of place. Too, the Balkanization of many parts of the world attests to the danger of viewing the world in Inda and Rosaldo's terms. There is resistance to attempts at deterritorialization, proving it to be much more a category of political strategy than a holistic analytic process. The Zapitista uprising is one of many instances Nash cites to show the importance of territorial resistance to globalization that denies the continuing priority of peoples' association with place. Those who naturalize the forced relocation of people undermine the basis of such struggles. For similar reasons, Mintz has objected to the popular use of *creolization* as the blending of Carribean cultures by many scholars of globalization, commenting:

> It stood for centuries of culture-building rather than culture mixing or culture blending by those who became Caribbean people. They were not becoming transnational; they were creating forms by which to live, even while they were being cruelly tested physically and mentally.... Resistance, both symbolic and real, figured importantly in the way such culture-building happened, because people in chains must deal with living meaningfully in one place, and with their chains, at the same time. (1998, 19)

Englund cautions us: "We are never anywhere, anywhen, but in place" (Englund 2002, 267; Casey 1996, 39). He prefers to use the term *emplacement*, where "the subject is inextricably situated in a historically and existentially specific condition, defined, for brevity, as a 'place'" (Englund 2002, 267).

Thus, in a language of globalization that stresses deterritorialization and the free movement of capital and peoples, community-based organizations are necessarily viewed as inconsequential remnants, if not cultural survivals of the past, unable to confront the onslaught of multinational restructuring to provide comfort and resistance to community oppression or destruction. But communities are vibrant and changing sources of place, as Mintz (1998) reminds us, and the Everglades has a long history of organizations that provide services and support to both visiting and stable local populations.

The migrants, farmers, and other residents of the Everglades are, of course, deeply affected by changes in global strategies for capitalist accumulation. But as we shall see, these changes are substantially modified by national, local, and community forces that call into question the postmodern analyses of communities, capital, and production.

National Influences

The history of sugar, vegetable production, and Everglades environmental policy is global, national, and local in scope, but none has had a more powerful presence than the federal government and the halls of Washington. Congress passed the Everglades Restoration Plan in 2000, and to date over $1 billion in funding has been granted. The plan is under the direction of the Army Corps of Engineers, the federal agency charged with initially draining the swamps in the 1940s. Nationally, the Army Corp approves proposals for the draining and filling of streams, marshes, and other wetlands, and regularly approves over 99 percent of such requests, destroying more wetlands than any developer (Grunwald June 24, 2002, A16). As Grunwald reports, "This mind-set was on display after September 11, when the Chief Corps regulator sent an e-mail to staff nationwide: 'the harder we work to expedite the issuance of permits, the more we serve the nation by moving the economy forward'" (Grunwald June 24, 2002, A16). Indeed, while the Army Corps initially questioned a mining plan that is now destroying more wetlands than was permitted nationwide in 2001, as Grunwald tells us, "the Corps is not blocking the plan, or even fighting the plan. The Corps is promoting the plan as a key element of its 7.8 billion Everglades restoration project" (Grunwald June 24, 2002, A01).

Contradictions in stated policy and local reasoning have become acute. While Vice President Gore was campaigning on a platform that stressed the importance of the environment—a primary component of the Democratic Party's Platform—he refused to denounce an airport proposed at the edge of the Everglades because it was being proposed by powerful Cuban-American business organizations (Grunwald June 23, 2002, A16). Many believe that this refusal to defend environmental standards cost him the election, and environmental organizations split over the decision by many to campaign for Ralph Nader, who received more than 96,000 votes in Florida.

Further complicating the situation is the lack of knowledge about how true restoration would work. The Corps of Engineers has proposed numerous projects that have been criticized both by environmental organizations and by other federal agencies, such as the Fish and Wildlife Service, although the current director never forwarded staff critiques to Congress. Richard Harvey, the Environmental Protection Agency's South Florida manager, argues that the plan focuses on water quantity rather than water quality. He stated in an internal e-mail: "Getting the water quality right is critical to the restoration of the ecosystem and yet the two lead agencies—the Corps and the [South Florida] Water Management District—don't seem to have a clue about how to do it—and therefore choose to virtually ignore/hope it will go away—unless they are sued" (quoted in Grunwald June 24, 2002, A11).

Gore championed the Everglades Restoration Plan in Congress, with the assistance of U.S. Senator Bob Graham (Democrat from Florida) and Representative Clay Shaw (Republican from Florida). The plan and the politics surrounding it were shepherded through the initial stages by Bruce Babbitt. Among Babbit's greatest concerns was the pivotal role of Florida in both the 1996 and 2000 elections, moving him to lobby hard with stakeholders in the restoration process, including legislators, industry, and developers. As the plan stands, its wording plays homage to the need that water be redirected to the developing coast. In its first section justifying the plan, the house version of the bill declares, "the plan is approved as a framework for modifications and operational changes to the Central and Southern Florida Project that are needed to restore, preserve, and protect the South Florida ecosystem while providing for other water-related need of the region, including water supply and flood protection" (United States Congress September 7, 2000, H.R. 5121; 106 H.R. 5121, emphasis added).

The influence of the sugar companies in the halls of Congress and the federal agencies in Washington is now legendary. Not only did the final plan unveiled by Babbitt and Gore closely resemble the suggestions made by the sugar industry, but the $2 million that the U.S. Sugar Corporation and the Fanjul-owned Florida Crystals have pumped into federal election campaigns helped them to negotiate the placement of the restoration so it would not interfere with sugarcane production.

Locality and Sugar

First domesticated in New Guinea around 8000 BC, the history of sugar and the human dependence on its use is a complex one. Its role in U.S. national policy is less enigmatic. It starts with the American Revolution and the British Molasses Act, which in 1733 stipulated that all non-British sugar be heavily taxed. The current history starts with the revolution in Cuba, where U.S. investors had purchased the majority of all sugar production and created a one-crop economy, contributing "to a century of rebellions, dictatorships, coups, repression, and, finally, revolution" (Roberts 1999, 56). The Cuban revolution marked a new era in American sugar production, leading to the current debates over sugar subsidies, migrant worker rights, and the power of political interest groups.

Before the massive restructuring of the Everglades that took place in the 1940s and 1950s, what is now the Everglades Agricultural Area consisted of twenty million inland acres. By 1920, four large canals had been dug from Lake Okeechobee to the Atlantic Ocean, opening up what growers hoped would be fertile ground for agricultural production. As it turns out, they miscalculated. Sugar is a dry land crop, and the muck created by the draining was not suitable for cane growth. The problem was solved with the breeding of new strains of cane, and the enormous applications of phosphorous and nitrogen. Until 1959, the U.S. sugar crop remained small, with the U.S. Sugar Corporation, owned by the Mott family, as the primary benefactor of the reclamation efforts.

In 1959 the story changed. With Cuban sugar banned from sale in the United States, the federal government initiated substantial incentives for sugar production. The Army Corp drained more swamp. By the mid-1960s, Florida's sugar production had increased tenfold, and with the help of Washington, became the major player in Florida politics (Roberts 1999, 58).

Along with the expansion of sugar production came Cuban sugar producers, the most influential among them Alfonso Fanjul, who bought 4,000 acres of drained farmland. By 1990, the company had bought Domino Sugar and 90,000 new acres of Florida land along with 110,000 acres in the Dominican Republic, forming the Florida Crystals Corporation. Florida Crystals is now the largest sugar producer in the United States.

The Fanjuls became a major force in national and Florida politics. The movie *Strip Tease* was based on the Fanjul family, and their influence over national environmental policy has become legendary. Still, they faced obstacles. Sued by environmental and labor organizations for both their mistreatment of migrants and the pollution caused by phosphorus, the Fanjuls, along with U.S. Sugar, have sustained a political and media campaign to absolve themselves of any responsibility in the environmental problems that have occurred since the draining of the wetlands. Using the discourse of science, the sugar industry has claimed that phosphorus levels are not dangerous. Robert M. Baker Jr., a prominent sugar industry spokesman, has gone so far as to claim that:

Farming will have been taxed and regulated out of business in order to achieve water quality that is twice as pure as rain, while government policy encouraged suburban sprawl whose run-off has at least four times a much phosphorus as sugar cane's. And the discharge from the best sewage plants has six times as much.… The Everglades need a solution, not a scapegoat. (*Sugar y Azucar*, March 1992)[3]

But community and environmental organizations disagree. Phosphorous levels have been blamed for a multitude of diseases and disorders, including not only the skin rashes and asthma generally recognized, but arthritis and cancer as well. Everglades' vegetation that is sensitive to phosphorous contamination, such as saw grass, have quickly died out in favor of more phosphorous adaptive plants, such as cattails. As Roberts reports:

In fact, the sugar industry knows good and well that water quality and water quantity are inseparable. By draining the saw-grass muck, engineers exposed underwater soils to the air, allowing fertilizers and natural nutrients to oxidize, thus freeing them up to blow away as dust or float off in rainstorms. Over time, up to six feet of phosphorus laden topsoil has washed from the farms into the Everglades. (Roberts 1999, 60)

The original reclamation plan created large reservoirs for urban settlements, and in 2001, faced with a shortage of drinking water, Florida appealed to the Environmental Protection Agency to waive safety rules on drinking water.

Meanwhile, as if to flaunt the relations of power in the discourse of environmental policy, in August of 2002, the Army Corps of Engineers granted approvals for limestone mining that will destroy 4,500 acres of wetlands. The limestone will be used for housing developments and roads. As the attorney for the Natural Resources Council put it, "We're committing an act of environmental cannibalism of really historic proportions" (Flesher 2002. 1A). Like the standard rebuttal to issues of development, the answer lies in jobs. The mining companies claim that the mines employ 7,000 people, and another 7,000 are employed in trucking, construction, and allied work. The immediate explanation is that they must expand their quarries or go out of business, at great cost to Florida's economy. The mining companies, which are based from West Virginia to as far away as Athens, Greece, argue that "if you want Florida to continue to grow, if you want tourists, if you want jobs, you've got to have new schools, churches, shopping centers" (Flesher 2002, 14A).

The mining industry has also been a major contributor to Florida's political campaigns, including those of U.S. Senator Bob Graham and U.S. Representative Clay Shaw, both of whom played a major role in the development of the restoration plan. The Florida newspaper the *Sun-Sentinel* reports that the state legislature stripped local communities of the right to set environmental standards for blasting, and Congress in 2000 declared the mining pits "reservoirs" in the Everglades Restoration Plan. "It's horrendous," said the chair of the Florida Sierra Club. "If you have the right lobbyists and the right politicians, you can get anything you want. You can turn mining the Everglades into Everglades Restoration" (Flesher 2002, 14A).

THE IMPLICATIONS OF EVERGLADES RESTORATION

That the Everglades still exists is a collective illusion shared by both those who care and those who don't. People used to say that nothing like the Everglades existed anywhere else in the world, but it doesn't exist in South Florida either. The Park, which millions of people visit and perceive to be the Everglades, makes up only 20 percent of the historic Glades and is but a pretty, fading afterimage of a once astounding ecosystem, the remaining 80 percent of which—drained, deiced, and poisoned—has vanished beneath cities, canals, vast water impoundment areas, sugarcane fields, and tomato farms. Ninety percent of the wading bird population has disappeared in 50 years, and gradually (quickly) "one of the rarest places on earth" (as it is so frequently described) located conveniently (unfortunately) one hour from

Miami, has become a horror show of extirpated species. On land, a water park with no water; at sea, a sick marine estuary turning into a murky, hyper-saline, super heated lagoon. (Joy Williams 1999, 9)

The Comprehensive Everglades Restoration Project (CERP) integrates levels of policy and decision making that tie community interests to the concerns of industry and developers. The mining, agricultural, and development companies that are fighting for environmental control are global and national; the labor that supplies agricultural and development companies is local in scope. Jobs and tax revenues in a state that boasts no income tax are pitted against the more abstract notion of what the environment represents. While communities measure survival in terms of both their ability to function and maintain sustainable infrastructures, corporations and government agencies take the cost-accounting approach, testing possible costs of cleanup and lawsuits against the profitability of their businesses and their ability to show growth in the next accounting quarter.

The Everglades have become the symbolic focal point in the differences among federal and state legislators, local community and community organizations, and environmental groups. The initial reengineering of the Everglades was assigned to the Army Corps of Engineers in 1947, and backed by $200 million allocated by Congress to build levies and dams and provide Miami's growing population with flood-free drinking water. Once labeled "unfit for man or vermin," the area between Interstate 75 and the Fort Meyers Airport now boasts the highest concentration of golf holes per capita on earth (Grunwald June 25, 2002, A01).

If the current plan sounds eerily familiar to the first plan, it is not by accident. The Army Corps of Engineers is again involved in a replumbing project—a plan that is designed more to provide water to Florida's growing population than to "restore" what was the Florida Everglades. The region's population is expected to again double by 2050.

The relationships among the federal agencies, the Florida state legislature, environmental groups, and community-based organizations are multifaceted. While Congress and federal agencies define the playing field, some environmental groups fear that if they do not engage these sources of power, they will lose all voice. Organizations such as the Audubon Society believe that they have a say in the making of environmental policy, as long as they stay on the good side of federal environmental chiefs. Others, such as Friends of the Everglades (a large coalition of environmental activists), decry the collaboration of environmental organizations with federal and state governments, claiming that working within the system will only hurt the cause of true restoration.

The growing divide among environmental groups and community organizations attests to the complexity of local integration into national policies. "There is a growing rift within the Everglades Coalition, the network of conservation groups that helped push restoration into law." Grunwald reports: "Some environmentalists want to work with the system to persuade the Army Corps of Engineers and the South Florida Water Management District to improve the plan. Others say the only hope for real ecological benefits will be tough legal requirements of restoration progress—or barring that, public opposition and litigation." As Grunwald's report continues:

> The most enthusiastic environmentalist advocates for the plan work for the National Audubon Society and its Florida chapter. Richard Pettegrew, the chairman of the commission that proposed the plan's blueprint, is on Audubon's Board; former Audubon staffer Naciann Regalado is head of the Everglades outreach for the Corps.

> But several environmental groups, including Friends of the Everglades and the Biodiversity Legal Foundation, opposed the plan in 2000, and now fed-up officials at such groups as Environmental Defense and the National Resources Defense Council also criticize it. (Grunwald June 26, 2002, A13)

In March of 2002, the Bush White House relaxed rules on the protection of wetlands, making it easier for developers and mining companies to obtain automatic permits to fill wetlands. Environmentalists are complaining that the Bush administration's rhetoric about protecting the wetlands and the Army Corps of Engineers promise to maintain "no-net-loss" of Everglades marshes is being undermined even as the official commitment is voiced. The contrast between the stated rhetoric of governmental agencies and the action they take are indicative of the contrasts in values and viewpoints among community, environmental and governmental organizations. Industry and government are linked in relationships of power that would, on the surface, seem to overshadow the concerns of other stakeholders. Federal and state legislators and agencies (particularly the Army Corp and the South Florida Water Management District) regularly yield to developers. Jeb Bush's administration is particularly close to real estate interests (Grunwald

June 25, 2002, A01). The reality of the situation, of course, is more contentiously nuanced.

POLITICS AND STRATAGEMS

The sheer number of community-based organizations in the EAA speaks to the involvement of the community in global, national, and local affairs. The Glades Interagency Directory lists 92 service-provider agencies, or one agency for every 152 residents—one of the highest per capita ratios in the country. These agencies are overwhelmingly grassroots based, ranging from the Belle Glade Housing Authority to Centro Campesino and Florida Rural Legal Services. Most are funded by grants and donations, as well as widely fluctuating federal and state funding. When I asked one agency director why the organization no longer provided transportation to and from AIDS testing and counseling centers, she answered that they had lost their state funding, and could not tell me why or even exactly when. Most of the agencies are housed in small, run-down offices that service walk-ins looking for help. As I arrived to interview another agency head, she asked me to wait while she e-mailed a friend of hers who she thought might be able to help a recent walk-in who was hysterical but could not tell her the reason. As in this case, much of the help provided is accomplished through personal and professional networks that exist within the community. Participation by community members is informal and by word of mouth. Some of the more active organizations attend interagency meetings and state and federal outreach meetings. By and large, the meetings frustrate them. All of the organizations, from housing to AIDS, are affected by the restoration process and the politics that is integral to its development and implementation. Funding is being diverted, while the community is faced with a deluge of information and attention needing to be negotiated. Too, the fate of skill-specific workers and the migration patterns of workers affect families and their support systems—the community as a whole.

Federal and state agencies are mandated by law to include community outreach programs that can be quantified in the number of people they serve and the types of meetings that are held. This is particularly true of the agencies that are directing the Everglades restoration project, which must show that they have implemented standards for participation by community members. How this mandate is interpreted by the agencies and by community organizations differs by stakeholder, although it is fair to conclude that the integration of community concerns has not been a priority for planning purposes, and at times, has been actively subverted.

The Public Outreach Program Management Plan for the Comprehensive Everglades Restoration Plan (CERP), produced in August 2001 by the Army Corps of Engineers and the South Florida Water Management District, defines the components of public outreach as "information and involvement" (Army Corps of Engineers, August 2001). Included in the reasoning for these components are media attention and legal mandates. It also includes the statement "Concerned communities, including stakeholder groups, state and federal agencies, tribes, and the general public, need to learn about and better understand each other's views and concerns in order to build consensus solutions" (August 2001). It cites expanding outreach through colleges and other educational institutions, and as a result, the South Florida Water Management District entered into an agreement with Florida Memorial College in late 2000. Florida Memorial is a small, Baptist college in Miami that has few resources for environmental studies and even less for advocacy and coalition building. It is an example of what one community-based activist called "manufactured participation," pointing to an appearance of compliance with regulations regarding community input without actually soliciting differing points of view.

The organizational chart for the South Florida Ecosystem Restoration Group, organized by the Environmental Protection Agency, depicts the attempts at diffusion that are pursued by federal agencies. The chart is a series of arrows pointing in various directions and ending up in a circle. Utterly confusing, the chart depicts a "task force," a "working group," and various "teams." I obtained the chart at a meeting held by the Army Corps of Engineers. The meeting was held at 9:00 am on a Tuesday morning in Fort Lauderdale, far from any community stakeholders and insuring that only civil service members of the federal agencies could attend (parking cost $8.00). Billed as an information and outreach meeting, a colleague and myself were the only obvious outside people in attendance. The meeting consisted of various speeches by members of the Army Corp about general planning, funding, and timetables, but did not actively seek comments by members of the audience.

Community organizations also have differing viewpoints on what is needed and who is controlling the flow of information. Like the mainstream environmental organizations, some strongly believe that they should work with those who hold power, while others are more comfortable expressing their points of view while building grassroots efforts. Many of these differences focus around jobs and the future of those that have been displaced by mechanization or will be displaced by the restoration process. The primary community development corporation, for example, is focused on the development of tourism, the magic bullet for many communities around the world that are undergoing transformations in the productive sphere (Kirsch 1998). As one organization's manager told me, "People need to be aware of how quaint the community is." But even she becomes frustrated at the process in place. "We're sick and tired of being assessed," she complained, "people are getting frustrated with systems."

It is noteworthy that most of the leaders of community-based organizations are African-American women. There is agreement among community-based organizations that the area is underserved and by some descriptions, oppressed. "It's like a third world country," one agency director remarked, commenting on the relationships of power that exist among the various federal, state, and local agencies. Too, many do not trust the motives of the larger environmental organizations, which they view as naïve and uninformed. One officer of an activist organization quipped:

It's the "stupidity position" of the traditional environmental groups, who thought that they were going to be getting something, and didn't. In their arrogance, being predominately white, they thought they would be treated differently—told the truth. They presume that we aren't them, so we can't collaborate. They didn't take into consideration that this is the United States of America; it's a process. They thought they were having conversations in good faith, and they became part of problem and the victim of action to which I am unsympathetic towards.

This director believes in coalition building, but not with the agencies of power. She believes that the restoration managers are focusing on wildlife, "because birds and fish can't talk." The funding agencies, she maintains, don't care about people. "They're just doin their job ... the fight for community is continually undermined because they are those experts who think they know how and can do it better." Despite the negative tone of her remarks, this director is optimistic about the possibilities for building sustainable opposition and gaining input into the process. Part of the optimism comes from what many community leaders recognize as the bad science inherent in the restoration plan, which will have to be addressed and will leave new openings for counterpoint perspectives. Their views seem to be backed by the National Academies' National Research Council whose report, released on

262 • Inclusion and Exclusion in the Global Arena

December 18, 2002, concluded that more money for scientific reviews of the restoration process is necessary, along with significant management improvements in conducting scientific reviews (Lipman Palm Beach Port, December 19, 2002). "The process has to play itself out," the director points out, "over and over and over again." The challenge, as she sees it, is "having everyone know that we're here and that we're here to stay. The tendency in oppressed communities is that once our light bulb goes off to not acknowledge what's occurred and discount the history—we therefore repeat history, mistakes are continually repeated. The challenge here is to go forward because of the road and the vastness of the project."

CONCLUSION

A current story in the Florida media describes a "cultural divide" that exists in South Florida. The schism is represented by a tragedy involving a young Mayan illegal immigrant. In her own country of Guatemala, family and generations of experience in child bearing would have surrounded her as she was about to give birth. Alone in this country and unable to speak English, she was unaccompanied when the labor started. The baby died, and she is being charged with murder. The police provided her with a Spanish interpreter—a language that she does not speak. The incident symbolizes the contradictions that characterize South Florida and is very much the story of the Everglades. While the area is growing exponentially, and new urbanism and shopping centers proliferate, so does the migrant labor that supports their growth, and the drive for profit that militates against true restoration. Migrant labor arrives with the dream of finding a safer and better life. They come to find that until they are integrated into their own cultural communities, there is no social support or safety net. Mayans, many of whom emigrated from Huehuetenango (the poorest province in Guatemala) during the period of the country's civil war, maintain their ties with each other through fierce obstacles. While the men often learn Spanish in the fields to which they must migrate, the women are confined to the domestic household and community where they speak their own language. There is severe discrimination. Yet in this area, as in areas around the globe, indigenous groups, even outside their home countries, are starting to agitate for their rights and their dignity. While illegal status often makes individuals hesitant to organize, community-based organizations are forming to represent their rights and to defend their status.

The new language of globalism and globalization in the form of capital transfer and deterrorialization rarely conveys the complexity of local communities and their maintenance. A level of analysis that relies on the global transfer of capital and power is consistently depressing, as it most often results in an analysis that overplays the power of capital to overwhelm community maintenance and localized needs. Particularly in the Everglades, where community, crops, and labor are all integrated on multiple levels of local, national, and supranational organization, it is easy to forget that local populations still participate and influence the policies that are developed around them. Even when there is a significant attempt to exclude localized voices, communities invariably still manage to demand input into the process. A more productive approach to the study of communities and regions undergoing change is to incorporate levels of integration that distinguish and combine the abstract with the concrete, in an attempt to provide a holistic picture of on-the-ground activities in the light of rapid social change. Nash proposes that using Bourdieu's notion of habitus, or the "space through which we learn who or what we are in society" (Bourdieu 1977, 163), is useful in illuminating the complex set of interactions in the nexus that is the present human condition. In her words:

> By retaining a sense of generative cultural practices within any given habitus and their interconnectedness through interactions and exchanges in the global ecumene, we may arrive at the structuring principles in global affairs. The flux of the human condition can be captured for each moment in a time-space continuum in a way that can illuminate the forces at work.... One of the ways to problematize this is through a "community of practice" approach. This takes into account all of the places in which people who are the subjects of study engage in and interact in the process of social reproduction. (Nash 2001a, 219)

The restoration of the Everglades has opened up the long-standing discontinuities between the communities and their inhabitants that exist in the area, and the industrial corporations and developers that have interests in expanding their control over the region's resources. The active participation by local and national government agencies has exacerbated these differences. While the effect of localized organizing on the planning and implementation process and the contention over voice remains to be seen, the result will be no less than the fate of the Everglades and South Florida.

REFERENCES

Abram, S., J. Waldren, ed. 1998. *Anthropological Perspectives on Local Development.* London: Routledge.

Amit, V. 2000. *Constructing the Field.* London: Routledge

Appadurai, Arjun. 1986. "Introduction: Communities and the Politics of Value." In *The Social Life of Things: Commodities in Cultural Perspective,* ed. Arjun Appaduari, 3–63. Cambridge: Cambridge University Press.

———. 1990. "Disjuncture and Difference in the Global Cultural Economy." *Public Culture* 2: 1–24.

———. 1991."Global Ethnoscapes: Notes and Queries for a Transnational Anthropology." In *Recapturing Anthropology: Working in the Present,* ed. R. G. Fox, 191–210. Santa Fe: School of American Research Press.

Army Corps of Engineers and South Florida Water Management District. 2001. *Public Outreach Program Management Plan, Comprehensive Everglades Restoration Plan.*

Barboza, J. 2002. Everglades Plan Defies Free Trade Logic. *New York Times,* May 6, 1.

Bourdeiu, Pierre. 1977. *Outline of a Theory of Practice.* Cambridge: Cambridge University Press.

Brown, L. G. 1993. Totch: A Life in the Everglades (with a forward by Peter Matthiessen). Gainesville: University Press of Florida.

Burns, Alan. 1993. Maya in Exile: Guatemalans in Florida. Philadelphia, PA: Temple University Press.

Castells, Manuel, Sherjro Yazawa, and Emma Kiselyova (1995–1996). "Insurgents against the New World Order: A Comparative Analysis of the Zapatistas in Mexico, the American Militia and Japan's Aum Shino." *Berkeley Journal of Sociology* 40.

Cockburn, Alexander. 1995. "'Win-Win' with Bruce Babbitt: The Clinton Administration Meets the Environment." *New Left Review* 201:43–55.

Douglas, M. S. 1947 [1997]. *The Everglades: River of Grass.* Sarasota, FL: Pineapple Press.

Englund, Harry. 2002. Ethnography after Globalism: Migration and Emplacement in Malawi. *American Ethnologist* 29(2):2261–86.

Flesher. 2002. "Environmental Debate Stirs Controversy." *New York Times,* April 3, 2002, 1A.

Friedman, J. F. 1995. "'Comment' on Scheper-Hughes, N. (1995). The Primacy of the Ethical: Propositions for a Militant Anthropology." *Current Anthropology* 36(3):421.

Glades Community Development Corporation (1998). *Final Report: Glades Vision to Action Forums.* September.

———. 2002. *Town Hall Meetings Project: Final Report,* Belle Glade. January 30, 2002.

Griffith, David. 2000. "Work and Immigration: Winter Vegetable Production in South Florida." In *Poverty or Development*, ed. Richard Tardancio and Mark B. Rosenberg, 139–178. New York: Routledge.

Grunwald, Michael. 2000. "How Corps Turned Doubt into a Lock." *Washington Post*, Sunday, February 13, A01.

———. 2000. "Engineers of Power: An Agency of Unchecked Clout." Washington Post, Sunday, September 10, A01.

———. 2000. "Pentagon Rebukes Army Corps." *Washington Post*, Thursday, December 7, A01.

———. 2001. "Plan to Revive Everglades Brings Renewed Dispute." *Washington Post*, Saturday, December 29, A03.

———. 2001. "Norton Closes Everglades Renewal Office." *Washington Post*, Wednesday, November 7, A03.

———. 2002. "White House Relaxes Rules on Protection of Wetland." *Washington Post*, Tuesday, January 15, A02.

———.2002. "A Rescue Plan, Bold and Uncertain." *Washington Post*, Sunday, June 23, A01.

———. 2002. "Among Environmentalists, the Great Divide." *Washington Post*, Wednesday, June 26, A13.

———. 2002. "An Environmental Reversal of Fortune." *Washington Post*, Wednesday, June 26, A01.

———. 2002. "Growing Pains in Southwest Florida." *Washington Post*, Tuesday, June 25, A01.

———. 2002. "How Enron Sought to Tap the Everglades." *Washington Post*, Friday, February 8, A12.

———.2002. "Interior's Silence on Corps Plan Questioned." *Washington Post*, Monday, January 14, A05.

———. 2002. "Oversight Favored for Corps Projects." *Washington Post*, Friday, July 26, A31.

———. 2002. "The Everglades." *Washington Post*, Monday, June 24, Washington Post Online Discussion.

———. 2002. "To the White House, by Way of the Everglades." *Washington Post*, Sunday June 23, A16.

———. 2002. "Water Quality is Long-Standing Issue for Tribe." *Washington Post*, Monday June 24, A11.

———. 2002. "When in Doubt, Blame Big Sugar." *Washington Post*, Tuesday June 25, A09.

———. 2002. "Between Rock and a Hard Place." *Washington Post*, Monday, June 24, A01.

Harvey, David (1990). The Condition of Postmodernity. Malden MA: Blackwell

———. 1998. "What's Green and Makes the Environment Go Round." In *The Cultures of Globalization*, ed. Frederic Jameson and Masao Miyoshi, 327–355. Durham, NC: Duke University Press.

Inda, Jonathan Xavier and Renato Rosaldo, eds. 2002. "Introduction." In *The Anthropology of Globalization: A Reader*, 1–36. Malden, MA: Blackwell Publishers.

Ingold, T. 1992. "Culture and the Perception of the Environment." In *Bush Base: Forest Farm*, ed. E. Croll and D. Parkin . London: Routledge.

Jefferson, Jon. 1993. "Cane Workers Accord Means Big Job Loss." *National Law Journal* 16(November 8):10.

King, R. P. 2001. "Restoration Plan Threatened." *Palm Beach Post*, October 29, 1.

Kirsch, Max (1998). *In the Wake of the Giant: Multinational Restructuring and Uneven Development in a New England Community*. Albany: State University of New York Press.

Kirsch, Max. 2002. Unpublished fieldnotes.

Maanen, J. V., ed. 1995. *Representation and Ethnography*. Thousand Oaks, CA: Sage Press.

McCally, D. 1999. *The Everglades: An Environmental History*; foreword by Raymond Arsenault and Gary R. Mormino. Gainesville: University Press of Florida.

McCally, David Philip . "Cane Cutters in the Everglades." Masters thesis, University of South Florida.

McKinley, James C., Jr. 1999. "Sugar Companies Pay a Pivotal Role in Effort to Restore Everglades." *New York Times*, April 6, 1999, National Desk.

Mehra, Rekha. 1984. "International Labor Migration and Florida Sugarcane Production: A Political Economic Analysis." PhD thesis, University of Florida.

Milton, K. ed. 1993. *Environmentalism: The View from Anthropology*. London: Routledge.

Mintz, Sidney. 1985. *Sweetness and Power: The Place of Sugar in Modern History*. New York: Penguin.

———. 1998. "The Localization of Anthropological Practice: From Area Studies to Transnationalism." *Critique of Anthropology* 18(2):117–133.

Murphy, Martha Celeste. 1997. "An Empirical Study of Farm Workers in South Florida: Environmental Injustice in the Fields?" PhD thesis, Florida Atlantic University.

Nash, June. 2001a. *Mayan Visions: The Quest for Autonomy in an Age of Globalization*. New York: Routledge.

———. 2001b. "Globalization and the Cultivation of Peripheral Vision." *Anthropology Today* 17(4):15–22.

Nash June and Max Kirsch. 1986. "Polychlorinated Biphenyls in the Electrical Machinery Industry: An Ethnological Study of Community Action and Corporate Responsibility." *Social Science and Medicine* 2(1):131–138.

———. 1988. "The Discourse of Medical Science in the Construction of Consensus between Corporation and Community." *Medical Anthropology Quarterly* 2(2):158–171.

_____. 1994. "Corporate Culture and Social Responsibility: The Case of Toxic Wastes in a New England Community." In *Anthropological Perspectives on Organizational Culture*, ed. T. Hamada and W. S. Sibley . Latham, MA: University Press of America.

Portes, Alejandro and Alex Stepick. 1985. "Unwelcome Immigrants: The Labor Market Experiences of 1980 (Mariel) Cuban and Haitian Refugees in South Florida." *American Sociological Review* 50:493–513.

Prato, G. B. 1993. "Political Decision Making: Environmentalism, Ethics and Popular Participation in Italy." In *Environmentalism: The View from Anthropology*, ed. K. Milton, 174–188. London: Routledge.

Redclift, M. 1992. "At Work in the Greenhouse: ESRC's Global Environmental Change Programme." *Global Environmental Change* (December): 341–344.

Report to Congressional Requestors . 1992. *Labor Action Needed to Protect Florida Sugar Cane Workers*. Washington DC.

Resnick, Rosalind. 1991. "Cane Cleanup. (Florida Sugar-Cane Industry Labor Policies)." *National Law Journal* 13(May 13):36.

_____. 1992. "$50 Million Win for Cane Cutters. (*Bygrave v. Sugar Cane Growers Cooperative*)." *National Law Journal* 14(3), July 13:43.

Roberts, Paul. 1999. "The Sweet Hereafter." *Harper's* 299(1794):54–68.

Rodman, Margaret C. 1993. "Empowering Place: Multilocality and Multivocality." *American Anthropologist* 94:640–656.

Rose, J. 1991. *Environmental Concepts, Policies and Strategies*. Philadelphia: Gordon and Breach.

Sassen, Saskia. 1998. *Globalization and Its Discontents*. New York: The Free Press.

Scheper-Hughes, N. 1995. "The Primacy of the Ethical: Propositions for a Militant Anthropology." *Current Anthropology* 36(3):409–439.

Scully, J. 2001. "Restoring the Fragile Everglades, Evermore." *Chronicle Review*, January 12, 2001, B13–14.

Simmons, G. and L. O. 1998. *Gladesmen*. Gainesville: University Press of Florida.

Sinclair, M. Thea, ed. 2000. *Gender Work, Tourism*. New York: Routledge.

Sugar y Azucar. 1992. "Has Sugar Harmed the Everglades?" March.

Tardanico R. and M. B. Rosenberg, eds. 2000) *Poverty or Development: Global Restructuring and Regional Transformations in the U.S. South and the Mexican South*. New York: Routledge.

Taylor, B. 1991. "The Religion and Politics of Earth First!" *Ecologist* 21(6):258–266.

United States Congress . 2000. H.R. 5121. 106th Congress, 2nd sess. (House Plan), September 7.

United States Congress . 2000. H.R. 5121; 106 H.R. 5121. Comprehensive Everglades Restoration Plan, September 7.

United States General Accounting Office. 1992. *Foreign Farm Workers in U.S.: Department of Labor Action Needed to Protect Florida Sugar Cane Workers. Report to Congressional Requesters.* Washington, DC.

Wallerstein, Immanuel. 1994. *The Modern World System: Capitalist Agriculture and the Originals of the European World Economy in the Sixteenth Century.* New York: Academic.

Wilkinson, Alec. 1990. *Big Sugar: Seasons in the Cane Fields of Florida.* New York: Vintage.

Williams, Joy. 1999. *Ill Nature: Rants and Reflections on Humanity and Other Animals.* New York: Lyons Press.

Yearley, S. and Milton K. 1990. "Environmentalism and Direct Rule: The Politics and Ethos of Conservation and Environmental Groups in Northern Ireland." *Built Environment* 16(3):192–202.

NOTES

1. For a full discussion of Babbitt's environmental strategy, see Alexander Cockburn's 1995, "'Win-Win' with Bruce Babbitt: The Clinton Administration Meets the Environment" New Left Review, 201.

2. Appadurai (1990) quoted in Nash (2001b). As Nash notes, "Unfortunately, this has instead focused a slide in the nearest convenient ethnoscape, often forgetting the capitalist framework that propels mobility. In this change of focus, some ethnographers have come to treat deterritorialization as a force in itself...Given this mode of inquiry, the resistance and protest of people confronting globalization processes may tend to be ignored in the rush to affirm what have become the imperatives of the new discourse on globalization. Attempts to bring the conflict into focus are cast as naïve or worse, essentializing" (Nash, 2001b:16).

3. It is an interesting paradox that while the philanthropic foundation created by the Mott family supports environmental issues, including a $900,000 grant to save wetlands in Latin America, they have not contributed to any environmental efforts in the Everglades.

11

POLITICAL STRUGGLES IN LEGAL ARENAS
Some African Instances

Sally Falk Moore

INTRODUCTION

There are two ways of contending: one by using laws, the other, force.

Machiavelli

In contemporary Africa politics turns on the instrumentalization of disorder,.

Patrick Chabal and Jean-Pascal Daloz

This paper will describe some shocking, legally irregular situations with which I had contact in Africa. Two such case histories will be reported in some detail. Their general national context, as well as some concurrent international activities in the human rights domain will be noted. The potential large-scale implications of local, microlevel events are evident. Attempts have been made to create global legal institutions that address crimes against humanity wherever they take place, but the question of whether such laws and institutions as they exist can be effective, is not clear. The African cases described here put the issues in perspective. At this moment in history, there is a huge disparity between the idea of an effective world legal order, and the corrupted reality actually visible.

Many African states have made efforts to reconfigure their constitutions and laws since the end of the Cold War, but the practical effects of these enunciated legal reforms have been variable, to say the least (Zoethout, Pietermaat-Kros, and Akkermans 1996). Unlawful government manipulations manifest themselves frequently. Uncontrollable eruptions of disorder appear. States often lack the capacity or the will to implement their legislative and constitutional declarations, and, in fact, often contravene their own pronouncements. One can only conclude sadly that the national legal frameworks in place in many African settings have often turned out to be, at best, more aspirational than realizable (Young 2003).

Parallel with the national constitutional reforms seen in Africa in the past two decades, there have been a series of human rights–related developments in international law. Institutions have been put in place that build toward a supranational normative order. This is particularly visible in relation to political accountability. The United Nations (UN) has been active, especially in the creation of UN special courts, and the long awaited International Criminal Court has come into official existence. There has been an increasing interest in the possible uses of the doctrine of universal jurisdiction, but at the same time there have been some notable failures in the attempts to implement it. The future of the doctrine is now uncertain.

The push for regularity in transnational and supranational affairs is also manifest in the ongoing proliferation of regional and international treaties, agreements, charters, declarations, conventions, and the like. All of these developments epitomize a commitment to building social order with law as its formal instrument and embodiment. But in Africa, the reality on the ground does not correspond to these ambitions. Violence and disorder are commonplace. Weapons are widely available and are used. The abuse of power is not unusual. The rot of corruption pervades many governments.

Government awareness of human rights in Africa is anything but new, but doing something about it is another matter. Decades ago, the Organization of African Unity drafted the Charter on Human and People's

Rights (adopted in 1981). A human rights commission was later instituted, but "[w]ith limited powers of investigation and no right to prosecute, the Commission is a toothless tiger" (Hyden, in Cohen, Hyden, and Nagan 1993, 264). African leaders have readily acknowledged these difficulties. In 1994, for example, heads of state and other leaders held a meeting to discuss corruption, democracy, and human rights (Aderinwale 1994). To better address the persistent dilemmas of governance, a new African Union was constituted on May 26, 2001 to substitute for the old Organization of African Unity. The problems continue.

African states are weak, and their leaders have preoccupations other than government management: "Over the years in Africa the state has proven to be the main channel for personal wealth accumulation and securing privileged position in society," (Aderinwale 1994, 6). "The state faces quite substantial competition from alternative decision-making centres.... The courts have neither the purse nor the sword. Why should the armed man obey them?" (Mattei 2002, 292).

On one side are the African governments, which have repeatedly deprived their citizens of basic liberties in order to stay in power; governments that do not hesitate to beat up, imprison, and torture the opposition, yet invoke law, saying that they are only acting to fulfill their legal mandate to maintain public order. In the same countries, human rights activists try to use the law to bring such regimes into disrepute. They fight for justice in individual cases, not just to alter the fate of particular victims, but with an eye to eventually dislodging the government.

The general background of abuse in Africa is not hard to find. The one-party structure that prevailed in many countries until recently, frequently produced an arrogance of power. Some of this centralized control emerged from the anticolonial struggle and its aftermath. However, the extreme form it eventually took was greatly exacerbated by the Cold War. In the 1990s, to try to reverse this, there was palpable Western pressure on African countries to hold multiparty elections. This technical requirement was conceived as an effort to get more African countries to move toward democratic organization. Many countries did hold elections that appeared to offer electoral choices, but few of these were genuine enfranchisements of opposition parties. There was merely a mechanical fulfillment of multiparty arrangements. Often the same governments or factions continued in office. As a 2002 editorial in the *Zimbabwe Daily News* said, "Elections do not a democracy make."[1]

Today, activist opposition inside these states must look to an international audience for support. Talk about the internationalization of modes of redress is beginning to surface. Sometimes the only recourse for dissidents is to appeal to a supranational arena, or to somehow presume that even without reaching its agencies directly, the supranational will eventually come to the rescue.

It is significant that there has been a great increase of informal communicative activity about these matters. Thus, in addition to the legal measures invoked, the litigations undertaken, and the legal talk in law journals, pressing information about human rights abuses reaches interested international organizations by other avenues. This enlarges the public record and alerts influential outsiders. Among the many agencies that listen for, receive, and publicize such materials, are the UN, the U.S. Department of State, Human Rights Watch, Amnesty International, the Lawyers Committee for Human Rights, and the Committee to Protect Journalists. They cannot always help particular victims directly, but they do what they can to publicize the injustices involved.

The information collected is regularly made known to foreign governments. Sometimes agents on the spot can work quietly behind the scenes through diplomatic and unofficial channels to considerable effect. Sometimes there is official international action, such as the establishment of international courts. But there are many obstacles that impede international action. Some recent efforts in this direction will be briefly reviewed here to put the activist's work in perspective.

African human rights activists in the professional classes, the journalists, the lawyers, and the civil servants, surely derive hope from their knowledge of the international information network that reports serious violations of law. For the privileged, there is a blizzard of human rights material on the Internet. Less privileged people are, of course, less visible, their concerns less audible, and their problems more acute.

Even though international interest cannot often provide direct protection, and only occasionally results in official pressure on persecuting governments, the mere global spread of knowledge—the awareness that there are like-minded people elsewhere—gives the professional activists inside these states encouragement. They know they are not alone in the struggle for civil liberties. They can hope for more.

Recent events in Burkina Faso and Kenya illustrate this proposition. In both countries, although I was on an entirely different research mission, I stumbled into ongoing politicolegal struggles and briefly met some of the protagonists. Seeking to understand the highly censored political story, I followed up on what I could. The details were instructive. In both countries there had been serious human rights violations, and during the past decade, there have been increasingly public demands that the governments be held accountable. A significant part of the struggle over the regimes in power have been conducted in legal terms. The underlying objectives are, however, political.

BURKINA FASO

I was in Burkina Faso as a consultant on development-related problems during the mid-1990s, when information about a number of human rights matters came my way.[2] One case concerned the assassination of a man in broad daylight in front of the Hotel Independance in Ouagadougou; he was driving past and stopped for a red light. This had happened in 1991, four years before my visit there. Why was he killed? Who was he? He was Oumarou Clement Ouedraogo, former rector of the University of Ouagadougou, former minister of education and research. As a prominent opposition leader, he was a credible political challenger of President Blaise Campaore.

During my visit, I noticed an article in a local newspaper that referred to the Ouedrago assassination.[3] The article demanded that an international commission of inquiry, which was supposed to investigate the murder, get moving and make its report public. The newspaper asked why, after years, nothing had been done. Surprised by the boldness and government-defying tone of this article, I set out to interview the newspaper editor.

I met him and he seemed eager to talk, not only about the Ouedraogo shooting, but about another case that was immediately urgent, perhaps hoping that I could be of some help. What he told me had to do with a colleague, E.O., who was in prison. The colleague had asked publicly how it happened that President Campaore could be building a very lavish house for himself in Ziniare on his modest salary. For this political impertinence (with its little-concealed intimation of corruption), E.O. was arrested and vanished from sight. His friend, the editor, told me that inquiries about the whereabouts of the prisoner, and about the stage of the legal process in which he was involved, were unavailable. The editor said that he thought it unwise to publish the story of E.O.'s plight at the time. Instead, he decided to print the one about the 1991 murder with its strong reference to human rights, as an oblique criticism of the case of his recently disappeared friend.

The editor was also the president of an organization for the furthering of democracy. I asked him where the organization got its funds. First he said, "from the membership, from the intellectuals in Ouagadougou." I pressed him. He then offered more plausible details. He said that the organization's funds were supplemented by the U.S. Embassy. He explained that if he asked for a certain level of francs, they would give it to him without delay. But if he asked for more, it took a little time because the person he dealt with had to consult Washington.

My Ouagadougou handler (the man who arranged my appointments) told me as we left to get into his car, that the American with whom the editor dealt was well known in Ouagadougou as the embassy's CIA (Central Intelligence Agency) man. I inferred that the reason this newspaper editor was bold enough to ask for the release of a report on the murder of Ouedraogo was that he counted on his U.S. sponsors for protection.

These bits of information came my way unofficially. What I found remarkable was how easy it was to elicit. I feared inquiring more deeply. My official assignment was quite different—to report on the progress of local political decentralization. These two cases, E.O.'s and Ouedraogo's, were representative of many, many more human rights abuses, a number of which are documented in U.S. Department of State reports (1998 and 1999), and an Amnesty International Report of 2002.[4] Killings, torture, detention, and the like are reported. Improper pressure on voters to reelect Blaise Campaore as president is noted as well. In fact, in 1998, Campaore was elected to a second seven-year term.

One of the sources of violence was also clear. In a casual conversation I was told in the 1990s that if I had any use for an AK-47, such a weapon could be obtained in Ouagadougou for $100. I thought this might be a joke. It wasn't. The trade in diamonds for weapons was a big West African business. "Ouagadougou was [for geographical and political reasons] the main transit point for weapons fueling wars in the region."[5] I had been told in confidence a few years earlier that the United States had objected to the President Campaore privately about the weapons trade, but that this reproof had little effect. Trying to have a practical impact, Denmark reduced its contribution of aid to Burkina in 2002 saying that it had violated a UN arms embargo.[6]

The existence of the arms trade was widely known, but that was not the only thing that President Campaore had to hide. There were some inexplicable deaths. A highly respected journalist, named Norbert Zongo, was investigating the scandals that surrounded President Campaore. He looked into the fate of some of persons who had died in the custody of the Presidential Guard, and Zongo, himself, received death threats while inquiring into these matters.

He must have come too close to uncomfortable truths because in December 1998, Zongo, his brother, and two other men were killed in a mysterious car fire on an isolated road. These deaths sparked major demonstrations in Ouagadougou and the other cities of Burkina.

Rioters sacked the headquarters of the ruling party in the capital, and burned and looted the homes of prominent party officials in other cities. The government was forced to respond and appointed a commission to investigate the deaths.

The U.S. Department of State reported that, "A collective of human rights groups, opposition political parties, journalistic organizations, student groups and trade unions that formed in response to Zongo's death rejected the government commission claiming that it was not sufficiently independent. ... The collective set up its own commission."[6] The State Department report continues with some pessimistic statements about what might come of this: "The major problem with law enforcement remains a general climate of impunity for human rights abusers by the failure of the government's investigations to result in guilty findings and appropriate sanctions. Inquiries tend to continue until they are overshadowed by subsequent incidents or quietly shelved. Appeals by human rights organizations generally go unanswered. The failure to prosecute previous abuses remains the most important hindrance to further human rights progress." The same report indicates that, " [t]he Constitution provides for an independent judiciary; however in practice the judiciary is subject to executive influence."

In 2002, Amnesty International reported that the government of Burkina Faso had established a national human rights commission in 2001, no doubt to enhance its public face, "to raise awareness of human rights and to organize human rights education."[7]

I first heard about the killing of Zongo and his brother from a Malian journalist in Cambridge. Such news travels quickly across national borders. Among other things, there is now the international Committee to Protect Journalists with a website that monitors attacks on the press. The head of Burkina's Presidential Guard was eventually charged with the Zongo killing. He was already serving a twenty-year sentence for killing an employee of the president's brother. He died in prison before he could be tried for the Zongo murder.

What is interesting about President Campaore's subsequent strategy in response to the pressures on him was to declare a National Pardon Day in the spring of 2001. He convened a crowd of 30,000 in a Ouagadougou stadium, asked for forgiveness, and expressed "deep regret for tortures, crimes, injustices, bullying and other wrongs."[8]

Many people did not find this display of presidential contrition convincing. They called for a counterdemonstration, for a National Mourning Day, and held a ceremony at the grave of Norbert Zongo. Dramatizing the whole affair were the widow of Norbert Zongo and the widow of the previous president, Thomas Sankara. Sankara had been killed under dubious circumstances involving Campaore in a coup just before Campaore took over the government. Both widows refused to participate in Campaore's Day of Pardon, and their refusal was publicized. (Loc.cit.). I do not know what has happened since, but it is not only clear that the illegalities committed by Campaore and his thugs have generated serious opposition, but that he has had to acknowledge them.

His misdeeds have also come to international attention. In October 2001, when Campaore was on a visit to France, an NGO (nongovernmental organization) called Reporters sans Frontieres tried to prosecute him for crimes against humanity. Nothing came of this case, but it is noteworthy that the protracted political fight against President Campaore was conducted in a legal arena, but initiated by journalists, and that there was wide public knowledge of his illegal acts.[8] This intense political awareness does not seem to have dislodged the president. Campaore was still in office in December 2003.

What is evident is that in a regime of suppression, newspapers may exert more influence than their literal text implies. The journalists created a record that was available for inspection by the literate elite, but the information they produced, and the doubts they sowed, traveled much further. To a great extent the human rights movement in Burkina depended on the work of journalists. By contrast, in Kenya the avenue of protest was opened by the legal profession.

A KENYAN'S CAREER FROM THE 1980S TO THE PRESENT

The extraordinary biography of Gibson Kamau Kuria, a human rights lawyer in Kenya, illustrates a multiyear struggle that went from protest and persecution to power. I first met Kamau Kuria in the early 1980s when he was a member of the law faculty at the University of Nairobi. I knew that he was interested in customary land law, and had taken a number of cases that involved tenure questions. As I was then working on land issues on Kilimanjaro in Tanzania, I wanted to learn what I could about what was going on in Kenya at the same time, so I contacted him. I knew nothing of his human rights work, which had just begun, nor did he mention it.

In fact, the Law Society of Kenya, in which Kamau Kuria and his law firm were active, was a center of opposition to President Moi. By the 1980s, Moi's policies of suppression and violence against all critics had exceeded all bounds. Opponents of the regime were being incarcerated, tortured, and some were killed. In 1982, Kamau Kuria represented a number of students charged with sedition. In 1984 he was the attorney for four detainees, "saying that their detention was illegal and demanding their immediate release."[9] When I next heard of him in 1987, he represented Raila Odinga, who had been in detention since 1982. Kamau Kuria asked that the case be reviewed by an independent tribunal, that Odinga be informed of the grounds for his detention, and that the inhuman treatment to which Odinga had been subjected be acknowledged. The request was denied and the case was dismissed. Kamau Kuria also sued the government in 1987 on behalf of three clients whom he argued had been tortured and illegally detained.[10]

The government's response to this was to incarcerate Kamau Kuria himself. He was arrested and detained, but not charged. His wife did not know where he was or whether he was alive; he simply disappeared for nine months. When he was released in 1988, the circumstances of his arrest came to the attention of the Robert F. Kennedy Human Rights Committee in the United States.[11] That committee gave him an award that he could not collect because his passport had been confiscated. He was also dismissed from his position at the University of Nairobi.

Undeterred by his experiences, Kamau Kuria resumed his human rights work. In 1990 he appeared on behalf of three lawyers who were detained without trial "after actively participating in the move for multi-party politics."[12] The year 1990 was a one of serious and violent human rights violations by the Moi government. The situation became extremely tense after Foreign Minister Robert Ouko was murdered. A critic of the government, Bishop Alexander Muge, called for a full investigation of the murder. Subsequently, when Bishop Muge planned a trip to Busia, he was warned publicly by the Minister for Labor that he would die if he went and tried "to poison the minds of the people of Busia against the government."[13] Muge issued a press statement in response to this death threat, then he went to Busia and was favorably received there. But while he was being driven back to Nairobi, his car was hit by a truck and he was killed. This was widely understood to have been a government staged "accident."

The unrest produced by the prodemocracy movement in the summer of 1990 was sufficiently violent to lead to the cancellation of the 23rd Biennial Conference of the International Bar Association, which had been scheduled to be held in Nairobi. A press release from the Bar Association, was issued to the following effect: "Another matter of great concern to us is the state of human rights and the rule of Law in Kenya. A number of persons are detained without being charged, including four lawyers, at least one of whom was arrested when he went to a police station to interview his client. Many hold the view that proceeding with our conference the I.B.A. would be lending support to a regime that has suppressed those attempting peacefully to express their political views and exercise their recognized human rights."[14]

While Kamau Kuria and his law partners were accustomed to being generally harassed by the police over the years, in 1990 he became seriously alarmed when he learned that officers of the Special Branch were waiting for him both at home and at the office. Anticipating a new arrest he asked for and received refuge in the American Embassy. He then left Kenya and came to the United States. He spent some months as a Visiting Fellow in the Harvard Law School's Human Rights Program, and later was Schell Fellow at the Yale Law School. Accompanying him into exile was his law partner, Kiraitu Murungi.

After his period abroad, Kamau Kuria went back to Nairobi and resumed his legal practice and his human rights work. I visited him in Nairobi in 1993. He told me something about the rights cases he was working on. I asked him why he expended so much time and energy appealing cases that he knew he would lose. He said, with marvelous certainty, that the Moi government would not last forever, and that he wanted those Moi-appointed appellate judges to go on record as supporting Moi's policies and affirming its law-clothed illegalities. He wanted that record to be available later on so that the judges could be removed from the bench when Moi left.

Moi did leave office in 2002, after twenty-four years as president. Subsequently, the Constitution of Kenya Review Commission was formed, and under the chairmanship of Yash Ghai, began working on drafting a new constitution. Kiraitu Murungi, the human rights lawyer who accompanied Kamau Kuria into exile and was a member of his law firm, is now the Justice and Constitutional Affairs minister of Kenya. Raila Odinga, who, after years in prison, was represented by Kamau Kuria in 1987, is now the minister for Roads, Public Works, and Housing.

When asked whether the government would act against Chief Justice Bernard Chunga, Murungi, the Minister for Justice, said that "although he has his own personal views pertaining to the matter of the Chief Justice he has been forced to keep these to himself by virtue of his position in the Government."[1714] The newspaper report goes on to say that "Murungi was at the forefront in defending alleged members of the clandestine Mwakenya movement which was perceived to be out to overthrow the Moi regime in the 1980s. During that time, Chunga, who was the Chief Public Prosecutor, played a leading role in jailing the Mwakenya activists."[15] Thus, after more than twenty years of threats, jailings, torture, and persecutions, the human rights activists are now in power. It seems unlikely that Chief Justice Chunga will be on the bench much longer.

In Burkina Faso and in Kenya, the most effective activists were and are people inside these countries. If such people fail when they try to force their governments to change, are there institutions outside their countries that could take over the task? What international interventions could there be?

INTERNATIONAL TRIBUNALS AND AFRICA

In Africa, the human rights movement has not only permeated the consciousness of elite educated Africans, but given the reach of the transistor radio, the idea of human rights has sometimes touched the lives of ordinary, uneducated people. As Richard Wilson (1997, 1) recently wrote, "human rights could be seen as one of the most globalised political values of our times."

What is proving to be more difficult is to turn those values into effective legal action. The practical attempts to mount an international system of accountability have been discouraging. The International Criminal Tribunal for Rwanda (ICTR), set up by the U.N. Security Council, is such an instance. The ICTR came into being in 1994 to find and prosecute those responsible for the Rwandan genocide, in which it is estimated that 800,000 Tutsi and some educated Hutu died. The International Tribunal arrested fifty-nine persons but has, to date, actually convicted only eight.

The cost of the tribunal has been enormous—so far $536 million, with the budget for the year 2002–2003 exceeding $96 million.[16] Trials of 29 of the remaining detainees are still to be scheduled. It has been suggested that 25 of these be turned over to the national courts of Rwanda, but the national courts are already burdened with somewhere between 115,00 and 120,000 cases associated with the genocide. They have dealt with this massive problem by handing these cases over to village courts. There is serious question, however, as to whether these village tribunals are in a position to afford the defendants due process, but the numbers involved seem to preclude any other recourse.

In another instance, the United Nations established a special tribunal in December 2002 to try those accused of war crimes in Sierra Leone's civil war.[17] The *New York Times* reported that 50,000 people had been killed or wounded in Sierra Leone during a decade of civil war. Most of these victims were civilians. Most of the killing, rape and mutilation was carried out by Revolutionary United Front rebels and fighters of a former military junta; they were at least 47,000 strong. The article adds that the court will probably try about 20 people. It has, at the time of this writing, actually indicted 7 persons .

Assuming this legal process results in the conviction of 7 people for devastating crimes against 40,000 people, will it be enough? Enough for what? Is this a kind of symbolic judicial act designed to communicate the dismay of the international community in the face of the horrors perpetrated? Is it reasonable to do this without reaching anywhere near the number of actual perpetrators? This is a highly selective form of prosecution. These are the show trials of our time. One could answer that it is better to try some than none, and that the symbolic value of prosecuting the once powerful is very important. If the UN tribunals cannot handle the number involved, will national courts, or mixed national-international do so?

And last, one should mention the case being prepared against Hissene Habre, the former president of Chad, because unlike the Rwanda and Sierra Leone cases, this is not being brought in a UN court, but in a Belgian one. Belgium passed a law in 1993 opening its courts to cases of major crimes under international law. Various subsequent amendments gave Belgian courts the authority to prosecute these crimes regardless of where the crimes took place or whether the suspect or the victims are Belgian.

In 2002, Human Rights Watch gave an award to Souleymane Guengueng, one of Habre's torture victims, for having spearheaded the campaign to bring him to justice. For a while it looked as if all that would be necessary to bring a case against Habre in Belgium would be his extradition from Senegal. Thirty cases against other national leaders were also filed in Belgium and were waiting to be addressed.[2][17]

Now, however, Belgium has had reason to reconsider the legal door they opened. A case was filed in Belgium against Ariel Sharon for killings in the Beirut Sabra and Shatila refugee camps in 1982. The victims and their families were duly represented by legal counsel. The filing of this case led Israel to recall its ambassador from Brussels. A charge recently brought by a group of Iraqis against the first President Bush and Messrs. Cheney, Powell, and Schwarzkopf in connection with the bombing of a civilian shelter in Baghdad in the Persian Gulf War of 1991 has also had political repercussions. Then secretary of state Powell warned the Belgian government that "Belgium was risking its status as an international meeting place and the headquarters of NATO."[18]

The Belgian parliament reacted quickly after Israel's action and Powell's warning. On April 5, 2003 the Belgian Senate approved an amendment gutting the war crimes law, and greatly restricting the range of its application. The law now says that if the perpetrator or the victim has some direct connection to Belgium, the Belgian courts can hear the case. However, foreigners facing war crimes charges would be referred back to their own governments for trial "if these are democracies with a record of fairness in justice."[19] What is clear is that at present political considerations are more powerful in these matters than the idea of supranational legal norms.

In the discourse about crimes against humanity, the accountability of government leaders is often treated as if it were already a tenet of global morality, given the doctrine of universal jurisdiction. But the practical facts are displayed in the Belgian failure. Belgium tried to become the forum of choice for cases involving universal jurisdiction, but considerations of political standing ended that attempt. Such efforts raise obvious questions about jurisdiction. By whom, and how, is the question of jurisdiction to be decided.

UNIVERSAL JURISDICTION: THE THEORY

In 2001 an international group of distinguished jurists were assembled by the Program in Law and Public Affairs and the Woodrow Wilson School at Princeton University to "develop consensus principles of universal jurisdiction" (p. 25).[20] These were published as a restatement of the existing international law, with accompanying commentary, as *The Princeton Principles on Univrsal Jurisdiction*. The authors hailed universal jurisdiction, "as one means to achieve accountability and to deny impunity" (52). The argument is persuasive, but there are worrisome issues that surround the potential proliferation of prosecutions, and the potential multiplication of countries that could designate themselves as suitable venues, and as far as I know, the absence of any system of review. This last seems to me very serious.

Though they are enthusiastic about the expansion of loci of accountability, not everything that even the authors of the *Princeton Principles* have to say is reassuring. They state: "Universal jurisdiction holds out the promise of greater justice, but the jurisprudence of universal jurisdiction is disparate, disjointed, and poorly understood. So long as that is so, this weapon against impunity is potentially beset by incoherence, confusion, and, at times, uneven justice" (24).

The *Princeton Principles* themselves are intended to repair some of that. They are designed as a restatement of international law as it is, with due regard for the fact that it will surely develop further in the future. The statement seeks to bring clarity and order to the subject because it is evident that very soon many more cases will be brought under the umbrella of universal jurisdiction, and that there will be legislatures, judges, government officials, nongovernmental organizations, and citizens who will want the guidance that the *Principles provide* (26, 41). But the authors recognize that "all legal powers can be abused by willfully malicious individuals" and they assure readers that the *Princeton Principles* "do all that principles can do to guard against such abuses" (45). But are principles enough?

The admirable goal of enabling further accountability for serious crimes permeates the whole text of the *Princeton Principles*. National courts exercising universal jurisdiction are seen as "having a vital role to play" (55). But the serious matter of review, which I mentioned earlier, is not addressed. There is no discussion of the means by which the decisions of national courts that do not conform to the standards of due process could be overturned, reversed, and undone (29). What international bodies might be appealed to in such a case? As the authors of the *Principles* state: "Universal jurisdiction can only work if different states provide each other with active judicial and prosecutorial assistance, and all participating states will need to insure that due process norms are being complied with" (45).

The International Criminal Court (ICC, at The Hague) is an incomplete alternative to universal jurisdiction. It came into existence in 2002, and can only hear cases of crimes committed after its establishment.[21] Crimes committed earlier must be dealt with by other courts. Normally, those would be domestic courts in the state of the nationals involved. The ICC is expected to take jurisdiction only if the state involved is either unable or unwilling to act. However, given that there is no statute of limitations under the doctrine of universal jurisdiction, it provides a much broader temporal definition of prosecutable cases. This can be seen in the Belgian attempts to implement the doctrine.

The *Princeton Principles* emphasize the vital role of national courts in the prosecution and punishment of "crimes of such exceptional gravity that they affect the fundamental interests of the international community as a whole" (*Princeton Principles*, 23). While they speak of the Rome Statute establishing the International Criminal Court as a signal achievement, they indicate that even after it becomes effective, the primary burden of prosecuting alleged perpetrators of serious crimes under international law will still rest with national legal systems.

Presumably this is partly because one problem that could face the International Criminal Court is that of overload. The distribution of some prosecutions to national courts might relieve some of the pressure, but to do this on a massive scale implies another set of problems. If the people who actually carry out the atrocities are to be tried, not just their leaders, it is not clear how that could be done. Can international standards of due process be applied if there are many thousand defendants as in Rwanda?

The authors of the *Princeton Principles*, no doubt aware of what the UN special tribunals are facing, acknowledge that there may be "many practical limitations on the quest for perfect justice." They go on to say that there are disagreements within and between societies "about the culpability of alleged criminals, the good faith of prosecutions, and the wisdom and practicality of pursuing alleged perpetrators" (27). Moreover, they comment on the political context and timing of the exercise of universal jurisdiction saying that, "imprudent or untimely exercise of universal jurisdiction could disrupt the quest for peace and national reconciliation in nations struggling to recover from violent conflict or political oppression" (25). Thus they recommend that while universal jurisdiction should be exercised to promote greater accountability, it should be exercised "with a prudent concern for the abuse of power and a reasonable solicitude for the quest for peace" (25). The authors of the *Princeton Principles* seem very conscious of some of the potential difficulties of the exercise of universal jurisdiction.

In international law there are a number of alternative jurisdictions that could be used to make political leaders accountable for their crimes against humanity. More and more modes of mounting such trials are being discussed and seem to be theoretically on offer. But in the real world, what matters is not only that such legal venues exist, but that courts will potentially hear cases under international criminal law. It is also necessary that there are persons willing to pursue such cases who have the requisite finances and know-how to see them through.

CONCLUSIONS

Two arenas of law and political struggles have been involved in the materials reviewed here—one national, the other international. On the national side we had a glimpse of particular human rights abuses in Burkina Faso and Kenya, which took place in the past dozen or more years. Those abuses were clearly perpetrated by sitting governments to maintain their power. Among other techniques, they used the law and its associated institutions to remove obstacles to their monopoly. Any attempts to undermine government control or to expose the illegal activities of legal institutions was rapidly and peremptorily punished. Burkinabes and Kenyans have mounted an ongoing countereffort to fight for their civil rights, and they, too, have tried to use the law in their interest.

What was going on was closely observed by other countries and by international organizations. Communications networks made it possible to keep watch on the activists and their causes, almost in real time. In the same decade, pressure for multiparty elections, and for the formation of acknowledged and legitimate opposition parties, was exerted by international donors and diplomats. This encouraged the opposition without helping their members very much. In Burkina, the struggle to unseat the government is still unresolved. In Kenya, former human rights activists *are* the government.

The international legal domain has been expanding in the same period. Not only does it involve the establishment of new institutions to handle crimes against humanity—from special UN courts to the International Criminal Tribunal for Rwanda —but it also involves reviving existing doctrines of universal jurisdiction so that they can be applied to new purposes.

All these raise questions of universal standards of morality, as well as calls for a culture of accountability to replace a culture of impunity. The connection between struggles inside states and international events is made evident by these legal developments. Saskia Sassen points to them as part of the process of globalization. She stresses the importance of transboundary networks, "cross-border networks of activists involved in specific localized struggles with an explicit or implicit global agenda ... the use of international human rights instruments in national courts ... and ... non-cosmopolitan forms of global politics and imaginaries that remain deeply attached or focused on localized issues or struggles, yet are part of global lateral networks containing multiple other such localized efforts" (p. 15).[22] We see all of those characteristics in the specific events reviewed here. Worldwide connections are being created out of the episodes of local struggles. And those connections involve a common, diffuse, value-laden symbolic content, as well as implying that practical consequences may emerge for individuals, institutions, and organizations. But the future of this domain as a normative body of law remains uncertain given the political considerations that are bound to figure in any instance that arises.

REFERENCES

Aderinwale, Ayodele, ed. 1994. *Corruption, Democracy and Human Rights in East and Central Africa*, Africa Leadership Forum, Entebbe, Republic of Uganda, 12-14 December 12–14. Ibadan: Intec Printers Ltd.

Amnesty International, "Amnesty International Report 2002: Burkina Faso." http://web.amnesty.org/web/ar2002.nsf/afr/burkina%20faso!Open.

2002. *"Editorial."* Anthropology Today *18(5) October* .

Borneman, John, ed. 2004. *The Case of Ariel Sharon and the Fate of Universal Jurisdiction.* Princeton, NJ: Princeton Institute for International Studies.

Chabal, Patrick and Jean-Pascal Daloz. 1999. *Africa Works: Disorder as Political Instrument.* London: International African Institute in association with James Currey, Oxford; Bloomington: Indiana University Press.

Cohen, Ronald, Goran Hyden, and Winston P. Nagan , eds. 1993. *Human Rights and Governance in Africa.* Gainesville: University Press of Florida.

Human Rights Watch, "Belgium: Questions and Answers on the Anti-Atrocity Law," February 2003 .

Kenya, Taking Liberties, Africa Watch Report, New York, Washington, London, July 1991

Machiavelli, Niccolo. 1988 [1532]. *The Prince,* ed. Quentin Skinner and Russell Price. Cambridge: Cambridge University Press.

Mattei, U. 2002. "Patterns of African Constitution in the Making." In *Transnational Legal Processes,* ed. Michael Likosky, 275–294. Butterworths, Lexis Nexis, Cromwell Press, Trowbridge, Wilts .

Program in Law and Public Affairs and Woodrow Wilson School. 2001. *The Princeton Principles on Universal Jurisdiction,* Princeton, NJ.

Sassen, Saskia. 2002–2003. "Globalization or Denationalization?" *Items* 4, no. 1 (winter):15.

Wilson, Richard A., ed. 1997. *Human Rights, Culture and Context.* London and Chicago: Pluto Press.

Zoethout, Carla M., Marlies E. Pietermaat-Kros, and Piet W. C. Akkermans, eds. 1996. *Constitutionalism in Africa.* Rotterdam: Sanders Institute, Faculty of Law, Erasmus University Rotterdam.

NOTES

1. "Editorial." Zimbabwe Daily News, January 15, 2002, 1.
2. I was on an assignment as a consultant for the Club du Sahel, a Paris-based consortium of Sahelian countries funded by the OECD (Organization for Economic Cooperation and Development) and U.S. Agency for International Development (AID,.U.S. Department of State). In the 1990s the club's focus on economic development expanded to include political reforms.
3. L'Observateur, Ouagadougou, October 2, 1995, 3.
4. (a) C.I.A., 2002, The World Fact Book, http://www.cia.gov/publications/factbook/geos/uv.html, choose Burkina Faso.
   (b) U.S. Department of State, Burkina Faso Country Report on Human Rights Practices for 1998, http://www.globalmarch.org/virtual-library/usstate departmentreport/1998-report/burkina-faso.htm, Released by the Bureau of Democracy, Human Rights, and Labor, February 26, 1999, 1–6.

(c) Amnesty International, "Amnesty International Report 2002: Burkina Faso," http://web.amnesty.org/web/ar2002.nsf/afr/burkina%20faso!Open.

5. Committee to Protect Journalists, "Attacks on the Press in 2002: Burkina Faso," http://www.cpj.org/attacks02/africa02/burkina.html.

6. See note 5.

7, Amnesty International, "Amnesty International Report 2002: Burkina Faso." http://web.amnesty.org/web/ar2002.nsf/afr/burkina%20faso!Open.

8. See note 4 (b).

9. Kenya, Taking Liberties, Africa Watch Report. New York, Washington, London, July 1991, 180.

10. Seen note 9, p. 181.

11. The Robert F. Kennedy Human Rights Award was established in 1984 to "honor individuals who are often at great personal risk, engaged in strategic and non-violent efforts to overcome serious human rights violations." An international advisory committee of sixty members recommends those to be honored.

12. See note 9, p. 181.

13. See note 9, pp. 223–24.

14. See note 9, pp. 175–76.

15. East African Standard, Nairobi, February 5, 2003.

16. Anthropology Today, October 2002.

17. For details, see Human Rights Watch, "Belgium: Questions and Answers on the Anti-Atrocity Law," February 2003.

18. New York Times, International, April 1, 2003, A8.

19. Boston Globe, April 6, 2003; New York Times, April 7, 2003, A8; BBC News, April 6, 2003.

20. Program in Law and Public Affairs and Woodrow Wilson School, The Princeton Principles on Universal Jurisdiction, 2001, 25. See also, Borneman 2004.

21. United Nations, Rome Statute of the International Criminal Court, 1998, Article 11.

22. Sassen, Saskia. "Globalization or Denationalization?" Items 4, no. 1 (winter 2002–2003): 15.

12

DANGEROUS AND ENDANGERED YOUTH
Social Structures and Determinants of Violence

Nancy Scheper-Hughes

PROLOGUE: THE VIOLENCE OF EVERYDAY LIFE

For many years, my anthropological and ethnographic research has focused on the everyday forms of violence expressed toward the bodies, minds, reproductive capacities, and children of the socially displaced and the stranded, including the homeless, street kids, and the vulnerable residents of shack cities, invasion barrios, favelas, squatter camps, inner cities, and refugee camps the world over.[1-3] Violence cannot be understood in terms of physical force, assault, or the infliction of pain alone. In addition to physical violence, there is also structural violence, psychological violence (which I will not be dealing with here), and symbolic domination.

Structural violence, a term developed within the context of liberation theology in Latin America[4,5] refers to the invisible *social machinery* of social inequality and oppression[6] that reproduces pathogenic social relations of exclusion and marginalization via ideologies and stigmas attendant on race, class, caste, sex, and other invidious distinctions. Structural violence erases the history and consciousness of the social origins of poverty, sickness, hunger, and premature death, so that they are simply taken for granted and naturalized, and no one is held accountable except, perhaps, the poor themselves. Structural violence is violence that is permissible, even encouraged. Indeed, most everyday violent acts are not seen as such, and are condoned, misrecognized, and deemed as necessary to the maintenance of crucial cultural, social, and political institutions. Violence is always mediated by an expressed or implicit dichotomy between legitimate and illegitimate, permissible and sanctioned acts,[7] as when the "legitimate" violence of the state in its various manifestations is differentiated from the unruly, illicit violence of dangerous populations, including minorities and their hostile children and violent adolescents—the "children of the other." Thus, the global category of *street child* (i.e., wild children) contains an unmarked and unstated contrasting set—the *house child* (i.e., "our children").

Symbolic violence refers to assaults on human dignity, sense of worth, and one's existential groundedness in the world.[8,9] Symbolic violence operates by means of substitution, subversion, and hegemony. Its power derives from the ability to make the oppressed complicit in their own destruction. Most everyday acts of violence that I have observed in the slums, favelas, and shantytowns of Brazil and in the townships and squatter camps of South Africa (to be discussed below) took place among the poor themselves. (White South African commentators, even progressive ones, often refer with disdain to "black-on-black" violence without confronting the links between crime and structural violence, which mask the reality of continued "white-on-black" violence.) Meanwhile, the affluent and the powerful, tucked away in gated communities and in homes protected by armed guards and mechanical surveillance reminiscent of medieval fortresses, safely imagine themselves as endangered rather than as the endangering populations. This calculated dissembling of social and political realities obviously requires a great deal of bad faith and misrecognition. Attention to the violence produced in the structures and mentalities of everyday life shifts attention to what Paul Farmer[10] calls the pathologies of power—class, racial, and other social inequalities—which produce paralysis and powerlessness among vulnerable populations forced into complicity with the very social forces that are poised, intentionally or not, to destroy them. Violence is perhaps best thought of in terms of a continuum comprising a multitude of "small wars and invisible genocides"[2] conducted in the normative social spaces of schools, clinics, streets, court rooms, jails and prisons, youth detention centers, and in public morgues. The violence continuum also refers to the ease with which humans are capable of reducing the socially vulnerable (even those from their own class and position) into expendable nonpersons, thus allowing the license—even the duty—to kill (as for example when working-class people in northeastern Brazil express their support for the activities of genocidal death squads promising to "clean up" (i.e., exterminate) human "vermin" and "garbage" from the streets, some of whom may be their own sons). The continuum of violence reveals the capacity and the willingness, if not the enthusiasm, of ordinary people to enforce what are unrecognized crimes against humanity toward categories of people thought of as better off dead.

In the following case studies, drawn from my field research in Brazil and South Africa, I want to demonstrate the inadequacy of the distinction between political and criminal violence that has often been made with respect to the emergence of crime, gang violence, and internal wars during and following periods of political transition. As Franz Fanon[13] noted many years ago, with respect to postcolonial Algeria, revolutionary struggles in response to centuries of political repression and economic and psychological oppression are rarely "finished events," even after the official truces, peace pacts, truth commissions, and new states and governments have come into being. Chaos and criminal violence are often the legacy of revolutionary struggles and their unfinished business. Unmet socioeconomic and psychological needs, including the search for respect, as both Philippe Bourgois and James Gilligan, working in different but equally fraught contexts,[14,15] have made clear, are inevitably incendiary.

My topic is older children, especially the semiautonomous, prematurely "liberated" children of the favelas and the squatter camps, who live on the margins of and are largely excluded from, the benefits of two exemplary post-democratic-transition societies: Brazil and South Africa. Such youth are often viewed with suspicion and subject to an overprediction of violence. They are seen as "dangerous," that is, as likely to commit a violent crime and as justifying the murderous feelings toward them that are sometimes enacted directly (as in death squad attacks) or indirectly (as in child- and youth-hostile politics and legislation). While focusing on two ethnographic cases—postdemocratic Brazil and South Africa—I do not mean to redline the south to the exclusion of the north, where similar patterns have been described for excluded populations in American inner cities.[14]

BRAZIL: DEATH SQUADS AND DEMOCRATIZATION

Between 1964 and 1985 Brazil was a military police state. The 1964 coup, initially and euphemistically described as a "revolution," was a dictatorship of generals that justified itself as stabilizing a volatile and inflationary economy and a politically volatile and expanding population of rural migrants and urban poor. During the harshest period of the dictatorship—the mid to late 1970s—those suspected of subversive activities, such as participation in outlawed labor movements, were arrested and tortured and hundreds died in prison, forcing thousands more into exile. Though never approaching the situation in Argentina, where during the so-called Dirty War (1976–1982) the army turned its full force against ordinary citizens, the military dictatorship years in Brazil were ruthless enough, the aberrations of a large and "nervous" state gone haywire.

It was only when the "economic miracle" began to fail in the early 1980s that a broad-based consensus demanding a return to democratic structures took shape. Many people became accustomed to military "statesmanship" and internalized the state's hatred of certain classes of people. Thus, it was not considered paradoxical that the military oversaw and managed the slow transition to democracy, even though the transition resulted in a new constitution (1988) that recognized the social and economic rights of women, children, students, prisoners, rural workers, squatters, and shantytown dwellers. In addition to new laws, innovative democratic structures and institutions were created and put into place at the municipal level to make sure these new rights were implemented and protected. The 1990 Child and Adolescent Statute, for example, created children's rights councils and child rights advocates in all of Brazil's 5,000 municipalities. These councils, made up of representatives from grassroots organizations, churches, commercial institutions, and local government were designed, among other things, to prevent gross abuses against Brazil's semiautonomous street children and "loose" minority youth who, during the military years, were often rounded up and thrown into state reform schools that were often worse than prisons. In the new, democratic political climate social movements, such as the National Movement of Street Children founded by activists and street educators, struggled to organize and empower Brazil's street youth. Their achievements were impressive: exposing police brutality, organizing street schools and alternative employment, fostering AIDS education and prevention, and advancing model legislation.

Nonetheless, the democratic transition was incomplete and death squad attacks on poor people and on other marginal social groups did not cease, and in some cases resurfaced in new forms and with even greater vigor. By the early 1990s it was apparent that the targets of death squad executions were not "subversives" or activists, but rather ordinary people, some of them involved in petty crime, and most of them poor, semi-illiterate, and socially marginal, especially young black men from urban shantytowns and street children. These attacks were carried out in the absence of public outrage. The democratization and demilitarization of Brazil's government was not accompanied by a demilitarization and democratization of everyday life. Meanwhile, the democratic transition took place within the context of economic globalization and structural adjustment programs, which contributed to new waves of urban crime and public violence. While a drug trade existed in the late 1960s, it did not have the structured network and entrepreneurial organization that emerged in the 1990s. In Rio de Janeiro and São Paulo, crime was primarily an individual activity; gangs, so-called mafia, and police mafia emerged later.[16] Homicides, which were traditionally mostly crimes of passion, became an activity organized in the conflicts between drug-dealing gangs and clandestine activity by death squads and complicit police. Consequently, death squads that began in attacks on marginal adults and petty criminals began to point their revolvers at older kids and adolescents.

As Teresa Caldeira[17] has argued, to a great many affluent Brazilians the mere physical proximity of rural migrants, unemployed men, and unattached street children was perceived as a threat and an affront to "decent" people. Consequently, public spaces—the *rua* and the *praça* (the street and the square)—were redefined as the "private" domain of propertied people. Local street kids and unemployed young men (especially if black) were not seen by most Brazilian citizens as rights-bearing individuals, but rather as bandits, public enemies, and rubbish people (*lixo*)—those who were better off dead. The extension of human rights discourses and constitutional rights to Brazil's large population of street children, vagrants, the unemployed, and even to petty criminals struck many ordinary Brazilians as empowering bandits and endangering the freedom and security of their class of "decent people." Human rights initiatives were undermined by a strong popular backlash against street children and other subcitizens, who were generally perceived as having no rights at all. A stealthy campaign of *social hygiene*—a Brazilian version of *ethnic cleansing*—began to take place in Brazil's largest and most diverse cities (São Paulo, Rio de Janeiro, Recife, and Salvador) with the support of local police, political leaders, and new private security firms and armed response groups. By the early 1990s, attacks on street children in São Paulo, Rio de Janeiro, and Recife, among other urban centers, resulted in youth mortality statistics that rivaled those of South Africa during the years of the armed struggle against apartheid. It was the profile of a nation at war, which in a sense, it was.

I first became aware of the extent of the violence practiced with impunity against residents of the shantytown, Alto do Cruzeiro, in Timbaúba (Bom Jesus da Mata in my early writings), the site of my long-term anthropological and political involvements in northeast Brazil, during the Christmas holidays in 1987, when a half dozen young black men, each in trouble with the law for petty theft, drunkenness, or vagrancy, were seized from their homes by masked men. Two of the missing showed up several days later, their mutilated bodies dumped unceremoniously between rows of sugarcane. Local police arrived with graphic photos for family members. "How do you expect me to recognize my man in this picture?" Dona Helena screamed hysterically.

"Ah, but this is the fate of the poor," Helena said later. "Nem donos do corpo deles, eles estão" (they don't even own their own bodies). Finally, masked men came late one night for the teenage son of "Black" Irene (Irene Preto), the boy everyone on the hillside shantytown knew affectionately as Nego De. A death squad with close ties to the local police was suspected, but on this topic shantytown people were silent, speaking, when they did at all, in a rapid and complicated form of sign language. No one else wanted to be marked. The deaths, insofar as they were recorded in the municipal civil death registry at all, were attributed to gun play, knife fights, traffic accidents, and hypothesized suicides. Few were investigated.

During subsequent fieldwork in 1992, street kids in Timbaúba identified twenty-two of their cohorts who had been killed, some (according to their reckoning) by police (and thus officially classified as "legitimate" homicides), some by *pistoleiros* (hired guns), and some at the hands of other street kids. Despite new laws designed to protect minors from incarceration, a dozen street kids were confined in the local jail and in the same cells as adult offenders. The children's judge (*juiz de minores*) explained that the children were being detained for their own safety. They were castaway children who had been rejected by family members and who were hated by local merchants in this regionally famous market town. Some, he said, were already marked for extermination by local death squads.

As a guard at the local jail in Timbaúba reflected: "The life of a young marginal here is short. It's like this. For a street kid to reach thirty years of age, it's a miracle." More than 5,000 children were murdered in Brazil between 1988 and 1990 alone (*Journal de Comercio*, June 19, 1991). Most of the victims were adolescent males between the ages of fifteen and nineteen, a particularly dangerous time for the children of shantytown and slum dwellers.[19] In 1991 the Legal Medical Institute (the public morgue) in Recife received approximately fifteen bodies of dead children per month. Black and brown (mixed race) bodies outnumbered white bodies twelve to one, and boys outnumbered girls at a ratio of seven to one. In 80 percent of the cases, the bodies had been damaged or mutilated (p. 42).[20] These routine assassinations represented an unofficial state death penalty, one carried out with chilling cruelty and without any chance of defense.

Death squads and vigilante justice were not new in this part of Brazil.[21] Masked men and hired guns often worked hand-in-glove with the old plantation and *fazenda* owners of the *zona da mata* to keep their slaves and later, following abolition, their debt-slave workers cutting and milling sugarcane at the same levels of human misery. The democratic-transition years (roughly 1984 to 2000) were accompanied by the rise of drug cartels and new forms of organized crime, and by the resurgence of *pistoleiros* and *justiceiros*, who were themselves involved in transnational, transregional traffic in small arms, drugs, and what one might even call "traffic" in street kids who were recruited, kept, and used (like Fagan's boys) as thieves and as drug couriers, so-called *avioes* (planes).

One could say that democratization had provoked a crisis. The old military state had kept the social classes safely apart, and the "hordes" of "dangerous" street children contained in their favelas or in public detention. When these policing structures loosened, the shantytowns and slums ruptured and poor people (unemployed young men and street children in particular) descended from hillsides and the river banks and suddenly seemed to be everywhere, flooding the downtown streets, flaunting their misery and "criminalized" needs. Unwanted and perceived as human waste, shantytown youths and street children evoked contradictory emotions of fear, aversion, pity, and anger. Unlike other kinds of refuse, these "garbage" kids and young adults refused to stay in the dump (the favelas and slums) where they "belonged." Their new visibility betrayed the illusion of Brazilian modernity and made life feel very insecure for those with decent homes, cars, and other enviable material possessions. In Timbaúba the death squad killings reached a peak between 1995 and 2001 until the appointment of a new, tough-minded, female judge and an impassioned prosecutor who, with the assistance of local human rights activists, took the hitherto unprecedented step of arresting fourteen local men associated with the extermination group in a dangerous battle to wrest the town from the control of killers.

In spring 2001, I received a startling fax from Dra. Marisa Borges, Timbaúba's new judge, and from Dr. Humberto Da Silva Graça, the new prosecutor. The fax included the legal brief against Abidoral Querizoz and his band of accomplices, who had been terrorizing the interior market town of 58,000 inhabitants for the past decade. Abidoral's "public security" operation, the so-called Guardian Angels, was, in reality, the legal brief stated, "a hyper-active death squad of hired killers" who were charged with the summary executions of more than one hundred people, many of them street children and poor and marginalized young men from the shantytowns. Timbaúba, located in the sugar plantation zone near the border between the states of Pernambuco and Paraiba, where 80 percent of the population still lives in deep poverty, had become, during the 1990s, an important transit point for the regional traffic in drugs (mostly marijuana cultivated in the backlands of the arid *sertão*, but also counterfeit prescription drugs) small arms, stolen merchandise (especially cars), and babies to supply new markets in international adoptions. "Timbaúba is becoming famous as suppliers of "tudo que nao presta" (everything bothersome and worthless), I was told by a resident in the early 1990s. The outlaw status of the community had become so legendary in the region that young boys took to wearing baseball caps with "#1 Mafia" sewn across the front. "What does 'Mafia' mean?" I asked a cute little street urchin, who could not have been more than five years old. He replied, "E, eu sai—bonito, nao e?" (I don't know—beautiful, right?)

Most death squad activities, however, fell under publicly approved neighborhood vigilance and "street-cleaning" (*limpeza*), ridding the *municipio* of its vagrants, drifters, chicken thieves, trouble makers, "sexual deviants," and eventually just plain poor people. The only drug runners who were killed, however, were "disobedient" young couriers in the employ of the extermination group. Otherwise, the drug traffickers were safe. The local business community of Timbaúba was, by and large, grateful for the activities of the Guardian Angels, which they saw as a gift to their social class. As the band grew stronger, powerful groups and institutions fell under their control, including political leaders, police, and some who were involved in the local Catholic Church. Those who refused to pay for Abidoral's protection were added to the death list. In the space of a few years, the extermination squad had managed to kill most of Timbaúba's male street kids. Gildete, herself a former street child of Timbaúba (today a children's rights activist), explained Abidoral's reign of terror as follows:

This "street cleaning" was ordered by the businessmen who wanted to rub out all the street urchins who spent their days sniffing glue, stealing things, and getting into trouble. They wanted them gone because they were hurting businesses, keeping people away from shopping in Timbaúba. Business was declining because there were just too many "dirty flies" [street kids] in the marketplace. So Abidoral's gang took care of them, but only after they used the kids first. They recruited loose kids to steal for them and to run drugs, creating a pretext to justify their cleanup operations and to demonstrate to the shopkeepers that the kids really were drug-addled little criminals. It was a real scam.

Then suddenly in July 2000, the new judge, Dra. Borges, and Dr. Humberto, the prosecutor, armed with little more than the new constitution and the new discourse on human rights, initiated a campaign to round up and arrest members of the death squad. They were able to do so because the population began to recognize that Abidoral and his gang posed a threat to an increasingly broad spectrum of vulnerable people. In addition to attacks on "marginals" and "dangerous" street children, Abidoral's gang began to punish sexual outlaws, public homosexuals, *travesti* (cross-dressers), and single young women involved in affairs with married men.

In her fax to me, Dra. Borges explained: "We are trying to restore the rule of law in Timbaúba" and she recruited my help in identifying the victims and survivors of Abidoral's death squad. Many family members were afraid to come forward and testify. Consequently, only a small number of the executions were represented in the criminal processes against the murderers. Many of the dead were "disappeared" and their bodies deposited in clandestine rural graves owned and operated by small, renegade Protestant churches. Some of the deaths were registered and shelved at the local *cartorio civil* (the privately owned registry office), but no one had the time or skills to comb through the books. Couldn't I use the same skills to uncover these clandestine deaths as I had used in the past to uncover "invisible" infant and child mortalities, she asked. I hesitated, but in the end I hardly had a choice. I was told that my writings on everyday violence in Timbaúba and on an earlier phase of death squad–linked disappearances and deaths of young men and street children of the Alto do Cruzeiro were already "implicated" in the current legal proceedings against Abidoral and his henchmen. (A Spanish edition of *Death without Weeping* (1993) had reached members of the local intelligentsia and was shown to the judge, prosecutor, and even, to my horror, distributed to some members of the local police force, some of whom were undoubtedly complicit in the deaths.)

On my return to Timbaúba in the summer of 2001, accompanied by my husband (a social worker with many years experience working in the field of violence against children), I found the population of Timbaúba, as usual, quite mixed in its views. Some working-class people referred to the bandits as *justiceiros*, the representatives of popular justice. A taxicab driver said:

> Look, these people are like us, they came from "the base." The police should not have arrested them. If there was no peace under the *justiceiros*, today there is even more street violence. Today the police have their hands tied by the new woman judge and the little bandits [street kids] are free to roam the streets.

For those residing in the hillside shantytown of Alto do Cruzeiro, Abidoral and his band of outlaws had turned them into shut-ins, living under self-imposed curfews. Many of my friends recalled with horror a night in 1999 when six people were murdered on the Rua do Cruzeiro, the principal road of the hill. "During the revolution, said Black Irene, using the local idiom describing what they saw as a war or revolution against the poor and socially marginal, "we all went underground. The streets were deserted, we kept our doors locked and our wooden shutters closed tight."

Biu, my fifty-six-year-old *comadre* and key informant of many years, was among the last in Timbaúba to lose a family member or loved one to Abidoral's band. Emaciated from cancer, her face drawn and her skin stretched tight as a drum over her high cheek bones, Biu explained how her twenty-four-year-old son, Gilvam, had met his untimely end walking home along the main road leading up to the top of Alto do Cruzeiro. It was just after Christmas 2000, and Gilvam was returning from a party. Neighbors heard the shots and screams, but they were too frightened to leave their homes. The next morning it was left to Gilvam's older sister, Pelzinha, to discover what was left of his body, sprawled over a mound of uncollected garbage. A crowd of greasy winged vultures had discovered Gilvam's first, and Pelzinha could barely recognize her brother.

In addition to collecting testimonies from residents of the Alto do Cruzeiro who had been affected by Abidora's rein of terror, I reviewed all officially registered deaths in the *cartorio civil* between 1994 and 2000. At first I pretended to be looking for infant and child mortalities, according to my familiar role in the registry office. After a few weeks, however, I had to explain to the proprietor of the records, exactly what I was looking for, and though she expressed no judgment or emotion, she began to facilitate the search in subtle ways.

Many summary executions were concealed in the death records as traffic and train accidents. Gildete, a local human rights worker, reviewed the data on suspicious deaths that I had culled from the death registry books, adding her own observations and recollections:

> Yes, this man you have [recorded] here, Sergio Pedro da Silva, he was a crazy kid, suffering from mental problems. He lived in the streets of Timbaúba since he was a little child. Then suddenly he turned up dead. The people who saw what happened said that a sugarcane truck had passed by amidst a lot of commotion and traffic. It looked to them like Sergio just threw himself under the truck. We knew that they were afraid to say that he was thrown under that truck. One of the techniques of the death squads [is] to conceal the executions by inventing gruesome accidents with trains, busses, and cars. Sometimes they pushed them and sometimes they shot them first and then threw them under trucks or left them exposed on train tracks, so they had an alibi that allowed the police, who actually knew all along what was going on, to say that the death was an accident.

Working with Michael, Gildete, and a small team of local child rights advocates, we were able to identify an additional thirty-one homicides linked to Abidoral's death squad operations. The deaths had been recorded, the death certificates were signed and stamped with the official the seal of the *municipio*, and then shelved. No questions were raised. The owner of the civil registry office had previously told me that her job was to record deaths not to investigate them.

The average victim in this small sample of likely death squad executions was a young black or mixed-race (*moreno*) male between fifteen and thiry years old, unemployed, or casually employed, and from one of the informal marginal communities built on the hillsides and peripheries of Timbaúba. In the early 1990s, most of the suspicious homicides were of older street kids and vagrants; toward the end of the decade the homicides included young men (and even some women) who had gotten tangled up in petty crimes, sexual and personal vendettas, and drug deals gone wrong. We presented our findings to the prosecutor and to members of the municipal Ministry of Public

Security to be used in continuing investigations and litigation against members of the death squads.

Our matter-of-fact public involvement in the investigations of the death squads was seen by local rights workers as useful toward building a broader-based coalition. Our note taking about violent deaths, our conversations in public spaces, our visits to the homes of those who had lost family members to the squads, and to graveyards where they had been buried, began to reverse the regime that Dr. Humberto described as "the law of silence, the law of 'let it be,' and the law of forgetting" (a lei do silencio, a lei do deixa pra la, e a lei do esquecimento) among the frightened populace of Timbaúba. Local activists, sympathetic political leaders, Catholic nuns, teachers, and officials from the municipal Ministries of Education, Justice, and Public Security met to plan a public demonstration, a *camanhada* or march or procession, against death squad violence and the declaration, albeit premature, of a time of peace. The march was held in Timbaúba on July 19, 2001, exactly one year after the arrest of Abidoral and several of his accomplices. Because most residents were still too fearful of, or complicit with, the death squads (many members of which were still at large) to join the march, the secretary of education declared the day a public school holiday and led the *municipio's* several hundred grade school children and adult school youths in the *camanada*. Although the day was dark, rain swept, and windy, hundreds of local residents came out to watch the events from the sidewalk, registering their amazement and occasionally their excitement that such an event could possibly be happening in Timbaúba.

Leading the procession were some thirty surviving street kids of Timbaúba (between the ages of four and seventeen years) dressed in white, each carrying a crudely fashioned wooden cross bearing the name of a young victim, often a sibling or best friend, executed by Abidoral's group (figs. 7 and 8). Behind them marched a small group of middle-aged women, the mothers and wives of men and boys who had been murdered, making public for the first time what had happened to them. Biu, Black Irene, Marlene, and Severina were among them. Irene shook her head and laughed in disbelief that she could actually be so bold as to protest, in front of the world, the execution-style murders of her husband and two teenage sons, the latter who often found themselves on the wrong side of the law. Biu was more reluctant and she refused to carry the cross with the name of her son Gilvam. Several of us took turns carrying the cross honoring and memorializing his untimely death at the hands of Abidoral and his thugs.

The march terminated in front of the city hall (*prefeitura*) with spontaneous speeches by the new mayor and town councilors, who were presented with a large brass plaque memorializing the end of the most recent reign of death squad terror in Timbaúba. The plaque would be placed on the wall of a public square facing the town hall, which was to be renamed the Praça de Paz. The plaque reads, in translation: The Gratitude of the People for Those who Fought against Violence and for Human Rights. Commemorating One Year of Peace in Timbaúba. July 19, 2001. Violent deaths have not ended in Timbaúba, of course, but for now they are no longer organized by roving death squads. Street kids have returned to their normal haunts, sleeping in doorways and under the canvas awnings of the public market, if that can be seen as a sign of progress. But there are discouraging reports from Timbaúba of Abidoral and his henchmen rearming themselves in prison and communicating with other bandits by cell phones, a right allowed them under prison reform codes. So perhaps there was some truth, after all, to popular fears that human rights discourses would extend rights to bandits. Nonetheless, the courage and success of a small band of rights workers calls into question facile anthropological critiques of universalized notions of human rights (such as those enshrined in the United Nations Proclamation on the Rights of the Child). To paraphrase Margaret Mead, human rights discourses provide real openings for thoughtful and committed citizens trying to protect the vulnerable and transform the world in which they live.

SOUTH AFRICA: YOUTH VIOLENCE, POPULAR JUSTICE, AND HUMAN RIGHTS

I will now focus on three incidents of violence in South Africa during the dangerous interregnum—the year before the election of Nelson Mandela—as the first democratic leader of South Africa, in which youth were the primary actors. Two of the incidents concern the murder of whites by militant youths. The first was a mob scene; the second was a carefully orchestrated massacre in a public setting. The third and contrasting incident concerns the discipline and control of angry and disenfranchised young men in a new squatter camp in the western Cape. In each case the young men were targeted as savage and barbaric threats to the transitional society. With my less than perfect sense of timing, the day after my family and I arrived in South Africa in July 1993, where I was to take up a temporary post as professor of the Department of Social Anthropology at the University of Cape Town, hell seemed to break loose. Three township youths dressed in overalls and head scarves burst into the evening service of St. James Church, a mostly white and conservative congregation in a suburb close to the university. The men fired several rounds of ammunition and tossed nail-spiked hand grenades into the congregation of more than 400 worshippers while they were singing the hymn "Come to the Garden." In a few minutes, 11 people were dead and more than 50 were maimed, among them a Russian seaman who lost an arm and both legs after one of the grenades landed in his lap.

More people would have died in the St. James massacre (as it came to be called) if not for a young man seated in the balcony, who was carrying a revolver and immediately fired back at the assailants, who turned on their heels and ran out of the church, escaping in a getaway car that had been carjacked earlier in the day in Kayelitsha (a sprawling black township containing as many as one million refugees from the former apartheid homelands and accounting for almost a third of the entire population of the city of Cape Town).

One month later, on August 25, an American Fulbright student, Amy Biehl, was dragged from her car in Guguletu township in Cape Town and stoned to death by an angry mob of youths, shouting "Death to the Settler!" While a shower of stones continued to rain down on her car, Amy Biehl, dazed and wounded, crawled from her car and smiling broadly, approached the angry youths, identifying herself as a friend, a comrade. But the crowd of about forty youths chased her and backed her against a fence, while some continued to throw stones, until one young man came forward to stab her several times until she finally collapsed to the ground. Another of the boys stole her purse, while the high-stepping crowd of demonstrators shouted out their encouragement and approval.

Then, on New Year's Eve 1993, a tavern in the mixed race and bohemian student quarter of Observatory in Cape Town was attacked with grenades and automatic weapons by young APLA/PAC (Azanian Peoples' Liberation Army/Pan-Africanist Congress) militants. Four people were killed, two of them University of Cape Town students, one a grade school teacher from a Colored township, and the fourth an acquaintance of ours, the owner of a Portuguese restaurant we often frequented. By this time I had begun to internalize the relentless media images descrying a "lost generation" of African youths portrayed as dangerous, destructive, and deranged. In a response that could only be seen as a counterphobic strategy, I initiated an ethnographic study of the role of violence in the last stages of the antiapartheid struggle, which required multiple visits to the Salt River police mortuary. On the night of the tavern massacre[22] I was put to work by a young state pathologist,

Len Lerer,[23] in helping relatives to identify the dead. Among the relatives was Ginn Fourie, an occupational therapist at Groote Schurr Hospital of the University of Cape Town and the mother of a twenty-one-year-old young woman, Lindsay, one of the four people killed at the tavern. Initially, Ms. Fourie knew me only as the disembodied, strangely accented and hesitant voice that blasted into her life with a brutal phone message from the medical police headquarters of the Salt River Mortuary on New Year's Eve: "Mrs. Fourie, I am so sorry to have to tell you, but your daughter Lindy-Anne has been killed." Later, she became a research informant and then an independent researcher herself on the topic of violence, trauma, and recovery.

To be sure, many beautiful things also happened during that eventful and miraculous year, but the memory of those mutilated bodies overdetermined the focus of my primary ethnographic work—a study of democracy, youth, and violence. Political transitions are inevitably chaotic and dangerous. As in postmilitary Brazil, in South Africa the antiapartheid struggle and the democratic transition had initiated a crisis, a crisis of chronically unmet needs and of rising expectations for the oppressed, and a crisis of security for the privileged classes. With democratization there emerge new nations full of needs, and full of rage.

In the following account, I will contrast the formal court proceedings that determined the fate of Biehl's convicted murderers with the fate of the three young men caught red-handed stealing $125 from a local shebeen (a small, black-owned shop) handled by the informal peoples' court of Chris Hani shantytown, a forum in which politicized youths had a considerable say. Then I will return to the Cape Town massacres, a decade later, when during hearings of the South African Truth and Reconciliation, the young militants applied for amnesty and tried to explain themselves.

Amy Biehl's death was treated as a political watershed and South African leaders of all stripes began to worry that township youths were totally out of control. At the memorial service held the day after the killing at the University of the Western Cape, one of Amy Biehl's mentors, feminist activist Rhoda Kadalie, spoke angrily of Amy's death at the hands of "young monsters" created and set loose by the apartheid machine: "Now they are afoot in the land and no-one can stop them. They are eating us and eating each other." Immediately following the memorial service, members of the ANC (African National Congress) Women's League called for white and colored women to join a spontaneous march into Guguletu to take back the township from the young criminal elements that now held people hostage to senseless acts of violence. The idea was to make the township safe and open to people of all colors. Carrying an ANC poster reading "Stop the Violence," I joined the march from the Shoprite supera market over the bridge and through the squatter camp across the highway leading into Gugs. Less than twenty-four hours after Amy was extrajudicially executed, the small group of demonstrators anxiously toi-toiyed (a militant high-stepping dance–march) past hostile faces. Did our posters with their reference to senseless violence imply that the apartheid police were "sensible" in their violent attacks on black townships? Was *senseless* a racist code for irrational black violence as opposed to rational, sensible white and police violence? What could "take back the township" mean in this beleaguered place? No one from the township joined our pathetic little protest march.

We stopped in front of the murder site on a main road next to a brightly lit and modern gas station. The stoning happened in full view of a row of neat cement block houses. The signs of her murder were still evident: blood and hair still adhered to the fence where she was cornered. Why didn't anyone intervene? Did Amy's fresh-faced naïveté enrage the youths who had just marched off a packed train of toy-toy-ing demonstrators returning from the launch of a new Pan African Congress headquarters. Was it because she had approached the crowd claiming for herself the status of *companheira* in the struggle ("I'm Amy, a comrade," were her last words). Or was it just Amy's big, smiling white "settler" face that had gotten in the way?

White Justice: The Amy Biehl Trial

Of the seven youths originally identified and detained for questioning in the Biehl murder case, three young men finally stood trial in the municipal Supreme Court of Cape Town: Mongezi Manquina, "Easy" Nofemela, and Vusumzi Ntamo. Later, Ntbeko Peni, an intense young PAC (Pan-African Congress) intellectual, was also apprehended, brought to trial, and found guilty in the death. For Amy Biehl's single and solitary death there was a "royal" dispensation—three judges: a president judge flanked by two assessors, one white, one black. The judge was addressed reverently as "my lord" by both defense and state lawyers. The robes were red, and the court room was rich in polished hardwood benches and pews. The lawyers for the state were white Afrikaners; the lawyers for the defense were black and of radical political backgrounds. The trial moved at a snail's pace, focusing on the defense accusations of forced confessions from the boys.

During the first stages of the trial, when two witnesses came forward to describe in graphic detail Biehl's final agony, her pleas and groans as she was stoned and stabbed, young PAC supporters packed into the upper gallery of the court room, laughed and cheered. The judge expressed his revulsion at the outburst and cleared the courtroom, but not before the media were able to capture the image of those dancing and seemingly heartless youth. Left out of the news reports, however, was the reaction of Nofemela (defendant number two), who whipped around to correct the festive spirit in the gallery: "What's wrong with you? Why don't you all get out of here!"

"Why did the youth laugh?" I asked Nona Goso, the soft-spoken lawyer for the defense.

She responded, "the laughter was not acceptable to me, nor to anyone else, but it did not shock me. I live in a township and I know the extent to which apartheid has murdered human feelings. Their own people have been killed so often that it has the effect of reducing killing to nothing."

"What can you tell me about the defendants?" I asked.

She explained, "in every sense they are children ... lovely children, like any other. Under normal circumstances they would have had a wonderful life. But they are children of apartheid. They come from broken homes and families where no one is working. Education was out of the question.... They have experienced everything and been exposed to everything."

I thought immediately of the games played by the children of Chris Hani squatter camp: "funeral," "shack burning," and "shoot-out." Few South African camp children escaped the scenes of everyday violence: the burnings of shacks, public whippings, premature death, and even the discovery of corpses where garbage should be.

Who Counts?

White deaths counted, so news reports of the church and tavern victims of PAC youth violence recorded their names and their histories, accompanied by images of grieving family members. During the same period, black deaths were reported in the English, Afrikaans, and Xhosa newspapers alike, as faceless body counts: "Another 40 bodies found on the East Rand;" "Dozen Bodies Removed from Guguletu in Weekend Casualties;" "The charred bodies of seven people, including three children were found in Katlehong on Friday;" "The burned bodies of two young men were found at the Mandela squatter camp in Thokoza and another body at Katlehong railway station;" and even:

"Charred bodies of two witches found in Nyanga outside CapeTown." A black journalist told me with disgust:

> Last week the *Cape Times* reported that seventeen people were killed in a bus accident on Main Road. I knew immediately those who died were Black because the press did not bother to say who they were and made nothing of the accident. There would have been better reporting if a busload of chickens had died in the crash on Main Road. Instead, it was treated as just another one of those things that happens to the kind of people who ride public transportation, that is—to African people.

As for the inappropriate courtroom laughter by the PAC youth during the Biehl trial, the experience of the deaths of so many comrades, of so many political funerals attended, surely contributed to the numbing that Nono Goso alluded to. Sidney Kumalo, an ANC (and sometime PAC) youth leader in Chris Hani squatter camp explained it like this:

> I don't want to apologize for the PAC and what their comrades may have done. But in these days in which we are living it is very hard. You don't get shocked any more when you hear that somebody has died. I'm afraid that we are starting to learn to live with death. If I myself hear that a friend has died, I say, "Oh, that is too bad. I guess I won't see him again. Okay, lets go and have a few beers. We don't need to worry ourselves anymore."

In the end, the boys were convicted and sentenced to eighteen years in prison. An attempt by the defense to mitigate the length of the sentence because of the ages of the young men (from seventeen to twenty-one years) and the political and emotional turmoil of the times was rejected by the judge, who insisted on seeing the murder as a race crime alone. It was a burlesque court that revealed the fissures and illegitimacy of the apartheid state, and the impossibility of a fair trial even during its final days. Consent to be ruled had been withdrawn from all sides, and the trial had the appearance of a kangaroo court, by definition "a court ... operated by any improperly constituted body. A tribunal before which a fair trial is impossible; a comic or burlesque court."

Popular Justice and the Comrades

In the townships and squatter camps of South Africa, alternative forms of policing and justice were put into place during the struggle years (the 1970s through 1994). In acts of refusal to collaborate with the apartheid state, the so-called ungovernable townships instituted their own forms of surveillance and control. Discipline committees, self-defense units, and people's courts took the place of the formal institutions of community policing (by apartheid police) to which politicized township people refused to submit themselves.[24–28] Street committees and civic associations redefined and bolstered male identity,[29,30] producing an idealized image of the young ANC and PAC comrade as one who was strong, upright, disciplined, respectful of communal norms and of new political values, accountable to his colleagues, and who recognized the true enemy—the apartheid state and all its collaborators, black as well as white. Age was not a factor, and even very young men could usurp positions of authority and control in the townships. In fact, political socialization challenged the authority of parents and elders, who were often seen as passive or even complicit with the apartheid state. The willingness to resist, violently at times, was an important symbol of the South African version of the "new Socialist man." During the antiapartheid struggle, the distinction between revolutionary and criminal violence was blurred. Two members of the discipline committee of Chris Hani shantytown in the western Cape, a primary site of my field research, explained how they had been recruited and politicized by older boys to cause mayhem on the commuter trains going back and forth from the black townships to the center of Cape Town during the 1980s:

> We would begin singing and toyi-toying, and then we would push and shove people who wouldn't join us. Sometimes we even pushed the people who wouldn't join us out the car doors and onto the train tracks. We didn't stop to think what we were doing to people who were just ordinary people like ourselves.

Zolilie Matross, himself a former PAC activist, added:

> What you must understand is that the criminal element—the skollies—were a force that had to be taken in and used by us in the struggle. Without that criminal element, the struggle would not have been available to us. Only the criminal element had the ability to ban their private life. Only they would have the courage to do the things that we could not bring ourselves to do. Do you think that Temba here would have the courage to burn a person alive with petrol and tires? A skollie has got the courage to attack a man in daylight, to rape and to murder in front of all

the people. He has no inhibitions! He has no shame. He has that kind of crazy courage. It is in his blood! So we said, "Give him petrol! Give him matches! He'll do the job for us!" But that skollie element, it can improve, it can rise up! Today, many former skollies are today very high up in the army, and they are now very disciplined men. Yes, from a skollie to a gentleman—it's the truth! [Laughter.]

In a fraught political climate such as this, the task of alternative self-policing in the township and squatter camp was daunting to say the least.

The Problem of the Incident

Chris Hani, a new squatter camp, was built on the outskirts of the wealthy agricultural village of Franschhoek in the western Cape during the early 1990s, when both hope and fear for the future prevailed. The local leaders of Chris Hani camp were faced with the thankless task of trying to maintain order (without recourse to the state or local, apartheid police) among some six hundred multilingual squatters who had migrated with little more than the clothes on their backs from their former homelands. Forced to live on top of each other in degrading conditions, it was amazing how little criminal behavior there actually was in the camp. But the fear of crime, and the older residents' suspiciousness of the hot-headed and often troubled youth—unemployed, hungry, and ready to take what they needed, whether outside or inside the camp—was strong. In response to the implicit threat posed by "dangerous," unattached youths living in shared and often squalid bachelor shacks, older members of the camp tried to enforce an almost draconian code of conduct, one that resembled a kind of self-imposed police camp mentality, reminiscent of apartheid itself. Strict curfews were imposed. Visitors to the camp could not stay overnight. Identity cards had to be shown on demand to members of the security committee, who also claimed the right to enter people's shacks without warning to search for guns, weapons, drugs, and alcohol. There was even talk of building a fence around the camp to prevent new squatters from taking up residence.

Those accused of transgressing camp codes of conduct had to appear before informally assembled people's courts and had to comply with demands for public apologies, the restitution of stolen goods, and submit to corporal punishments (beatings and floggings) for crimes ranging from brawling and drunkenness, assault and battery, rape, theft, to complicity with hated apartheid personnel and institutions.

The most heinous punishment, reserved for those seen as enemies of the people, was the "necklace"—a rubber tire filled with gasoline that was placed over the shoulders of the guilty party and ignited with a match. Flaunting a box of matches was one way that township militants earned respect and fear. In the case I am about to describe, however, the threat of the necklace—indeed a triple necklacing—in Chris Hani camp was imposed in the heat of a mob scene following the capture of three young, single men who leaders of the camp felt had been up to no good for long enough. They were common thieves, disrespectful to elders and to women, and were seen as violent, dangerous, and incorrigible—better off dead once and for all. The incident was averted in the nick of time by the interventions of a small group of politicized youth.

The incident occurred on the night of January 24, 1994, when three teenage boys stole 400 rands (about $125) from a *shebeen*. The widow who owned the shop cried out for help, and the community assembled and demanded immediate punishment—initially it was to be death by necklacing. As the boys sat trembling awaiting their fate, a few youth leaders, invoking the ANC Bill of Rights, dangerously raised their voices in protest and successfully argued for public whippings over the death penalty. Further debate ensued, and the demand for one hundred strokes with a *sjambock* (a bullwhip very similar to the slave whips kept on display at the Sugar Museum in Recife, Brazil) was negotiated by the youth leaders down to fifty lashes for each boy caught red-handed. The floggings were laid on collectively by several designated older men of the camp.

The boys, bachelors who shared shack number 12 in the camp, had sometimes helped me out, pointing out camp leaders and indicating those who spoke some English. In all, there was enough interaction for me to sense hearts beating (now in terror) behind those makeshift, newspaper-covered shack walls with headlines displaying stories and photos of Chris Hani, General Holomisa, and Winnie Mandela. My local assistant, eighteen-year-old Sidney Kumalo, had recently returned (his skin still painted with red dye) from his month of initiation, isolation, and disciplined hunger in the bushes near the town of Paar. Freshly circumcised, Sidney was now a "made" man, and he stepped out in the confines of his camp world fairly beaming and wearing a new suit of clothes and a derby hat, which proudly announced his new status. Postinitiation rules forbade him from going out for thirty days without his derby, and he always brushed the dust off carefully before placing it jauntily on his shaved head.

"There is something you need to know," Sidney said in grave tones, "about our codes of discipline." He told me to accompany him on a visit to the boys who were being held prisoner in the camp, and I did so with great trepidation. The boys were not a pretty sight, though some thought they had gotten off easy with just fifty lashes. The whip lay limp and tired against the wall. Kept in isolation and denied food, water, and human company as a continuation of the punishment, the three prisoners lay on dirty rags on the dirt floor. Their eyes were dull and glassy with fever. They could not bend their legs, sit down, or walk without wincing, and three days later they still had trouble urinating. The smallest, Michael B., carried the mark of the lash across his neck and face. He scowled with pain and with revenge. "I'll kill them," he kept repeating of his tormentors.

The community, fearing police involvement, refused the boys access to medical attention. The parents and relatives were nowhere in sight, fearful that their shacks might be burned were they to show any sympathy toward their children who were seen as enemies of the camp. Acting on behalf of the ANC youth committee, Sidney urged me to take photos of the boys (for evidence) and to tape-record an interview to be used later at a civic association meeting. Sidney served as their interpreter:

Kumalo: They say that they stole 400 rands from one of the people's houses here, and with it they bought brandy and weapons. When they were caught the *pangas* (machetes) were in their hands and they still had 200 rand between them. Due to our codes of conduct, they had to be punished in our way. At first the community called for burnings, the people were waving *pangas* and sticks and they said that the boys must be burned because they are thieves. So they were just waiting to get killed. They couldn't run away because they were surrounded by the whole community. It's very quick. This is not our traditional way. In Transkei [the old apartheid reserve for the Xhosas] only a very old man with a lot of experience can stand up and speak out and give the punishment. But here it is too simple. If I don't like someone I can just say, "Give him eighty lashes." Other people who like him better may come up with a smaller number: "No, give them twenty lashes." It is very harsh.

Scheper-Hughes: Would they really be killed for stealing just 400 rands?

Kumalo: The boys say that the punishment was that they must get burned [necklaced] … but some people still had sympathy for them and they said, "No, no, just give them the lashes instead." And a lot of the young people here are in the PAC and the ANC youth committees and they are against these harsh discipline codes. The ANC leadership says that we shouldn't use the necklace or to put the lash on ourselves the way the police and the Boer [the Afrikaner farmers] did to us.

Scheper-Hughes: What about their relatives?

Kumalo: If their relatives speak out, the people here think, "Oh, so it was you who put them up to this, you set them up to steal." So the mothers and fathers, they can't defend their own children. If a mother speaks out for her son, the people have the right to burn down her shack. The people here are very strict in this discipline. They say we cannot afford to be soft.

Scheper-Hughes: Has anyone ever been burned [necklaced] here?

Kumalo: No, not yet. And that's what makes it a little bit difficult for them to kill. The youth committee here are very afraid of what will happen here after they take that step once.

Scheper-Hughes: Could you ask Michael what he has learned from this?

Kumalo: At this moment he don't think he will steal again. But the only thing that's going through his mind over and over is revenge. I told him that if he takes revenge he'll just be punished all over again. But right now he wants revenge, only he says that he doesn't have the power to do it. He says that he knows who were the people who did this to him, the ones who whipped him, because they don't even bother to cover their faces. He remembers all the faces. [This was said with great emphasis and a threatening tone of voice.]

Scheper-Hughes: Why did they decide to steal?

Kumalo: They say they were hungry and were sick and tired of having no money and no work. They are stuck because they don't even have the goats and sheep they need to be initiated. So they cannot even become men. The family [of the initiates] must prepare a big feast and everyone must be invited. And the clothes you wore before initiation, you must give them away, because now you are starting a new life. But you see, everything goes back to money, and these guys don't have any.

The next day I returned to Chris Hani with Rose, a mixed-race medical student intern from the University of Cape Town Medical School, a young woman of considerable courage and stamina. Two other doctors from Cape Town, both male, one white and one black, declined my request for help. After a careful examination and washing and dressing the considerable wounds of the young men, Rose decided that Michael's wounds had gone septic and required antibiotics to prevent a generalized infection.

We carried Michael by combi-taxi to the "white" hospital in Paarl, where he was reluctantly attended by a young Afrikaner doctor who agreed not to ask any questions about the incident. The Afrikaner doctor could not, however, refrain from expressing his disdain and he communicated his disapproval while he set up an intravenous antibiotic: "Yah, and these barbarians are the people who are going to be ruling us soon! Shame! They'll send us all back into the Stone Age." In contrast to the "primitive" and "unhygienic" squatter camp floggings, the white doctor explained the "proper procedure," which was used by local police who always brought their prisoners to the clinic for a medical examination before administering the lash. The attending doctor would decide how many lashes the prisoner could "safely" sustain. "But this," Dr. K. said, gesturing to Michael's exposed buttocks, "This way of going about it is barbaric." The doctor completed the examination, diagnosed an infection-related fever, and decided to keep the scowling (and very frightened) young patient in the hospital for a few days of observation and treatment. Michael's general health was poor, he said. The young man was severely anemic, malnourished, and dehydrated. "A few days of hospital fare won't hurt him," Dr. K. said and we left the hospital feeling that despite the racist commentary, Michael would be medically well attended despite his resistance to the regime.

Discipline and Punish

A decade of democracy has been celebrated, but South Africa remains a violent country. The legacy of apartheid includes the "renegade" social institutions created by people who tried to survive as best they could with informal institutions of popular justice that ran the risk of veering toward populist justice instead. The "incident" at Chris Hani camp illustrates a number of enduring problems, among them the disruptions resulting from the inversions of traditional power relations within the African community during the struggle years, as young people openly challenged the traditional codes of control by elders. In meetings of the civic association, cleavages between the older and younger residents of the camp, and between women and men were evident. The severity of discipline imposed on the three young thieves by the adult men who controlled the security committee was, in part, a displacement of their frustration and anger at their loss of control to politicized youths in the transitional society in formation.

The heightened surveillance toward, and overreactions to, the threats posed by young, loose men in the camp was a reflection of political tensions between the generations as well as a reflection of the impact (even in the squatter camp) of media images of "dangerous and savage youths." One could say that residents of the camp had become afraid of their own shadows, by which I mean the terrifying "double" produced in racist rhetoric still circulating in South Africa at that time.

Nonetheless, in a context where self-government was often invented on the spot and in response to specific crises, the security and discipline committees did an admirable job, and what might appear at first glance to be an unreflective and reactive mob rule (i.e., the initial demand for necklacing) was in fact open to negotiation based on argument and appeals to reason, mercy, and human rights.

Popular justice and people's courts are vulnerable on many counts. They are dependent on volunteers. Many residents are afraid to serve, fearing intimidation by relatives of the accused, paving the way for strong men with connections to usurp the roles. These grassroots institutions are not very good at fact-finding, and they rely heavily on accusations, counteraccusations, and on confessions of guilt. But much the same could be said of the Amy Biehl trial in the Municipal Supreme Court, and also of the official TRC (Truth and Reconciliation Commission) hearings, which represented another and more "cosmopolitan" version of popular justice.

Reconciliation—Letting Go

Eventually, the victims and survivors of the unruly end-stage anti-apartheid attacks, including Linda and Peter Biehl; Dawie Ackerman (who lost his wife in the St. James Massacre); and Ginn Fourie, whose only daughter died in the tavern massacre, had to confront the young men who killed their loved ones when they were summoned to appear and testify during the TRC amnesty hearings in Cape Town. Dawie Ackerman directly addressed the three young amnesty applicants to turn their heads and face him directly: "This is the first opportunity we have had to look each other in the eye while talking. I want to ask Mr. Makoma, who actually entered the church, a question. My wife was sitting at the door when you came in. [Dawie wept as his words seemed to be dragged from the roots of his shaking body.] She was wearing a long blue coat.... Please, can you remember if you shot her?"

Makoma looked up at Dawie terrified, as though seeing Hamlet's father's ghost. He bite his lower lip and slowly shook his head. No, he could not remember—not Marita nor her long, blue coat. But he, along with the other petitioners at the TRC hearing, apologized to Dawie. Makoma, having been singled out by Ackerman, was the most affected and the most defensive in his response: "We are truly sorry for what we have done. But it was not intentional.... Although people died, we did not do that out of our own will. It was the situation in South Africa we were living under. And now we are asking you please, do forgive us."

To his own amazement (Dawie later told me), Ackerman did forgive him, withdrawing on the spot his carefully prepared legal objections to the amnesty process. After the TRC hearing, Ackerman and several other survivors of the St. James massacre, including Bishop Reteif, the pastor of the church, were taken to a private room where they held a meeting with the young militants, each of whom walked around the table addressing each survivor in turn, shaking their hands, and whispering individual messages of condolence.

Brian Smart, a St. James survivor, was impressed by the ages of the militants at the time of the massacre: "They were only seventeen years old, and I could relate to that. When I was eighteen years old I was in the South Africa Air Force and sent out in defense of the realm, if you like. The only difference between myself and them was that I was operating under controlled military orders. So a massacre like the one we experienced would not have happened. In their case the command structure was very weak and, unfortunately, they had the soldier's normal ability to kill, just as I had." Bishop Reteif, who was not in the church until moments after the attack took place, and who subsequently suffered a great deal of pastoral survivor guilt, originally opposed the granting of amnesty to terrorists. His initial response to the massacre was to heroize the South African police and to demonize the PAC youth as "instruments of evil forces." After the TRC hearings the bishop was contrite and mindful of the blindness of his evangelical church to the suffering caused by apartheid, indirectly supported by his large wealthy church, which had benefited from their oppression. He later confessed to me: "It took me a while, but now I finally understand why the TRC was necessary." He also realized how offensive and patronizing his church's missionary work had been in the townships of Cape Town, and how their presence had contributed to young people's hostility toward the church.

As for Linda and Peter Biehl, their extraordinary faith in their daughter's "meaningful" death allowed them to move forward, as Peter put it in his Midwestern U.S., down-to-earth style. For them, this has meant not only facing, but embracing, their daughter's killers and devoting their lives to the townships within and outside Cape Town, especially Guguletu, where three of the young militants convicted in their daughter's death—Easy Nofemla, Mangesi, and Ntbeko Peni—have returned to live since the TRC amnesty panel released them from Pollsmor Prison.

In accepting amnesty for the killers, the Biehls, Ginn Fourie, and Dawie Ackerman—along with a multitude black South Africans called upon to do the same—allowed their own personal tragedies to serve as a symbol of national healing and reconciliation. Their ability to find some transcendent purpose, some beauty even, in the death of their loved one was a stepping stone in getting over the past in order to reach the other side.

But among the youth militants who came to the TRC in search of amnesty were those like comrade Makoma, who remained bitter and unreconciled; who felt abandoned by the paramilitary command structure and publicly humiliated. The very structure of the TRC equated the violent apartheid state and its operatives with the young PAC and ANC militants, pathologized and individualized the antiapartheid struggle, and turned everyone into either victims or perpetrators. What was written out of the TRC process was the act of political resistance itself. Following his TRC hearing, Makoma, who was serving a twenty-year sentence for his part in the St. James Church massacre, returned to prison to await the decision on his plea for amnesty. During that period, a visit was arranged between Mokoma and Dawie Ackerman's daughter. Leisel asked Makoma how he felt during his amnesty hearing when he was shown the graphic police photos "of all the people and all the blood" of those he had killed. Makoma replied frankly to the girl whose mother he had killed:

> Yah, I remember seeing that and I had bad feelings. It was bad. But no matter how I feel now, at this time, or at this moment, about what I did then was bad, there is nothing which I can do. The people are dead. Why ask me how I feel about that? How I feel cannot change anything, cannot bring them back to life.

As a disciplined PAC operative, Makoma considered these emotional demands and ritual performances both unseemly and beside the point. Dead is dead and what happened cannot be undone. The Ackerman family remains divided over the TRC and the role that Dawie played in forgiving Makoma and the other killers and supporting the amnesty that the young men received. Dawie himself concedes that "none of killers seemed really sorry about what they had done," but he accepted the amnesty process as necessary for the nation to move ahead.

Ntbeko Peni and Easy Nofemela, who petitioned for and received amnesty for their roles in the killing of Amy Biehl, expressed different sentiments about the TRC. In July 1999 the young men reluctantly agreed to meet with me in their rundown shacks in Guguletu township. I faced a solid brick wall of seething silence, and I began to speak about what I had seen and learned thus far, until silenced by Ntbeko, who explained his political position within the PAC command structure, his role in the killing of Amy Biehl, and his mistrust of the ANC-led TRC. Nonetheless, he decided to appear before the TRC because of the "heaviness" in his heart. Talking had not helped, and since being granted amnesty and returning to live in Guguletu, his days (he said) were very dark. He could not sleep. He could not have a girlfriend. He could not take up work. He could not study. He hid from people. Above all, he was full of shame. He asked if I could arrange a meeting with Amy's parents.

"What would you want to tell the parents of Amy Biehl?" I asked.

He answered: "I want to tell that Mr. Biehl that I did not take the death of his daughter lightly. That this thing has weighed heavily on me. And I want him to know that he is a hero father to me. That he has great strength. If you could get that Peter Biehl to listen to me and to release me from my suffering, that would be good, as good as bread."

The arranged meeting with Peter Biehl (his wife, Linda, was in California) at the home of Ntbeko Peni took an amazing turn. After a painful emotional standoff between Peter Biehl, Ntbeko, Easy Nofemela, and several of their comrades, the boys tried their best to explain themselves and to convey their sadness over a death they now say should never have happened. They told Peter about the youth group they had started in the township and they brought out photos of the hikes they took with the young people up and around Cape Town's famous Table Mountain.

Though his face remained stonelike, Peter Biehl accepted the boys' awkward attempts to approach him, and after conferring by phone with Linda Biehl, he invited Ntbeko and Easy to work for the Amy Biehl Foundation. Shaking their heads in disbelief, the boys eagerly accepted.

The young men were apprenticed as welders and construction workers, and they helped Peter Biehl organize the distribution and sale of "Amy's Bread" from the large communal bakery that Peter established near Guguletu. Linda Biehl was proud that Easy and Ntbeko shyly called her "Mama," a term of respect used by Xhosa youth for mature women, and that Ntbeko called Peter, who has since passed away, his "hero father." Ntbeko, Linda, and Peter referred to the great weight that was lifted, even though a permanent void and sadness remained.

POSTSCRIPT

During civil wars and wars of liberation—as in situations of extreme poverty (the favelas of Brazil)—childhood is often denied or foreshortened. After the civil war was over, the young township militants who were recruited by older revolutionary factions were expected to return quietly to normal lives in squatter camps and townships where very little has changed.[31] Some have resumed "normal" lives with great reluctance. Many initially felt sidelined by the new ANC government and abandoned by their militant leaders. Some have turned to crime, falling back on skills they learned as children in "making the townships ungovernable." Of the four men originally tried and accused of the murder of Amy Biehl, only two were able to accept the forgiveness and help extended by the Biehls in their extraordinary acts of reconciliation.

A third returned, almost immediately, to a life of crime and violent assault. The fourth exonerated killer of Amy Biehl disappeared. No one in Guguletu, including his former comrades, knows his whereabouts.

If there is a parable here, it concerns the fragility and extreme vulnerability of young black men—dangerous and endangered youths—whether in the shantytowns of Brazil, the townships of South Africa, or the inner cities of the United States. The invisible (because empowered) endangering classes and their dangerous discourses of "savage," "barbaric," and (above all) "dangerous" youth have yet to be exposed and displaced (or routed out), thus awaiting yet another struggle, another civil war.

REFERENCES

1. Scheper-Hughes, Nancy. 1993. *Death without Weeping: The Violence of Everyday Life in Brazil*. Berkeley: University of California Press.
2. Scheper-Hughes, Nancy. 1996. "Small Wars and Invisible Genocides." *Social Science & Medicine* 43:889–900.
3. Scheper-Hughes, Nancy and Daniel Hoffman. 1998. "Brazilian Apartheid: Street Kids and the Search for Citizenship in Brazil. In *Small Wars: The Cultural Politics of Childhood*, ed. N. Scheper-Hughes and C. Sargent, 352–388. Berkeley: University of California Press. Berkeley, CA.
4. Gutiérrez, Gustavo. 1979. "Liberation Praxis and Christian Faith." In *Frontiers of Theology in Latin America*, ed. Rosino Gibellini. Maryknoll, NY: Orbis Books.
5. McAffe Brown, Robert. 1993. *Liberation Theology*. Louisville, KY: Westminster/John Knox Press.

6. Farmer, Paul. 2004. "An Anthropology of Structural Violence." *Current Anthropology* 45(3):305–330.

7. Arendt, Hannah. 1969. *On Violence*. New York: Harcourt, Brace and World.

8. Bourdieu, Pierre. 1977. "Symbolic Power." In *Identity and Structure: Issues in the Sociology of Education*, ed. Denis Gleeson, 112–119. Driffield, England: Nafferton Books.

9. Benedict, Ruth. 1946. *The Chrysanthemum and the Sword*. Boston, MA: Houghton Mifflin.

10. Farmer, Paul. 2003. *Pathologies of Power: Health: Human Rights and the New War on the Poor*. Berkeley: University of California Press.

11. Girard, Irene. 1977. *Violence and the Sacred*. Baltimore, MD: Johns Hopkins University Press.

12. Sparks, Alister. 2003. "A Bitter Inheritance." In *Beyond the Miracle: Inside the New South Africa*. Johannesburg: Jonathan Ball Publishers.

13. Fanon, Frantz. 1963. *The Wretched of the Earth*. Grove Press.

14. Bourgois, Philippe. 1996. *In Search of Respect: Selling Crack in El Barrio*. New York: Cambridge University Press.

15. Gillian, James. 1997. *Violence: Reflections on a National Epidemic*. New York: Vintage.

16. Goldstein, Donna. 2003. *Laughter Out of Place: Race, Class, Violence and Sexuality in a Rio Shantytown*. Berkeley: University of California Press.

17. Caldeira, Teresa. 2000. *City of Walls: Crime, Segregation and Citizenship in São Paulo, Brazil*. Berkeley: University of California Press.

18. Allesbrook, Annie and Anthony Swift. 1989. *Broken Promise*. Sevenoaks, Kent: Hodder & Stoughton.

19. Nascimento, Maria Das Graças O. 1990. "Street Children, the Right to Become a Citizen." In *The Killing of Children and Adolescents in Brazil*, ed. André Papi, Marisa Brandão, and Jorge L.C. Jardineiro, trans. Vera Mello Joscelyne. Rio de Janeiro: Center for the Mobilization of Marginalized Populations (CEAP).

20. Filho, Mario Simas, Eliane Azevedo, and Lula Costa Pinto. 1991. "Infância de raiva, dor e sangue." *Veja* 29 (May):34–45.

21. Huggins, Martha. 1997. "From Bureaucratic Consolidation to Structural Devolution: Police Death Squads in Brazil." *Policing and Society* 7:207–234.

22. Scheper-Hughes, Nancy. 1994. "The Last White Christmas: The Heidleberg Pub Massacre (South Africa). *American Anthropologist* 96:1–28.

23. Lerer, Leonard B. N.d. "Homicide Associated Burnings in Cape Town, South Africa" (unpublished manuscript). Department of Forensic Medicine and Toxicology, University of Cape Town.

24. Crais, Clifton. 1998. "Of Men, Magic, and the Law: Popular Justice and Political Imagination in South Africa." *Journal of Social History* 32.
25. Hund, J. and M. Koto-Rammopo. 1983. "Justice in a South African Township: The Sociology of the Makgotla." *Comparative Journal of International Law in Southern Africa* XVI.
26. Manganyi, Chabani and Andre du Tout, eds. 1990. *Political Violence and the Struggle in South Africa*. London: Macmillan.
27. Scharf, Wilfred and Baba Ngcokoto. 1990. "Images of Punishment in the People's Courts of Cape Town: From Prefigurative Justice to Populist Violence." In *Political Violence and the Struggle in South Africa*, ed. Manganyi, Chabani and Andre du Tout. London: Macmillan.
28. Scheper-Highes. 1995. Who's the Killer? Popular Justice and Human Rights in a South African Squatter Camp." *Social Justice* 22(3):143–64.
29. Campbell, Catherine. 1992. "Learning to Kill? Masculinity, the Family and Violence in Natal." *Journal of Southern African Studies* 18:614–628.
30. Sitis, Ari. 1992. "The Making of the Comrades Movement in Natal, 1985–91." *Journal of Southern African Studies* 18:629–641.
31. Reynolds, Pamela. 1990. "Children and Tribulation: The Need to Heal and the Means to Heal War Trauma. *Africa* 60:1–37.

CONTRIBUTORS

Jack Goody is one of the major figures in British anthropology. He was William Wyse Professor at St. James College, Cambridge, in the United Kingdom. Perhaps best known for his work on the evolution of the household and family, and on literacy and the impact of literacy on nonliterate societies, he has also written many books on kinship, culture, and many other subjects, including the cultural role and function of flowers, food, religion, love, and death.

Saskia Sassen is the Ralph Lewis Professor of Sociology at the University of Chicago, and Centennial Visiting Professor of Political Economy in the Department of Geography at the London School of Economics. Having coined the term *global city*, she has written many books on globalization and the movements of capital and labor, including *Globalization and its Discontents* (1998), *Guests and Aliens* (1999), *The Global City* (2001), *Cities in a World Economy* (2000), and most recently, *Denationalization: Territory, Authority, and Rights in a Global Digital Age* (2005).

Jeffrey W. Mantz is an assistant professor of anthropology at California State University, Stanislaus. He holds a PhD in anthropology from the University of Chicago, and is currently involved in research on the Caribbean island of Dominica and in the Democratic Republic of the Congo. His research focuses on unmasking the cultural, religious, and cosmological phenomena that underlie various transnational economic structures and reorganized production frameworks, including coltan mining in the Congo (on which the present paper is based), and a comparative analysis of twentieth-century capitalisms through the banana trade. He is currently finishing a book on his Caribbean research entitled, *Lost in the Fire, Gained in the Ash: Voodoo Economies and the Culture of Exchange in Dominica.*

James Howard Smith is a member of the Spelman College Department of Sociology and Anthropology. He was a Rockefeller Visiting Research Fellow at the Joan B. Kroc Institute for International Peace Studies at the University of Notre Dame, and visiting faculty at the University of California, Santa Cruz. Smith's research has carried him to Kenya, Uganda, Tanzania, Rwanda, the Democratic Republic of the Congo (DRC), South Africa, and Senegal. His research has focused on African appropriations and transformations of Western development discourse and practice; the relationship between African occult beliefs and global social-structural transformations; religion, conflict, and peace building in Africa; and the productive dimensions of the digital age, with a focus on coltan mining in the Eastern DRC. He has completed a book manuscript entitled *Bewitching Development: The Disintegration and Reinvention of Development in the Taita Hills, Kenya,* and is finishing an edited volume titled *Religion in African Conflicts and Peace-building: New Insights on the Continent's Crisis and Promise.* His articles have appeared in the *American Ethnologist, Comparative Studies in Society and History,* and the *Journal of Religion in Africa.*

June Nash is Distinguished Professor Emerita at the City University of New York. Her early fieldwork was in Chiapas, Mexico, where she worked with Mayas, publishing *In the Eyes of the Ancestors: Belief and Behavior in a Mayan Community* (1970, 1986). She is the author or editor of over twenty books, including *Mayan Visions: The Quest for Autonomy in an Age of Globalization* (2001), *We Eat the Mines and the Mines Eat Us: Dependency and Exploitation in Bolivian Tin Mines* (1979), *Social Movements, An Anthropological Reader* (2005), and most recently, *An Anthropological Odyssey: From Structural Functionalism to Social Activism* (forthcoming). She is the recipient of the American Anthropological Association's Distinguished Service Award (1995) and the Latin American Studies Association's Silvert Award (2004). She is currently writing on human rights and militarization.

Richard B. Lee is University Professor of Anthropology at the University of Toronto. He is internationally known for his work on hunting-and-gathering societies, particularly the Ju/'hoansi-!Kung San of Botswana, with which he has worked since 1963. He is the author of over one hundred articles and many books, including *Man the Hunter* (1968), *Kalahari Hunter-Gatherers* (1976), *The !Kung San* (1979), *Politics and History in Band Societies* (1982), and *The Dobe Ju/'hoansi* (1993). In addition, he is coeditor, with Richard H. Daly of *The Cambridge Encyclopedia of Hunters and Gatherers* (1999). Lee is a past president of the Canadian Anthropological Society and a fellow of the Royal Society of Canada. He has lectured at over fifty universities in North America, Europe Africa, Japan, and Australia. His current research interests are in ecology, history, African Studies, indigenous peoples, AIDS, political economy, and the politics of culture.

Beth A. Conklin is Associate Professor of Anthropology at Vanderbilt University and Codirector of the Vanderbilt Ecology and Spirituality Project at the Center for the Study of Religion and Culture, a project exploring environmentalism as a focus for cooperation and community building across religious and political divides in contemporary society. She has carried out ethnographic and medical anthropological research with indigenous people in the Brazilian Amazon, and published *Consuming Grief: Compassionate Cannibalism in an Amazonian Society* (2001). Her current work focuses on the anthropology of place in Amazonia, politics of representation in indigenous activism and visual media, and models for ethical collaboration with native communities in field research and museum exhibits in North and South America.

Renee Sylvain is associate professor in the department of Sociology and Anthropology at the University of Guelph, Ontario. She has conducted fieldwork with the San in the Omaheke Region of eastern Namibia since 1996. Her work focuses on the intersections of race, ethnicity, gender and class inequalities, indigenous identity, and human rights. Her work has been published in *American Anthropologist*, *American Ethnologist*, *Anthropologica*, and the *Journal of Southern African Studies*.

Eric Wolf (1923–1999) was Distinguished Professor Emeritus at the City University of New York, and a major figure in contemporary American anthropology. Among his now classic works are *Sons of the Shaking Earth* (1962), *Europe and the People without History* (1982), *Envisioning Power: Ideologies of Dominance and Crisis* (1999), among many others.

Helen I. Safa is Professor Emerita at the University of Florida. She was formerly Director of the Center for Latin American Studies at the University of Florida and President of the Latin American Studies Association. She has worked in the Caribbean for over fifty years, producing more than one hundred articles and many edited books and monographs, including the now classic *The Urban Poor of Puerto Rico* (1974), *The Myth of the Male Breadwinner* (1995), and with June Nash, *Sex and Class in Latin America*, and *Women and Change in Latin America*.

Max Kirsch is UNESCO Chair in Human and Cultural Rights at Florida Atlantic University. He was the founding Director of the PhD Program in Comparative Studies: The Public Intellectual's Program at Florida Atlantic and past Associate Dean of the Graduate Faculty of Political and Social Science at the New School for Social Research. His publications include *Queer Theory and Social Change*, Routledge (2000), *In the Wake of the Giant: Multinational Restructuring and Uneven Development*, (1998), and with Mike Budd, *Rethinking Disney: Private Control, Public Dimensions* (2005). His current research involves environment, industry, and community in the Florida Everglades.

Sally Falk Moore is the Victor S. Thomas Research Professor at Harvard University. She is the author of many articles and books, including *Power and Property in Inca Peru* (1958), *Law as Process* (1978), *Social Facts and Fabrications* (1986), *Anthropology and Africa: Changing Perspectives on a Changing Scene* (1995), and *Law and Anthropology: A Reader* (2005). She served as the Dean of the Graduate School of Arts and Sciences at Harvard from 1985 to 1989, and in 1999 was named Huxley Memorial Medalist and Lecturer for by the Royal Anthropological Institute in London, only the second woman to be awarded the honor in the institute's one-hundred-year history.

Nancy Sheper-Hughes is Professor of Anthropology at the University of California, Berkeley. She is best known for her ethnographies, *Death without Weeping* (1992) and *Saints, Scholars, and Schizophrenics* (1979, 2000). She is widely acknowledged for her work on the traffic in human organs, and for her research and ethnographic studies of violence in Brazil and South Africa. She is the recipient of many awards, including the Staley Price, the Margaret Mead Award, the Wellcome Medal, a Guggenheim Award, and the Pietre Prize. Her most recent book is *Violence in War and Peace*, edited with Phillipe Bourgois (2004). Her contribution to this volume on dangerous and dangerous youth is the product of continuing research and political engagements in the plantation market town of Timbauba (Bom Jesus da Mata) northeast Brazil and in the western cape of South Africa. Her next book, *Parts Unknown: The Global Traffic in Human Organs,* will be published in 2007.

INDEX

A

Aboriginal Autonomy and Development in Northern Quebec and Labrador (Scott), 152

Aboriginal Rights and Self-Government: The Canadian and Mexican Experience in North America (Cook and Lindau), 151

Africa, human rights in, 270–272; *see also* South Africa

Afrodescendent women, 19, 22, 225–230
  Afro-Creole population, 231–233
  educational/occupational gains of, 232–233
  race and social exclusion, 226
  redressing inequities, 234–238
  welfare/social mobility, 231–234

Aguiar, Neuma, 103

Amnesty International, 272

Analytic borderland, 53

Angostura dam construction, 118

Anthropology, 3, 131–132, 150

Appadurai, Arjun, 78–79, 250

At the Risk of Being Heard (Dean and Levy), 151

Austin, Diane, 213

Autonomy, 10, 112–114
  autonomous development, 111–114, 162–163

B

Babb, Florence, 104–106, 123

Babbage Principle, 222

Ballard, Chris, 82

Banks, Glenn, 82

Banzer, Hugo, 106, 122

Barnard, Alan, 180

Barth, Fredrik, 210

Battiste, Marie, 151

Bauer, Peter, 121–122

Beneria, Lourdes, 103

Biehl death and trial, 301–304, 311–315

Biesele, M., 151

Birth rates, 36–38

Black consciousness/identity, 144, 227–228, 231

Blackman, Morris, 105

Blanqueamiento (whitening), 19, 226

Blaser, Mario, 152

Postmodernism, or, the Cultural Logic of Late Capitalism (Jameson), 76
Poststructuralism, 8
Poverty, 121–122
Power
  geography of, 55
  labor power, 222
  political power, 15
  structural power, 22
Primitive communities, 35
Primordial communalism, 35
Princeton Principles on Universal Jurisdiction, 281–282
Privatization, 56
Production and consumption, 78
Production process, 47
Property rights, 151–152

R

Racial consciousness, 227–231, 236
Ranger, Terence, 223
Reconciliation, 311–314
Redistribution of resources, 25
Reher, David, 36–39
Resistance, 212
Robbins, Steven, 181, 191
Rodriguez, Nemesio, 120
Rosaldo, Renato, 250–251
Rosenberg, M. B., 249
Rustow, Walter W., 6, 13, 100
Rwandan genocide, 23, 73–74, 77, 280

S

Sachs, Jeffery, 106
Sadr, Karim, 141
Safa, Helen I., 1, 18–20, 22, 102–103, 225
Saffioti, Heleieth E., 103
Sahlins, Marshall, 131, 142, 152–153
Said, Edouard, 111
Salinas de Gortari, Carlos, 108

San peoples, 12–13, 129, 137–139, 143–147, 177
  development difficulties, 190–193
  exploitation of, 189, 197–198
  identity/activism, 180–181
  status today, 184–187
  taming "wild" bushmen, 182–184
  tourism/ethnotourism, 194–199
Santiago declaration (2000), 225
Sassen, Saskia, 6–7, 43, 284
Saugestad, Sidsel, 152
Scheper-Hughes, Nancy, 25, 287
Schooling, 40
Schultz, Theodore, 101
Schweitzer, P., 151
Scott, Colin, 152
Self-determination, 12
Self-development, 120
Sen, Amaryta, 121
Sen, Gita, 103
Sheper-Hughes, Nancy, 22, 24
Sider, Gerald, 143
Sierra Leone, 279–280
Silk Road, 31
Simmel, Georg, 79
Simmonian, Ligia, 109
Simonelli, Jeanne, 120
Slavery, modern slavery, 21–22
Smith, Adam, 14
Smith, Andrew, 141
Smith, James H., 9–10, 18, 22, 71
Social cohesion, 10
Social integration/networks, 1, 3, 7
"Social life of things," 78–79
Social machinery, 287
Social planning, 15
Solway, Jackie, 142
South Africa
  Biehl's death and trial, 301–304, 311–315
  camp codes of conduct, 306–310
  discipline and punishment, 310–311